THE FARTHEST VALLEY

OSPREY
PUBLISHING

ESCAPING THE CHINESE TRAP AT THE CHOSIN RESERVOIR

THE FARTHEST VALLEY

JOSEPH WHEELAN

OSPREY PUBLISHING
Bloomsbury Publishing Plc
Kemp House, Chawley Park, Cumnor Hill, Oxford OX2 9PH, UK
29 Earlsfort Terrace, Dublin 2, Ireland
1385 Broadway, 5th Floor, New York, NY 10018, USA
E-mail: info@ospreypublishing.com
www.ospreypublishing.com

OSPREY is a trademark of Osprey Publishing Ltd

First published in Great Britain in 2024

A catalogue record for this book is available from the British Library.

ISBN: HB 9781472859792; PB 9781472859808; eBook 9781472859785; ePDF 9781472859778; XML 9781472859815; Audio 9781472859761

24 25 26 27 28 10 9 8 7 6 5 4 3 2 1

Plate section image credits are given in full in the List of Illustrations (pp. 7–8).
Maps by www.bounford.com
Index by Zoe Ross

Typeset by Deanta Global Publishing Services, Chennai, India
Printed and bound in Great Britain by CPI (Group) UK Ltd, Croydon, CR0 4YY

MIX
Paper | Supporting responsible forestry
FSC® C171272

Contents

List of Illustrations

Corsairs use napalm to clear the way for Marines during their breakout from Hagaru-ri. (USMC)

The MSR near Hagaru-ri during the Marines' breakout. (Photo by Underwood Archives/Getty Images)

Chinese prisoners of war. (USMC)

Delays in the breakout to the sea resulted in traffic jams on the MSR, and an opportunity for the exhausted Marines to snatch a short nap. (USMC)

With room needed in the convoy for freshly wounded men, the Marines prepare to bury 117 of their dead comrades at Koto-ri. (USMC)

This iconic photograph taken by *Life* magazine photojournalist David Douglas Duncan shows a cold, weather-beaten Marine during the breakout, trying to loose a single, frost-coated bean from the others in his can. When asked what he would have wanted if he could have had any wish, he raised his eyes to the gray sky. "Give me tomorrow," he said. (David Douglas Duncan Papers and Photography Collection, © Harry Ransom Center, The University of Texas at Austin)

The bridge blown by the Chinese over the 2,200-feet-deep chasm at Funchilin Pass. Bridge spans were parachuted to engineers, who built a new bridge, enabling the convoy to proceed. (USMC)

North Korean refugees crowd the waterfront at Hungnam. About 98,000 civilians were evacuated along with X Corps. (DOD)

List of Maps

Acronyms

AAA	Antiaircraft Artillery
ANGLICO	Air Naval Gunfire Liaison Company
AW	Automatic Weapons
BAR	Browning Automatic Rifle
CP	Command Post
CPVF	Chinese People's Volunteer Force
FEC	Far Eastern Command
KATUSA	Korean Augmentees of the United States Army
KMAG	Korean Military Advisory Group
MSR	Main Supply Route
NKPA	North Korean People's Army
PLA	[Chinese] People's Liberation Army
ROK	Republic of Korea
VF	Naval Fighter Squadron
VMF	Marine Fighter Squadron
VMF(N)	Marine Fighter Squadron (Night)
VMO	Marine Bomber Squadron

Prologue

In the garage of our home a faded green Marine Corps field jacket hung from a hook on the wall. Its right elbow was torn and blackened by old dried blood.

For many years, it was part of the garage's spartan decor, so much so that it eventually escaped notice. Its provenance was never discussed, but even to a child it was clear that it had belonged to my father.

In November 1950, he was hit in the elbow by a bullet from a .30-caliber Chinese machine gun during the Marines' desperate battle for survival at the Chosin Reservoir in North Korea's rugged mountains.

His hope of obtaining an appointment to the Naval Academy died that afternoon near Yudam-ni, where three Chinese divisions with orders to "annihilate the 1st Marine Division to the last man" surrounded two Marine regiments in some of the worst combat conditions imaginable: 30-below-zero temperatures exacerbated by shrieking winds out of Manchuria.

The gunshot cost my father his right elbow and eventually earned him a disability retirement from the Marine Corps. He adapted to his new circumstances and became a successful civil and soils engineer. But his life was cut short by Hepatitis B, which he contracted from a blood transfusion that he received after his evacuation to a Japanese hospital.

Staff Sergeant John R. Wheelan of Baker Company, Seventh Marines, was just one of thousands of Marines and soldiers who survived those savage battles in the brutal cold, but whose lives were forever changed.

Joseph Wheelan

LATE NOVEMBER 1950, WEST OF CHOSIN RESERVOIR

It had turned sharply colder on the North Korean highlands plateau and in the mountains around Chosin Reservoir.

Overnight temperatures were bottoming out well below zero, and during the daytime, the temperature did not reach 32 degrees. This was just the beginning of an unusually harsh winter; minus-20 and minus-30 readings would soon be commonplace, with the added misery of winds howling out of Siberia.

When the Seventh Marine Regiment marched into the desolate village of Hagaru-ri on the south side of the Reservoir on November 16, it was 21 degrees below zero at 10:30am. The temperature fell further that night.

"It was unbelievably cold," said Lieutenant John Yancey, who commanded an Easy Company platoon.[1]

Thanksgiving dinner, served to all but the most remote units of the 1st Marine Division on November 23, was well-intentioned, but impractical considering the extreme cold.

The menu featured turkey, sweet potatoes, fruit salad, fruitcake, mince pie, shrimp cocktail, stuffed olives, and coffee, along with a truckload of French bread.

Unfortunately, the bitter wind froze the steaming slices of turkey dished up on the men's mess kits before they reached the men's mouths.

"What you had," said Corporal Harley Trueblood of the First Marines, "was a kind of turkey popsickle."[2]

Some of the men made do with a more modest repast of canned beans, spaghetti, and sherbet.[3]

Lieutenant Colonel Ray Davis's 1st Battalion of the Seventh Marines, on the point of the division's 78-mile trek north from the Sea of Japan, got no turkey on Thanksgiving, frozen or otherwise. "The troops were bummed," recalled Davis.

Instead of eating turkey and all the trimmings on the 23rd, they were busy seizing high ground south of Yudam-ni. The tiny crossroads hamlet lay in a long, broad valley on the western side of Chosin Reservoir.

Yudam-ni was fated to become one of the division's most memorable battlegrounds.

The Seventh Marines commander, Colonel Homer Litzenberg, was determined that his men would have Thanksgiving turkey, even a day late. But when the turkeys were delivered, there was another complication: they were frozen solid. The cooks threw up their hands and said that thawing and cooking them was impossible.

Lieutenant Colonel Davis, an optimist and an improviser, believed otherwise. He put his men to work erecting two tents, one over the other, with two stoves inside. The stoves were lit, and the birds were stacked around them so that they would thaw and could be cooked.

Davis's creative solution worked. His battalion dined on turkey in a deep gulley at the base of Hill 1419 three miles south of Yudam-ni. When they were finished eating, the Marines made no attempt to police the premises. Instead, the turkey carcass-littered hillside became known as "Turkey Hill."

It was the last decent meal that Davis's men would eat for ten days.[4]

At 3,500 feet above sea level, Yudam-ni was surrounded by five ridges rising to nearly a mile in height, separated by smaller valleys that fanned out from the valley's main road. The Marines called the road the Main Supply Route, or MSR. The dirt road originated at Hamhung, near the Sea of Japan, and rolled northward for 78 miles to Yudam-ni – over gorges and plateaus, and through forests and mountains.

The Marines named the ridges that ringed Yudam-ni according to their orientation to the village: North Ridge, Northwest Ridge, Southwest Ridge, South Ridge, and Southeast Ridge. They were riven by draws, and lumpy with knobs and spurs. It was extremely rugged terrain.[5]

Immediately north of Yudam-ni the MSR divided, with one fork continuing north, skirting the western side of Chosin Reservoir, and the other turning west toward the forbidding Taebaek Mountains.

Down the latter road the Marines were to embark on a strategic march of 55 miles on November 27 to join the United Nations' 130,000-man

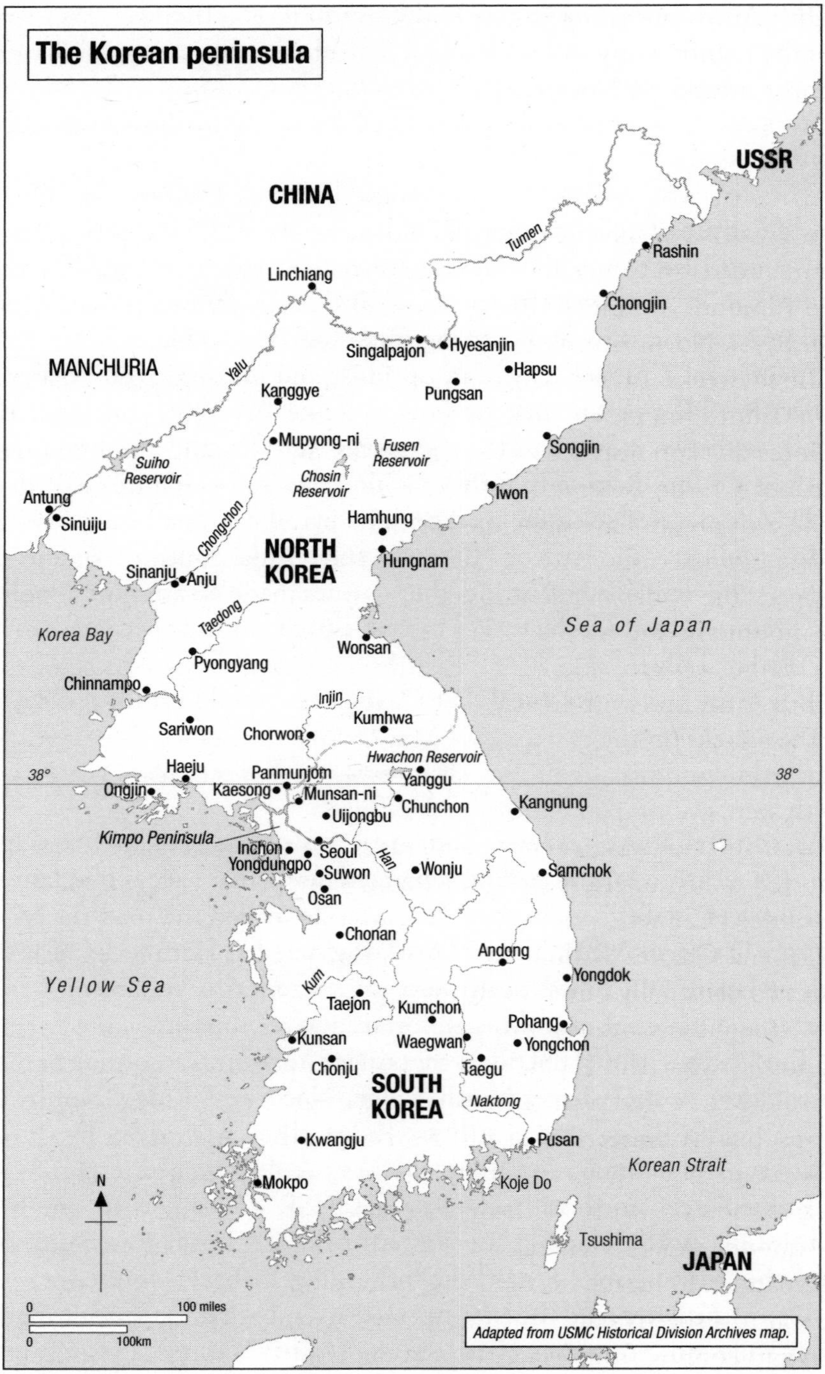
The Korean peninsula
USSR
CHINA
Tumen
Rashin
Linchiang
Chongjin
Singalpajon
Hyesanjin
MANCHURIA
Yalu
Hapsu
Kanggye
Pungsan
Mupyong-ni
Fusen Reservoir
Songjin
Suiho Reservoir
Chosin Reservoir
Iwon
Antung
Sinuiju
Chongchon
Hamhung
NORTH KOREA
Hungnam
Sinanju
Anju
Taedong
Sea of Japan
Korea Bay
Wonsan
Pyongyang
Chinnampo
Injin
Kumhwa
Sariwon
Chorwon
Hwachon Reservoir
38°
Haeju
Panmunjom
Yanggu
38°
Ongjin
Kaesong
Munsan-ni
Chunchon
Kangnung
Uijongbu
Kimpo Peninsula
Inchon
Seoul
Yongdungpo
Han
Suwon
Wonju
Samchok
Osan
Chonan
Andong
Yongdok
Yellow Sea
Kum
Taejon
Kumchon
Pohang
Kunsan
Waegwan
Yongchon
Chonju
Taegu
SOUTH KOREA
Naktong
Kwangju
Pusan
Korean Strait
N
Mokpo
Koje Do
Tsushima
JAPAN
0
100 miles
0
100km
Adapted from USMC Historical Division Archives map.

Eighth Army, operating in western Korea. The Marines were unaware that the Eighth Army was recoiling in disarray from devastating Chinese surprise attacks on November 25.

Five divisions fought in northeast Korea under the aegis of X Corps, commanded by General Douglas MacArthur's chief of staff, General Ned Almond. Almond's 90,000 troops advanced northwest toward the Yalu River, North Korea's boundary with China.

Three weeks earlier, China had fired a shot across the bow of MacArthur's forces. For three days the Seventh Marines had battled a Chinese division near the village of Sudong on the MSR about 30 miles south of Chosin Reservoir. The Marines had sustained 344 casualties, while claiming to have killed 800 Chinese soldiers.

The Chinese toll was probably much higher, for when the fighting stopped, the badly mauled 124th Division abruptly disappeared into the mountains and forests.[6]

On the western side of the peninsula, Chinese forces struck the Eighth Army and withdrew.

The attacks on the two arms of MacArthur's advancing forces caused MacArthur and his aides to briefly re-evaluate their strategy. The drives north were put on pause, but not for long.

After interrogating enemy prisoners, X Corps commander Almond reported to his superiors in Tokyo that the enemy arrayed against them was indeed Chinese.

General Charles Willoughby, MacArthur's intelligence chief, flew to Korea to personally question the prisoners.

Willoughby routinely provided MacArthur with intelligence that supported what the Pacific area supreme commander wanted to do. He told MacArthur that the prisoners were not regular Chinese army troops, but "volunteers" that had gone to the aid of North Korea.

Weakened by heavy casualties, they were withdrawing all of the way back to the Yalu River, Willoughby confidently reported.[7]

Almond urged General O.P. Smith, the 1st Marine Division commander, to hasten his division's march to the Yalu in order to bring the war to a speedy end. The men would be "home for Christmas," was the word coming from MacArthur's command.

"If successful this should for all practical purposes end the war, restore peace and unity to Korea, and enable the prompt withdrawal of United Nations military forces ..." MacArthur's headquarters announced optimistically.[8]

Smith did not buy this rosy scenario. He strongly suspected that the Chinese were luring his men into a trap.[9]

Warning signs abounded for anyone who cared to see them. Weeks earlier, China's Communist Party had issued a broadside under the banner "Aid Korea, Protect Our Homes."

It stated that "the main objective of the U.S. aggression in Korea is not Korea itself, but China ... To save our neighbor is to save ourselves."[10]

Toward that end, Chairman Mao Tse-Tung had ordered Song Shihun, commander of the 150,000-man 9th Army Group in northeast Korea, to stop the enemy at "Changjin Lake" – the Korean name for the "Chosin Reservoir," – so named by the Japanese during Japan's occupation of Korea from 1910 to 1945.

Mao went on to write: "Your first priority is to attack the U.S. 1st Marine Division, or at least destroy two of its regiments."[11]

General Song's three armies had begun crossing the Yalu in early November. While his 26th Army remained in reserve at the border with Manchuria, the 20th and 27th made forced, 100-mile marches through the Rangrim and Kaema mountain ranges to the Chosin Reservoir area.

The 20th Army traveled 60 miles in four nights over difficult terrain, and encountered unexpected problems during their march.

For example, the horses accompanying the artillery batteries refused to walk over the dangerously icy paths along the cliffs. The soldiers hit upon the idea of laying comforters on the ground to cover the snow and ice, and the horses went ahead.[12]

Traveling only by night, they hid in the forests and in peasant huts during the daytime to avoid snooping US surveillance planes. The Chinese marched under radio silence and observed a ban on the use of bugles and whistles.

The Chinese intended to massively disrupt MacArthur's end-of-war plan.

PART I

Prelude to Chosin

Chapter 1

West of Chosin Reservoir

June–October 1950

There's no reason for having a Navy and Marine Corps. General [Omar] Bradley tells me that amphibious operations are a thing of the past.

DEFENSE SECRETARY LOUIS JOHNSON.[1]

The slightest resistance brought down a deluge of destruction, blotting out the area. Few people have suffered so terrible a liberation.

REGINALD THOMPSON, A CORRESPONDENT FOR THE LONDON *DAILY TELEGRAPH*, DESCRIBING THE BATTLE FOR SEOUL.[2]

The atomic bombing of Hiroshima and Nagasaki in August 1945 radically changed the thinking of American military leaders about how to fight future wars.

General Omar Bradley, chairman of the Joint Chiefs of Staff (JCS), believed that the atomic bomb made amphibious operations obsolete, and that profound changes to the military establishment were warranted.

President Harry Truman was emphatic about wanting "the antiquated defense setup of the United States ... to be reorganized quickly."

The former World War I Army artillery officer was blunt about wishing to reduce the Marine Corps to a skeletal force, if even that.

"The Navy had its own 'little army that talks Navy' and is known as the Marine Corps," Truman wrote deprecatingly.[3]

The Army's hostility toward the Navy and Marine Corps was nothing new, but the advent of nuclear weapons, and the possibility that conventional warfare was becoming obsolete, had put wind under its wings.

Truman supported replacing the Joint Chiefs of Staff – which had been improvised on a non-statutory basis during World War II – with a "unified command" that would plan and coordinate land, sea, and air operations.

Truman, Bradley, and Generals George Marshal, Dwight Eisenhower, and Henry "Hap" Arnold supported the proposal. The Navy's senior admirals steadfastly opposed it. They feared that naval aviation would be absorbed by the Army Air Corps, and that the Marine Corps would cease to exist.

Indeed, the admirals were not far off the mark.

During congressional hearings in 1946, Marine Commandant Alexander Vandegrift's compelling testimony thwarted that year's attempt to diminish the Marine Corps.

Afterward, Vandegrift organized some of the top officers that had served with him on Guadalcanal – General Merritt "Red Mike" Edson, the famed Marine Raider and Congressional Medal of Honor winner; General Gerald Thomas; and Colonel Merrill Twining – along with Colonel Victor "Brute" Krulak to brainstorm ways to save the Corps from extinction.

The strategy group, led by Edson, was serendipitously called "The Chowder Society," the namesake of a mythical institution appearing in a popular comic strip. It met in a conference room at Marine Corps Headquarters.[4]

Stung by the failure of the unification proposal in 1946, the Joint Chiefs of Staff issued an order forbidding testimony by naval and Marine officers on the unification bill when congressional hearings resumed in 1947, hoping to quash opposition.

Edson circumvented the prohibition by retiring from the Marine Corps before appearing before Congress. He advocated civilian control of the military, and spoke against the "militarization" of America and what he saw as a sinister shift toward a German general staff system that would centralize military power.

Edson's strong, eloquent testimony safeguarded the Corps – for the time being, anyway – as a military service within the Department of the Navy. Red Mike's Marine Corps career was over, though.[5]

However, the unification campaign continued, pressed by the Army and the Air Force, the latter now a separate service branch under the National Security Act of 1947.

Manpower reductions had begun in 1946, when the Corps' wartime peak of 485,053 men was slashed to 155,592. By 1949, Louis Johnson, the new defense secretary and no friend of the naval services, was calling for cutting the Fleet Marine Force by 14 percent, to 30,988.

Moreover, Johnson proposed that in 1950 it be cut again, to 27,656 men in eight infantry battalions comprising two skeletal divisions, and its 23 air squadrons slashed to 12 – a 48 percent drop in air strength. Colonel Krulak wrote that Johnson was determined to "starve" the Marine Corps.

About this time, Johnson told Admiral Richard Connolly, "Admiral, the Navy is on its way out … There's no reason for having a Navy and Marine Corps. General Bradley tells me that amphibious operations are a thing of the past. We'll never have any more amphibious operations. That does away with the Marine Corps. And the Air Force can do anything the Navy can nowadays, so that does away with the Navy."[6]

Johnson also told newspaper correspondents in April 1949 that plans had been drawn up to transfer Marine aviation to the Air Force.

Congressman Carl Vinson of Georgia, chairman of the House Armed Services Committee, summoned Johnson and pointedly informed him that Marine aviation would not be abolished or transferred to the Air Force without congressional approval.

Marine Commandant Clifton Cates, summoned to testify before Vinson's committee, said the budget and the armed forces' strategic plan were "devices to destroy the operating forces of the Marine Corps," leaving it with "minor units around the world assigned to duties which ignore their special training and unique offensive capabilities."[7]

Indeed, the Marine Corps's prospects appeared bleak as 1950 began.

Then, in June 1950, 90,000 North Korean People's Army (NKPA) troops invaded South Korea, overrunning the Republic of Korea troops posted along the 38th Parallel. They quickly pushed south toward the capital, Seoul.

North Korea falsely claimed that South Korea had started the war, and that it was only counterattacking.[8]

At the Potsdam Conference in July 1945, the United States and the Soviet Union had agreed that the 38th Parallel would be the temporary dividing line across Korea when Japan's 35-year occupation of the peninsula ended with its defeat.

The agreement stipulated that north of the 38th Parallel, the Soviet Union would accept the surrender of Japanese forces, and the United States would have that responsibility in the south.

Korea ostensibly would become unified and democratic under the joint trusteeship of the US and USSR.

That was not to be. The Soviets blocked nationwide elections and sent communist-trained Korean officials to Pyongyang.

In the south, a National Assembly was elected in May 1948, and the US-backed authoritarian anti-communist Syngman Rhee, 73 years old, was installed as president in August. The Republic of Korea came into being.

The next month, the Soviets established the Democratic People's Republic of Korea in the north under 36-year-old Kim Il-Sung, who had led guerrilla forces against the Japanese from 1937 to 1940, and had served thereafter in the Soviet Red Army until the end of World War II.[9]

Two police states hostile to dissent of any kind confronted one another across the 38th Parallel as the Cold War deepened.[10]

Below the 38th Parallel, South Korea was predominantly agricultural, with 42 percent of the land area and two-thirds of Korea's 30 million people. In the mineral-rich north, Japanese-built petroleum refineries and hydroelectric works were features of the thinly populated area.

The Soviet Union sent 3,000 military advisors to ready the NKPA for offensive warfare. Between November 1949 and May 1950, the North Korean army doubled in size to 180,000 men and was transformed with Soviet materiel from a light infantry force into a combined-arms force with 180 aircraft, T-34 tanks, and mobile artillery and mortars.

After Mao's triumph over the Nationalists in 1949 that ended China's civil war, 50,000 North Korean troops that had fought alongside the Red Chinese forces returned to North Korea with weapons and sometimes as intact units.

In South Korea, the US had drawn down its occupying force to a regimental combat team of 7,500 men and 472 advisors under the aegis of the United States' Korean Military Advisory Group (KMAG). The US had "little strategic interest" in maintaining bases in Korea, the Joint Chiefs of Staff stated. The US military priority during the late 1940s was the defense of Europe against the Soviet Union.

KMAG was tasked with training the South Korean army, but there were too few advisors to inspire the unmotivated Republic of Korea forces, or ROKs as they were nicknamed. The people were restive, South Korean President Rhee was unpopular, corruption was endemic, and inflation was a problem.

In June 1950 KMAG reported that just four infantry battalions were as much as 70 percent combat-ready. It went so far as to warn the Joint Chiefs of Staff that the South Korean army could defend South Korea for no more than 15 days.

"Korea is threatened with the same disaster that befell China," KMAG wrote, referring to the communist civil war victory over Chiang Kai-Shek's army in 1949.[11]

The US had armed South Korea only for defense and internal security, because of Syngman Rhee's bombastic prediction that if there were a war, he would capture Pyongyang in three days.

Because the US did not want to be blamed if South Korea attacked North Korea, South Korea was not equipped with tanks or aircraft, but had only light artillery and mortars.[12]

In June 1950, Secretary of State Dean Acheson sent John Foster Dulles to Korea, where he met with Rhee and toured the 38th Parallel. Dulles was a special advisor to President Harry Truman, a Democrat, despite being a prominent Republican who had advised Thomas Dewey, Truman's opponent in 1948.

It proved to be an extremely timely visit. To the South Koreans he pledged that the Free World would come to its aid if needed.

"You are not alone," Dulles said. "You will never be alone so long as you continue to play worthily your part in the great design of human freedom."[13]

North of the 38th Parallel, Kim Il-Sung was eager to invade. Soviet Premier Joseph Stalin had approved Kim's plan, but with the caveat that if the United States intervened, the Soviet Union would not come to North Korea's aid for fear of triggering a world war.

North Korea needed a firm commitment from China, Stalin told Kim. China's leader, Mao Tse-Tung, reluctantly assented.[14]

The invasion began on June 25, 1950. The NKPA, equipped with heavy weapons and 150 T-34 tanks, and supported by combat aircraft, blitzed through Seoul. It was a chaotic scene: the South Koreans blew up a Han River bridge with their own troops on it. The NKPA drove down toward Pusan, at the peninsula's southern tip.

During the war's first week, 44,000 South Korean troops were lost. Prisoners were tortured, hanged, shot, and burned alive. It appeared that South Korea would soon cease to exist.[15]

The United Nations Security Council condemned North Korea's invasion, and two days later approved a US-sponsored resolution to provide military assistance to South Korea. The Soviet Union boycotted the meeting.

President Truman's promise to provide South Korea with air and naval support signaled that the United States would lead the defense of Syngman Rhee's young nation.[16]

General Douglas MacArthur, the legendary Supreme Commander of Allied Powers who had overseen Japan's post-war rehabilitation from Tokyo, was named commander of the United Nations forces that would aid South Korea.

Sixteen nations pledged to support allied forces in Korea. Besides the United States, notable participants included the United Kingdom, Australia, South Africa, France, Greece, and Turkey.[17]

During World War I, MacArthur had commanded the 42nd Division, which he nicknamed the Rainbow Division because its National Guard units from 26 states "stretch over the whole country like a rainbow."

War Secretary Newton Baker said MacArthur was the American Expeditionary Force's "greatest fighting front-line officer." Gassed twice, MacArthur won seven Silver Stars, two Distinguished Service Crosses, two Purple Hearts, and two Croix de Guerre. The French honored him as a commander of its Legion of Honor.

In 1932, MacArthur, then the Army chief of staff, was criticized for sending regular troops to eject the so-called "Bonus Marchers" from their encampment in Washington, DC. The penniless World War I veterans had descended on the capital to collect wartime bonuses that had been promised them.

MacArthur was military advisor to the Philippines when Japanese forces overran the archipelago in 1942. Ordered to evacuate to Australia, he became commander of Allied forces in the Southwest Pacific Theater. They captured Papua New Guinea during their drive north, which culminated in the recapture of the Philippines in 1944–45.

Following Japan's surrender in 1945, MacArthur ruled Japan as a benevolent despot for five years. Given wide latitude by Washington, he had retained the emperor; permitted the Japanese to disarm themselves, rather than be disarmed by the Allies; broken up industrial monopolies; and limited the profits of foreign traders.

He acted through the emperor, cabinet, and Diet – the Japanese parliament, striving to preserve a semblance of Japanese rule. He also rewrote the Japanese constitution, creating a parliamentary democracy. As 1950 dawned, MacArthur was the most popular man in Japan.[18]

In July 1950, he sent the US 24th, 25th, and 1st Cavalry Divisions to the Korean peninsula to bolster the shattered South Korean divisions. The American divisions, all drawn from US occupation troops in Japan, formed the basis for what became the Eighth Army.

The Eighth Army would always remain predominantly American, but in the months ahead it would also include a large contingent of South Koreans, as well as troops from British Commonwealth nations, Turkey, the Philippines, Thailand, Holland, Ethiopia, Greece, Columbia, and Belgium.

The first arrivals slowed, but could not stop, the North Korean juggernaut.

The moment had arrived for the Marine Corps to justify its existence. The Department of Defense called on the downsized Marines to help stem the flood from the north.

A provisional brigade was hastily formed, consisting of the Fifth Marine Regiment – the Corps's only intact regiment – along with attached air and artillery elements. The brigade sailed July 14 for the Korean peninsula. It became known as the "Fire Brigade," commanded by General Edward Craig.[19]

On August 2, after 19 days at sea, the 6,534-man 1st Provisional Marine Brigade landed at Pusan, where it was greeted by its commander, Craig; Pusan's mayor; a South Korean band playing "The Marines Hymn"; and 20 US embassy guards from Seoul, the only other Marines in Korea at that time.[20]

Alongside the Army's 25th Division, the Marine brigade now occupied the Pusan Perimeter, the last bastion against North Korea's conquest of the entire peninsula. The Pusan pocket covered 70 air miles north to south, and 60 miles east to west.[21]

Five days after arriving at Pusan – and eight years to the day after Marines landed at Guadalcanal – the 1st Provisional Marine Brigade led the first counteroffensive of the new war.

Hill 342 was the counterattack's interim objective. The Marine brigade and three Army regiments comprised Task Force Kean, named for the 25th Division's commander, General William Kean.

Seizing and holding Hill 342 was critical to the operation; if the NKPA captured it, the task force could be cut off from the Pusan Perimeter and face annihilation.

Two fighter squadrons from Marine Air Group 33 carried out 100 close-air support missions on the first day, flying so low that spent machine-gun cartridges fell on the Marines below. Hill 342 was secured August 9.[22]

The North Korean troops quickly learned to respect and fear the Marines' aggressiveness and firepower. They distinguished them from the other allied troops by the Marines' distinctive yellow leggings, earning them the nickname "Yellow Legs."

Task Force Keane's counteroffensive was fought in 112-degree heat and suffocating humidity amid rugged hills and swamps that sapped the combatants' strength. Water shortages and heat casualties became as much a menace as the NKPA ambushes.

By August 11, Keane's drive had run out of steam. Three days later, the North Koreans responded with an offensive of their own, crossing the Naktong River and establishing a bridgehead.

The NKPA attack created a bulge in the opposing allies' lines and threatened their main supply route between Taegu and Pusan.

To counteract the dire threat to the entire Pusan Perimeter, the allies seized Obong-ni Ridge, the strongpoint of the North Korean salient.

They had to take it again a week later after the enemy, determined to drive the allies from the peninsula, recaptured it.

In later years, General MacArthur wrote that he conceived the bold strategy of an amphibious landing behind the NKPA's lines while watching the South Korean troops' panicked retreat from Seoul in late June from a hill outside the city.

He foresaw a "turning movement deep into the flank and rear of the enemy that would sever his supply lines and encircle all his forces south of Seoul."

The time would be mid-September, and the place would be Inchon.[23]

MacArthur insisted that the 1st Marine Division lead the assault, although it had been hollowed out by the draconian cutbacks imposed by Congress.

At a meeting with MacArthur in July, General Lemuel Shepherd, commander of the Fleet Marine Force, Pacific, promised that he would have the division ready by September 1. MacArthur formally asked the Joint Chiefs of Staff to authorize its resurrection.[24]

There were many reasons why Inchon appeared to be one of the worst amphibious assault objectives imaginable. It had a 29-foot tidal range, one of the world's most extreme; at low tide, massive mud flats made the shoreline virtually unapproachable.

To reach the beaches, landing craft would have to maneuver through the tricky, 34-mile-long Flying Fish Channel after first capturing the small outlying island of Wolmi-do. It was defended by an estimated 500 North Korean troops. Another 2,500 enemy troops occupied Inchon, a city of 250,000.

The Joint Chiefs of Staff initially opposed Operation *Chromite*, as it was code-named, because of their serious misgivings about the tide.

Yet, despite Inchon's many drawbacks, MacArthur won over the chiefs at a meeting in Tokyo at which he guaranteed that Inchon would succeed – simply due to the fact that North Korea would not expect an assault there – and that it would save 100,000 lives.[25]

Indeed, Kim Il-Sung had discounted the possibility of an amphibious assault at Inchon, even though warned by China of its likelihood, based on the activity of US Navy ships in the Yellow Sea.

On August 22, General O.P. Smith, the 1st Marine Division's commander, arrived in Tokyo to confer with MacArthur at the Dai Ichi* about the Marines' role at Inchon. At this meeting, Smith learned that D-day would be in just three weeks.

MacArthur told Smith the assault would be part of a hammer-and-anvil operation that would destroy the North Korean army and quickly end the war. Serving as the anvil would be Smith's Marines and the Army's 7th Infantry Division, together comprising a new entity, X Corps, under the command of General Ned Almond, MacArthur's chief of staff. The Eighth Army, attacking north from Pusan, would be the hammer.[26]

Smith and Almond were both major generals, although Almond had a year's seniority over Smith.

Their relationship began on a sour note. During their first meeting in Tokyo, Almond irked the white-haired Smith by calling him "son."

Inchon would secure the Marine Corps's future, MacArthur assured Smith, insisting that the 1st Marine Division, which he greatly admired, lead Operation *Chromite*. The downsized Marine Corps, however, was struggling to form one division of the size that MacArthur remembered from World War II.[27]

In 1943–44, the 1st Division, previously under Navy control, had briefly fought under MacArthur's US Sixth Army on rain-drenched Cape Gloucester on New Britain.

MacArthur was so impressed by the Marines' capabilities that he had fought to keep the division under his Southwest Pacific Area command. However, his naval counterpart, Admiral Chester Nimitz, had won the argument and gotten the division back under Navy control.

With little time to complete the task, Smith had to rebuild the 1st Marine Division at Camp Pendleton, California, nearly from the ground up – all of it except the Fifth Marines, currently in heavy combat near Pusan.

To form the core of the other infantry units – the 1st and 7th Regiments – Smith expropriated 7,182 men from the 2nd Marine Division at Camp Lejeune, North Carolina. To them were added a

*This was an insurance building used as the headquarters for SPAC (Southwest Pacific Area Command).

flood of called-up reservists, some of them World War II veterans, and 1,500 short-timer regulars whose enlistments were extended.[28]

Working at top speed, the Marines loaded men and equipment on 19 ships in California by August 18 and departed forthwith for Inchon. D-day was scheduled for September 15.[29]

General Smith said that he would oppose the Inchon landing unless the Fifth Marines were part of the assault force, and so MacArthur directed General Walton Walker, the Eighth Army commander in Korea, to release them from Pusan for Operation *Chromite*.[30]

As the principal component of the 1st Provisional Marine Brigade, it was unclear when the Fifth Marines would be free to begin its second Korean campaign.

Determined to snuff out all resistance in the Pusan Perimeter, elements of four NKPA divisions again lunged across the Naktong River on August 31. They punched a six-mile hole in the lines of the just-arrived US 2nd Infantry Division and sent it into chaotic retreat.

General Walker tried to rally the 2nd Division and stem the onslaught. Flying low in a two-seat L-5 with his star flag fluttering in the breeze, he yelled at his men to turn around. "Get back there, you yellow sons of bitches!" he shouted. "Get back there and fight!"

In desperation Walker deployed the Marine Brigade, although it was scheduled to load for Inchon in just two days, to plug the hole in the 2nd Division line.[31]

On September 3, the Fifth Marines' 1st and 2nd Battalions crossed a rice paddy and with the 2nd Division assaulted Obong-ni – nicknamed "No Name Ridge" – its objective during the first battle of the Naktong.

Supported by Corsairs from Marine Air Group 33, the Fifth Marines stormed the heights, losing 37 killed and 157 wounded during the first day. The attack drove the North Koreans into disorderly flight.

When the North Koreans re-formed for a counterattack on the 5th, the Fifth Marines hit them again. After more bloody, intensive fighting, the North Korean survivors retreated across the Naktong River on September 7.[32]

Afterward, American forces came upon a gully where the enemy had stripped 26 captives of the US 1st Cavalry Division of their supplies and shoes, tied their hands behind their backs, and massacred them.[33]

The Fifth Marines hastily prepared to embark for Inchon. Lieutenant Colonel Robert Taplett's 3rd Battalion was the first to leave on September 8. Its mission was to capture Wolmi-do, the island guarding Inchon's harbor.[34]

Upon its deployment from Pusan, the 1st Provisional Marine Brigade was officially disbanded. During its month at the Pusan Perimeter, the brigade had lost 903 men killed or wounded.[35]

Congressman Gordon S. McDonough was inspired by the brigade's performance at Pusan to write a letter to Truman asserting that the Marine Corps had proved its worth. The Marine commandant should be given a seat on the Joint Chiefs of Staff, McDonough said.

Truman angrily replied that "... the Marine Corps is the Navy's police force and as long as I am President that is what it will remain. They have a propaganda machine that is almost equal to Stalin's ... Nobody desires to belittle the efforts of the Marine Corps but when the Marine Corps goes into the army it works with and for the army and that is the way it should be."[36]

Truman would rue his intemperate words. McDonough inserted the letter into the Congressional Record, and letters objecting to the president's outburst flooded the White House.

Aware that he must quell the uproar with midterm elections looming in two months, Truman went before the Marine Corps League, which was then meeting at the Statler Hotel in Washington, and apologized for the letter. The Marines may have accepted the president's apology, but they did not forget his disparaging words.[37]

For such a bold, complex operation where so many things might go wrong, the amphibious assault at Inchon was at many levels a slapdash affair.

Intelligence was practically nil. There were no rehearsals because the 1st Marine Division's three assault regiments – the so-called "Minutemen of 1950" – were converging on Inchon from different locations.

The most battle-tested of them, the Fifth Marines, was embarking without a break after a month of combat in Pusan, minus hundreds of casualties from the Naktong River battles. The other landing regiment, the First Marines, had only recently been hastily assembled in San Diego with Marines from all over the United States. These Marines had never acted together as a regiment.

The third regiment, the Seventh Marines, was activated on August 10 at Camp Pendleton and cobbled together from combat-ready reservists from around the United States and men from the 2nd Marine Division at Camp Lejeune and the Sixth Marines based in the Mediterranean. It was not part of the *Chromite* assault force, but was scheduled to land on September 21, six days after D-day.[38]

If the gathering of assault forces was rushed and at times chaotic, the planning was thorough, and the objectives clear: control of the port of Inchon on the Yellow Sea, and a short campaign whose object was the recapture of South Korea's capital, Seoul, 16 miles from Inchon.

Senior Marine officers knew that even more was at stake: the survival of the Marine Corps, believed by Army leaders to be an anachronism in a nuclear age in which there would be no more amphibious landings. They had not counted on Operation *Chromite*.

For *Chromite*'s 70,000 troops, the transit from Yokohama through Typhoon Kezia was a stomach-churning journey through rough seas.

And at Inchon, there were formidable obstacles at every turn.

Inchon's enormous daily tidal fluctuation meant that during the nearly 12-hour low tide, the shoreline was virtually unapproachable from the sea, barred by miles of mud flats. An assault force landing at high tide would be cut off from reinforcements and resupply until the tide turned.

Then there were the seawalls that rose from the water's edge, requiring the landing troops to climb scaling ladders, probably under enemy fire.

Army General Matthew B. Ridgway, at that time Army deputy chief of staff, assayed the operation to be a "5,000-to-one gamble."[39]

MacArthur, however, liked to cite British General James Wolfe's ascent of the cliffs of Quebec in 1859 that culminated in his army's capture of the French citadel. The assault had been a gamble, but it ultimately won Canada for Great Britain. Wolfe and the French commander, Louis de Montcalm, were both mortally wounded during the fighting.[40]

MacArthur's command ship, *Mount McKinley*, set out from Sasebo for Inchon on September 13, an auspicious date, for that was the same date of Wolfe's audacious assault at Quebec.

The general had alarmed the Truman administration in August by meeting Chinese Nationalist president Chiang Kai-shek in Formosa and sending him three jet fighter squadrons – without first consulting with Washington. While the administration was attempting to remain on friendly terms with Red China, MacArthur's visit implied US support for Formosa, where Chiang's Nationalists had taken refuge after losing the civil war to the Reds in 1949.

Red China believed that Formosa was an intrinsic part of China.

In late August, MacArthur told the Veterans of Foreign Wars convention that Formosa was the fulcrum of American defensive operations in the Far East. The administration feared that MacArthur's words, coupled with his visit to Formosa, would drive Red China into an alliance with the Soviet Union.[41]

Operation *Chromite* commenced with air attacks on Wolmi-do beginning September 10, followed by a series of intensive naval bombardments by the operation's 260-ship armada.

At 6:33am on the 15th, the Fifth Marines' 3rd Battalion stormed Green Beach at Wolmi-do. MacArthur, wearing his trademark "smashed-down" hat and sunglasses and puffing on a corncob pipe, watched the assault from the *Mount McKinley*'s bridge.[42]

By 8:30am, the Marines had captured Wolmi-do and adjacent Swolmi-do at a cost of just 17 wounded. Taplett's 3rd Battalion reported having killed 108 North Koreans and capturing 136.[43]

When the tide went out, the Fifth Marines, as expected, were isolated on Wolmi-do, but there was no North Korean counterattack. The Inchon landing had been a complete surprise.

Naval ships resumed their heavy shelling of the Inchon waterfront late in the afternoon, and fired 6,000 rockets. Corsairs lifting off from the escort carriers *Sicily* and *Badaeng Strait* added their firepower to the onslaught. Smoke and drizzle obscured the shore at times.

At 5:30pm, the First Marines landed on Blue Beach to the south of Wolmi-do, climbing cargo nets draped over the seawall after their aluminum scaling ladders buckled. The Fifth Marines' 1st and 2nd Battalions went ashore on Red Beach to the north of Wolmi-do and got over the seawall with wooden scaling ladders. Cemetery Hill and Observatory Hill fell to the Fifth after brief hard fighting.

The First Marines maneuvered through smoke-filled streets and blazing buildings in Inchon and seized a hill overlooking the Inchon–Seoul highway.[44]

Late on September 15, MacArthur, highly pleased with *Chromite*'s success – with just 20 Marines killed in action – wrote to Admiral Arthur Struble, commander of the naval task force, on the cruiser USS *Rochester*: "The Navy and Marines have never shone more brightly than this morning."[45]

The Army 7th Infantry Division's participation in *Chromite* began September 18 when General David Barr's division landed south of Inchon to secure the 1st Marine Division's right flank.

The "hammer" in MacArthur's plan to crush the NKPA was delayed by bad weather. Storms held up the Eighth Army's breakout from the Pusan Perimeter for one day when its air support was grounded.

On the 16th, the Eighth Army began crossing the Naktong River, where it faced 13 North Korean divisions arrayed to the north of the Pusan Perimeter. However, within days the enemy formations began breaking up, after news reached them of the America landings in their rear at Inchon.

The Eighth Army charged north through the crumbling North Korean units. As the US 2nd, 24th, 25th, and 1st Cavalry Divisions; the 1st ROK Division; and the British 27th Brigade advanced, the US 7th Infantry Division's 32nd Regiment wheeled south from the Inchon area to join them.[46]

The First and Fifth Marines marched east toward Seoul from Inchon. After daybreak on September 17, a North Korean tank and infantry column blundered into the path of the Fifth Marines.

Platoons had been outposted on a knoll overlooking where the Inchon–Seoul highway passed through a road cut. The Marine positions bristled with rocket launchers, machine guns, 75mm recoilless rifles, and a platoon of M-26 tanks.

The enemy column had been dispatched to block the Marines. The North Koreans evidently did not know their location because some of the soldiers were sitting on the tanks, eating breakfast, while others laughed and talked as they walked down the road.

As they approached the knoll, the Marines counted six T-34 tanks and 200 infantrymen. They waited until the column reached a bend in the road before opening up with a hurricane of gunfire. Within minutes, all of the enemy tanks were destroyed, and the 200 infantrymen lay dead.[47]

The slaughter had no sooner ended when, from behind the Marines, a column of jeeps appeared – MacArthur making his first visit to the battlefront, accompanied by a galaxy of top brass and newspaper correspondents.

The group included Army Generals Almond, Henry Hodes, and Edwin Wright, Marine Generals Smith and Shepherd, and Admiral Struble. Also present was *New York Herald Tribune* correspondent Marguerite Higgins, and General Frank Lowe, President Truman's personal observer.[48]

When the entourage reached the Fifth Marines CP, Lieutenant Colonel Ray Murray told MacArthur that if he drove ahead he would see freshly destroyed tanks. MacArthur was keenly interested.

They came upon the scene of burning T-34 tanks and scores of North Korean bodies heaped along the road. MacArthur leaped from his jeep, surrounded by newspaper photographers snapping pictures of the general.

"This is a wonderful sight for my old eyes," MacArthur said, striding through the area for a closer look at the wrecked tanks and dead enemy soldiers.[49]

With a feeling of deep unease, General Smith anxiously scanned the area for signs of live enemy, aware of how unlucky it would be if an enemy mortar team were to wipe out America's military command in Korea, while Smith was responsible for the group's safety. But the column successfully moved on without drawing fire.

After the MacArthur party's departure, a Marine platoon flushed seven armed North Korean soldiers from a culvert – the very culvert on which MacArthur's jeep had been parked.[50]

Later in the day on the 17th, the Fifth Marines' 2nd Battalion reached Kimpo airfield, a primary objective of the Inchon–Seoul campaign. It set up perimeters on the southern tip of the airfield. A North Korean counterattack that night was repulsed, with the survivors streaming toward the Han River and Seoul.

The Fifth Marines secured Kimpo airfield at 10am on September 18, enabling allied air squadrons to operate from Kimpo rather than from the carriers in the South China Sea. As the Marines closed on Seoul, close-air support was now minutes away.[51]

Eight North Korean infantry and heavy weapons battalions were dug into the heights around Seoul, where the Marines' initial problem was getting over the Han River. It flowed around Seoul's southern outskirts, and its bridges had been blown by the retreating enemy.

North Korean troops made a stand at Yongdungpo, a Seoul industrial suburb on the Han's south bank. They slowed the Marines' advance, but did not stop it.

Because X Corps had no bridging material, the Fifth Marines crossed the Han on September 20 in amtracs. Tanks made the crossing on large improvised rafts built by Marine engineers, and the First Marines got across on the 24th.[52]

Fated to have to work together in the months ahead, Smith and Almond were a mismatched pair, and conflict between the two was inevitable.

Smith was cool, deliberate, and even cautious when he needed to be. Almond seemed to be everywhere at once trying to ensure that MacArthur's orders were carried out.

In his haste to capture Seoul, Almond, during his unceasing visits to the front lines, had begun giving orders directly to Smith's regimental commanders rather than going through the division, the usual protocol. When Smith called him out on it, Almond stopped.[53]

Almond was determined to fulfill MacArthur's wish to declare the city "liberated" on September 25, three months to the day from North

Korea's invasion. He pressed Smith to hasten the Marines' advance into the city in order to meet that deadline.

Smith instead proposed encircling the city to isolate the defenders, while sparing Seoul from destruction.

Almond rejected the proposal; the deadline must be met, he insisted.[54]

"He wanted that communiqué," Smith said of Almond's demand for Seoul's liberation by September 25. "I said I couldn't guarantee anything – that's up to the enemy." The North Koreans did not abide by MacArthur's timetable; intensive fighting raged in Seoul throughout September 25. MacArthur, however, did not let that stop him from issuing the communiqué.

"By 1400 hours 25 September the military defenses of Seoul were broken ... The enemy is fleeing the city to the northeast."

From atop lamp posts and utility poles, North Korean troops dropped Molotov cocktails on the Marine M-26 tanks. Thereafter, the tanks knocked down every pole and shot the enemy soldiers perched there.[55]

Seoul's North Korean defenders belonged to the 18th Division's 70th Regiment, mainly inexperienced troops that were on their way south to the Naktong River battle when Inchon was invaded. They fought surprisingly well and were joined by the 78th Independent Regiment and the 25th Brigade.[56]

The Marines battled house-to-house, street-to-street – savage, elemental combat – along with the Army's 32nd Infantry Regiment and 187th Airborne Regimental Combat Team, and the ROK Marines' 1st Battalion.[57]

General Almond, eager to make good on MacArthur's communiqué, ordered the Marines to attack the "fleeing" North Koreans during the night of September 25–26 and crush them before they could escape. Marine officers were appalled, believing this was inviting ambushes on dark, unfamiliar streets, with attendant high casualties.

It turned out that civilians – not enemy troops – were fleeing the city, while the North Korean troops were preparing to counterattack.

At 1:45am on September 26 they launched their assault with 300 men and ten tanks. A Marine who had served during the Pacific War compared it to a Japanese banzai attack. Like most banzai attacks, the North Korean counterattack failed.[58]

The Americans repelled the desperate attack with tanks and tremendous firing by the Eleventh Marines artillery regiment, which burned out cannon barrels that night. At dawn, the enemy broke off the attack, leaving hundreds of their dead in the streets.[59]

The fighting continued in the narrow streets during the day of September 26. The enemy had blocked the main streets with 5-foot-thick rice-bag barriers rising to 8 feet in height. The streets were sown with mines, and enemy soldiers fired rifles and submachine guns from rooftops, windows, and side streets. Suicide squads darted from doorways to hurl satchel charges at the Marine tanks.

The Marines improvised a three-step method for eliminating the roadblocks: engineers cleared the mines so the tanks could ram the barriers, as infantrymen provided covering fire. It was effective but laborious work.

"Progress was agonizingly slow," said Colonel Lewis B. "Chesty" Puller, commander of the First Marines. Its 2nd Battalion advanced just 1,200 yards on September 26. Corsairs from Kimpo airfield bombed and strafed enemy troops in the city.[60]

"The slightest resistance brought down a deluge of destruction, blotting out the area," wrote Reginald Thompson, a correspondent for the London *Daily Telegraph*. "Few people have suffered so terrible a liberation."

The 7th Division's 32nd Infantry stormed South Mountain, killing 500 enemy soldiers, while Puller's 1st Battalion cleared Seoul's railyard and drove the defenders from the rail station. Inside, they found the bodies of women and children the North Koreans had executed.

At 3pm on the 27th, the Fifth Marines' 3rd Battalion secured Seoul's government complex. Marines lowered the North Korean flag and raised the Stars and Stripes. Except for scattered firefights, the battle for Seoul was over – at a cost to the 1st Marine Division of 711 casualties in three days.[61]

Three days after MacArthur had pronounced Seoul liberated, it was finally safe for him to return to Seoul in triumph with Syngman Rhee by his side.

General Smith's staff proposed that the Supreme Commander of Allied Powers and South Korea's president enter Seoul by helicopter from Kimpo airfield, as the North Koreans had destroyed all of the Han River bridges. Only military pontoon bridges assembled by Marine engineers spanned the river, and they were unsuitable for a parade of cars and jeeps.

MacArthur's staff spurned the proposal. MacArthur and Rhee would enter the capital in a vehicle procession, General Smith was told.

Smith, who was busy directing his regiments' efforts to drive the enemy from Seoul, was now expected to build a bridge over the Han that would support a motor vehicle convoy consisting of MacArthur, Rhee, and their entourage of Korean and United Nations dignitaries.

Lieutenant Colonel John Partridge's 1st Marine Engineer Battalion flew in industrial-strength pontoons from all over the Far East and built a new floating bridge, completing it just before midnight on the 27th.

MacArthur and Rhee arrived the next morning in a Chevrolet sedan, trailed by four staff cars and more than a dozen jeeps carrying reporters and US diplomats. They drove directly to the Government Palace.

A former Seoul embassy official, Harold Noble, was shocked by his first look at the city since North Korean troops captured it in June. "The sight of the wreckage sickened me," he wrote, believing the destruction to be worse than that of Yokohama and Tokyo in 1945.[62]

Distant artillery and gunfire could be heard during MacArthur's five-minute opening address, which ended with the "Lord's Prayer." Audience members could be seen glancing apprehensively at the shattered dome 100 feet above them.

"Occasional falls of glass from the dome and drifting smoke and ashes were part of the scene," wrote a Marine officer. "Unheeded noise of rifle shots punctuated the talks. Grim Marines from Puller's regiment surrounded the seated audience."[63]

After MacArthur officially reinstated Syngman Rhee as president of the South Korean republic, he presented Almond with the Distinguished Service Cross and two Air Medals.[64]

When the spare ceremony ended, MacArthur returned to Kimpo airfield and flew to Tokyo.

After Seoul's recapture, MacArthur concluded his report to the United Nations Security Council on the campaigns of the Eighth Army and X Corps by writing: "A successful frontal attack and envelopment has completely changed the tide of battle in South Korea. The backbone of the North Korean army has been broken and their scattered forces are being liquidated or driven north with material losses in equipment and men captured."

On September 29, X Corps alerted its major units to the likely prospect of a new amphibious landing – on Korea's east coast. The

Eighth Army continued driving northward against crumbling North Korean opposition and reported taking 23,600 prisoners.[65]

Before MacArthur split his forces, sending General Almond's X Corps to northeastern Korea and the Eighth Army continuing to drive north of Seoul, the Joint Chiefs of Staff authorized him to cross the 38th Parallel, the Korean demarcation line established in 1945 by the United States and the Soviet Union.

The Chiefs' decision on September 27 reflected their faith in MacArthur's ability and judgment following the Inchon triumph. It expanded the scope of the war and opened the door to a host of unintended consequences.

By the barest of margins, the allies had managed to repel the North Koreans' invasion of South Korea. Now, the JCS told MacArthur, his "military objective is the destruction of the North Korean armed forces. In attaining this objective, you are authorized to conduct military operations north of the 38th Parallel."[66]

The JCS attached an important clause to its authorization: "... that at the time of such operations there has been no entry into North Korea by major Soviet or Chinese Communist Forces, no announcement of intended entry, nor a threat to encounter our operations militarily in North Korea."

Moreover, it stipulated that "no non-Korean ground forces will be used in the northeast provinces bordering the Soviet Union or in the area along the Manchurian border."[67]

Defense Secretary George Marshall more congenially told MacArthur in a telegram sent on the same day as the JCS authorization, "We want you to feel unhampered tactically and strategically to proceed north of the 38th Parallel."

MacArthur replied to Marshall, "Unless and until the enemy capitulates, I regard all Korea as open for all military operations."[68]

The South Korean 3rd Division crossed the 38th Parallel on October 1, when MacArthur issued a menacing message to North Korea's commander-in-chief: "The early and total defeat and complete destruction of your Armed Forces and war-making potential is now inevitable."

North Korean forces must lay down their arms and cease hostilities "to avoid the further useless shedding of blood and destruction of property." There was no response from North Korean President Kim Il-Sung.[69]

Two days later, Chinese Foreign Minister Zhou Enlai summoned Indian ambassador K.M. Panikkar to a midnight meeting and told him that although the ROK incursion was inconsequential, if US troops crossed the 38th Parallel, China would be justified in entering the war.

"The Chinese people absolutely will not tolerate foreign aggression, nor will they supinely tolerate seeing their neighbors being savagely invaded by the imperialists," Zhou said.

Although Red China had no diplomatic relations with the United States, the warning was received in Washington through both allied and neutral sources.[70]

On October 7, the United Nations, by a vote of 47–5 with seven abstentions, authorized MacArthur with the rest of his forces to cross the 38th Parallel. Invading North Korea to defeat its army was a logical outcome of the UN's June 27 resolution to intervene in Korea, the delegates agreed.

In quick succession, the US 1st Cavalry Division crossed the 38th Parallel, and the JCS authorized MacArthur, if necessary, to engage Chinese forces in Korea "as long as, in your judgment, action by forces under your control offers a reasonable chance of success."[71]

On October 9, MacArthur for a second time publicly urged the North Korean army to capitulate, implying that dire consequences would ensue if it did not. When his message was met by silence, MacArthur proceeded with his plan for conquering all of North Korea, disregarding China's warning.

Henceforth, MacArthur would ignore the few guardrails the JCS tried to impose on his operations.

And who would call him to account? The magnificent success of Operation *Chromite* at Inchon appeared to have inoculated MacArthur to supervision from higher-ups, much less to mere guardrails.

In his later revisionist account of his decision-making, MacArthur suggested that crossing the 38th Parallel was a pre-emptive move that anticipated Chinese intervention, and sought to disrupt it.

"It would be simultaneously a mopping up of the defeated North Korean forces and a reconnaissance in force to probe the intentions of the Chinese," MacArthur wrote. "If our forward movement should prematurely expose Chinese involvement, my troops would have the necessary freedom of action to escape its jaws."[72]

X Corps began redeploying its divisions to northeast Korea by sea and land. Dividing one's forces in the middle of a campaign normally violates conventional warfare principles.

However, the war appeared to be speedily nearing its conclusion, and MacArthur believed he had good reason for sending X Corps across the Korean peninsula – albeit too far to either support the Eighth Army, or to receive its support.

First, the port of Inchon, with its tremendous tides and tricky approach, was incapable of supporting both the Eighth Army and X Corps.

However, Wonsan, on Korea's east coast, was regarded as a splendid port for unloading resupply ships from Japan to meet X Corps's logistical needs.[73]

There was also the issue of General Ned Almond and X Corps answering directly to MacArthur – and bypassing General Walton Walker's Eighth Army chain of command, much to Walker's irritation. Separating X Corps geographically from the Eighth Army made this anomaly appear almost reasonable.

Thus, two United Nation armies, separated by 50 to 80 miles of the rugged Taebaek Mountains, were going to march north and bring North Korea to heel. But if China intervened, the enterprise would be imperiled by the inability of the two armies to coordinate with or support one another.[74]

As X Corps's redeployment began, the 1st Marine Division sailed from Inchon on October 17 for Wonsan. The Army's 7th Infantry Division marched to Pusan and boarded ships, also bound for Wonsan, as the Army 3rd Infantry Division, X Corps's reserve, sailed from Japan for northeast Korea on November 7.

By land, the ROK 3rd and Capitol Divisions crossed the 38th Parallel and proceeded up the eastern Korean coast against light opposition.

President Truman arranged to meet MacArthur on October 15 at Wake Island to promote a better relationship. It was their first meeting.

Truman brought five 1-pound boxes and one 5-pound box of Blum's candy for Mrs MacArthur, and a fourth Oak Leaf cluster for the general's Distinguished Service Medal.

When meeting in Hawaii in 1944 with President Franklin Roosevelt, MacArthur had deliberately kept the president waiting for his arrival; this time, SPAC was waiting to greet Truman.

The men held three congenial meetings that day. *Time* magazine described the interaction: "Truman and MacArthur seemed, at the moment, like the sovereign rulers of separate states, approaching a neutral field with panoplied retainers to make talk and watch each other's eyes."[75] At their first meeting that day, MacArthur apologized for any problems caused by his August Veterans of Foreign Wars speech that had asserted the supposed primacy of Formosa to America's defense of the Far East.[76]

The apology would have cleared the air between the men and buoyed the spirits of Truman, who had hoped that the meeting would soothe Red China's anxiety over the touchy issue of Formosa by demonstrating that Truman was clearly MacArthur's boss.

At another meeting that day, MacArthur was invited to speculate on the possibility of Soviet or Chinese intervention in Korea.

"Had they interfered in the first or second months it would have been decisive. We are no longer fearful of their intervention. We no longer stand hat in hand."

MacArthur estimated that China had 100,000 to 125,000 soldiers stationed along the Yalu River, but predicted that just 50,000 to 60,000 would cross into North Korea. "If the Chinese tried to get down to Pyongyang there could be the greatest slaughter," he said.

Yet there was "very little" chance of Chinese intervention, said MacArthur. He expected organized resistance to cease by Thanksgiving.

One division might be transferred from Korea to Western Europe as early as the end of January, MacArthur said.

They discussed the disposition of United Nations troops, with MacArthur suggesting that none would advance more than 20 miles north of Pyongyang or Hamhung. Truman did not press him on the matter.[77]

When they parted, Truman said the conference was the most satisfactory of his presidency, and MacArthur professed to have enjoyed the meeting.[78]

The 1st Marine Division's expected two-day transit from Inchon to Wonsan lasted a full eight days – eight days of diminishing food supplies and rampant dysentery on the transports, eight days of lengthening daily sick call lists reaching the hundreds.[79]

The reason was that the North Koreans had sown Wonsan harbor and its approaches with 2,000 Soviet-made mines, laid down by shallow-draft sampans, junks, and wooden barges.

Mine-sweeping began October 8. Four days later, two sweepers hit mines and were destroyed; 13 men were killed, and 87 were wounded.

Besides laying conventional contact mines, the North Koreans had also planted magnetic mines that might permit a dozen ships to safely pass before detonating – adding peril on top of an already fraught situation.[80]

Aboard the transports, there was elation when the ships first turned around on October 19 and began to sail south. Rumors swept the below-decks troops. "War's over! They're taking us back to Pusan for embarkation to the States" was a favorite.

Twelve hours later, the 72-ship convoy turned again and began to sail north. Then, after another 12 hours, it reversed course and headed southward. And so it went, day after day while the minesweepers did their work.

In the official Marine Corps history, the peripatetic sea journey became known as "Operation *Yo-Yo*."[81]

Meanwhile, the ROK I Corps entered Wonsan on October 10 after rapidly marching up Korea's eastern coast.

Conditions steadily deteriorated aboard the transports. When the food ran out on one ship, mustard sandwiches were served three times a day. More amply supplied ships were reduced to serving the same fare repeatedly – on one vessel, it was canned bacon, powdered milk, and green scrambled eggs.[82]

Seasickness was pervasive, and the stench of vomit polluted the below-decks areas of the transports. The transport *Marine Phoenix* reported a sick call of 750 men in just one day.[83]

Lieutenant Chew-Een Lee, the US Marine Corps's first Chinese-American officer, swapped his machine-gun platoon's C-rations for the fare eaten by the LST Q1010's Japanese crew. The exchange was a failure: "We nearly starved" on the low-calorie Japanese food, recalled Lee. The food also wreaked havoc on his men's digestive systems.

On the *George Clymer*, just one movie, *Broken Arrow* starring James Stewart, was available for screening; it was shown repeatedly. A line in the movie that the Marines picked up and made a catchphrase was uttered by a Native-American character who refused to sign on to a treaty and said, "I walk away."

"Whenever you didn't want to do something, you could always say, 'I walk away,'" said Pfc Patrick Stingley, "although in the Marines you couldn't actually do so."[84]

The Eighth Army marched up Korea's western coast against scattered North Korean opposition.

On the 19th, the 1st Cavalry Division and the 1st ROK Division entered Pyongyang, the North Korean capital. It was secured two days later.

MacArthur came from Tokyo to watch the 187th Airborne Regimental Combat Team parachute into an area 30 miles north of Pyongyang to cut off the enemy's escape route.[85]

The Marines were still at sea when Bob Hope and the 1st Marine Air Wing ground crews arrived at Wonsan Airfield. Hope headlined a USO show on October 24, lacing his monologue with jokes about the absent seaborne Marines.

The 1st Division conducted an "administrative landing" at Wonsan on October 26. It was uneventful but for the two Marines blown to pieces by booby-trapped driftwood while gathering firewood on the beach. They were the first two Americans to die in northeast Korea. What was left of them was buried in a common grave.[86]

If the Marines believed that the war was over, they were disabused of the notion during the night of October 27–28. North Korean troops pushing north through the area assaulted the First Regiment's 1st Battalion 30 miles south of Wonsan at Kojo, where the Marines had been sent to relieve a South Korean army unit. During the pitched battle, the battalion lost 23 killed and 47 wounded.[87]

Sailing from Pusan, the Army's 7th Infantry Division was diverted from Wonsan and landed on October 31 at Iwon, 178 miles to the north. The 17th Infantry was the first regiment ashore, followed by the 31st and 32nd Infantry Regiments.[88]

Mountain ranges rose precipitously to the west and north of Wonsan, Hamhung, Hungnam, and Iwon. The Taebaek Range stood like a wall far to the west, while the Yangnim Range sprawled northward to the Yalu River. Both ranges boasted peaks of 7,000 to 8,000 feet.[89]

The 17th Infantry Regiment boarded trucks that transported them to Pungsan, 120 miles north of Iwon. The soldiers were eager to reach the Yalu River just 50 miles away.

At daybreak on November 1, an hour-long artillery barrage crashed into the 17th's perimeter, and the 71st NKPA Regiment stormed the American lines.

US artillerymen fought desperately to keep their guns out of enemy hands and, with the aid of the ROK Capital Division and Marine close-air support, the line held.[90]

The 17th Infantry pushed on toward the Chinese border. Previous prohibitions on American soldiers trespassing within 40 miles of the border were brushed aside with the war's end seemingly so near at hand.

After landing at Wonsan on November 7, the Army's 3rd Infantry Division was sent to relieve the First Marines of road security duty between Wonsan and Hamhung. It was ambushed by North Korean troops, with the 96th Field Artillery Battalion receiving a thrashing.

Enemy troops overran part of the American lines and commandeered vehicles, went joy-riding in them, and then set them on fire.[91]

X Corps's main combat units – the 1st Marine and 7th Infantry Divisions – were now ashore in northeastern Korea. They began advancing on their assigned objectives: Chosin Reservoir for the 1st

Marine Division; Fusen Reservoir, 20 miles east of Chosin, for the 7th Infantry Division. The reserve 3rd Division would remain near the coast.

It appeared that the North Korean army had shot its last bolt and that MacArthur's "home by Christmas" prediction would soon be realized.

The First Marines traveled by rail to Hamhung, where they fell in behind the Seventh and Fifth Marines on the road to Chosin Reservoir, 70 miles to the north, ostensibly to close out the Korean War.

PART II

The March Upcountry

Chapter 2

The Chinese Menace

Early November 1950

... pretend that we [are] weak so as to let the enemy advance, make them overconfident, and lure them in deep.

PENG DEHUAI, CHINESE PEOPLE'S VOLUNTEER FORCE COMMANDER.[1]

We can expect to meet Chinese Communist troops, and it is important that we win the first battle.

COLONEL HOMER LITZENBERG, SEVENTH MARINES COMMANDER, AT SUDONG.[2]

Everywhere you turned there were Chinese

SEVENTH MARINES SERGEANT ROBERT OLSON, FIGHTING AT SUDONG.[3]

Blue-eyed, white-haired and whip-thin at 6 foot 1 inch tall and 150 pounds, General Oliver Prince Smith, 57 years old, had been a Marine officer for 33 years. After two years as Marine Corps assistant commandant, Smith became commander of the 1st Marine Division in June 1950.

Smith was reserved, dignified, and unflappable. Being a devout Christian Scientist, he rarely drank and never cursed, but he smoked a pipe, favoring Sir Walter Raleigh tobacco. In his free time, he was a dedicated gardener and raised roses. Smith was no archetypical career

Marine, but "an intellectual with common sense," as he was once described by fellow officers.

He had commanded Marines in combat during World War II. He led the 1st Division's Fifth Marines on New Britain, was promoted to brigadier general, and was the assistant division commander on Peleliu. On Okinawa, Smith acted as the Marines' liaison to the Tenth Army.

Smith had lived on a west Texas cattle ranch until he was six, when his lawyer father died. His mother moved Smith, his brother, and his sister to Santa Cruz, California, where she supported the family as a seamstress.

Smith worked in logging camps during the summertime to help pay the family's bills and to finance his education at the University of California-Berkeley.

Upon graduation, he was commissioned a Marine officer, and received orders to go to Guam. While stationed on Guam, he married his fiancée, Esther King, the daughter of a California fruit farmer, but he missed active service in Europe during World War I.[4]

During the interwar period, Smith spent three years in Haiti with the Garde d'Haiti, then was sent to the Army Field Officer's Course at Fort Benning, Georgia, and the French École Supérieure de Guerre. He wrote a paper during the 1930s that challenged the bayonet's effectiveness in battle, citing medical officers' reports that demonstrated that there had been few bayonet wounds during World War I.

In May 1941, then-Lieutenant Colonel Smith sailed to Iceland as commander of the Sixth Marine Brigade's 1st Battalion. It replaced the British garrison that had been posted there to discourage German depredations on the northern convoy route between Great Britain and North America.[5]

After World War II and his service in the Pacific Theater, General Smith commanded the Marine Corps School at Quantico, Virginia, and in 1947, as a two-star general, he became assistant commandant to General Clifton Cates during a period when the Corps's future was in doubt.

Outside of official Marine Corps channels during the late 1940s was the Chowder Society, an unofficial group of high-ranking Marine officers dedicated to saving the Corps from extinction.

Smith approved of the Society's aims, but not its means, which often offended his sensibilities. For their part, the Chowder Society members viewed Smith as too strait-laced. He was never one of them.

He was "a serious problem at Marine Corps Headquarters," wrote Colonel Robert Heinl, a Chowder Society member and historian. "He was an individual of extreme propriety, extreme circumspection, extreme caution, who was habituated to extending to all people around him the benefit of the doubt. He was a Christian man in the literal sense of the word."

Heinl rather caustically added that "the Chowder business ... frequently involved what, by his definition, was impropriety, and there was just nothing worse in O.P.'s book than impropriety."[6]

Smith's subordinates, however, praised his abilities and managerial style. Although a meticulous planner, he gave his staff latitude to carry plans to completion, so long as they met the stated goals. Smith always made sure that the work got done, and he did not brook failure.[7]

"He never raised his voice, yet was firm in his decisions," said Colonel Alpha Bowser, the 1st Division's operations officer in Korea. "As a result, the conduct of operations in the division was accomplished with quiet confidence."

"The people that I know that worked for him and with him ... listened for any expression of opinion that he gave and took it on themselves as a directive," said George Good, Smith's chief of staff at the Marine Schools and later a general.[8]

General Frank Lowe, an Army Reservist sent to Korea as President Truman's personal representative, characterized Smith in a confidential letter to Truman as "a very *kindly* man, always calm and cheerful, even under the greatest strain. He is always professorial and this characteristic is apt to fool you because he is an offensive tiger."[9]

General Smith had reconstituted his 1st Division and with it executed an amphibious landing at Inchon in an unbelievably short time. The so-called Operation *Yo-Yo* had tried his patience, but the transports had finally landed his division in northeast Korea, where it now faced ascending ranks of soaring mountain ranges, with winter closing in fast.

A daunting new set of challenges loomed on the horizon for Smith's 24,300-man division.[10]

Despite MacArthur's assurances to President Truman at Wake Island, China planned to intervene in Korea, although Mao Tse-Tung's higher priorities were seizing Tibet and Taiwan.

Kim Il-Sung expressly requested Chinese assistance days after the US amphibious landing at Inchon on September 15. Soviet Premier Joseph Stalin promised to send China arms and air support if it deployed troops to North Korea.[11]

After the war, Mao described to a Soviet delegation how he reached the decision to send troops into North Korea: "Should American imperialists intervene, and would not cross the 38th Parallel, we would not intervene; should they cross the 38th Parallel, we would certain[ly] send troops to Korea."

The Chinese government had explicitly and repeatedly warned of the possibility of intervention during September and October through various intermediaries. The warnings were disregarded.[12]

Peng Dehuai, commander of the Chinese People's Volunteer Force (CPVF) – the misleading name given by the Chinese government for Chinese Red Army regulars fighting in Korea – described China's grave concerns about the presence of American troops in North Korea: "If the American military places itself along the Yalu River and in Taiwan, it could find an excuse anytime it wants to launch an invasion."[13]

Chinese troops began crossing the Yalu River into North Korea in mid-October. A week later, China's government announced that it was sending "volunteers" to Korea in a "War to Resist the United States and Aid Korea."

Mao notified Peng Dehuai by telegram on October 27 that his 9th Army Group would be sent by train November 1 to the northeast China border region.[14]

Lacking hard intelligence on the numbers and fighting ability of the American troops, the Chinese launched limited attacks in late October and early November to test the Americans.

In the west, Chinese troops lit forest fires that sent plumes of thick smoke into the air, concealing troop movements from aerial reconnaissance during the daytime.

Then, on October 25, the Chinese 13th Army Group forces launched a series of attacks on the Eighth Army, nearly wiping out the 1st Cavalry Division's Eighth Regiment and crushing the ROK 6th Division.

In northeast Korea, the Chinese 42nd Army began probing the X Corps zone.

General Smith met in Hamhung on November 1 with Colonel Homer Litzenberg, the Seventh Marines' commander, who was "rightly concerned over the situation," Smith wrote. "By this time word had trickled in of the reverses suffered by the Eighth Army in the west."[15]

Nonetheless, Litzenberg's regiment continued to advance north toward Chosin Reservoir. It relieved the 3rd ROK Division's 26th Regiment on November 2 near the village of Sudong, 29 miles north of Hamhung.

The South Koreans had recently fought intensive back-to-back battles against Chinese troops, sustaining heavy casualties. A Chinese prisoner told the South Koreans that about 5,000 enemy troops were in the Sudong area.

When a Marine advance party reached the 26th Regiment headquarters, it learned that the South Koreans had 16 Chinese prisoners belonging to a regiment of the 124th Chinese Communist Forces (CCF) Division of the 42nd Field Army.

Under interrogation, the prisoners recounted crossing the Yalu River around October 16, and marching south over the next ten days to the Chosin Reservoir area, undetected.

General Almond's staff discounted the intelligence.

"This information has not been confirmed and is not accepted at this time," an X Corps assessment said. It stated that it was likely that the prisoners were replacements and not from CCF units, and that they were serving in "groups, thereby giving rise to the erroneous impression that CCF units may be engaged."

Almond personally questioned some of the prisoners, and even attempted to order them to stand in formation and march. They were "not intelligent," he concluded.[16]

In reality, the 42nd Army's three divisions had been sent on a "delaying mission" to buy time for the deployment of "larger and more effective forces" to the area.[17]

The ROK troops, more than happy to let the Marines take over from them, quickly withdrew toward Hamhung.

The Eighth Army's heavy losses from Chinese attacks in northwestern Korea did not effect any change in the Marines' orders to speedily march north.[18]

Sudong was known as the gateway to the Taebaek Mountains, which loomed over North Korea's coastal plain from the west. Sudong consisted of a cluster of mud-and-wattle huts surrounded by rice paddies. South of the village lay a steep, boulder-strewn gorge.

Pine-scented air from the nearby uplands buoyed the spirits of the Seventh Marines, who settled into bivouacs along a dry river bed.

"There was great energy in the ranks," as befitted "healthy young men on the way to adventure," wrote Lieutenant Joe Owen, a mortar platoon commander with the Seventh's Baker Company.

Colonel Litzenberg, a prematurely white-haired man known as "Blitzen Litzen" and "The Great White Father," was a no-nonsense officer who had led Marines during World War II on Saipan and Tinian during the Mariana Islands campaign.

Gathering his officers and senior NCOs on a knoll near his tent, he warned them that they might soon be fighting the first battle of World War III.

"We can expect to meet Chinese Communist troops," he said, "and it is important that we win the first battle. The results of that action will reverberate around the world, and we want to make sure that the outcome has an adverse effect in Moscow as well as Peiping."[19]

Rumors were also flying through the Marine ranks about Chinese soldiers in the area, which had everybody on edge.

"We were afraid to close our eyes. We were looking for Chinese behind every rock and tree," said Lieutenant Harrol Kiser, a Baker Company platoon commander.

At midnight on November 2, the tense silence was shattered by bugles, whistles, and the crash of cymbals.

Lieutenant Colonel Ray Davis's 1st Battalion, the Seventh Marines' forward unit, was bivouacked on the lower slopes of Hills 698 and 727 bracketing the MSR, less than a mile south of Sudong.

Enemy flares lit up the battleground as Chinese troops from the 42nd Army's 124th Division suddenly poured down Hill 727 and through the Marine positions on Hills 698 and 727.

The Marines were driven into the valley as grenades exploded all around them. Three Marines were killed in their sleeping bags. It was an adrenaline-pumping moment after weeks of relative quiet.

"Everywhere you turned there were Chinese," said Sergeant Robert Olson of Able Company.[20]

Davis's battalion bore the brunt of the assault by the 370th and 371st Regiments of the 124th Division.

The enemy had followed the ridgelines above the MSR until they came abreast of the Marine positions, their approach muffled by their rubber-soled sneakers. They pounced on the Marines in a classic double envelopment.

On Hill 727, Able and Fox Companies were engulfed by shouting enemy troops, while Baker Company was swamped on the lower levels of Hill 698.

As the gunfire rose to a deafening crescendo, the roiling melee spilled the troops into the valley and onto the MSR in tangled confusion.

Chinese troops established a roadblock on a finger of high ground that separated the Marines' 2nd and 3rd Battalions.[21]

A roaring North Korean T-34 tank suddenly appeared on the MSR, searchlight blazing. It and four other T-34s were all that remained of the North Korean Army's 344th Tank Regiment, once made up of three armored and three infantry companies.

The road to the north was bordered by cliffs and gorges, and was too narrow to accommodate tanks. Consequently, the remaining T-34s and their crews faced oblivion in the lowlands.[22]

The tank had driven past a Marine roadblock unchallenged – the Marines believing it was a friendly bulldozer – and it proceeded to the Seventh's 1st Battalion headquarters.

There, it was pummeled by a 75mm recoilless rifle round and a 3.5-inch rocket. The tank responded with an 85mm shell at pistol range that wiped out most of a Marine antitank crew.

The tank turned around and headed north, "trailing flame and sparks as it clanked around a bend in the road and disappeared." It was found abandoned the next day.[23]

Amid the Chinese attack, Lieutenant Chew-Een Lee, a Baker Company machine-gun section commander, taunted the attackers in the Mandarin Chinese that he had learned as a boy.

The enemy momentarily fell silent, suspicious of Lee's dialect, and Lee followed his overture with a string of shouted insults. A Chinese soldier cursed Lee in Cantonese, and someone opened up with a Soviet-made PPSH-41 submachine gun, commonly known as a burp gun because of the sound that it made when fired.

Lee's ploy had succeeded in drawing enemy fire so that he could pinpoint their positions and deploy his machine guns effectively. Throwing grenades and firing his carbine, Lee led a counterattack that briefly threw the Chinese into confusion – and was wounded while doing so.[24]

At the center of the Chinese attack on Baker Company was Kiser's platoon. As it made its stand, Kiser's Guadalcanal veteran platoon sergeant, Archie Van Winkle, led a dash to reach one of Kiser's isolated squads. They ran through "withering fire" that wounded Van Winkle and all of the other rescuers.

They were able to help the squad fend off Chinese attacks. Van Winkle wielded his '03 Springfield rifle as a club until he was shot in the elbow, rendering one of his arms useless. He was then wounded in the chest by grenade fragments.

Van Winkle survived to become the first Marine to be awarded the Congressional Medal of Honor during the Chosin Reservoir campaign; 14 Marines were eventually so honored.[25]

Dawn revealed a chaotic scene on the MSR. "We found that we were in a dickens of a mess," said Major Webb Sawyer, the 2nd Battalion's executive officer. "The rifle companies were well up in the hills, and the Chinese were occupying the terrain between the CP and the companies."

The attackers had severed the MSR between the Seventh Marines' 1st Battalion and the rest of the regiment.

With morning, the overwhelming firepower of the Marines' supporting arms enabled them to seize the initiative. The Divison Reconnaissance Company flanked the Chinese.

Close-air strikes by the Marine Fighter Squadron VMF-312 followed, and then heavy shelling by 4.2-inch mortars and three howitzer batteries of the Eleventh Marines 3rd Battalion, which fired 1,431 rounds.[26]

Close-air support operations for the 1st Battalion continued throughout the Chosin Reservoir campaign. As the number of missions grew, the Marine pilots continually refined and improved their operations.

General Field Harris's 1st Marine Air Wing had begun operations in northeast Korea on October 19. After Wonsan's capture by the ROK I Corps, Marine Air Groups 12 and 33 went into action with six squadrons.

It was an inauspicious beginning for what became a supreme test of the Marine Corps's close-air support (CAS) system of pilots attached to infantry units directing air strikes.

The system was first utilized during the Banana Wars of the 1920s and 1930s and improved upon during the Pacific War's island-hopping campaigns.

During the Korean War, CAS and its ground-air teamwork would prove superior to the cumbersome Air Force paradigm of centrally controlled air operations in supporting ground troops.[27]

Because the North Koreans had heavily mined Wonsan harbor, for nearly two weeks the squadrons lacked their usual arming and fueling equipment and had to instead rely on muscle power.

Five-hundred-pound bombs were hand-loaded onto Corsairs until the harbor was cleared and refuelers, trucks, and machine shop trailers became available.

During this time, ground crews fueled aircraft manually from 55-gallon drums that they had to roll to the planes from the fuel dump a mile away.

From Wonsan, and later Yonpo airfield at Hungnam, when the Marine Air Wing (MAW) was moved there, and from escort carriers in the Sea of Japan, VMF-214, 311, 312, and 323 flew Vought F4U Corsairs to support ground troops. The land-based VMF(N)-513 and 542 flew twin-engine F7F-3N Tigercats – heavily armed fighter-bombers that were radar-equipped for nighttime operations.

From Yonpo, Marine Observation Squadron 6 deployed ten OY-2 observation planes and nine HO3-1 helicopters for aerial reconnaissance, combat rescues, and medical evacuations. VMO-6 flew the four-seat HO3-1 helicopters; the Marine Corps initiated the use of helicopters in combat zones, with Colonel Victor Krulak an enthusiastic early advocate.

The helicopters were initially used for observation and for rescuing downed airmen, but they later directed air strikes and evacuated the wounded.[28]

Major Mike Wojcik, who during World War II flew observation planes over Saipan, Guam, and Iwo Jima, patrolled the Marine front lines along the MSR, directing artillery fire and watching for the enemy.

On one artillery spotting mission, Wojcik saw a Chinese company laying an ambush for an approaching Marine battalion.

Upon alerting the Marines on the ground by radio of the ambush ahead of them, Wojcik guided them along a route that bypassed the Chinese ambuscade, leading to its rear. He then called in an air strike on the enemy.

Corsairs raked the Chinese with machine-gun fire, artillery joined in, and the enemy soldiers broke and hastily withdrew – into the path of the Marine battalion that they were supposed to ambush. "They got clobbered," said Wojcik.[29]

The fighter-bomber squadrons conducted armed reconnaissance missions over northeastern Korea. VMF-214 (the famed "Black Sheep" squadron) and VMF-323 (nicknamed the "Death Rattlers") for a time flew combat air patrols from the escort carriers *Sicily* and *Badoeng Strait*, which lay offshore in the Sea of Japan while minesweepers cleared Wonsan harbor.[30]

The MAW initially had to first clear its missions through the Fifth Air Force in Seoul. It was an inefficient procedure; communications lapses between Seoul and X Corps in northeast Korea made it nearly impossible to receive permission in a timely fashion; permission was sometimes granted up to two days late.

General Harris, however, persuaded General Earle Partridge, commander of the Fifth Air Force, to authorize him to immediately green-light air strikes so long as he kept Partridge informed by filing the paperwork afterward. Partridge later allowed Harris to direct the 1st MAW missions virtually without Air Force oversight.[31]

During four days in early November, the Marine Air Wing flew 148 close support sorties, wiped out enemy soldiers dug in on a ridge overlooking the Marine positions, and knocked out a T-34 tank.

The *Sicily* and *Badoeng Strait* served as platforms for Marine Corsair squadrons. In addition, 15 Navy air squadrons, predominantly Corsairs but also a smaller number of Douglas AD Skyraiders, operated from three of the Seventh Fleet's full-size carriers: *Leyte*, *Boxer*, and *Philippine Sea*.[32]

The Corsairs were the close-air-support work horses. With a flying time of two and a half hours, a Corsair typically carried 800 rounds of 20mm ammunition; eight rockets; and two 150-gallon napalm pods.

The less numerous Skyraiders, which could remain aloft for four hours, carried 400 rounds of 20mm ammunition; three napalm pods; and either 12 rockets or 12 250-pound fragmentation bombs.[33]

Integral to close-air support was the Marine forward air controller (FAC) on the ground. He was a trained pilot who might sometimes orally guide the pilot overhead to his target via visual landmarks.

Each Marine battalion had an FAC, accompanied by a radio operator; by contrast, Army units had one Air Force controller per division. To request an air strike, the Marine controller contacted his Direct Air Support Center, which would assign a strike aircraft to carry out the mission.[34]

Beginning November 1, MiG-15 jets began appearing over the Yalu River crossings when Corsairs and Skyraiders conducted missions to destroy the Yalu bridges.

Navy Lieutenant Commander William Amon, flying a Grumman F9F-2 Panther jet, claimed the first MiG kill in mid-November.

MiGs were encountered during nearly every mission over the Yalu River from November 11 onward. It was conceded that the MiG, if competently flown, was superior to the Panther.

Later, when the Panthers saw wider use in close-air support operations, Chinese infantrymen grew to fear the "blue airplanes" that struck before they even knew they were there.[35]

By mid-morning of November 3, the Seventh's 1st Battalion had cleared the low ground around Sudong of Chinese troops, but three more days of sporadic fighting lay ahead. The 2nd Battalion's Dog Company destroyed a Chinese roadblock on the spur of Hill 727, while Easy Company secured Hill 698 with the assistance of an air strike after being initially repulsed by a hailstorm of Chinese grenades.[36]

Undoubtedly to the relief of the exhausted Marines, the Chinese broke off contact with them late November 3 and withdrew to a defensive line established by their 372nd Regiment two miles north of Chinghung-ni.[37]

When the shooting stopped, one Marine praised the Chinese: "They were a helluva lot better than the North Koreans – better trained, better equipped, and better led."

Sergeant Richard Danforth of the Seventh Marines' Fox Company said, "If these were the goddamn stragglers, don't even show me the diehards."

The Seventh Marines were the first US combat troops to defeat the Chinese Communist Forces in battle. The cost was 61 Marines killed in action, 283 wounded, and one missing.[38]

Following a directive issued September 27, there had been an understanding that non-Korean troops could not approach within 40 miles of the Yalu River. On October 24 MacArthur announced that the restriction no longer existed, and that US and UN troops could now march all the way to the Chinese border.

The Joint Chiefs of Staff bridled at MacArthur's action and demanded an explanation. It was a matter of "military necessity," MacArthur replied. ROK units lacked the strength and leadership to carry out the mission, he said, and his mission was to rid all of Korea of enemy troops.

The Joint Chiefs decided to drop the matter, not wishing to interfere with the theater commander's operation.[39]

On November 4, MacArthur ordered the Far Eastern Air Force to destroy the international bridges abutting the North Korea side of the Yalu River. He also ordered the bombing of the region immediately south of the Yalu so that the Chinese could not live off the land.

MacArthur believed that Chinese "volunteers" were aiding the NKPA in order to maintain a foothold in North Korea, but that the Chinese attacks in late October and early November fell short of full-blown intervention.

The Joint Chiefs of Staff countermanded MacArthur's bombing order, declaring the bridges to be off-limits and limiting bombing missions to targets five miles or more from the border.

MacArthur shot back angrily: "Every hour that this is postponed will be paid for dearly in American and other United Nations blood ... I cannot overemphasize the disastrous effect, both physical and psychological, that will result from the restrictions which you are imposing."

The outburst persuaded the Joint Chiefs of Staff to authorize B-29s to bomb the Yalu River bridges at Andong. "Men and materiel in large force are pouring over the Yalu bridges from Manchuria," MacArthur wrote the Chiefs, and they threatened "the ultimate destruction of the forces under my command."

The bombing raid damaged the bridge spans, and incendiary bombs wiped out the adjacent Korean city of Sinuiju.[40]

MacArthur was having his way in Korea.

The Seventh Marines' Reconnaissance Company and a section of 70mm recoilless rifles led the advance on November 4 from Sudong to Chinhung-ni, the next milepost on the MSR to Chosin Reservoir.

There, the Marines encountered the North Koreans' remaining tanks. A T-34 camouflaged by brush along the roadside was transformed by grenades into a smoking hulk. When another tank burst from its hiding place inside a thatched hut, a Corsair summoned by a forward air controller dipped out of a formation of the gull-winged planes overhead and took it out with rockets. The crews of two other North Korean tanks surrendered.[41]

North of Chinhung-ni, Hills 987 and 891, defended by soldiers from the battered Chinese 124th Division, towered over both sides of the MSR on the steep ascent to Funchilin Pass.

The Seventh Marines' 3rd Battalion took the point on November 5 from Lieutenant Colonel Davis's 1st Battalion, which had moved to higher ground. The 3rd Battalion's "I" and "G" Companies were stopped by intensive enemy fire when they attempted to advance on 987 and How Hill on the southern spur of Hill 891.

The Eleventh Marines' guns smothered the Chinese positions with 943 shells, silencing their 122mm mortars and blowing up an ammunition dump. A Marine fighter squadron, VMF-312, flew 37 sorties, hitting ridges bristling with enemy troops, with "extremely effective" bombing, strafing, and rocket-firing runs.

Nonetheless, "advance was negligible," said the Seventh Marines' after-action report for November 5.

Small advances were made on the lower reaches of Funchilin Pass the next day, November 6.

Then, after a night of stygian darkness, the Marines discovered in the morning of November 7 that the Chinese no longer occupied the heights. The enemy was gone.

A Marine Corps Board report concluded that "the 124th CCF Division was estimated to have been rendered militarily ineffective." The Seventh Marines had killed about 1,500 enemy soldiers and captured 62 others.

Chinese prisoners said that just 3,000 of the 124th Division's original force of 12,500 men remained able to fight.[42]

The Chinese echelons that had mauled two divisions of the Eighth Army days earlier at Unsan in northwest Korea had also vanished.[43]

The withdrawals were intended to signal vulnerability in order to lure the allies deeper into North Korea – into a trap that they could not escape.

As General Peng Dehuai had once told his assembled top officers, "In order to hook a big fish you must let the fish taste your bait."[44]

During the now-ended First Offensive, Peng wrote that his armies "adopted combat tactics to pretend that we were weak so as to let the enemy advance, make them overconfident, and lure them in deep."[45]

Marshal Nie Rongzhen wrote, "The [CPVF] troops pulled back in order to lure the enemy further north and to find the opportunity to annihilate it."[46]

In northeastern Korea, the 42nd Army had served as bait and tested American combat capabilities. Its sister armies in the 13th Army Group, the 38th, 39th, and 40th Armies, had tested the Eighth Army in northwestern Korea where CCF attacks had smashed the 8th Cavalry Regiment and ROK units on November 1 and 2.

The 13th Army Group's losses in western Korea were relatively modest and its planned withdrawal bought time to quickly recover. The army group was reinforced by the restoration of the 42nd Army from northeastern Korea and the addition of the 66th Army. On the western Korean front, five Chinese armies now faced the Eighth Army.

Chinese officers were decidedly unimpressed by the Eighth Army's conduct during the First Offensive.

The Americans displayed weakness by quick withdrawals when Chinese forces were detected nearby, the officers said, and by their dependence on supporting arms. They were poor night-fighters who recoiled from hand-to-hand combat. The officers rated the Eighth Army below "capable" Chinese Nationalist troops.[47]

The enemy troops' sudden appearance and disappearance puzzled the allies. They could not agree on what it meant or portended, if anything.

For two or three days, MacArthur was uncharacteristically subdued, telling the Joint Chiefs of Staff that he wished to take "accurate measure" of enemy strength before sending his armies farther north.

Yet he did agree to a preposterous proposal by General Almond, calling for the 65th Infantry Regiment of the Army's 3rd Division to march from the northeastern Korean coast 80 miles through the mountains to make contact with the Eighth Army. When Almond issued the marching order to the 65th's commander, Colonel William Harris, Harris was "appalled."[48]

Chinese prisoners shared details of their army's deployments with interrogators for the Eighth Army and the 1st Marine Division. The information was discounted by MacArthur's senior officers.

It was inconceivable to them that peasant foot soldiers would possess such knowledge. Moreover, MacArthur's staff continued to firmly believe that the Chinese who had launched attacks in North Korea were "volunteers" – and not regular Chinese army units, despite what the prisoners told their captors.

They did not understand that in the People's Liberation Army (PLA), distinctions in rank were de-emphasized, and Chinese officers shared with their men all of the information available about a planned operation beforehand.

In 1950, the Chinese Communist Forces remained a proletariat army. Its soldiers displayed no insignia denoting rank, except for the red piping on officers' uniform sleeves, front, collar, and trouser seams. Officers and men ate the same food, and had the same sleeping arrangements.[49]

In 1938, Marine Lieutenant Colonel Evan Carlson, who later commanded the 2nd Marine Raider Battalion on Guadalcanal, had traveled with Mao's Eighth Route Army on a 1,000-mile trek through China. In private letters to President Franklin Roosevelt, Carlson described how the Chinese Red Army operated: "Leaders [officers] take the fighters [enlisted men] into their confidence and constantly explain to them what the situation is, why the army is taking certain action, etc. Before a battle the men are assembled and the military situation is explained to them so that they go into battle with their eyes open ... The result is a strong bond of understanding between leaders and fighters."[50]

The Chinese army's culture had changed little since Carlson's experiences with the Eighth Route Army, and it was altogether alien to the experiences of US Army senior officers in 1950.

The Chinese prisoners said that the conscripts in the 42nd Army that fought at Sudong received more political indoctrination than field training. They were told that US forces planned to march to the Yalu River and invade Manchuria, and that any Chinese soldier that surrendered would be decapitated immediately.[51]

MacArthur's Dai Ichi staff did not act on the intelligence provided by the prisoners, and merely forwarded the information to the Department of the Army.

Meanwhile, General Almond met with the commanders of the 1st Marine Division, the Army 7th Infantry Division, and the ROK I Corps to elicit their opinions.

Reflecting MacArthur's concerns and thinking at that time, Almond said that he wished to shrink X Corps's perimeter. He listened with interest to General O.P. Smith's suggestion that X Corps pull back for the winter to an enclave within the confines of Wonsan, Hungnam, and Hamhung.[52]

To assess the degree of the Chinese presence in North Korea, United Nations reconnaissance planes crisscrossed the area looking for signs of Chinese troop concentrations.

The flights failed to accurately assay the extent of the enemy infiltration. This was by design. Chinese troops moved at night, and during the daytime concealed themselves in native huts, in caves, and in dense forests.

In November, MacArthur's headquarters estimated Chinese troop strength in North Korea to be between 64,000 and 72,000 men, augmented by an estimated 82,000 North Korean soldiers – certainly an overestimation – that had found sanctuary in the far north.[53]

MacArthur's intelligence chief was General Charles Willoughby – a man utterly devoted to MacArthur. Willoughby had known MacArthur since 1940 in Manila, and then had acted as his chief of intelligence during World War II.

Born Adolph Karl Tscheppe-Wiedenbach in Heidelberg, Germany, he had adopted his Baltimore-born mother's surname after his emigration to America, and changed his first name to the Anglicized version. Lieutenant Colonel James Polk, who worked for Willoughby as an intelligence officer in Tokyo, described him as a loner and a bachelor who had no real friends.[54]

Willoughby was an admirer of Francisco Franco, the Spanish dictator whom he once toasted as "the second-greatest military genius in the world" – MacArthur, of course, being the greatest. Years later, Willoughby became an advisor to Franco.

As MacArthur's intelligence chief, he appeared to believe that his job was to supply MacArthur only with information that aligned with his boss's preconceptions.

In his earlier assessments of Chinese strength and intentions, Willoughby had consistently erred. He had declared that the movement of Chinese troops to Manchuria was no more than "diplomatic blackmail."

China and the Soviet Union, Willoughby also said, were opposed to "further expensive investment in support of a lost cause." If asked by North Korea, the Chinese would provide replacements for North Korean units "through discrete integration."[55]

Willoughby now refused to acknowledge that Chinese regulars had attacked the Eighth Army and X Corps in early November, even when told by Almond that the Marines held 50 Chinese soldiers as prisoner at Sudong.

"Those aren't Chinese soldiers," Willioughby reportedly asserted. "That's a Marine lie." They were "volunteers," not regulars, he believed.

He told the Pentagon that no Chinese intervention would occur at this late date, when the "auspicious time for intervention had long since passed" – in his view, that time had been during the Pusan fighting.[56]

The Chinese attacks, however, alarmed MacArthur, who weeks earlier had exuded the utmost confidence.

On November 6, MacArthur hyperbolically described the Chinese attacks as "one of the most offensive acts of international lawlessness of historic record."

After being given permission to bomb the Yalu River bridges, B-29s damaged or destroyed some of the bridge spans. But most of the Chinese forces being deployed to North Korea by Peng for his Second Offensive were already there, moving by night and hiding by day.[57]

Moreover, bombing the bridges did not stop Chinese troops from entering North Korea. Some units got across the river on special pre-fabricated wooden bridges painted to match the color of the river, and submerged just below the water surface.

Trucks drove over the improvised bridges at night through water reaching the tops of their wheels. Soldiers removed their trousers, shoes and socks, and tied them to their backs before crossing. These infiltrations began at nightfall and usually ended by 4am.[58]

By November 9, when three days had passed without further enemy attacks, MacArthur's alarm subsided. It was now urgent, he said in a secret cable to Washington, that the Eighth Army and X Corps resume their "end of-war" offensive.

Failure to do so, he said in an outburst of exaggeration, would have the direst consequences. It "would completely destroy the morale of my forces and its psychological consequences would be inestimable. It would condemn us to an indefinite defense line in North Korea and would unquestionably arouse such resentment among the South Koreans that their forces would collapse or might even turn against us."[59]

In Washington, the Chinese withdrawal was interpreted just as Peng had intended – a sign of Chinese weakness. Call the Chinese bluff with an all-out offensive to the Yalu River, senior military officials advised.[60]

In mid-November, ten days after Chinese forces disappeared following their First Offensive, MacArthur told John Muccio, the US ambassador to South Korea, that he believed there were just 30,000 Chinese troops in Korea; if there were more, he told Muccio, air reconnaissance would have detected them. He boasted that he could clear the remaining areas held by the communists in just ten days.[61]

But air reconnaissance had not detected the huge Chinese presence in North Korea. From mid-October to November 1, between 180,000 and 228,000 Chinese troops had gone over the Yalu River into North Korea, with the crossings increasing in subsequent weeks.[62]

Indeed, on October 31, Mao had ordered the 9th Army Group's 20th and 27th Armies to move from southeast China to northeast Korea and set a trap for X Corps during the impending Second Offensive.

Peng had given Song Shilun, the 9th Army Group commander, specific orders to "entice the Americans deep into Kujing-ri and Changjin line [an area north of Chosin Reservoir] and wipe out two regiments of the US 1st Marine Division ... With such deployment, the deeper the 1st Marine moves north into Kujing-ri, the better. Two armies (yours) should use two divisions to hold the front while the other seven divisions attack the enemy from flank and rear."[63]

But after the Marines' destruction of the 124th Division during the First Offensive battles at Sudong and Chinghung-ni, Mao believed that more troops would be needed in northeast Korea besides the 20th and 27th Armies. Unlike the Eighth Army, the Marines were dangerously capable, the Chinese now believed.

In a telegram to Peng on November 12, Mao wrote, "It is said that the American Marine First Division has the highest combat effectiveness in the American armed forces. It seems not enough for our four divisions [from the 20th and 27th Armies] to surround and annihilate its two regiments. [You] should have one to two more divisions as a reserve force. The 26th Army of the Ninth Army Group should be stationed close to the front."[64]

Meanwhile, the Seventh Marines' after-action reports noted dwindling contacts with Chinese troops as the regiment led the march north to Koto-ri, Hagaru-ri, and the Chosin Reservoir.

The Marines captured Funchilin Pass on November 8, when General Almond dropped in on the Marines to award a Silver Star to Captain Thomas Cooney, wounded while charging the enemy on Hill 891. Discovering that he had no medals in his pocket, Almond scrawled on a scrap of paper, "Silver Star Medal for Gallantry in Action – Almond" and pinned it to Cooney's jacket.[65]

Enemy troops would occasionally fire on the aggressively patrolling Marines, but when they returned fire, the Chinese quickly withdrew.[66]

Rather than evidence of Chinese weakness, the enemy movements in fact were a demonstration of the opening of one of Mao's best-known military gambits: "Enemy advancing, we retreat." The lines that followed would be put into action in the coming weeks: "... enemy entrenched, we harass; enemy exhausted, we attack; enemy retreating, we pursue."[67]

China had steadily protested American involvement in the war to the United Nations since late August. Foreign Minister Zhou Enlai telegrammed the UN Secretary General claiming that the United States had started the Korean War and was impeding its resolution. He also demanded that the UN compel the withdrawal of the US Seventh Fleet from the Formosa Strait. There were, too, complaints about US planes strafing airfields and railroads in Manchuria.

In late September, China announced that it had released "battle-trained" Korean soldiers from Manchuria to "defend their motherland." On September 30, Zhou Enlai pronounced the United States to be "the most dangerous enemy of the People's Republic of China," and avowed that China would not "supinely tolerate" North Korea's destruction.

China's warnings continued throughout October, when Zhou said, "The Chinese people love peace, but in order to defend peace, they will never be afraid to oppose aggressive war."[68]

"The Americans can bomb us, they can destroy our industries, but they cannot defeat us on land," declared General Nie Rongzhen.[69]

In an attempt to quash the tensions that had culminated in the Chinese First Offensive in late October and early November, the United Nations' Interim Committee on Korea on November 7 announced that UN troops would honor the Manchurian frontier.

Three days later, the UN Security Council went further, weighing a resolution pledging to hold the frontier "inviolate" and to protect both Korean and Chinese interests in that zone.

On the 11th, US Secretary of State Dean Acheson said neither the UN nor US had "ulterior designs" on Manchuria. Any misunderstanding by China, he said, would ignite "a world-wide tragedy of the most colossal nature."

But China categorically rejected the assurances, accusing the United States of aggression in Formosa and North Korea.

"To help Korea in its resistance ... is to defend our own country," the Chinese government said. What the allies contemplated, China charged, was "an American advance right up to the Chinese frontier and eventually across it."[70]

Throughout this exchange, the Chinese continued to withdraw to the north, and UN troops continued their march to the Yalu River.

The MSR was a busy two-lane road between Hamhung and Chinhung-ni, but it then narrowed to a one-lane road as it began to climb into the mountains. A narrow-gauge railroad ran beside the MSR to Chinhung-ni, where it became a cableway for the eight-mile, 2,500-foot climb to Funchilin Pass.

And beyond the pass lay a 4,000-foot-elevation plateau and the mountain village of Koto-ri. In the fall of 1950 the cableway was inoperable, the cable severed.[71]

The narrow road between Chinhung-ni and Koto-ri was literally carved out of a mountainside, with a cliff on one side of the road and a nearly vertical drop of several hundred feet on the other side.

It was a heart-stopping journey either on foot or in a jeep or truck. The road was later widened to one-and-a-half lanes to accommodate M-26 tanks.[72]

The Seventh Marines reached Koto-ri on November 10, the Marine Corps's birthday. Being a tight-knit fraternity, the Marines celebrated the milestone each year with a birthday cake. Tradition required that it be cut by the commanding officer, with the first slice served to the senior Marine present.[73]

The Seventh Marines sent patrols into the hills surrounding Koto-ri. While patrolling north of the village on November 11, "C" Company clashed with a Chinese unit.

The Marines lost four men killed and four wounded during the firefight; 40 Chinese soldiers were killed. It would be the Marines' last hostile encounter with the Chinese for the next 16 days.

Meanwhile, Chinese troops continued to pour into North Korea each night. During early November an estimated 100,000 soldiers crossed the Yalu River from Manchuria.[74]

On November 14, Xie Fang, Peng Dehuai's chief of staff, wrote, "Our 9th Army Group main forces have successfully entered Korea from J'an and Linjiang to assume eastern front operations. ... We have over 150,000 men on the eastern front, the enemy [X Corps] over 90,000, giving us a 1.66 advantage over him. We have 250,000 men on the western front, the enemy 130,000, giving us a 1.75 advantage over him."[75]

Just before the attacks began October 25 in western Korea, a patrol from the 7th ROK Regiment managed to reach the Yalu River – the only Eighth Army unit to reach the Manchurian border during the war. The South Koreans reported the milestone, but did not tarry.[76]

Nearly a month later, the 7th Division's 17th Regiment accomplished the same feat in northeastern Korea, but with more panache. On the morning of November 21, Colonel Herbert Powell and his regiment reached the Yalu at the deserted village of Hyesanjn, known as the "ghost city of broken bridges."

On hand for the occasion were General Almond, who had arrived at the 17th's CP the previous evening in his L-17 aircraft, the *Blue Goose*; General David Barr, the 7th Division commander; and Barr's assistant, General Henry Hodes.[77]

Almond, Barr, and Hodes walked behind the lead company to the riverbank and, along with Colonel Powell, anointed the Yalu with a ritual urination, following the example of General George Patton watering the Rhine.

Across the river, Chinese sentries pointedly ignored the Americans. When Almond radioed MacArthur with the news, he replied with congratulations, "and tell David Barr the 7th Division hit the jackpot."

Now encouraged that the war would end very quickly, MacArthur ordered Almond to prod General Smith to move faster to the Chosin Reservoir, and thence to the Yalu River.[78]

A week later, a patrol from the 32nd Regiment's 3rd Battalion, led by Lieutenant Robert Kingston, reached the Yalu at Singalpajn after a house-to-house fight with North Korean troops. Kingston's men, too, took turns urinating in the river.

The patrol reported just one casualty – the strange, violent death of a soldier mauled by a Siberian tiger. It was a disturbing omen, perhaps portending the fate awaiting MacArthur's legions as they marched ever farther north.[79]

Chapter 3

The March North

I do not like the prospect of stringing out a Marine division along a single mountain road for 120 air miles from Hamhung to the [Manchurian] border. I believe a winter campaign in the mountains of Korea is too much to ask of the American soldier or Marine.

General O.P. Smith to Commandant Clifton Cates.[1]

Extensive air and ground reconnaissance around Koto-ri had yielded reports of only small groups of Chinese soldiers, encouraging Almond to issue "X Corps Operation Order 6 on November 11" – the immediate advance of all major units to the Yalu River.

Almond envisioned three "flying columns" charging to the Manchurian border. On the right was the ROK I Corps, which would march up the northeastern Korean coast. In the center was General Barr's 7th Division. The 1st Marine Division constituted the left prong, advancing northward past Chosin Reservoir to the Manchurian border.[2]

Although this dispersal of X Corps's 90,000 men across such a broad front might have appeared ill-advised, Almond and MacArthur believed that it faced nothing that could stop the drive to the Yalu. The war would be over by Christmas.

"We became 'land happy.' All units were racing to see who could cover the most mileage every day. The Yalu River became THE objective," said Ellis Williamson, one of Almond's senior planners.[3]

The 1st Marine Division, however, was quietly applying the brakes to its march to Chosin Reservoir.

General Smith had tried to convince Almond to slow the advance, arguing that consolidating X Corps's far-flung units made them less vulnerable to ambushes and large-scale Chinese attacks. Smith told Almond that "In the 1st Marine Division he had a powerful instrument, but that it couldn't help being weakened by the dispersion ..."

Seeing no threats, immediate or distant, to X Corps's drive north, Almond told Smith that he was being too cautious. Almond refused to slow down the advance.[4]

General Lemuel Shepherd, in charge of Fleet Marine Force, Pacific, and Smith's superior, sided with Almond.

Like Almond, Shepherd was a Virginia native and an alumnus of the Virginia Military Institute. He also badly wanted to become the next commandant of the Marine Corps, and believed it best to remain in the good graces of Almond and MacArthur.

In his oral history, Shepherd recalled having dinner with Smith, and advising him, "O.P., play the game, don't get so mad with Almond, he's trying to do the right thing." Shepherd urged Smith to expedite the 1st Marine Division's march to the Yalu.[5]

In ostensible obedience to Almond's November 11 Order 6, Smith directed the First Marines to capture Huksu-ri; the Seventh Marines to seize Hagaru-ri at the southern end of Chosin Reservoir; and the Fifth Marines to guard the MSR to Koto-ri.

At the same time, Smith surreptitiously slowed down his division's march north.[6]

"We pulled every trick in the book to slow down our advance, hoping the enemy would show his hand before we got even more widely dispersed than we already were," said Colonel Alpha Bowser, Smith's operations officer. "At the same time, we were building up our levels of supply at selected dumps along the road."[7]

Now aware that his immediate superior officer, Shepherd, was in agreement with Arnold and MacArthur, Smith recognized that it was pointless to address his concerns to him. Known for doing everything by the book, Smith for once did not.

He jumped the chain of command and wrote directly to Marine Commandant Clifton Cates to express his deep unease with Almond's demand that he swiftly march north without regard to dispersing his units.

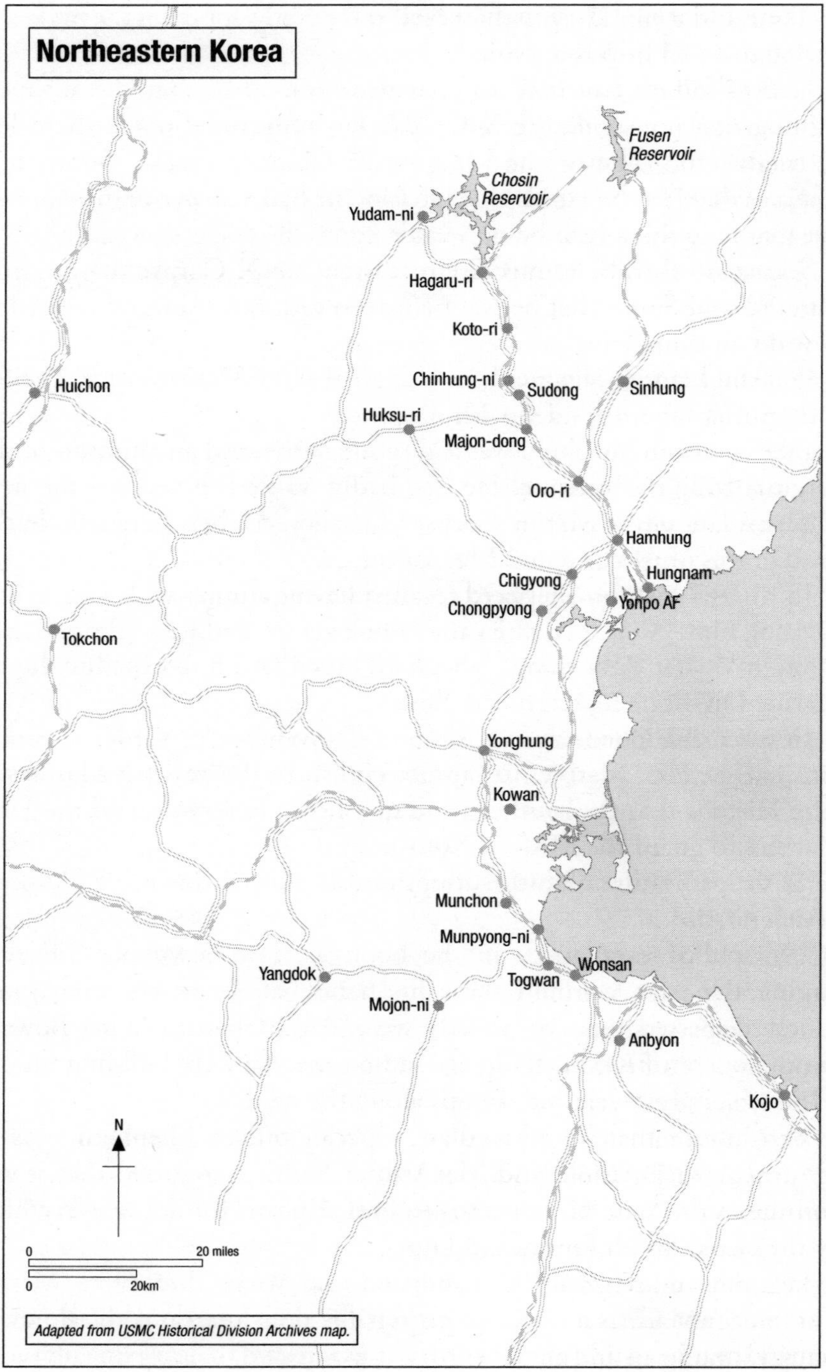
Northeastern Korea
Fusen Reservoir
Chosin Reservoir
Yudam-ni
Hagaru-ri
Koto-ri
Chinhung-ni
Sudong
Sinhung
Huichon
Huksu-ri
Majon-dong
Oro-ri
Hamhung
Hungnam
Chigyong
Yonpo AF
Chongpyong
Tokchon
Yonghung
Kowan
Munchon
Munpyong-ni
Wonsan
Togwan
Yangdok
Mojon-ni
Anbyon
Kojo
N
0
20 miles
0
20km
Adapted from USMC Historical Division Archives map.

"Time and again I have tried to tell the Corps Commander that in a Marine division he has a powerful instrument, but that it cannot help but lose its full effectiveness when dispersed," Smith wrote.

Of particular concern, he wrote, was the division's gaping left flank.

"There is no unit of the 8th Army nearer than 80 miles to the southwest of [the Seventh Marines]. When it is convenient the [X] Corps can say there is nothing on our left flank. If this were true, then there should be nothing to prevent the 8th Army from coming abreast of us. This they are not doing."

"I do not like the prospect of stringing out a Marine division along a single mountain road for 120 air miles from Hamhung to the [Manchurian] border," he wrote, especially in wintertime when bad weather would complicate supplying troops with food and ammunition and evacuating the wounded.

"I believe a winter campaign in the mountains of Korea is too much to ask of the American soldier or Marine," Smith told Cates.[8]

Smith's letter did not prompt Cates to act.

The Far Eastern Command (FEC) in Tokyo ordered X Corps to make plans to cut the Chinese supply route to the Eighth Army battle zone in western Korea. MacArthur's headquarters expected X Corps to advance 35 air miles north of Chosin Reservoir and then turn west to sever the enemy's supply line from Manchuria.

General Almond objected. Carrying out the FEC's plan would stretch X Corps's MSR too far. Almond ordered his staff to develop a different plan – for the 1st Marine Division to attack west from Yudam-ni on the reservoir's western side to Mupyong-ni and then to Kanggye, the temporary seat of Kim Il-Sung's government.

The objectives were 55 miles west of Yudam-ni through heavily forested mountains rising 7,000 feet or higher. Under Almond's plan, the Army's 7th Division would traverse the reservoir's eastern side and continue to the Yalu River, while protecting the Marines' right flank.

Completed on November 23, the plan was approved by MacArthur the next day and scheduled to be put into action on November 27.[9]

As Smith's Marines pressed north on the one-lane dirt and gravel MSR from Chinhung-ni and then Koto-ri, engineers widened and improved the road, which in places clung to nearly vertical mountainsides that cast shadows even at noon.

Before the improvements, NKPA tanks had been unable to negotiate the hairpin turns on the 2,600-foot climb to Funchilin Pass. The twisting road sequestered the tanks near Chinhung-ni and doomed them to destruction by the Marines.

The engineers' road work made it possible for six Marine M4A Sherman tanks to reach Koto-ri by November 18. On the 19th, five large bulldozers pushed on to Hagaru-ri, where Marine engineers planned to build an airstrip.[10]

At this juncture, an airstrip might have appeared superfluous to General Almond's insistence on a headlong, war-ending drive to the Yalu River. However, events would demonstrate the Hagaru-ri airfield's surpassing importance to the survival of the strung-out regiments, as Smith's worst fears were realized.

Chapter 4

Arctic Cold Arrives

November 10–27, 1950

We turned on the lights of Jeeps and stood or sat on the hoods and ate our meal. You had to eat fast because everything was turning cold. The gravy and then the mashed potatoes froze first.

CORPSMAN BILL DAVIS, WITH THE SEVENTH MARINES, DESCRIBING THANKSGIVING DINNER.[1]

Cold weather unlike anything ever experienced by most of the Marines suddenly swept down on them at Koto-ri during the night of November 10–11. The temperature plummeted from 32 degrees to minus 8 as 35mph winds whipped across the Siberian plains into Korea.

The combination of the cold temperatures and strong winds produced a wind chill of minus 38 degrees. "The initial shock of subzero temperatures stunned personnel and over 200 turned in for medical treatment," a Seventh Marines' after-action report said.[2]

The powerful wind gusts blew down some men. Many went into shock; some men wept; others simply collapsed as though from exhaustion. Navy corpsmen described the dazed cold-weather victims as "shook."

The raw, wet cold "made people daft," said Lieutenant Joe Owen. "They stopped talking, except to blaspheme the goddamn fools who sent us out into this miserable, cold country."[3]

The Marines erected tents and lit stoves inside them. They rotated the stunned men through them for a few minutes of warmth and hot coffee before turning them back out into the cold.

After the initial shock, the men slowly adapted to subzero cold. In the weeks ahead, the cold would only deepen, but the "shook" symptoms did not recur.[4]

The Chosin Reservoir area lies in the Kaema Highlands, the most remote, isolated, and coldest part of Korea. It is cut off from warmer air from the Yellow Sea to the west and from the Sea of Japan to the southeast, while being fully exposed to cold fronts charging down from the north out of Manchuria and Siberia.

The winter of 1950 would be remembered as one of the region's coldest, with the temperatures bottoming out at minus 40 and lower. Before 1950, the coldest recorded temperature was 46 degrees below zero at Hagaru-ri.[5]

Winters were cold on the North Dakota farm where Private Eugene Timseth was reared, but "on the farm you get shelter out of the cold, like going into a barn where cattle were to stay warm. But at Chosin we had no shelter. We had to live, try to sleep and survive in the snow and cold, day and night."[6]

Navy Lieutenant Henry Litvin, a battalion surgeon, said he did not notice the extreme temperature change until he began eating breakfast outdoors one morning in a strong wind.

After quickly consuming his scrambled eggs, he picked up his tin canteen coffee cup. "The tin was so cold my fingers stuck to the metal and there was a film of ice on the coffee itself," he said. "For the first time in the campaign I wondered if the weather might turn out to be a medical problem."

Commanders submitted requests to higher-ups for parkas, woolen socks, heavy underwear, and hot food for their men, who continued to go out on reconnaissance patrols from Koto-ri despite freezing, wet, foggy conditions.[7]

They encountered small Chinese units in the jagged hills miles from Koto-ri. Often, the enemy fired on the Marines and then vanished like wraiths into the swirling mists, but sometimes they put up a stiff fight and the Marines suffered casualties.

The morning after the Seventh Marines' Baker Company returned from a long, exhausting patrol outside Koto-ri in rain and sleet, the Marines awakened to find their poncho bed wraps buried under a half-foot of snow. An icy wind shrieked over the plateau as Baker came to full wakefulness.

"The men groaned, coughed, wheezed, and hawked big gobs of phlegm," wrote Owen. A corpsman ministered to a long line of sick men at the company CP. Each man was given an APC pill (aspirin, phenacetin, caffeine) and a swig from a canteen containing diluted sick-bay alcohol.

After sick call, the shivering men, blasted by wind and snow, marched north, still wearing their ponchos in an attempt to keep warm. The ponchos froze stiff and crackled in the wind as the men once more cursed the powers-that-be responsible for their plight.[8]

Beneath the ponchos they wore unlined field jackets and lightweight dungarees that they had been issued while fighting in South Korea's summer heat months earlier. Their summer-issue footwear consisted of thin socks under boondockers.

Marine Quartermaster General William Hill had anticipated the division's need for cold-weather gear. He was familiar with northern Asia's penetrating cold, having served in China before World War II and explored the Gobi Desert.

In early October, Hill had begun shipping heavier clothing to Korea, remembering northern Asia's early winters from his time in the region.

Their cold-weather gear arrived the day after the first wintry blast. Each man received a heavy knee-length, pile-lined parka with a hood; winter-weight storm trousers; a new set of dungarees to wear underneath them; flannel shirts; long johns; woolen gloves; leather and canvas mittens with trigger fingers to wear over the gloves; and three pairs of woolen socks.

The Marines walked around their bivouac in their new gear to become accustomed to carrying the additional weight before going out on their next patrol. With all of the clothing layers to peel back to perform bodily functions, even urination became a challenge.[9]

The new boots, Shoe-pacs, with thick, heavily cleated soles, replaced the Marines' boondockers. They weighed nearly twice as much as the boondockers and would become the bane of the foot soldiers fighting in North Korea. They slipped on ice, and they were cumbersome and clumsy for hill-climbing.

But worst of all, when the Shoe-pac's leather tops were laced tightly from the ankle over the shin, there was no air circulation. Exertion produced sweat, and when the man stopped moving, the sweat froze.

Casualties from frostbite would exceed those from combat wounds in the weeks ahead. To pre-empt frostbite, men were urged to change their socks often – not always practical when marching or in combat.[10]

In late October, the Far Eastern Command quartermaster's office had optimistically stated that the war would end before cold-weather clothing would be needed.[11] Yet on November 14, a cold front swept across North Korea, driving down temperatures to 35 below.

The winter gear shortage pinched Army units hard across X Corps.

On November 17, General Almond informed the Far Eastern Command in Tokyo that the 7th Army Division had an "urgent need for 250 squad tents complete and 400 stoves with oil burners ... Soldiers are freezing for lack of shelter."

The same day, the 7th Division requested 6,705 mountain sleeping bags for US personnel, and an additional 6,855 for its ROK troops.

The extreme cold forced a re-evaluation of weapons capabilities. The Marines disliked the M-1 and M-2 carbines because the safety and clip release were close to one another and a mittened hand could inadvertently activate either or both. The men preferred the M-1 Garand, and took them from the dead and wounded whenever possible.

They were lubricated with hair oil, which was lighter than the usual lubricant. When it got colder, the weapons were wiped dry and "the barest touch of oil" was applied.[12]

Air-cooled machine guns had to be fired every two or three hours to keep them operational. They also tended to burn out barrels quickly in the cold.

However, the water-cooled .30-caliber machine gun worked well when the water jacket was filled with antifreeze.

When carbon buildup caused a machine gun to seize up, urinating on the front of the barrel often resolved the problem.[13]

The cold especially affected the howitzers. Besides the near-impossibility of digging their trails into the frozen ground, their firing rate slowed considerably; two to three minutes elapsed, instead of mere seconds, while a gun crept back into battery to fire again. Moreover, their effective range decreased by 20 percent.[14]

Extreme cold drained radio batteries and cracked open 3.5-inch rocket launcher rounds. Frozen mortar parts sometimes simply broke, and there was an alarming number of mortar duds.

Tank machine guns had to be hand-loaded for the first few rounds before they would fire automatically. Diesel engines were run continually, with motor transport personnel keeping watch around-the-clock so that the truck engines would not freeze up.[15]

C-ration meat, beans, hash, and stew froze solid and had to be carefully thawed in a pot of hot water before it could be eaten, or a man would suffer from a gnawing pain in his gut, or diarrhea.

Consequently, the Marines carried their "wet" rations close to their bodies so that they would not freeze solid and could be consumed in small amounts. For the most part, only the dry rations were routinely eaten, with the result that riflemen lost 15 to 30 pounds on average while running up and down North Korea's craggy hills on such a sparse diet.[16]

"If you were lucky, you had a can of beans," said Sergeant Joe Demarco of the Seventh Marines. "You'd keep this under your armpits all day, then warm it up over a fire at night."[17]

Going into a firefight, corpsmen carried their morphine syrettes in their mouths so that they remained fluid and could be immediately jabbed into a wounded man if needed.

The extreme cold had one major benefit: battle wounds temporarily froze shut, stopping blood loss until the wounded man's body temperature returned to normal. Undoubtedly, the cold enabled many wounded men to survive who ordinarily would not have.[18]

Colonel Litzenberg's Seventh Marines continued pushing into the looming North Korean mountains, described by author James Brady as a place of "shadow and shade, a gloom, a darkness, over the snow and the land."

Beyond each hill rose yet another, taller hill. It was "bandit country," perfect for ambushes, said one Marine. Another said the roads took the Marines into a "mysterious Oriental kingdom" where he expected to see "a giant ogre lurking on the sawtooth horizon."[19]

Litzenberg's men took advantage of a brief interlude in November of unusually warm Indian summer weather to wash up, shave, and use their toothbrushes. Patrols roved the front lines, and working parties brought up supplies, but otherwise it was like being in a rest camp where little was required of the men.[20]

The prospect of relying on a single-lane mountain road to receive supplies and evacuate the wounded troubled General Smith, whose instincts warned him that major Chinese forces were gathering nearby, preparing to attack his division. In a letter to his wife Esther, he wrote, "Our only answer is to build an airstrip on the top of the mountain."[21]

The Seventh Marines reached Smith's "top of the mountain" – Hagaru-ri, at the southern end of 30-mile-long Chosin Reservoir – on November 14 and 15 and secured it. The village lay in a shallow bowl through which the Changjin River flowed north into the reservoir a mile and a half away.[22]

The Seventh established perimeters north and south of Hagaru-ri, while the Fifth Marines followed a branch of the MSR that traced Chosin Reservoir's eastern shore.

On the 16th, patrols engaged small groups of Chinese troops one mile west of Hagaru-ri and, aided by artillery and close-air support, drove about 200 enemy soldiers from entrenchments three miles to the northwest.[23]

In a meeting with General Almond, Smith said that an airstrip would be indispensable, but must be large so that transport planes could airlift casualties from Hagaru-ri to hospitals in Hungnam and Japan.

"What casualties?" Almond asked, clearly puzzled. He believed that the North Korean army was on the run, and that the war would end in just weeks.

Almond grudgingly consented to the construction of an airfield at Hagaru-ri, but told Smith to expect no assistance from X Corps. Marine engineers alone would have to build the airstrip, Almond said.

"Division Engineers are not normally required to construct fields for transport planes, but no aid was forthcoming," Smith wrote to his wife.

The Marine engineers began clearing ground for the airfield on the day that the bulldozers reached Hagaru-ri, November 19.

X Corps eventually set a deadline for the airstrip's completion, a tacit acknowledgment that it would be useful, but it still would not aid in its construction.

"The fixing of deadlines was normal practice for the X Corps. Our Engineer Battalion had been working night and day on the construction of the airstrip. The fixing of a deadline would make no difference in the date of completion of the strip," he told Esther with a trace of irritation.[24]

Smith and General Field Harris, the commander of the 1st Marine Air Wing, had walked the ground at Hagaru-ri on November 16 to evaluate potential airfield sites. They found an area south of the village that was flat and large enough to accommodate an airstrip. The soil consisted of "thick, black loam." "If the ground freezes," Smith wrote in his log, "it will probably be all right for a strip."[25]

Smith and Harris had located the airfield site after Smith persuaded a skeptical Almond to permit him to build it.

Now it was up to Lieutenant Colonel John Partridge, the 1st Marine Engineer Battalion commander, to get it built. Partridge had proven his resourcefulness two months earlier at Seoul, where he had gotten the Marines across the Han River on pontoon bridges.

Smith set a December 1 deadline for completing the airstrip. All day long and under floodlights at night the rumble of bulldozers and earth-moving equipment filled the air – as did the crack of enemy snipers' gunfire aimed at the heavy equipment drivers.

Explosives were used to break through the ground, which was frozen to the consistency of stone. The work proceeded slowly around-the-clock.[26]

Engineering field manuals recommended a 3,600-foot-long runway for transport planes at sea level – and 1,000 additional feet for each 1,000 feet of elevation. At Hagaru-ri's 4,000 feet, the runway ideally should have been 7,600 feet for twin-engine transport planes to land and take off. But 7,600 feet of flat ground simply could not be found around Hagaru-ri. A 3,200-foot runway would have to suffice.

When the bulldozers began work on November 19, the engineers had just 12 days to complete a durable, usable airstrip under Smith's tight deadline.

Initially, it was designed to be just 50 feet wide with no taxiways, and to accommodate two planes at once. With expansion, six planes could load and unload men and cargo on the airstrip simultaneously.[27]

Until the airstrip was completed, VMO-6's nine helicopters and ten light planes airlifted casualties from Hagaru-ri, Koto-ri, and later from Yudam-ni. VMO-6 would evacuate 152 casualties before Hagaru-ri's airfield was completed.[28]

Hagaru-ri was a humble village of 500 people before it was suddenly transformed into a busy military base bristling with combat and support troops, bulldozers, trucks, and artillery.

Oxen had tilled the stony soil until it sprouted fields of millet and barley, now dead and rustling in the cold wind. The village's buildings consisted of shacks and some concrete structures lining dirt streets.

Smith's decision to build an airstrip at Hagaru-ri established the hamlet as not only a crucial transit point, but also the 1st Division's forward base, field hospital, communication center, and ammunition and supply depot.

A strongly defended perimeter ringed Hagaru-ri as ammunition and supplies arrived by truck convoy.

Smith intended to accumulate ten units of fire at Hagaru-ri – one unit equal to one day's aggregate firepower – and to bring his tanks into the village.[29]

His foresight would enable his division to survive amid incessant enemy attacks and arctic cold, while in the future flying out casualties.[30]

The Seventh Marines broke camp on November 25 and resumed their advance north. The weather turned again, and wind-driven snow pellets stung the Marines as they climbed the MSR toward Toktong Pass, seven miles west of Hagaru-ri.

An estimated 150 to 200 Chinese soldiers that had dug in around a rock formation near the pass fired on the Marines. Close-air support was summoned.

The Corsairs on station overhead made a napalm run, described as "a spectacle of awesome and terrible beauty." In its wake, "Chinese soldiers were aflame, running about in frenzied circles. They threw themselves, flailing, into the snow," an eyewitness said.

The survivors scattered. When the Marines reached the pass, they found only charred bodies. "I think we were all awed by the power of that close-in napalm strike," said Lieutenant Joe Owen.[31]

North of Toktong Pass, the road narrowed and writhed through gorges on the approach to Yudam-ni, seven miles distant. Enemy resistance stiffened.

Roadblocks appeared, and each one had to be cleared mainly by rifle squads and machine guns, as air support became spottier because of the weather, and the Marines passed beyond range of the heavy artillery, still in Hagaru-ri.

At a roadblock and a hairpin turn, enemy troops hidden above the road, which was devoid of concealment, raked it with sleeting machine-gun and rifle fire.

Summoned by Lieutenant Colonel Ray Davis, the Seventh's 1st Battalion commander, Lieutenant Joe Owen's mortarmen came up the road singing a parody of the Army marching song, "Sound Off." They set up on the open road as bullets spanged around them and fired two rounds that silenced the Chinese position.

"You tell your men their shooting is right on, lieutenant," Davis told Owen. "But tell them that their singing is way off key."[32]

The Marine Air Wing moved its tactical air direction center to Hagaru-ri, which was closer to the action and a better place for controlling aircraft.

Pilots warned the 1st Division as it approached the Yudam-ni valley of large bands of enemy troops, some of them in plain sight. And thousands of footprints were visible in the snow.

Flying cover for the division vanguard, the fighter-bomber pilots reported five roadblocks between Hagaru-ri and Yudam-ni and an enemy buildup in the area. As many as 50 to 60 Chinese soldiers were seen crowding into a peasant's hut.

On November 21, they observed hundreds of troops west and southwest of Yudam-ni; nine large holes blown in the MSR; four stone roadblocks between Hagaru-ri and Yudam-ni; and Chinese troops, now attired in their white winter uniforms instead of summer green, digging defensive lines in the area.[33]

It all pointed to an impending attack.

Even though he expected Chinese columns to pounce upon his division at any time in the soaring North Korean mountains, Smith had no choice but to follow General Almond's orders. His division would continue advancing toward the Yalu River, but cautiously.

If attacked, he told his officers, they were to fight from high ground in the steep hills and mountains. They were not to be tethered to the roads, where the Chinese hoped to find them.

Artillery and close-air support would counteract the enemy's numerical advantage. The division would move primarily by day, when both were available, and dig in at night.[34]

"The country around Chosin was never intended for military operations," Smith told Army historian S.L.A. Marshall. "Even Genghis Khan wouldn't tackle it."[35]

Aggressively patrolling in all directions from Hagaru-ri, the Seventh and Fifth Marines continued to search for the enemy to determine his strength, but were unable to ascertain his numbers and intentions.

In the meantime, the Army's 3rd Infantry Division relieved the First Marine Regiment in the low country near the coast. The 3rd initially was to have protected the MSR from Hamhung to Hagaru-ri, but persistent guerrilla activity around Wonsan kept it in the lowlands, guarding the road between Hamhung and Sudong.

Colonel Puller's regiment moved into the highlands, dropping off a battalion at Chinhung-ni, and another battalion and the regimental headquarters at Koto-ri. On November 26, its third battalion, minus George Company, marched into Hagaru-ri. Smith's plan to consolidate his division during the drive north was as complete as it would ever be.[36]

General Almond made certain that Thanksgiving Day, November 23, was observed in every unit of X Corps. The feast included a tom turkey, cranberry sauce, shrimp cocktail, candied sweet potatoes, and mincemeat pie – and often the additional ingredient of improvisation to compensate for the cold and the spartan setting. It was an impressive logistics feat that many men would remember for the rest of their lives.

Thanksgiving was celebrated a day late, on the 24th, by Davis's 1st Battalion, alongside the road to Yudam-ni. The stacks of turkeys delivered to the battalion cooks were frozen, through and through, as hard as concrete.

"It was so cold no one could figure out how to do it," Davis said. "Everyone, from the chief cook on down, said it couldn't be done."

They finally made a mountain of the frozen birds around two field kitchen stoves in two pyramidical tents – one inside the other – until the turkeys were thawed enough to be cut up and cooked.

Davis's men feasted on the turkey and trimmings throughout the day when they were not patrolling or ferreting out snipers.[37]

Some ate later than others. After a day of patrolling, the Seventh Regiment's Baker Company got in at nightfall. The cooks served the Thanksgiving dinner and fixings on tin trays.

"We turned on the lights of Jeeps and stood or sat on the hoods and ate our meal," said corpsman Bill Davis. "You had to eat fast because everything was turning cold. The gravy and then the mashed potatoes froze first." Enemy snipers shot at the Marines as they tried to quickly finish the meal before it froze solid.[38]

Besides being an unusual celebration of a national holiday, it was an occasion for morbid humor. "We kind of wondered: Were we just being fattened up for the kill?" said Pfc Hector Cafferata of the Seventh Marines' Fox Company.[39]

At X Corps headquarters at Hamhung, General Almond threw a sybaritic feast. General Smith was one of the invited guests. In his log, Smith described the meal: "The dinner was complete with cocktails served from a cocktail bar, tablecloths, napkins, Japanese chinaware, regular silverware, place cards, etc." Also attending Almond's dinner were General David Barr of the Army's 7th Infantry Division; Admiral Arthur Struble, commander of the Seventh Fleet; and General Field Harris of the First Marine Air Wing.[40]

Almond was still relishing his ritual urination in the Yalu River two days earlier, when he joined the 7th Division's 17th Infantry there.

He believed it was an historic milestone, marking the beginning of the end of the Korean War. Almond was certain that his soldiers and Marines would all go home soon.[41]

While the Americans feasted, the Chinese troops cleaned their weapons and foraged for food.[42]

Except for minor patrol actions, the North Korean front was quiet everywhere on November 24 – the day that MacArthur announced the beginning of the Eighth Army's end-of-the-war offensive in western Korea. His expansive communiqué was read to all of the United Nations troops on the Korean peninsula. Senior Chinese officers quickly learned of it as well.

"The United Nations massive compression envelopment in North Korea against the new Red Armies operating there is now approaching its decisive effort," the communiqué began portentously. MacArthur said UN aircraft had successfully interdicted enemy supply lines over the previous three weeks.

On the morning of the 24th, the western pincer was moving forward "to complete the compression and close the vise" with X Corps in the northeast. Almond's X Corps had now reached a "commanding envelopment position, cutting in two the northern reaches of the enemy's geographical potential ... If successful, this should for all practical purposes end the war," the communiqué triumphantly concluded.[43]

Evidently, no one had considered Red China's intentions.

The Eighth Army offensive did make impressive gains on the first day. But then, on November 25, the Chinese counterattacked.

Attacking in astonishingly large numbers, enemy soldiers stopped General Walton Walker's troops in their tracks. The ROK II Corps was flung back at Tokshon, about 70 miles southwest of Yudam-ni.

The counterattacks in western Korea prompted MacArthur to revisit X Corps's end-of-war plan and change the 1st Marine Division's mission.

X Corps Operation Order No. 7, developed by Almond's staff, stated that instead of marching farther north before turning west, the Marines would drive west from Yudam-ni and join the Eighth Army in the Taebaek Mountains.

Beginning at 8am on November 27, the Fifth Marines, acting as the eastern pincer of MacArthur's touted "massive compression envelopment," was to lead the attack to Mupyong-ni before turning north to the Yalu River.[44]

Lieutenant Colonel Ray Murray, the Fifth's commander, was nonplussed by his orders to march west into the forbidding North Korean mountains in northern Asia's notoriously brutal winter weather.

"It was unbelievable," he said. "The more you think about it, the more unreal it becomes." It was a "crazy" plan, he said.[45]

"It was an insane plan," General Clark Ruffner, Almond's chief of staff, later wrote. "You couldn't take a picnic lunch in peacetime and go over that terrain in November and December."

But the order had come from MacArthur's Dai Ichi Tokyo headquarters, and it would not be retracted. MacArthur believed that the Chinese counterattack in western Korea was a temporary setback that would be reversed.[46]

First Division intelligence officers predicted stiff resistance. "He [the enemy] will defend at all costs our debouchment in his rear," the Periodic Intelligence Report for November 27 predicted.

General Smith drily commented that the road to Mupyong-ni "passed through the central mountain chain and was narrow, steep, and winding. Our line of communication promised to be very tenuous."[47]

On the 27th, Smith did not yet know that the Eighth Army had failed to reach its initial objective under MacArthur's "pincer movement" plan and was instead chaotically falling back before the attacking Chinese forces on the western front.

Smith's regiments would find no friendly forces at Mupyong-ni.[48]

General Barr's 7th Division was ordered to attack north to the Yalu River, with the 32nd Infantry's 1st Battalion relieving the Fifth Marines east of the reservoir so that it could spearhead the attack to Mupyong-ni.[49]

MacArthur continued to profoundly underestimate the size of the Chinese forces in North Korea. He was influenced by General Willoughby's willfully shoddy intelligence, and unaware of the extent of the enemy's stealthy nighttime infiltration into the North Korean mountains.

So far as MacArthur and his staff were concerned, the drive to the Yalu River was still achievable and would yet signal the war's end.[50]

Lieutenant Colonel Hal Roise's 2nd Battalion of the Fifth Marines was redeployed in motor transports from east of Chosin Reservoir to Yudam-ni on November 26. A battalion of the 32nd Infantry of the Army's 7th Division had relieved the Fifth.

The ambitious objective set the next day for Roise's men was a mountain pass ten miles distant.

The Fifth's 1st and 3rd Battalions reached Yudam-ni in the afternoon and evening of the 27th and bivouacked in an assembly area near town.

During the night of November 26–27, colder air aloft on strong winds from Manchuria whipped through the Marine positions.

In wind-blown tents, Roise gave his company officers last-minute instructions about the next day's attack to the west, and Seventh Regiment officers learned of their roles in protecting Roise's flanks by occupying the formidable Northwest and Southwest Ridges.[51]

Chapter 5

The Chinese Prepare to Attack

Kill these Marines as you would snakes in your home!
CHINESE POLITICAL COMMISSAR'S PAMPHLET.[1]

Three Chinese soldiers from the Chinese 20th Army's 60th Division, captured on the 26th southwest of Yudam-ni by Lieutenant Colonel Ray Davis's 1st Battalion, provided alarming intelligence. They told their interrogators that the 58th, 59th, and 60th Divisions of the 20th Army had been in the Yudam-ni area for a week.

After the Fifth and Seventh Marines had passed them by, Chinese forces were under orders to drive south and southeast from Yudam-ni and cut the MSR, the prisoners said.

General Almond rejected the report out of hand. There were no more than 10,000 to 20,000 Chinese soldiers in the Yudam-ni area, he declared.[2]

The 1st Division periodic intelligence report for November 26 contributed to the illusion of weak Chinese forces in the area, capable of causing only "a token delay" to the planned advance to Mupyong-ni.

The anticipated weak resistance, the report said, was "a direct result of his [the enemy's] preoccupation with the western front," one that "may well prove fatal."

The authors couldn't have been more wrong.[3]

In fact, six Chinese divisions had been positively identified in northeast Korea, but X Corps and 1st Division intelligence officers believed that they would withdraw before the advancing allied troops.[4]

The Chinese 9th Army Group's intelligence regarding X Corps's strength, its units' locations, and its capabilities was just as flawed as Almond's assessment of Chinese strength and intentions in the Chosin Reservoir area.

The army group commander, Song Shilun, sought a more ambitious victory than just destroying two Marine regiments; he wanted to encircle and wipe out all of the allied regiments in the Chosin Reservoir area, of which he believed there were four. In actuality, there were six.

After his divisions surrounded the X Corps forces, Song planned to test the strength of each regiment, determining which could be eliminated first and which ones next, rather than concentrating all of his troops against the two Marine regiments.

This divide-and-conquer strategy, abetted by mobile and nighttime operations, had succeeded against the Nationalists during the Chinese Civil War.

During the civil war, the 9th Army Group had distinguished itself in 1948 at the Battle of Ji'nan, and in 1949 at the Battle of Shanghai. Song believed that the strategy could also produce a decisive victory in North Korea.[5]

In their haste to move into their assault positions without being detected by allied air reconnaissance, the Chinese left behind most of their supplies, winter clothing, and food, just as arctic cold began to grip the region.[6]

At his front-line command post, Song exhorted his officers and staff to overcome every hardship and, if necessary, sacrifice their lives to drive the invaders from Korea over the next three to six months.

The 9th Army Group had never faced American firepower and supporting arms. Song's prediction of a swift, annihilating victory would prove to be fanciful.[7]

Song's political commissar wrote a pamphlet that was distributed to 9th Army Group troops before they attacked. It said, "Soon we will meet the American Marines in battle. We will destroy them. When they are defeated, the enemy will collapse and our country will be free from the threat of aggression. Kill these Marines as you would snakes in your home!"[8]

On November 26, Song ordered the 20th Army "and main force of the 27th Army to destroy the main force of the U.S. 1st Marine

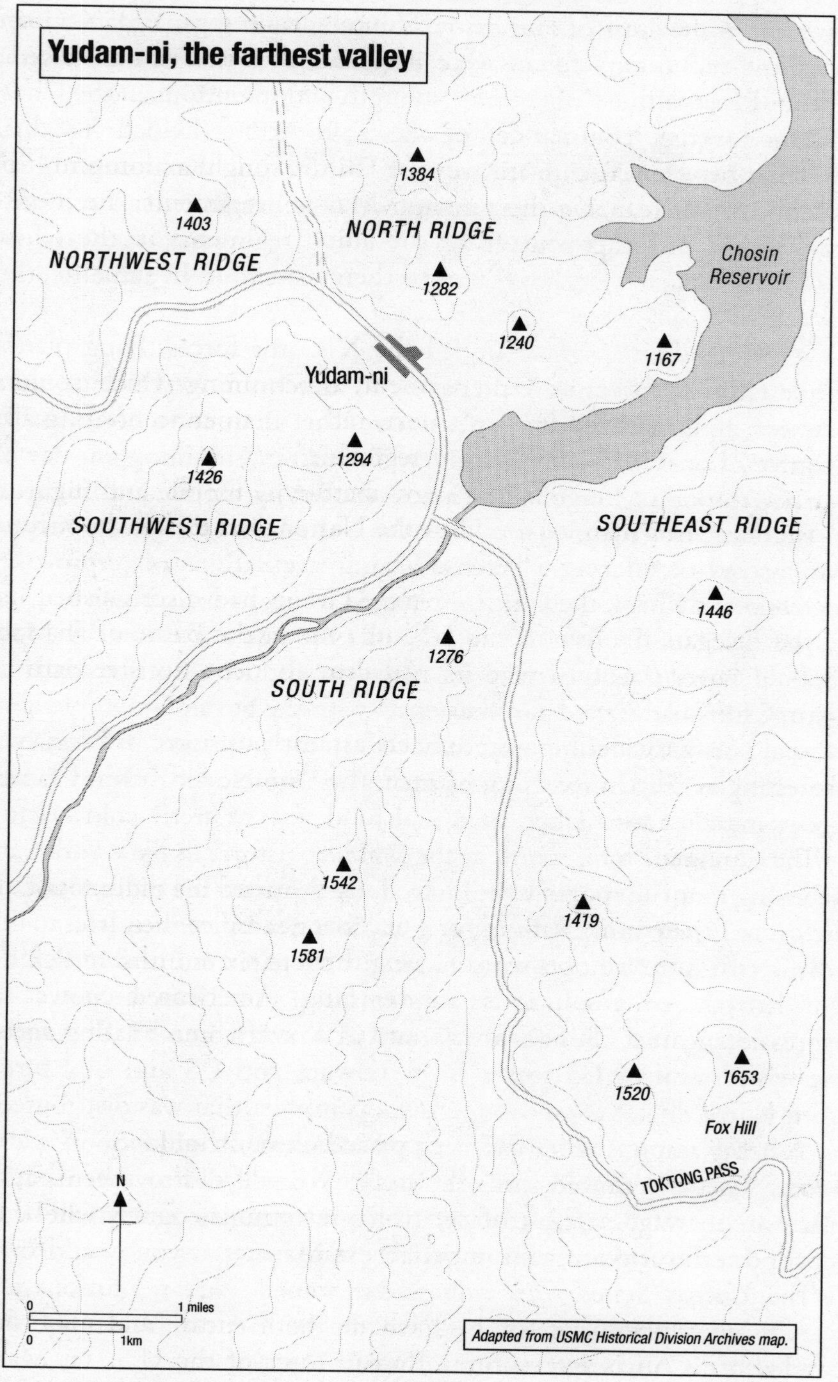
Yudam-ni, the farthest valley
1384
1403
NORTH RIDGE
NORTHWEST RIDGE
1282
Chosin Reservoir
1240
1167
Yudam-ni
1294
1426
SOUTHWEST RIDGE
SOUTHEAST RIDGE
1446
1276
SOUTH RIDGE
1542
1419
1581
1520
1653
Fox Hill
TOKTONG PASS
N
0
1 miles
0
1km
Adapted from USMC Historical Division Archives map.

Division in the areas of Hagaru-ri, Shina-ri, Kujing-ni, Yudam-ni and Singhung-ni." Song's forces were dispersed at five locations around Chosin Reservoir.

Peng Deqing, commander of the 27th Army, divided his three divisions between Yudam-ni, west of Chosin, and Singhung-ni, east of Chosin, not realizing their manpower was insufficient to achieve a quick victory in either place.[9]

While Chinese forces were preparing to attack the 1st Division, nine Chinese diplomats led by Ambassador Wu Xiuquan, a confidant of Premier Zhou Enlai, arrived in New York after a draining ten-day air journey through Mongolia and across the Soviet Union and Europe.

The delegation planned to address the United Nations at Lake Success. But instead of offering a defense against accusations of unprovoked aggression in Korea, the Chinese planned to go on the offensive.

The delegation's visit to the UN was the latest overture by Mao's year-old government to take its place on the world stage. Early in 1950, China had signed a military pact with the Soviet Union pledging mutual assistance if either were attacked. In early October, as China was protesting at the United Nations incursion into North Korea, Chinese troops marched into Tibet.[10]

The diplomats took rooms at the Waldorf-Astoria in New York City. Believing that the rooms were bugged, they played the radio loudly to drown out their conversations, or went to a nearby park to talk.

In a two-hour 20,000-word harangue prepared for him in Peking, Wu introduced resolutions condemning the United States for aggression against China, Taiwan, and in North Korea. He demanded the withdrawal of US forces from Taiwan, and US and UN forces from Korea.

"A heavy responsibility had been placed on our shoulders," Wu later wrote. "We had moved from the military battlefield to the debating platform to wage a face-to-face, tit-for-tat struggle against the then most powerful and arrogant imperialist state."

The United States' UN ambassador vetoed Wu's resolutions and introduced a resolution of his own at the General Assembly that condemned China's aggression in Korea.

The Chinese delegation walked out in protest. It would be 21 years before China returned to the UN.[11]

The Seventh Marines' 14-mile advance to Yudam-ni from Hagaru-ri was punctuated by sharp firefights with Chinese units as the Marines neared Yudam-ni.

"Friendly natives" reported that "many, many" Chinese were massing at Hansong-ni, a small village in a valley leading to Yudam-ni from the southwest.

On November 26, Lieutenant Colonel Davis dispatched Able Company to patrol that area.

Lieutenant Frank Mitchell's platoon was on point when Able Company was ambushed. Mitchell's men fought off the attack with automatic weapons and grenades, but Chinese reinforcements poured in from Hansong-ni.

Able's commander, Lieutenant Eugenous Hovatter, ordered a withdrawal as daylight waned, with Mitchell's platoon in an especially exposed position. Although wounded, Mitchell led a hand-to-hand counterattack and began withdrawing his platoon. While single-handedly covering his men's withdrawal, Mitchell was killed by small-arms fire.[12]

Above Yudam-ni loomed five ridges like castle battlements, each a tortuous complex of peaks, spurs, and draws. The desolate hamlet lay in a broad valley from which roads fanned out to the north, west, and south.

Litzenberg believed that the village had been defended by at least a battalion. Furthermore, air reconnaissance had spotted another battalion entrenched north of the town, and civilians reported that the enemy occupied defensive positions on high ground seven miles to the northwest.[13]

It appeared that the Chinese captives were right: the crossroads town was surrounded by possibly three enemy divisions. But the very windy night of November 26–27, when temperatures plunged far below zero, was relatively quiet nonetheless.

At daylight on November 27 Litzenberg's companies resumed their aggressive patrolling among the steep hills and valleys around Yudam-ni. Captain Myron Wilcox's Baker Company was sent to the area where Able Company had been ambushed the previous day.

Captain Thomas Cooney's George Company seized Hill 1426, a peak on Southwest Ridge, without meeting opposition initially. The hill mass dominated the road west to Mupyong-ni, the final objective of the Fifth Marines' 2nd Battalion when it began its march later that morning.

Steep-sided Hill 1426, and Hill 1403, a peak on Northwest Ridge north of the Mupyong-ni road, girdled the road west of Yudam-ni, and constituted a potential chokepoint. By mid-morning on November 27, both hills were in Marine hands.[14]

The Fifth Marines' advance toward Mupyong-ni began. The Marines found that each step westward met increased resistance and hailstorms of enemy fire. Marine engineers began tackling nine unmanned roadblocks barring the way.[15]

The advance to the west became a running battle.

Small-arms fire from a draw and a spur at the foot of Hill 1403 held up the advance. Marine mortars and 75mm recoilless rifles hammered the crest of the spur and bunkers on the forward slopes.

Then, VMF-312's Corsairs blasted the positions with rockets and bombs. The Fifth Marines' Fox and Dog Companies struck both ends of the draw, and most of the Chinese fled to the west.[16]

An observation plane reported that Chinese troops held positions all across the Fifth Marines' front.

When Dog Company rounded a road bend at the south end of the Hill 1403 spur, enemy machine-gun fire slammed into the column from Sakkat Mountain, dead ahead to the west.

From their places of concealment, the Marines observed with trepidation that heavily armed Chinese occupied tier upon tier of bunkers on the eastern slopes of the towering mass.

The bunkers were constructed of logs wired together to double thickness, and reinforced by rock and soil several feet thick. They were virtually impervious to all but direct rocket fire.[17]

The strong resistance, the daunting terrain, and the rising casualties persuaded Lieutenant Colonel Roise at 2:30pm to discontinue the attack. It had advanced just 1,500 yards, less than a mile.

Fox Company established night positions north of the Mupyong-ni road on Hill 1403, while Dog Company dug in across the road on a spur of Southwestern Ridge.[18]

General Almond, crackling with his usual energy, arrived in Yudam-ni by jeep on the 27th to check on the progress of the Marines' drive. He had helicoptered to Hagaru-ri from Hamhung and then endured the jolting jeep ride over the unpaved 14-mile road to Yudam-ni, weaving through the truck and jeep traffic that clogged the MSR.

At Seventh Marines headquarters, Almond pinned medals on several men and then asked the regiment's intelligence officer, Major Don France, for an update on the situation.

France typically delivered a sober, business-like summary, but this time he blurted out, "General, there are a fucking lot of Chinese in those hills!" Almond received the news without betraying any emotion. He left the tent and walked to the nearby airstrip, where he boarded a helicopter waiting to fly him back to Hagaru-ri.[19]

The stalled drive to Mupyong-ni appeared to bear out the dour observation of an Almond staff officer, Lieutenant Colonel Bill McCaffrey, about the "insanity" infecting the X Corps command during the end-of-war drive to the Yalu.

"From the time we headed to the Yalu it was like being in the nut house with the nuts in charge," he later said. "You could only understand the totality of the madness if you were up there in the north after the Chinese had entered in full force, and we were being hit and hit again by these immense numbers of troops."[20]

In the jumbled terrain southwest of Yudam-ni, the Seventh's Baker Company Marines worked up a sweat while toiling through fresh snowfall covering the steep hills around Southwest and South Ridges. Baker's objective was Hansang-ni, where Able Company was ambushed the day before and Lieutenant Frank Mitchell had been killed.

Lieutenant Colonel Davis had ordered the reconnaissance in force to assess enemy strength and, if possible, to recover Mitchell's body.

A Congressional Medal of Honor would be awarded posthumously in recognition of Mitchell's retrieval of his wounded while under fire, and his valiant one-man rearguard action that had cost him his life.

Leading the long patrol was Lieutenant Woody Taylor's 1st Platoon. Taylor was an Alabaman who had been in Korea just three weeks, but he had served in the Pacific during World War II. At 32 he was practically ancient by the standards of the young Marines that he commanded. Historian Eric Hammel described Taylor as a distant but dependable leader.[21]

About 3pm, Baker Company, passing through the valley between Southwest and South Ridges, struggled up a steep slope west of Hill 1426.

There, Taylor's platoon was suddenly hit by long-range machine-gun fire from Sakkat Mountain, as well as enemy gunfire from the north and south. Baker had marched into an ambush.

Taylor threw his platoon into a skirmish line, and it charged up the slope, the attack designed to relieve enemy pressure on the rest of the company. The assault poked a hornets' nest. Chinese troops spilled off the ridgelines, swarming Baker from every direction.[22]

Pfc Raul Rendon's light machine-gun squad deployed behind a rock outcropping and began firing at white-uniform-clad Chinese soldiers as they began to grapple with the Marines. Enemy bullets stitched Rendon in the legs and lower abdomen, and he tumbled down the hill.

Corpsman Bill Davis injected Rendon with morphine, numbing the pain. Minutes later, Davis himself required treatment after being sprayed with mortar fragments. He was dragged to safety.[23]

With the enemy menacing it from every direction, Baker Company formed a 360-degree perimeter to ward off the repeated attacks.

The wounded were dragged by their parkas to the makeshift aid station in the middle of the perimeter, where corpsmen cleaned wounds with bloodied hands and jabbed the men with morphine syrettes.[24]

Captain Myron Wilcox, Baker's commander, was shot through the mouth and Lieutenant Joe Kurcaba took over. He ordered his platoon commanders to prepare for a fighting withdrawal to the MSR, but he needed air cover.

Baker's forward air controller, Lieutenant Joe Hedrick, had been futilely trying for hours to flag down Corsairs for close-air support, but they had been engaged in supporting the Fifth Marines' advance to the west.

When the advance was discontinued late in the afternoon, Corsairs laden with unused ordnance that they hoped to discharge before dark became available.

Four Corsairs guided by Hedrick plastered the ridgetops that were alive with Chinese troops, and then scoured a path down the valley toward the MSR with rockets, bombs, and machine-gun fire. Baker Company moved out quickly as the planes continued to make passes in front of the column.

The company slipped and slid down the valley as nightfall approached. The Chinese thrusts waned and, over several hours, the Marines were able to reach the main road.[25]

Lieutenant Colonel Davis was waiting there with Charlie Company, which occupied a draw on the other side of the MSR at the base of what they christened "Turkey Hill."

Davis ordered mortarmen to fire white phosphorus rounds to mark Baker's withdrawal route.

Ambulances and trucks arrived from Yudam-ni to retrieve the wounded. Davis told his officers that the Chinese had cut the MSR between Yudam-ni and Hagaru-ri, south of Turkey Hill.

Baker Company assembled on the MSR and marched the three miles back to Yudam-ni, arriving around midnight. It had been a brutally cold day with too many Marines lost for no apparent gain. They hiked down the road in silence.[26]

At a cost of up to two dozen men killed or wounded, Baker Company's reconnaissance had revealed that Chinese forces were massing in the hills south of Yudam-ni and along the road to the west. As events would reveal, large numbers were gathered to the north as well.[27]

On the advance north from Hagaru-ri, the three companies of the Seventh Marines' 2nd Battalion had become fragmented.

Captain William Barber's Fox Company had been sent to Toktong Pass, the vital strategic feature midway between Hagaru-ri and Yudam-ni, while Dog and Easy Companies had proceeded to Yudam-ni.

There, Dog and Easy had dug in on North Ridge, one of the topographical masses that surrounded the hamlet.

The 2nd Battalion commander, Lieutenant Colonel Randolph Lockwood, and his headquarters company had remained in Hagaru-ri, confident that they would soon join their rifle companies.

On the 27th, a Dog Company patrol hiked over North Ridge to reconnoiter the area northwest of Chosin Reservoir.

Heavy machine-gun and mortar fire stopped the patrol two miles from Yudam-ni, and Marine Corsairs were summoned to provide close-air support.

The pilots alerted the patrol that an entrenched company-size force lay ahead of it. The patrol withdrew with several casualties at 4:45pm to its company lines on North Ridge's southern tip.[28]

By dusk, large Chinese forces menaced the Yudam-ni Marines from the south, west, and north.

That evening, five trucks laden with ammunition, rations, and weapon lubricants left Hagaru-ri, crossed Toktong Pass, and by good luck reached Yudam-ni.

The materiel was welcome; Yudam-ni's supply stockpile was shrinking. It consisted of three days' food; fuel for three days; and a two-day supply of small-arms ammunition, in addition to what each unit and individual carried.[29]

Later that night, Lieutenant Colonel Olin Beall, commander of the 1st Motor Transport Battalion, led a caravan of empty trucks back to Hagaru-ri, leaving 40 to 50 trucks behind at Yudam-ni. Beall's convoy reached Hagaru-ri unmolested.

These were the last supplies to arrive in Yudam-ni by truck before the roof fell in on the Fifth and Seventh Marines and their supporting arm, the Eleventh Artillery Regiment.[30]

PART III

The Trap Closes

Chapter 6

A Night to Remember

November 27–28, 1950

My feet and legs gradually grew numb. The strong wind kept biting my nose and ears, and the tears from the biting pain immediately became ice cubes on my face.

Yang Yizhi, platoon leader with the 79th Division, describes lying in the snow in 25-below-zero cold waiting to attack.[1]

You never saw so much movement. They were loading up to attack, that whole field stood up and started running at us, screaming, "Marine you die tonight, you die tonight!" We just kinda leveled in and let them have it.

John Cole, Item Company, Fifth Marines, at Yudam-ni.[2]

Silently, they approached through the draws and the stream beds, deploying whenever they encountered resistance.

The Chinese assault troops lay down in the snow, waiting for the signal to attack the Marines guarding the Yudam-ni perimeter.

Beginning about 9pm, groups of a dozen or so drifted along the Marine lines, probing for soft spots. The Marines could hear them talking softly among themselves, and they reeked of garlic. When they found a seam, they attempted to exploit it.

Then, forming in columns, they attacked amid a roar of rifle and submachine-gun fire, and exploding grenades, hitting the ground when the Marines returned fire.

During a lull in the action, they rose and pressed the attack with a storm of unnerving bugle and duck calls, and piercing whistles.

"It was eerie, scary," said Lieutenant Colonel Ray Murray, the Fifth Marines' commander. "I heard all these bugles and all the hell raising. They were screaming and shouting and then I heard the firing start."

An enemy machine gun stitched the top of his headquarters tent. Murray grabbed a radio and crawled away.[3]

Three divisions – the 89th, 79th, and 59th, from two Chinese armies of the 9th Army Group – had moved into their assault positions on November 27 as darkness enveloped the picturesque Yudam-ni valley.

It was a bitter-cold, moonless night. The attackers wore quilted cotton uniforms that were mustard-brown on one side, white on the other; visored, cotton-padded caps with pile lining on the ear and neck flaps; and canvas, high-topped tennis shoes with rubber soles – scant protection against frostbite.

With temperatures falling to 20 to 30 degrees below zero, the Chinese soldiers normally were not permitted to sleep more than one hour at a time so that they would not freeze to death.

When they did lie down to sleep, the soldiers held a mate's feet to keep them warm, or bear-hugged two companions for warmth. When circumstances permitted, they would jog in place hourly during the bitter-cold nights.

Chinese cold weather casualties – frostbite in particular – would surpass combat casualties in the weeks ahead.[4]

Many of the Chinese soldiers were also in the first stages of starvation. Upon crossing the Yalu River, they had been issued a two- or three-day ration of cooked wheat flour, soybeans, rice, or a combination thereof and, of course, garlic as a preventative against colds.

A week of marching had exhausted their provisions, and they were now reduced to foraging and swapping their blankets and medicine for North Korean rice, corn, and vegetables – when they could find it.[5]

The 9th Army Group had been sent from southeast China to northeast Korea in October after United Nations forces crossed the 38th Parallel.

Many of its soldiers had fought in Chiang Kai-Shek's Nationalist army, which was defeated by communist forces in the civil war that ended a year earlier. In Shanghai alone, after Mao Tse-Tung's People's Liberation Army took control, 15,000 Nationalists were inducted into the PLA. After two months' political indoctrination, they joined the 9th Army Group's ranks.[6]

Although equipped with World War II-era rifles, machine guns, and mortars, as well as artillery when terrain permitted its deployment, the People's Volunteer Force was essentially a peasant army, and a throwback to an earlier era both strategically and tactically. In 1950 it lacked air support, tanks, and sufficient motor transport.

Yet it had one thing in abundance: manpower. The 9th Army Group's 12 divisions mustered 150,000 men.

When Mao named him commander of the intervention force, 53-year-old General Peng Dehuai was vice chairman of the Central Military Commission and commander of the First Field Army. As a teenager, Peng had served in a warlord army in Hunan Province – his birthplace was not far from Mao's – and had risen to officer rank and attended Hunan Province Military Academy.

He joined the Communist Party in 1928 and had served in the Chinese Red Army during the 22 years since. In 1940, as commander of the First Front Army, he launched the "Hundred Regiments Campaign" against Japanese forces – initially successful, but ultimately a defeat.

After the Japanese surrender, and before he was chosen to command the Chinese armies in Korea, Peng led communist forces in Inner Mongolia and northwest China during the civil war.[7]

The Chinese speedily deployed the 9th Army Group – so quickly that the troops reached the Yalu River still clad in their summer uniforms. They would pay dearly for their haste.

The 27th Army left Shandong Province on October 25 and eight days later reached Linjiang near Korea's northern tip. On November 2, its 50,000 troops crossed the Yalu River.

The 20th Army, reinforced by the 89th Division, entered Manchuria on November 6, crossed into North Korea on the 10th, and entrained to Mupyong-ni, from where it began marching east to Yudam-ni.

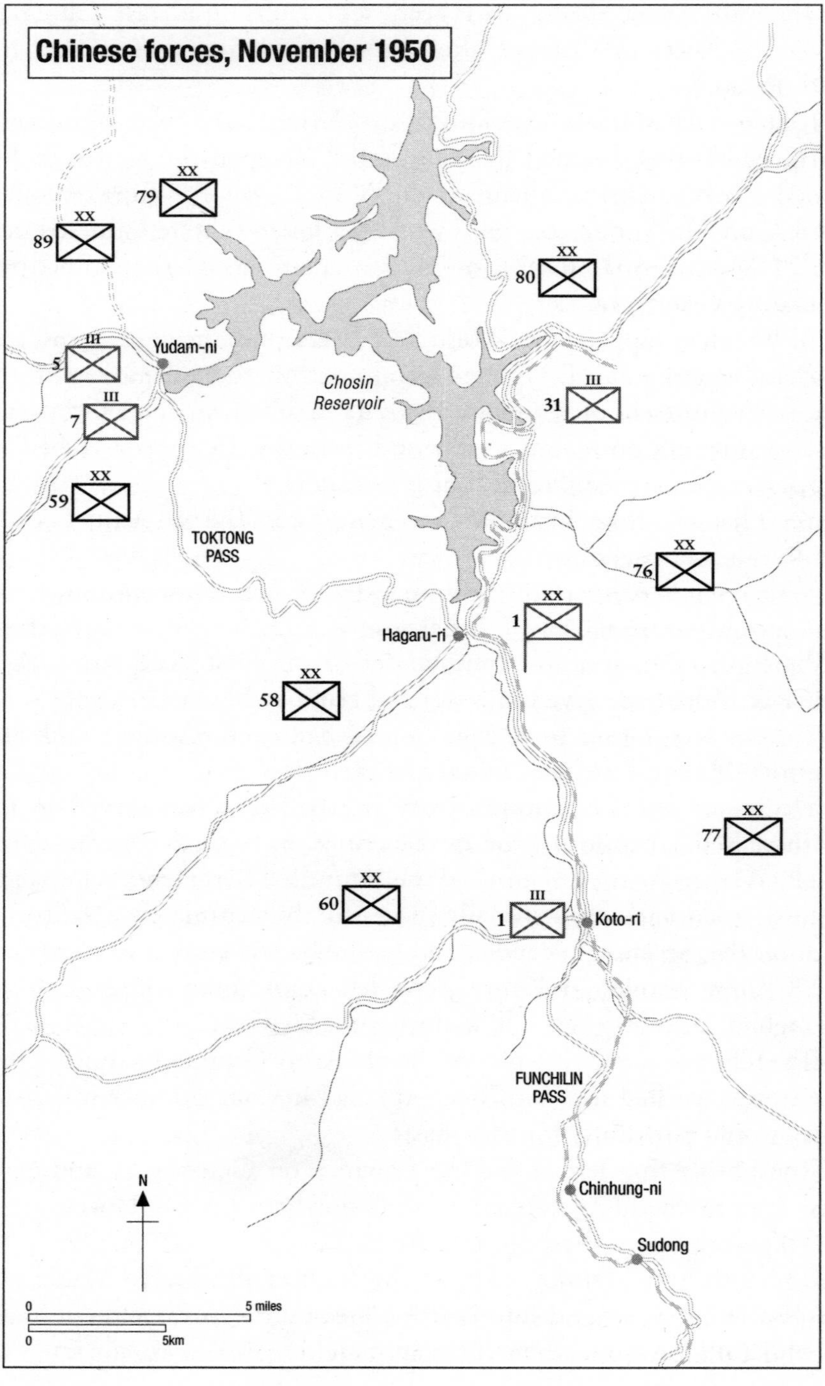
Chinese forces, November 1950
XX
79
XX
89
XX
80
III
5
Yudam-ni
III
7
Chosin
Reservoir
III
31
XX
59
TOKTONG
PASS
XX
76
XX
1
Hagaru-ri
XX
58
XX
77
XX
60
III
1
Koto-ri
FUNCHILIN
PASS
N
Chinhung-ni
Sudong
0
5 miles
0
5km

The 26th Army, the last of the 9th Army Group to reach the Yalu River area, went into reserve near Linjiang, still wearing the uniforms that the soldiers had been issued that summer in southeastern China.[8]

Each army had its three original divisions plus a fourth division from the former 30th Army, which had been disbanded. Thus, the 20th Army consisted of the 58th, 59th, and 60th Divisions, and the 89th from the 30th Army; the 26th Army, the 76th, 77th, and 78th Divisions, and the 88th Division from the 30th Army; and the 27th Army was made up of the 79th, 80th, and 81st Divisions, and the 94th Division from the former 30th Army.[9]

Upon entering North Korea, the Chinese traveled quickly and carried minimal equipment. Each division brought a handful of 75mm field pieces, but relied mainly on mortars and pack howitzers for heavy firepower.

Each regiment was equipped with eight or nine 92mm rocket launchers to be used as antitank weapons. Limited ammunition was doled out: 40 shells for each 82mm mortar, 90 shells for a 60mm mortar, 80 bullets per rifle, 2,000 rounds for each heavy machine gun, and 600 rounds per light machine gun.[10]

A Chinese soldier captured on November 26 told his Marine captors that the 20th Army had an artillery regiment of horse-drawn 122mm mountain guns. That involved a lot of draft animals. In a properly equipped Chinese artillery battalion, 26 horses were assigned to each platoon, and 20 horses were assigned to carry ammunition.[11]

The Chinese lacked reliable maps, and they sometimes had no maps at all. Without radios, they were unable to communicate with other units or even with their own command posts; bugles, whistles, flares, and messengers conveyed orders to attack or withdraw.

Thus, the simplest coordination was beyond reach, and sometimes, for lack of accurate maps, Chinese assault companies even attacked the wrong hill.[12]

Confusion that might have been cleared up by radio contact delayed the 79th Division's 236th Regiment attack by two hours on November 27.

On November 8, when Peng met with his top commanders to plan the Second Offensive, General Xie Fang, chief of staff of the CPVF, said there were nine Chinese armies in North Korea. They consisted of 30 divisions and more than 380,000 men.[13]

The Chinese possessed a fairly accurate estimate of the United Nations' strength – 90,000 on the eastern front; 130,000 on the western front (actually, 120,000) – but General MacArthur's intelligence on Chinese strength was wanting. Aware that hundreds of thousands of enemy soldiers were arrayed near the Yalu River in Manchuria, US intelligence was unsure how many had crossed over.

General Peng anticipated modest gains in western Korea from the Second Offensive planned for late November.

"We must be content ourselves for the moment with establishing a line just beyond the 39th Parallel," he said. "We don't have the logistics to back up an advance much more."

His 13th Army Group might drive the Eighth Army to Pyongwon, midway between the Chongchon River estuary and the capital city of Pyongyang, Peng wrote.

In northeastern Korea, he believed X Corps could be lured into the northern mountains and destroyed.[14]

Mao expressed reservations about the planned attacks on the 1st Marine Division's two regiments west of Chosin Reservoir. He wanted more divisions to be available to assault what he believed was America's best division.

Mao had well-established views on warfare, honed during his years of battling the Nationalists and the Japanese. In his *On Protracted Warfare*, Mao wrote that he believed it better to attack a moving enemy than a stationary one.

The fact that the Fifth and Seventh regiments – heavily armed US Marines – were dug in at Yudam-ni was worrisome. Better to deploy a large force alongside the route that the enemy was expected to take and launch a surprise attack to obtain a quick victory than to attack prepared defenses.[15]

If US intelligence was doing a poor job of monitoring Chinese troop movements and pronouncements, Mao, Peng, and Chinese leaders were closely watching and listening to their adversary.

Peng had fought delaying actions in western Korea after the First Offensive in early November, but the fear that the enemy might discover his actual strength farther north compelled him to order the harassing attacks stopped, and the rapid withdrawal of the Thirteenth Army Group.

Aware that MacArthur's staff had grossly underestimated Chinese strength, Peng and his generals did not want to ruin the surprise that they had in store for the United Nations allies.[16]

The Chinese were very much aware of MacArthur's blustering declaration of his intention to carry out a "massive compression" envelopment in the far north, with X Corps "cutting in to the northern reaches of the enemy's geographical potential."

MacArthur's words caused a two-day delay in General Song's 9th Army Group's planned attacks around the Chosin Reservoir.

The 9th Army Group, which had expected the 1st Marine Division to continue to march north from Yudam-ni to the Yalu River, now needed time to reposition its troops to meet a Marine thrust westward to Mupyong-ni.

It now planned to launch its main assault at Yudam-ni on November 27th, two days after the 13th Army Group's attack in the west on the Eighth Army on November 25 – the very day that a US air raid on the Chinese army's general headquarters killed Mao's elder son, Mao Anying. He was Peng's Russian interpreter and the headquarters secretary.[17]

At Yudam-ni, the 79th, 89th, and 59th Divisions faced the two Marine regiments, the Fifth and the Seventh, while at Hagaru-ri the 58th Division menaced General Smith's southwest perimeter. The 60th Division was erecting roadblocks between Hagaru-ri and Koto-ri, and air reconnaissance spotted 37 roadblocks west of Yudam-ni over six miles.

Two divisions – the 80th and 81st – were poised to overrun what the Chinese believed to be three companies immediately east of Chosin Reservoir, but in fact were the three battalions of the US Army's 31st Regimental Combat Team – RCT-31.

Thereafter, those two Chinese divisions planned a rapid march south to Hagaru-ri to join the 58th Division in overwhelming the vital 1st Marine Division base.

The anticipated quick victory east of Chosin Reservoir, however, would become a bloody slugfest lasting five days.[18]

In the runup to the 9th Army Group's attacks of November 27–28, Peng Dehuai, commander of the Chinese CPVF, urged his armies to "create a striking superiority" when planning their attacks.

"We will use one regiment to pin down [the] enemy's three regiments, and concentrate our three regiments to annihilate one enemy regiment, creating a superior striking power," he said.[19]

At Yudam-ni, however, three Chinese divisions of more than 30,000 troops surrounded 8,214 Marines that occupied a shallow bowl ringed by rugged hills.

The Chinese enjoyed a nearly 4-to-1 numerical superiority, and planned to exploit their advantage with battalion-size attacks against a narrow front.

They planned to crawl within grenade-throwing distance and simply overwhelm the defenders through this sheer weight of numbers.[20]

Yet, as historian Xiaobing Li noted, the extreme cold – 25 to 30 degrees below zero – confounded the usual Chinese practice of a battalion first sending a platoon to test enemy defenses for weak spots while the main force lay in the snow awaiting the attack signal.

On this night, the assault troops were freezing to death; they had to either move or die.

Before beginning the attack, Yang Yizhi, a platoon leader in the 1st Battalion of the 237th Regiment, 79th Division, said he and his men lay in the snow without coats, gloves, or winter shoes.

"My feet and legs gradually grew numb," he said. "The strong wind kept biting my nose and ears, and the tears from the biting pain immediately became ice cubes on my face."[21]

Facing the choice of his men either dying of the cold or being killed in a mass attack, the commander of the 235th Regiment's 2nd Battalion chose to send all 800 of his men into a frontal attack against the Marine hilltop defenses.

It was a debacle. The Marines held their fire until the Chinese were 15 yards away and then unleashed a fusillade of lead and metal that crushed the assault. Repeated assaults met the same fate. Overnight, the 2nd Battalion lost 650 men.

In Yang's attack on Northwest Ridge that night, his 3rd Company lost 80 percent of its men. His 1st Battalion reported 1,600 soldiers killed.

Had the Chinese adopted the tactic of flowing around fortified defensive positions rather than attacking them head-on, they might have been more successful.

But they remained wedded to their frontal attacks, believing that numbers and "fighting spirit" would overwhelm superior firepower.[22]

This proved to be a tragic fallacy: during the first ten hours of the 9th Army Group's attacks throughout the night of November 27–28, ten thousand Chinese soldiers were lost – so high a cost that the Chinese did not hazard another major attack the next night.[23]

On Northwest Ridge, the 89th Division assaults began at 9:30pm as the Marines shivered in their icy foxholes under frost-covered parka hoods, trigger fingers aching, their feet lumps of ice in their Shoe-pacs.[24]

Suddenly, the Chinese seemed to be everywhere at once. They were armed mostly with American weapons captured from Nationalist forces during the civil war: American "Lend-Lease" Thompson submachine guns, heavy and light machine guns, and 60mm and 81mm mortars.

Not every enemy soldier had a weapon, though. The unarmed men, as though by design, picked up the weapons of comrades cut down by the Marines' gunfire.[25]

"They were on top of us so fast, screaming," said Corporal Gerald Boyd of the Seventh Marines' How Company, which occupied Hill 1403, part of Northwest Ridge. His buddy was asleep in his bag when they hit.

In a panic, Boyd's mate struggled to get out of the bag, but the zipper was frozen, and he was bayoneted to death. A concussion grenade blew Boyd down the hill and left him nearly blind.[26]

The adrenaline-fueled Marines fired back as fast as they were able. Tracers streaked the night everywhere. "It looked like Christmas, red and green, with blood," said one Marine.[27]

Attacking from the west, the Chinese approached in columns until they were within grenade range and wedged a salient between the Fifth Marines' Easy and Fox Companies.

Chinese concussion grenades exploded around Corporal John Smith of Fox Company, which had been part of the advance to the west earlier in the day.

They overran James M. Brown's weapons company at the foot of North Ridge. A .30-caliber machine gunner, Brown went through three barrels that night. Donning asbestos gloves, he changed inoperable ones for fresh ones.[28]

Fortunately for the Easy Company Marines, they had had time to carefully prepare their defenses on Northwest Ridge, having been held in reserve during the 2nd Battalion's advance westward.

By nightfall, they were positioned along a natural, brush-covered corridor that crossed a frozen streambed lined by a few houses. The approach corridor became known as "Easy Alley."

There was nothing easy about it for the Chinese. Marine machine guns set a local hut ablaze, backlighting the attackers, and transforming Easy Alley into a bloody gauntlet where the grenade-throwing, burp gun-firing enemy was cut down by the hundred.[29]

"I didn't comprehend the magnitude or the scope of the attack until I saw the bodies in the morning," said Lieutenant Jack Nolan of Easy Company. He counted 201 dead in front of his machine guns. Some of the bodies lay just 5 feet from the Marine positions.[30]

John Cole's Fifth Marines Item Company was on the north side of Yudam-ni when it detected men moving around a building in a field between two hills. It was "a thick, shuffling, shadowy movement." The Marines fired flares and blasted the building with bazooka fire.

"You never saw so much movement," said Cole. "They were loading up to attack, that whole field stood up and started running at us, screaming, 'Marine you die tonight, you die tonight!' We just kinda leveled in and let them have it."[31]

When the attack began, some Marines bolted from their sleeping bags in their socks.

Corporal Arthur Gentry of Easy Company said the first attack by the 89th Division lasted 30 minutes. Subsequent assaults came at 30- to 40-minute intervals. "We were outnumbered 10 to 15 to 1," he said.

It was the beginning of nights without sleep and days of constant movement. Gentry quickly learned how to sleep standing up.[32]

Easy's commander, Captain Samuel Jaskilka, had happily anticipated leaving the next morning for the States for the birth of his child. The night's attacks and the events that followed would delay his departure by two weeks.

During the first attack, the Chinese advanced in assault columns to within grenade range, targeting the juncture of Easy and Fox Companies. Marine machine gunners mowed down the attackers as they rapidly approached while hurling grenades and firing burp guns.

Despite heavy casualties, the white-clad Chinese persisted in their wild onslaught until their losses became so heavy that they were unable to continue. They dug in about 900 yards away from the Marine lines as temperatures fell to 30 below zero.

A second attack on Easy began at 3am, but lacked the punch of the first, as the Chinese tried to draw the Marines' fire and pinpoint their positions.

"These tactics failed because our Marines participated in no promiscuous firing and were always ready with their own hand grenades when the frustrated, jabbering Chinese rushed our positions," wrote Jaskilka, who that morning counted at least 300 enemy bodies in front of Easy Company.

Amazingly, Easy reported just one man killed, 14 wounded, and 24 frostbite cases.[33]

Some of the attackers bypassed the Marine positions on Northwest Ridge and raced downhill to the medical tents in the valley.

When three enemy soldiers burst into one of them, a Navy doctor calmly informed them, "We're operating," and the Chinese humbly bowed and departed.[34]

Pfc LeRoy Hintsa, resting in a Fifth Marines medical tent after carrying wounded men on stretchers from the hills to the aid tent, was shocked by the sight of a Marine staggering toward him.

"His lower jaw was missing. All he had was frozen red icicles on his face," said Hintsa.

A corpsman examined the man and told him that he would die when he thawed out; he advised the Marine to write a letter home while he could. Hintsa said the Marine sat down outside the aid tent and began writing.[35]

Hill 1403, the highest point on Northwest Ridge, overlooked the rear of the Fifth Marines' 2nd Regiment and loomed over the Yudam-ni road junction from the north.

Defended by Captain Leroy Cooke's How Company of the Seventh Marines, it became a primary Chinese objective in the belief that seizing it would crack open Yudam-ni's defenses. At 10pm, the 89th Division's 266th and 267th Regiments struck How Company and drove it from Hill 1403.

Captain Cooke was killed while leading a counterattack, and Lieutenant Howard Harris, recently discharged from a hospital in Hamhung, took over and led the company's reserve platoon to the hilltop.

From an observation point, Harris could see enemy and Marine tracer fire flickering in the dark in every direction, and concluded that this was much more than a localized attack.

Chinese troops also struck How Company during a second attack at 3am, while attempting to dislodge Easy and Fox Companies.

How Company held, but by 4am, severely weakened by casualties, it was no longer capable of holding onto Hill 1403, and was withdrawn. The hill's loss posed a mortal threat to Southwest and North Ridges, and to the 2,000 Marines deployed on the valley floor.

But the perimeter remained intact, at least for the present.[36]

During the same night, two regiments of the Chinese 59th Division captured several hills on the MSR south of Yudam-ni, cutting off access to Hagaru-ri. A 59th Division company sent to guard a roadblock was found the next morning with every man frozen to death at his post.[37]

While the Yudam-ni perimeter was under siege from heavy attacks, the Chinese struck Captain John Morris's understrength Charlie Company of the Seventh Marines three miles south of Yudam-ni. Lacking one platoon that had been borrowed to guard the regimental CP, it was trapped by enemy gunfire in a gulley near the MSR.

In a tight perimeter on the western slope of Hill 1419 – forever known as Turkey Hill because of the turkey carcasses littering the area from the Thanksgiving Day feast – the Marines were raked with gunfire by the Chinese holding Turkey Hill's crest. Then, the enemy attacked the company's left flank. Morris's lines held, but his radio was disabled, and everyone in his headquarters platoon was either killed or wounded.

Lieutenant Colonel Ray Davis, Charlie Company's battalion commander, later observed that "in any large fighting unit one of its elements seems to be a 'hard-luck' outfit," and that Charlie Company was one of those outfits.[38]

Chapter 7

The Longest Night

Yudam-ni

The extreme cold made me feel like I was wearing nothing at all. I was chilled to the bone.

Zou Shiyong, political officer with the 237th Regiment.[1]

By 0200, as the first attack began to taper off, the northeastern slopes of Hill 1282 lay buried under a mat of human wreckage.

Description of fighting on North Ridge outside Yudam-ni.[2]

I couldn't believe my eyes when I saw them in the moonlight. It was like the snow came to life, and they were shouting and shaking their fists – just raising hell. They came in a rush, like a pack of mad dogs.

Corporal Arthur Koch.[3]

Menacing though the loss of Hill 1403 and the pressure on Northwest Ridge were to the sanctity of Yudam-ni's perimeter, the Marine lines had held.

But an even graver threat arose a short distance to the east, at North Ridge. Its hills were closest to Yudam-ni and thus its defense was critical to the preservation of the regimental headquarters and the Eleventh Marines' artillery batteries in the valley below.

North Ridge's east side was bounded by the Chosin Reservoir; to its west, a valley separated it from Northwest Ridge. On the right rose Hill 1167, and on the left, a massive spur to Hill 1384. The two center heights, Hills 1282 and 1240, with a 1,000-yard saddle between them, were occupied, respectively, by Easy and Dog Companies of the Seventh Marines.[4]

Earlier in the day, when a patrol had clashed with Chinese troops on the north side of North Ridge, the Marines discovered that one of the enemy soldiers that they had killed was a captain who possessed surveying instruments and maps. He evidently was plotting artillery and mortar registrations.

The Marines on North Ridge had been forewarned.[5]

The Chinese 235th Regiment of the 79th Division was assigned to assault Hill 1240, but strangely no units had been ordered to strike Hill 1282.

Instead, the 236th and 237th Regiments were ordered to hit Hills 1167 and 1384 on either side of Hills 1282 and 1240, but the targeted hills were unoccupied. The 79th Division's orders to the regiments reflected senior officers' recognition that North Ridge was the key to Yudam-ni. After capturing the hills, the orders said, Chinese troops were to "... annihilate the enemy at Yudam-ni."

Besides being the headquarters for the Fifth and Seventh regiments, the Yudam-ni valley floor was the location of three battalions of the Eleventh Marines artillery regiment: Lieutenant Colonel Harvey Feehan's 1st Battalion, with 18 105mm howitzers; Major Fox Parry's 3rd Battalion, minus one battery remaining at Hagaru-ri, with 12 105mm guns; and Major William McReynolds' 4th Battalion of 18 155mm howitzers. The 4th Battalion was the last unit to reach Yudam-ni on the 27th.[6]

On paper, this was a lot of firepower, but there was an ammunition shortage. Fifteen trucks sent from Yudam-ni to Hagaru-ri on the 27th for more ammunition were unable to return after the Chinese 59th Division cut the MSR between the two villages.

Artillery ammunition was now rationed. With the goal of greater efficiency, the three battalions were combined into a "groupment" led by Lieutenant Colonel Feehan, the senior artillery officer.[7]

Major Fox Parry, the 3rd Battalion commander, said the big guns would play a minor role in Yudam-ni's defense because of the ammunition shortage – and because the artillery units' radios were losing battery strength daily because of the extreme cold and "unavoidable misuse."

Consequently, Parry said, many artillerymen would eventually be sent into the infantry ranks or be "forced to defend themselves almost continuously."

"Into this breach stepped the fired-up Marine airmen who flew to our aid time and time again under the most horrendous conditions," wrote Parry. For good reason, Marine close-air support was called the "flying artillery."[8]

The 12,000 men in the 79th's three regiments advanced on North Ridge in battalion-strength columns along a two-mile front, an impressive sight when they could be glimpsed by the light of the waning gibbous moon.

Yang Yizhi of the 237th Regiment dreaded lying in wait in the snow because he knew that he might not be able to get up again. He had seen men lie down, intending to take just a short break. "But they could never get up"; they had frozen to death.[9]

"The extreme cold made me feel like I was wearing nothing at all," said Zou Shiyong, a political officer with the 237th. "I was chilled to the bone."[10]

The 237th Regiment reached Hill 1384's crest unopposed by the Marines and awaited further orders. When they came, the regiment was told to prepare to sweep down the ridge into Yudam-ni.

Darkness, the confusingly broken terrain, and poor maps now combined to cause the 235th Regiment's 1st Battalion to veer off course.

Instead of assaulting Hill 1240, as it had been assigned, the unit began ascending its neighbor, Hill 1282, held by Captain Walter Phillips's Easy Company. Maintaining contact with the 1st Battalion, the 236th Regiment's 3rd Battalion, which was to attack Hill 1167, found itself facing the larger Hill 1240, occupied by Captain Milton Hull's Dog Company.

The Chinese battalions foundered in the deep snow before the unfamiliar objectives.[11]

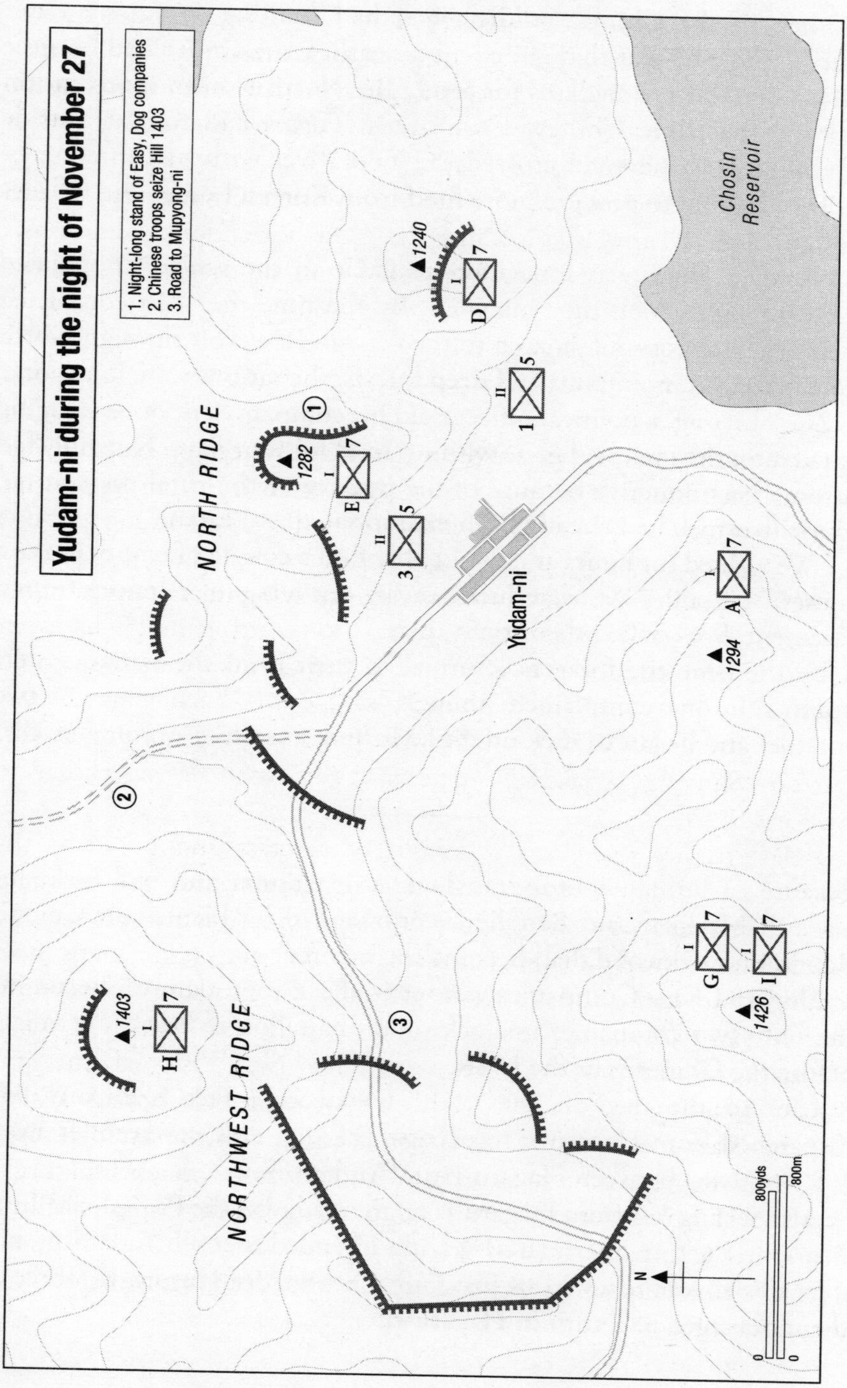
Yudam-ni during the night of November 27
1. Night-long stand of Easy, Dog companies
2. Chinese troops seize Hill 1403
3. Road to Mupyong-ni
NORTH RIDGE
NORTHWEST RIDGE
Chosin Reservoir
Yudam-ni
1240
1282
1294
1403
1426
D 7
E 7
A 7
H 7
G 7
I 7
3 5
1 5
N
0
800yds
800m

Some of the Chinese soldiers had had nothing to eat for days. During the civil war that ended a year earlier, the armies had become reliant on Chinese civilians for food. The North Korean intervention was the first time Chinese Communist Forces had fought outside of China, and they had crossed the Yalu River with just three days' rations, hoping to procure more food from Korean homes and villages along the way.

However, there was little food available in the sparsely populated areas through which they marched. By the time they had completed their grueling 100-mile march to the Chosin Reservoir through North Korea's rugged mountains and deep forests, the rations were long gone.

Zuo Shiyong, a political officer, said his company sent out a foraging squad after the men had gone without food for four days. Foraging had become unproductive because of the poverty of the rural population, whose livestock had already been expropriated and eaten.

"We walked for hours and could only find a couple of empty peasant houses," he said. "We were lucky to dig out a bag of potatoes from a basement. We cooked them right there."

By the time the foragers returned to their unit, the potatoes were frozen. No one complained, though, said Zuo. "Each man got two potatoes and began to suck on it like licking a rock."[12]

Because of limited motor transport at Hagaru-ri and bad luck, the Seventh Marines' 2nd Battalion, commanded by Lieutenant Colonel Randolph Lockwood, had become fragmented.

Dog and Easy Companies were sent ahead to Yudam-ni, becoming the only two companies in Lockwood's battalion to reach the village before the Chinese cut the MSR.

Late in the day on the 27th, Lockwood's Fox Company was dispatched from Hagaru-ri to occupy Toktong Pass, seven miles away. It lay midway between Hagaru-ri and Yudam-ni.[13]

Also setting out from Hagaru-ri on the 27th was the Provisional Tank Platoon. The four Sherman M-4 tanks intended to reach Yudam-ni, but they all slid off the icy MSR just four miles west of Hagaru-ri. Three of them managed to return to Hagaru-ri.

Lieutenant Richard Primrose had brought a platoon of heavier Pershing M-26 tanks to Hagaru-ri, and he believed that he could get them over Toktong Pass to Yudam-ni.

But rather than commit the entire platoon, he and driver Sergeant Clyde Kidd made a test run with one M-26. After slowly weaving through the MSR's heavy truck traffic, they managed to roll into Yudam-ni.

The test run being a success, Primrose and Kidd then helicoptered back to Hagaru-ri, intending to bring the other Pershings to Yudam-ni. The Chinese cut the MSR that night, and no other tanks reached Yudam-ni.

The lone tank in Yudam-ni was known as D-23. With Primrose and Kidd now back in Hagaru-ri, D-23 needed a crew. Colonel Litzenberg radioed a request for a tank crew, and Sergeant Russell Munsell and a crew from "C" Company of the 1st Marine Tank Battalion were flown by helicopter to Yudam-ni.[14]

The orphaned Dog and Easy Companies at Yudam-ni were placed under the temporary command of the 1st Battalion's Lieutenant Colonel Davis. They would own the unhappy distinction of absorbing the most powerful Chinese assaults at Yudam-ni during the night of November 27–28.

Two of the 79th Division's three regiments devoted themselves to driving the companies from Hills 1282 and 1240.[15]

When the 235th Regiment's 4th Battalion assaulted Hill 1282 on North Ridge early November 28, the Marines held their fire until the Chinese were ten yards away before letting them have it. The battalion lost 480 men in 20 minutes.

Lynn Montross's and Nicholas Canzona's official account of the attack noted: "When one formation was cut to pieces by machine-gun fire and grenades, another rose out of the night to take its place. By 0200, as the first attack began to taper off, the northeastern slopes of Hill 1282 lay buried under a mat of human wreckage."[16]

In the crosshairs of the first Chinese attacks by the 235th Regiment was Lieutenant John Yancey's Easy Company platoon.

Yancey, 32, a reservist like many men in the Seventh Marines, had served with distinction in the Pacific War. As a member of Lieutenant Colonel Evans Carlson's elite 2nd Marine Raider Battalion, Yancey had participated in the Makin Island raid, the first major US raid of World War II.

On Guadalcanal during the 2nd Raiders' four-week "Long Patrol" of November and December 1942, Corporal Yancey led a seven-man attack in a torrential downpour on a Japanese bivouac. Seventy-five Japanese soldiers were killed, and Yancey was awarded the Navy Cross and a battlefield commission for his actions.

He later fought on Iwo Jima, and when the war ended, he was discharged into the reserves and opened a liquor store in Little Rock, Arkansas.[17]

Although Yancey's thin mustache might have given him the appearance of a gigolo, as some of his men joked, he was anything but that; he was profane, hot-tempered, and stockily built – he had played football at the University of Arkansas after World War II. Known as a perfectionist, he embodied Easy Company's motto, "Easy for us, tough for others." Most importantly, Yancey knew how to fight.[18]

Yancey's platoon looked to the northeast from Hill 1282's crest, while another platoon, led by Lieutenant Leonard Clements, faced northwest. The platoons formed a crescent, with Phillips's command post and the mortar platoon in the middle. Easy Company's third platoon, that of Lieutenant Robert Bey, was posted farther to the right toward Hill 1240, along a portion of the saddle separating the hills.

Light probes by the Chinese preceded the first serious attack, which fell on Yancey's platoon about midnight. In the runup to it, Yancey heard crunching noises on the brittle-hard snow, "like hundreds of feet walking slowly across a big carpet of cornflakes." He ordered his men to fix bayonets.

Then, one of the attackers shouted in Chinese-accented English as the first wave approached: "Nobody lives forever. You die!" Amid a cacophony of blaring bugles, whistles, and shepherds' horns, the Chinese front ranks charged through the snow. As they drew closer, they touched off the Marines' trip flares.

The bright, wavering lights revealed a hillside swarming with white-clad enemy troops that stretched from one flank to another. Ranks of attackers were spaced at 15-yard intervals behind the first wave.[19]

"I couldn't believe my eyes when I saw them in the moonlight. It was like the snow came to life, and they were shouting and shaking their fists – just raising hell," said Corporal Arthur Koch. "They came in a rush, like a pack of mad dogs."[20]

The attackers flung so many grenades into the air that "it looked like a big flock of blackbirds overhead," said Yancey.[21]

Amid exploding grenades and gunfire, Yancey and Captain Phillips darted from one Marine foxhole to another, shouting encouragement.

A nearly spent bullet lodged in Yancey's nose. He calmly removed a glove and plucked out the bullet. Blood flowed and then froze. He resumed shouting encouragement to the dwindling number of Easy Marines still capable of fighting.[22]

Yancey tried to assemble his platoon in a line with a squad borrowed from Lieutenant Clements. As Yancey turned to leave, a bullet struck Clements in the middle of his forehead, and he fell to the ground. Believing Clements to be dead, Yancey left him there. Clements survived. The bullet penetrated Clements's helmet, but not the helmet liner, and bloodied the side of his head.[23]

There was a break in the action, and then the Chinese attacked again, intent on crashing through Easy's paper-thin lines.

As they ascended the hill, they began to chant eerily in a minor key, "Sonuvabitch Marines, we kill! Sonuvabitch Marines, you die! Nobody lives forever!" The chants were followed by a cacophony of bugles, whistles, shepherds' horns, cymbals, and drums – a veritable "witches' conference," said one Marine.[24]

Two Chinese battalions were now fully committed to overrunning Easy Company on Hill 1282 and racing into Yudam-ni.

"It was like Custer's Last Stand," said Yancey. "I kept wondering where did all those fucking Chinese come from?"[25]

Corporal Earl Pickens Jr, part of a machine-gun squad in Clements's platoon, said, "The sergeant told us to get to the point of attack with the machine gun and fight for our lives."

The gunner and assistant gunner ran to the point with the machine gun and tripod, and dove into a shallow foxhole to begin firing. Seconds later, two Chinese grenades landed in the hole, severely wounding them.

Pickens and the other crew member then jumped into the hole and began firing the machine gun along with a carbine, and throwing grenades.

Clements's platoon threw back attack after attack, but the enemy soldiers kept coming.[26]

Yancey was wounded a second time while distributing bandoleers of M-1 ammunition foxhole to foxhole. A grenade blew him off his feet, and a fragment sliced into the roof of his mouth, sending a bolt of blood down his throat. He hawked and spit blood while encouraging the survivors to keep fighting.[27]

Captain Phillips slammed his bayonet-tipped rifle into the ground and bellowed, "This is Easy Company, and we hold here!" An instant later, he was shot dead.

Lieutenant Ray Ball, Easy's executive officer, was badly wounded and forced himself into a rifleman's sitting position next to his foxhole. He shot down the attackers until he lost consciousness and died.[28]

After firing all of his mortar rounds, Lieutenant William Schreier, Easy's mortar section leader, sent his men down the hill to get more shells. The mortar men were ambushed on the way back, and Schreier was at their position alone when the Chinese broke through the line "and came right at me. I shot about 10 of them" with his carbine and .45, briefly stopping the attack.

Reporting to the company CP and apprehending the dire situation there, Schreier gathered up some men, "and we lay down on the snow. They were throwing hand grenades and mortars at us."

Scheier was wounded by a concussion grenade, and then sprayed with shrapnel from a 60mm mortar round that lacerated one side of his body.[29]

The 235th Regiment's battalions swept the Easy Company survivors off the crest of Hill 1282.

Yancey gathered nine men and led a counterattack, shouting the Chinese motto that was a battle cry of Carlson's Raiders, "Gung Ho!" which meant "work together."

The counterattack failed, and Yancey was wounded a third time – shot in the face, causing his eyeball to dangle from its socket; he pushed it back into place. With a .45-caliber pistol taken from a Japanese officer on Guadalcanal eight years earlier, Yancey killed his assailant while he was reloading his weapon.[30]

Because of a weird acoustical anomaly caused by the terrain, Lieutenant Robert Bey's Easy platoon, which occupied the extreme right of Hill 1282, was unaware of the mortal crisis that had befallen Yancey and Clements.

The first inkling came when some riflemen from Yancey's platoon stumbled into Bey's position and excitedly related what had occurred.

Bey's platoon sergeant, Daniel Murphy, wanted to round up every available man and go to Yancey's assistance, but Bey reacted more cautiously because he had heard nothing to suggest that there had been a pitched battle on the hill. He dispatched Murphy with 17 rifleman and a corpsman, hardly enough men to turn the tide of battle.[31]

However, they were able to fight their way to the Easy Company CP, near where Phillips and Ball lay dead, and their corpsman began treating the wounded.

More help was on the way.

After the first attack, Captain Phillips had radioed Lieutenant Colonel Davis and requested help. The Fifth Marines' Charlie Company, composed of Salt Lake City reservists, was bivouacked in the valley between Hills 1282 and 1240 and the Eleventh Marines batteries, and was the only available reserve.

At 4am, Litzenberger and Murray sent platoons from the Fifth's Able and Charlie Companies, led by Captain Jack Jones, to Hill 1282. Lieutenant Harold Dawe led a third platoon, which was dispatched to Hill 1240.

It took two hours for Jones's relief column to reach Sergeant Murphy's group, which had been driven 100 yards below 1282's summit.[32]

When informed of the gravity of the situation on 1282, Lieutenant Colonel John Stevens, commander of the Fifth Marines' 1st Battalion, sent the rest of Charlie Company to Jones to recapture the hill.[33]

Jones led a furious attack against the crest of 1282, destroying two Chinese platoons in bloody, close-in fighting.

When the Charlie Company platoon reached the hilltop, it "found a confused and disorganized situation," with most of Easy Company's officers and NCOs killed or wounded.

At one point, Lieutenant Nick Trapnell's Able Company platoon was forced to re-form on higher ground because the 235th Regiment did not break off its attacks at daybreak despite its grievous losses.

The 235th's 3rd Company had just six or seven survivors, and when the 2nd Company was sent to reinforce them, the Marines wiped it out in just ten minutes with rifle fire and grenades.

Pfc Win Scott of Charlie Company said frozen Chinese bodies lay everywhere – so many that when he fired his .30-caliber machine gun downhill, the gunfire was deflected by piled-up corpses. Scott had to move some of them to create a clear field of fire.[34]

When Scott's machine gun jammed, he and his foxhole mate held their position with an M-1 rifle fed by the machine gun's belted ammunition.

"The guy beside me and I decided we weren't going to live, but do the best job we could," Scott said. "We lined up our sugar and cigarettes around our hole and fired at the enemy and ate the sugar and smoked the cigarettes."[35]

With daylight, Corsairs appeared overhead and scorched the attackers with napalm and rockets.

Yet the wild close-in melee, fought hand-to-hand and with grenades, continued intermittently during the day throughout several Chinese assaults. The attacks destroyed what remained of the 235th Regiment's 1st Battalion.[36]

As many as 400 Chinese soldiers lay dead in the snow when Easy Company began leaving Hill 1282 at 4pm on the 28th.

With the help of 100 men from Stevens's Headquarters and Service Company, about 200 wounded Marines were carried from Hill 1282 to the aid tents below.

While descending the hill, Pfc Scott was wounded; shrapnel split the M-1 that he had slung across his back. The carbine probably saved his life.[37]

Of the 175 men of Easy Company that ascended Hill 1282, only 30 left it under their own power. A sergeant led Lieutenant Yancey down the hill, each man grasping an end of a stick. Lieutenant Schreier also managed to stumble into a first aid station in Yudam-ni.[38]

When the flood of wounded men began coming down the hills to the medical tents, Pfc James Hester and Corpsman Joseph Pancamo drove out in a jeep to pick them up – and vanished. The next day, their bullet-riddled jeep was found, but there was no sign of Hester or Pancamo. They were listed as missing in action.[39]

On adjacent Hill 1240, things were even worse, if that were possible. Separated from Hill 1282 by a broad saddle, Captain Milton Hull's

Dog Company fought a separate battle that began at 1am when two battalions of the enemy's 236th Regiment struck with terrific power. By 2:30am, the attackers had overrun Hull's defenses on the northwest end of the hill. A half hour later, the weapons company command post fell to the enemy.

The survivors of the enemy's whirlwind attacks withdrew halfway down the hill. Hull was ordered to organize a counterattack.

When he informed his superior that he had just 20 or 30 effectives remaining, he was told that the Chinese must be stopped at all costs.

The stakes were high: if the Chinese broke through, they could capture the artillery pieces in the valley immediately behind Dog Company.

Although wounded, Hull led a counterattack that surprised the Chinese and drove them from the crest. The enemy recovered and retaliated with attacks from three sides that pushed the Dog Company remnant to a spur of the hillcrest, to which it clung while awaiting help.[40]

"You get chills down your spine thinking you were there," Pfc Thomas Cassis later said. "Sometimes you think it was actually a dream."[41]

Just in time, reinforcements arrived.

At 4am, Lieutenant Harold Dawe began to lead a platoon of the Fifth Marines' Charlie Company up the steep, slippery hill. The relief troops, sweating from the exertion of lugging extra ammunition to Hull's company in spite of the 20-below-zero cold, reached the crest where they battled enemy troops that fought from the cover of the reverse slope.

The Charlie platoon had missed Hull's tiny remnant on the way up, so it backtracked until it found what remained of Dog Company. When combined, Hull's and Dawe's men numbered no more than 50 exhausted men, many of them wounded.

Determined to regain control of 1240, Hull led the tiny combined force in a counterattack that, against all odds, reached the hillcrest. It did not remain there for long.

From the northeastern spur Dawe was chilled by what he saw: large numbers of Chinese soldiers massing for another attack. He was astounded by how many there were.

"It was just like kicking over an anthill; there were so many of them," Dawe said.

When the Chinese struck at 11am, the Marines realized they could not hope to hold Hill 1240 against such numbers, and they withdrew to a more defensible position halfway down the hill.

Dawe, whose helmet was shot from his head, lost about half of the 54 men that he had led up the hill. Just 16 Dog Company Marines remained able to fight. They clung to their position until more reinforcements arrived.[42]

The 79th Division's 237th Regiment, ordered to capture Hill 1384 northwest of Hills 1282 and 1240, found its objective undefended.

Lieutenant Colonel Robert Taplett's 3rd Battalion had reached the Fifth Marines' assembly area in Yudam-ni earlier in the day, expecting to join the regiment's renewed march to Mupyong-ni in the morning.

The battalion occupied positions on Yudam-ni's north side, beneath the knobs and spurs of North Ridge and Hill 1384. Because no major hostile action was expected, the Marines did not deploy in a continuous line.

As the day progressed, Taplett's uneasiness grew over the situation on Hill 1384 and its spur.

Despite the assurances of regimental staff that a Seventh Marines company was posted there, Taplett believed that the hill was undefended.

He sent a platoon from "I" Company, along with a South Korean police platoon, up the hill to investigate.[43]

Shortly after 2am on the 28th, one or two Chinese companies swept down Hill 1384's spur, with the object of seizing the road junction north of Yudam-ni. Enemy troops overran the "I" Company platoon outpost, and drove a wedge between the 3rd Battalion's Weapons Company and the South Koreans, who withdrew after cutting down many attackers with their two machine guns.

Taplett's command post happened to lie in a no-man's-land between the approaching Chinese and one of Taplett's rifle companies.

From his darkened operations tent, Taplett continued to consult his maps while directing the movement of his men by radio – oddly, without interference from the enemy, who apparently believed that the tent was unoccupied.[44]

Pfc Red Parkinson of the Weapons Company fired his rifle until the barrel was steaming and had to be thrust into the snow to cool. Around him, wounded Marines moaned and wailed, and an emotional Marine had to be restrained from executing Chinese prisoners.

The Chinese attack down Hill 1384 was stopped by the Weapons Company Marines' massive firepower. The enemy left behind 200 to 300 dead.[45]

The 79th Division's massed, battalion-size attacks failed to break the Marine lines anywhere, or to drive the Marines from the hilltops into Yudam-ni.

Although heavily outnumbered, the Marines compensated for the disparity in numbers with their enormous firepower advantage. The Chinese attacked frontally, rather than flowing around some hilltop defenses, making it easier for the Marines to repulse them.

The 79th Division's losses were shocking; in just one night, it lost five of its nine battalions, about 4,500 men. The remnants of two regiments were combined into three companies. The losses severely hampered the division's effectiveness in the days ahead.[46]

The Fifth and Seventh Marines' casualties during November 27 and November 28 totaled 136 killed in action, 675 wounded, and 60 missing. There were also 355 non-battle casualties, nearly all of them due to frostbite and cold weather injuries.[47]

With daylight on the 28th, soldiers of the Chinese 89th Division could be seen atop Hill 1403 to the west, the one from which the Seventh Regiment's How Company was driven overnight. The loss of 1403 had the potential to undermine Yudam-ni's defensive network.[48]

Lieutenant Colonel Ray Murray postponed the scheduled resumption of his Fifth Regiment's advance to Mupyong-ni to the west.

In the aftermath of the night's bloody attacks by the Chinese, it was evident to Murray and the Seventh Marines' Colonel Homer Litzenberg that their regiments in the Yudam-ni valley and the surrounding hills were surrounded and heavily outnumbered.

Without orders from the division or X Corps, Murray and Litzenberg agreed to consolidate their regiments and to go on the defensive at Yudam-ni.

Ordinarily, General Edward Craig, the 1st Division's assistant commander, would have been sent by General Smith to take command, but Craig had been ordered home two days earlier to be with his father, who had suffered a cerebral thrombosis and was not expected to live.[49]

"We intermeshed, we planned together what we were going to do to come out, and everything worked out fine," said Murray. "He [Litzenberg] never did say, 'I'm going to take charge here. I'm the senior regimental commander.'"[50]

Although neither China nor the United States had formally declared war, and both countries were careful about how they characterized the fighting, to the men fighting and dying on the battle lines in subzero cold, it certainly felt like war.[51]

Chapter 8

Fox Hill

November 27–28

Here they come!
SHOUTED CORPORAL THOMAS ASHDALE,
A SQUAD LEADER.[1]

I would not be here today if it had not been for (Lieutenant) Don Campbell and How Battery.
CAPTAIN WILLIAM BARBER, GRATEFUL FOR THE ARTILLERY PROTECTION ON FOX HILL.[2]

Roughly equidistant between Yudam-ni and Hagaru-ri loomed 5,454-foot Toktong Pass, the Chosin Reservoir area's highest point.

Even the lowliest private could grasp the importance of seizing the pass, which funneled the 1st Marine Division's vehicles and supplies between the two towns via the one-lane main supply route, or MSR. If the Chinese captured the pass, it would become a chokepoint rather than a conduit.

Fox Company of the Seventh Marines' 2nd Battalion was sent from Hagaru-ri to occupy the hill, which rose abruptly from the MSR and was covered in knee-deep snow. Below the crest, the hill was wreathed in dwarf pines; its upper reaches and summit were covered by patches of dense brush.[3]

On November 27 Captain William Barber, Fox's 30-year-old commanding officer, and Lieutenant Colonel Randolph Lockwood, the 2nd Battalion commander, drove the seven miles from Hagaru-ri to the mountain pass in a jeep.

They studied the ground with an eye to preparing a temporary defensive perimeter. Barber expected that his company would spend just one night on the mountain pass before moving on to Yudam-ni the next day and joining its sister companies, Easy and Dog.

Neither Barber nor Lockwood had been in Korea very long, but both men had served in the Marine Corps during World War II. Lockwood did not see combat, and had spent just one day in the Pacific during the war; that day happened to be December 7, 1941, at Pearl Harbor.

Barber, however, had seen action in the Pacific. The Kentuckian was an enlisted man for two years and had gone to Marine Parachute School. Later, after his leadership qualities were recognized, he was sent to Officer Candidate School.

He was commissioned in February 1945, in time to land on Iwo Jima with the 5th Marine Division's 26th Regiment. His rifle company's high attrition of officers resulted in Barber's rapid promotion to company commander. Twice wounded, he won two Purple Hearts, and also a Silver Star for rescuing two wounded Marines from Japanese-held territory.[4]

Barber and Lockwood selected Toktong Pass's 4,800-foot-elevation northern shoulder as the place where Barber's company would set up its temporary defensive perimeter. It was an 80-by-300-yard area that provided a sweeping view of the innumerable ridges, valleys, and gulleys that rolled away in all directions. The alpine countryside was at once severely beautiful and fraught with unseen danger.

The isolated hillside rose sharply from the north side of the MSR. From the hill's highest point was a narrow saddle that extended 900 yards northward to a curved ridge.

Barber remained at Toktong Pass, awaiting the arrival of his company, while Lockwood returned to Hagaru-ri in the jeep.

Barber's men were still in Hagaru-ri. They had had a problem rounding up motor transportation, and the men grumbled at the prospect of having to march seven miles uphill with all of their gear.

However, Lieutenant Don Campbell, the forward artillery observer assigned to Fox Company, was able to borrow nine six-by-six flatbed trucks from How Company, the artillery unit that would support Fox Company.

Barber's Marines climbed aboard and arrived at the pass at 5pm, as the day was ending.[5]

Reinforced by the heavy machine-gun and mortar sections of the battalion Weapons Company, Barber commanded 240 men.[6]

After weighing the pros and cons, Barber decided to insist that his men dig in – an unpopular order with darkness fast approaching, the ground frozen, and Fox Company scheduled to move on to Yudam-ni the next morning, The order "seemed foolish at the time," Barber later acknowledged, and it elicited much grumbling in the ranks.

"But something made me order them to break out those entrenching tools and turn to, even though it was growing dark and we were all dog-tired." He added, "But you do whatever you think is going to be the most effective in the long run."[7]

In what proved to be a prescient decision, Barber designed a V-shaped perimeter whose closed end – and strongest point – faced northward toward Hill 1653, and a promontory that would be nicknamed Rocky Ridge.[8]

By 9pm, the Marines had settled into their sleeping bags in their foxholes. There were no warming tents, no fires. Two hours later, the moon rose. The night was now clear, bright "and miserably cold," said Lieutenant Robert McCarthy, who commanded Fox's 3rd Platoon.[9]

Barber was commanding a guard company at the Marine barracks in Philadelphia when he got his orders on September 15 to go to Korea. He arrived November 13 and took charge of Fox Company near Koto-ri.

He was clean-shaven and wore clean, starched, and pressed dungarees when he introduced himself to his Marines, who were dirty and unshaven after weeks in the field. They suspected that he might be a poster Marine, while he judged them to be slovenly and "largely untrained." Many were reservists, and some of them had not even gone to boot camp.

Barber ordered his platoon leaders to have their men clean their weapons, field-shave in cold water, and prepare for a conditioning hike beginning at 6am the next day.[10]

Over the ensuing days, he attempted to rectify his company's weaknesses. After observing one of his platoons firing at three Chinese soldiers and not hitting them, he began holding remedial target practice sessions, with his men shooting at cans. Their marksmanship improved. He focused too on physical conditioning and on getting his men to work together as a team.[11]

"Here they come!" shouted Corporal Thomas Ashdale, a squad leader in McCarthy's 3rd Platoon, which held the center of Barber's perimeter. It was 2:30am on November 28.[12]

A company or more of 59th Division soldiers armed with Russian burp guns and American Thompson submachine guns swarmed McCarthy's platoon.

In groups of ten or more, they charged down Rocky Ridge, northwest of the perimeter. Opening fire from 50 yards away, the Chinese forced McCarthy's platoon back with grenades that knocked out three 60mm Marine mortars, killing and wounding more than a half-dozen members of Ashdale's squad.

In short order, McCarthy's 35 men were reduced by casualties to eight effectives, with 15 men killed, nine wounded, and three missing.[13]

It was the first of several headlong enemy assaults whose object was to wipe out Fox Company. The initial attacks came from both Rocky Ridge and the MSR, the latter thrust forcing Barber to hastily relocate his command post to a less exposed place farther uphill.

"They came at us in a mass formation," said Barber. "They had bugles blowing, using them for maneuver signals."

After the attacks from the MSR were bloodily repulsed, subsequent attacks came predominantly from Rocky Ridge.

Flares revealed a daunting spectacle. "We saw we had a battalion out there – five to six hundred Chinese," said Barber.[14]

To the left of McCarthy's platoon and facing west, Lieutenant Elmo Peterson's 2nd Platoon clung to its position as the Chinese crowded around Peterson's men.

"I ran into one of them. He shot me and I shot him," said Peterson, who was hit in his left shoulder joint by a slug from the enemy soldier's Thompson submachine gun. The wound bled a lot but he could still carry a rifle with his right hand.

Peterson was wounded again the following night – shot in the back. The bullet ranged through Peterson's ribs and into his abdominal cavity. It felt like being slammed by a baseball bat; the sharp pain became a dull ache after a day or two. Peterson remained in command in spite of his wounds.[15]

The Chinese plowed through the deep snow flinging grenades. One went off in the trench connected to Pfc Ernest Gonzales's foxhole. "I saw the flash and felt the shock waves," he said.

The explosion wounded six nearby Marines, but the trench curved before Gonzalez's foxhole and that spared him. "I had butterflies in my stomach" as he fought the enemy, Gonzales said, "and my shivering was not caused by the cold."[16]

"The whole hilltop was alive with grenades," said Lieutenant McCarthy. Three landed in the foxhole of one Marine, and a fourth exploded atop his helmet, knocking him out. When he came to, the Marine resumed directing his fire team.[17]

They fought the attackers hand-to-hand. Everything became a weapon: entrenching tools, knives, fists, and elbows.

Barber refused to take cover, although urged to do so by a sergeant. "They haven't made the bullet yet that can kill me," he said, but he was later wounded in the hip.[18]

Pfc Bob Kirschner was returning to his platoon from the CP, where he had identified the body of a friend whose face had been blown off, when Pfc Roger Gonzales approached him.

Suddenly, Gonzales went down spurting blood from a bullet wound in the neck. Kirschner dragged him into his foxhole, Gonzales asked for water, and Kirschner rubbed snow on Gonzales's lips.

Gonzales died in Kirschner's arms. Afterward, Kirschner used Gonzales's frozen body as a sandbag for his foxhole. The searing memory never left him, necessary though his act was in the extreme circumstances.[19]

Two northern New Jersey Pfcs, 6-foot-3, 220-pound Hector Cafferata – called "Moose" or "Big Hec" – and his bespectacled friend Kenneth Benson occupied a forward listening post on the right flank of Peterson's 2nd Platoon. The 25-below-zero icebox cold and whistling wind out of Siberia had frozen their edible food, so their dinner consisted of frozen Tootsie Rolls.[20]

Cafferata and Benson had become friends while playing semi-pro football in New Jersey. While Cafferata loved hunting, fishing, and trapping in the northern New Jersey woods, Benson was an athlete who enjoyed sports.

Together, they enlisted in the Marine Corps Reserves, and when the Korean War broke out, they traveled cross country together by train to Camp Pendleton, California.[21]

When the first attack came at 1:30am on the 28th, their platoon was overrun, and Chinese soldiers were all around Cafferata and Benson.

Having emerged from his sleeping bag stocking-footed, Cafferata, an excellent marksman from his years of hunting, immediately shot five or six of the enemy with his M-1.

He and Benson began to crawl back to the main platoon line when a potato masher fell in front of Benson. It exploded when he picked it up and threw it; the blast shattered Benson's thick glasses, blinding him.[22]

Cafferata continued crawling toward the 2nd Platoon's main defenses, with the sightless Benson clutching Cafferata's foot and following him.

They occupied a new position, and the Chinese attempted to overrun them again in order to break through the intersection of Peterson's 2nd Platoon and McCarthy's 3rd Platoon.

Snatching up an entrenching tool, Cafferata clubbed two attackers, and he then grabbed a Thompson submachine gun dropped by an enemy soldier and emptied it into the swarming Chinese.

Unable to see and shoot, Benson did what he could – methodically loading M-1s with eight-bullet clips and handing the rifles to Cafferata, who added to his mounting body count. So many Chinese corpses piled up in front of their position that Cafferata was able to take cover behind them.

When the enemy soldiers flung potato mashers at them, Cafferata batted them away with his entrenching tool and continued to fire the Benson-loaded rifles at anything that moved.

When a potato masher exploded as Cafferata was throwing it back at the Chinese, he lost a finger and his right arm was severely injured.

At dawn, Cafferata was the only 2nd Platoon Marine still fighting when Australian P-51s arrived and broke up the enemy attack with rockets and bombs.

Cafferata, Benson, and Pfc Gerald Smith were credited with preventing the Chinese from driving a wedge between Peterson's and McCarthy's platoons.[23]

That morning, 100 or more Chinese corpses lay before Cafferata's and Benson's position.[24]

Cafferata was shot through the right arm and chest as he returned to the listening post to retrieve his boots. The bullet punctured his right lung.

"Moose" walked to the medical tent in his stocking feet after fighting boot-less for five hours. He lost all of his toes to frostbite.[25]

Barber's platoon leaders reported 450 dead Chinese on the ground around Fox Company. The Marines lost 20 men killed in action and 54 wounded. Three Marines were reported missing.[26]

During the morning of November 28, Lieutenant Peterson was alarmed to discover that Fox had an ammunition shortage.

"We only had enough ammunition so that every rifleman had four or five rounds and the light machineguns had half a belt. We only had enough ammunition for ten to 15 minutes of Chinese attacks," he said.

He could only hope that the Chinese wouldn't attack again before Fox was resupplied with ammunition. "It would have been bayonets."[27]

So that it wouldn't come to that, Peterson sent foraging parties out to collect weapons and bandoleers from the dead Chinese soldiers. "They had fairly decent weapons," Peterson said, but many of them were foreign-made and required different calibers of ammunition.[28]

The 105mm howitzers of the Eleventh Marines' How Company, commanded by Captain Ben Read, fired at maximum range from its position on Hagaru-ri's northwest perimeter.

The exposed position where Read placed his guns enabled How to provide decisive heavy firepower to help keep the enemy at bay on Fox Hill.

How Company had a surplus of ammunition because the 15 trucks loaded with artillery shells that were to go to Yudam-ni's batteries had remained in Hagaru-ri when the Chinese cut the MSR between Hagaru-ri and Yudam-ni. How possessed more ammunition than its sister companies George and Item in Yudam-ni.[29]

Lieutenant Campbell, the forward artillery observer on Fox Hill, was able to accurately guide the long-range 105mm howitzer fire from the How Company battery in Hagaru-ri into the masses of attacking Chinese because he had earlier worked out the firing coordinates.

He had the area "zeroed in perfectly," he said. During the long night, Fox Hill rumbled and shook with exploding artillery shells.[30]

In later years, Barber expressed his gratitude for the artillery protection. "I would not be here today if it had not been for Don Campbell and How Battery," he said.[31]

Campbell was not immune from the attacking Chinese, however. At one point during the attacks, enemy soldiers so menaced Campbell and his support team that he ordered his men into their foxholes and brought down How Battery artillery fire onto their observation positions.[32]

Barber and his officers now knew that their company was surrounded and could not expect to receive any relief soon. It must depend on its own resources. "The odds weren't very good," Peterson conceded.[33]

The Marines erected tents for the two dozen men who had been severely wounded during the first night's attacks. They converted the company oil-burning cooking stoves to wood stoves to heat the tents and protect the patients from the 25-below-zero cold. Two corpsmen tended to them full-time.

Dozens of others who were not as badly wounded remained on the battle line, as did men who were unable to walk but could defend fixed positions.

In an attempt to prevent frostbite, squad leaders made certain that the Marines changed their socks every day.

Two non-coms inspected every weapon every morning and fired them. The men's lives depended on their weapons, which had to be kept clean with just a touch of oil. Too much oil, and the weapon would become inoperable.[34]

Chapter 9

East of Chosin Reservoir

November 27–28

Immediately, the high explosive shells burst in the column of men, and I ordered fire at full automatic [about 240 high-explosive rounds per minute]. In only seconds there was no movement from the column.

Captain James McClymont, AAA Automatic Weapons Battalion commander, describing the destruction of a Chinese column of 80 men east of Chosin Reservoir.[1]

While Fox Company and the Fifth and Seventh Regiments at Yudam-ni were fighting for their lives during the night of November 27–28, east of Chosin Reservoir the Chinese 80th Division was poised to attack three US Army battalions belonging to the 7th Division's 31st and 32nd Regiments.

The 7th Division's deployment in northeastern Korea had been a scattershot affair. It began landing on October 29 at Iwon in northeastern Korea, about 150 miles north of where the 1st Marine Division came ashore at Wonsan.

The 17th Regiment, which landed first, was ordered to march north to the Yalu River. The 31st and 32nd Regiments arrived next, and infantry battalions from those regiments were dispatched from Hamhung northwest to the Chosin Reservoir area.[2]

General Ned Almond dispersed his X Corps divisions across 4,000 square miles of northeastern Korea under the assumption that organized opposition to the UN forces was nearly ended. Almond and MacArthur believed that the United Nations forces must only reach the Yalu River for organized resistance to cease entirely.

However, the entry into the war of several Chinese armies was proving the optimism emanating from General MacArthur's Tokyo command to be as insubstantial as a dream.

Chinese forces had smashed the Eighth Army in northwestern Korea on November 25, sending it reeling backward. Now, two days later, it was X Corps's turn. Almond's men faced three Chinese field armies.[3]

Before the attacks at Chosin, General Almond had ordered General David Barr to send a regiment of his 7th Infantry Division east of Chosin Reservoir. It was to relieve the Fifth Marines being sent to Yudam-ni to lead the march west to Mupyong-ni.

The 32nd Regiment's 1st Battalion, commanded by Lieutenant Colonel Don Faith, arrived first on November 25, before the 31st Regimental Combat Team led by Colonel Alan MacLean.

On November 26, MacLean and some of his staff officers arrived at Faith's command post on Hill 1221 ahead of the rest of RCT-31. MacLean's men were still toiling up the MSR from Chinghung-ni and were expected to arrive the next day.

Upon MacLean's arrival, Faith's 1st Battalion became part of the composite 31st Regimental Combat Team, or RCT-31 – "Task Force MacLean." It consisted of Faith's infantry battalion, MacLean's 3rd Infantry Battalion of the 31st Regiment, and the 57th Field Artillery Battalion – 3,200 officers and men.[4]

MacLean's RCT-31 included not only his 3rd Battalion, commanded by Lieutenant Colonel William Reilly, but Lieutenant Colonel Raymond Embree's field artillery battalion, and an assortment of other units: Battery D of the 15th Antiaircraft Automatic Weapons Battalion; the 31st Heavy Mortar Company, with 12 4.2-inch mortars; the 31st Tank Company, consisting of 16 M-4A Sherman tanks and two 105mm howitzer tanks. The 31st's 2nd Infantry Battalion was expected to arrive at any time, but no one knew for certain where it was.[5]

MacLean's eight crew-served heavy weapons carriers gave RCT-31 a tremendous firepower advantage that the Marines west of Chosin Reservoir lacked. They would be of critical importance to the survival

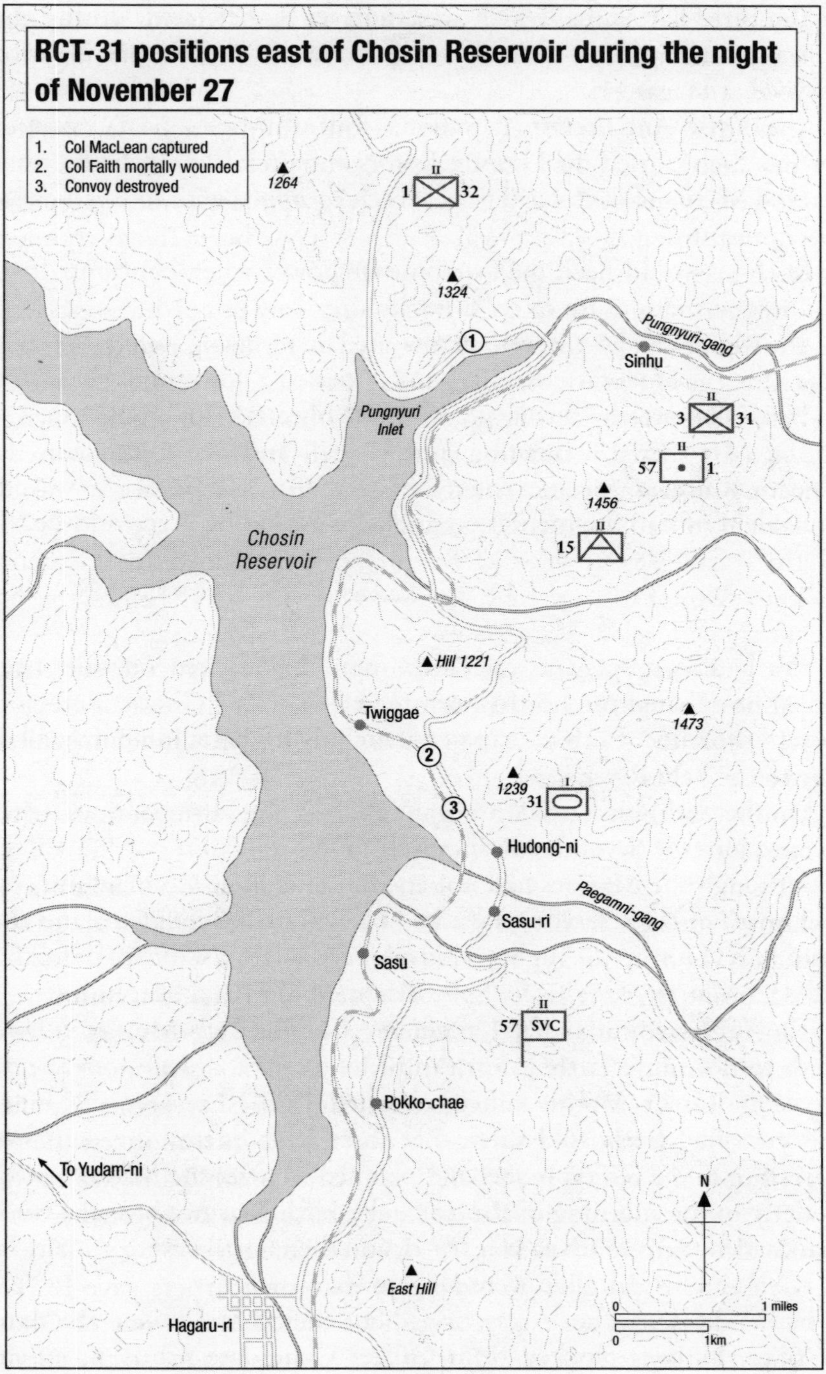
RCT-31 positions east of Chosin Reservoir during the night of November 27
1. Col MacLean captured
2. Col Faith mortally wounded
3. Convoy destroyed
1264
1 32
1324
Pungnyuri-gang
Sinhu
Pungnyuri Inlet
3 31
57 1
1456
15
Chosin Reservoir
Hill 1221
Twiggae
1473
1239
31
Hudong-ni
Paegamni-gang
Sasu-ri
Sasu
57 SVC
Pokko-chae
To Yudam-ni
N
East Hill
0
1 miles
0
1km
Hagaru-ri

of the three battalions, which were not yet battle-tested, during their coming trial by fire – and, by extension, the 1st Marine Division's survival at Hagaru-ri.

The 15th Antiaircraft Battalion's four full-track M-19 weapons carriers each carried dual 40mm Bofors antiaircraft guns. Its four half-tracked M-16 quad-50 carriers were each equipped with four .50-caliber machine guns.

RCT-31 would need the awesome firepower when confronted with Chinese formations up to six times its size.

The M-19s and M-16s were all mounted on revolving turrets. When the M-16 fired all four of its machine guns, it spewed 1,800 rounds per minute, and was "like a scythe cutting grain," wrote historian Roy Appleman.

The M-19 fired a bursting 40mm shell and could also aim flat-trajectory fire at specific enemy targets. On automatic, it was the equivalent of 240 fragmentation grenades exploding every minute.[6]

Faith's battalion spent a quiet first night bivouacked on Hill 1221, which dominated the north-south road that traced Chosin Reservoir's eastern shoreline. Faith anticipated marching his battalion north, all the way to the Yalu River.

On the 26th, his battalion began relieving the Fifth Marines, which were to join the Seventh Marines west of the reservoir.

Although the Marines had not encountered large Chinese units east and north of the reservoir, there had been scattered incidents and they were wary. During the night of November 25–26, a Chinese patrol had pulled a Marine from his foxhole, disarmed him, and beat him.

The Fifth's commander, Lieutenant Colonel Ray Murray, advised Faith to not move farther north until he received orders from the 7th Division. Other Marine officers warned Faith that several Chinese prisoners had freely told them that three fresh enemy divisions were operating in the reservoir area and planned to sever the MSR.

Early in the morning of the 27th, the Fifth Marines boarded trucks that carried them south to Hagaru-ri, and then northwest to Yudam-ni.[7]

Faith and his battalion were now on their own.

Faith, the son of an Army brigadier general, had joined the Army in 1941. He was plucked from Officer Candidate School – missing the Infantry Advanced Course and the Command and General Staff College – to become aide-de-camp to General Matthew Ridgway. Faith jumped into Normandy with Ridgway and the 82nd Airborne Division on D-Day.

Although Faith had led the 32nd Regiment's 1st Battalion for less than one year, he was awarded the Distinguished Service Cross for his leadership at Inchon and Seoul.

What the 32-year-old lacked in experience and infantry and command training, he more than compensated for with aggressiveness and courage, his fellow officers agreed.[8]

Like Faith, Colonel MacLean, who was 43, had served as a staff officer during World War II. He was a large, robust man who graduated in 1930 from the US Military Academy, where he played tackle on the football team.

Early in his career, MacLean served with the 31st Infantry in the Philippines and, after the war ended, he commanded the 32nd Infantry in Japan. Following the Battle of Seoul two months earlier, he was assigned to lead the 31st Infantry.

"He was a bull of the woods, a great guy," said Colonel Charles Beauchamp, who attended West Point with MacLean. "He possessed ceaseless energy, a dynamic personality, and an uncompromising will to get things done."[9]

MacLean approved Faith's plan to move his 32nd Regiment battalion six miles north of Hill 1221 to occupy the Fifth Marines' former positions. MacLean said that when his task force arrived the next day, he intended to attack north as well.[10]

MacLean established his command post in a schoolhouse a mile south of Hill 1221.

The next morning, November 27th, MacLean, his staff officers, and Faith drove the six miles north to the foxholes and bunkers that the Fifth Marines had vacated just hours earlier. Faith's battalion was in the process of making them its own, on the north side of the Pungnyuri Inlet of the Chosin Reservoir.

When the 31st Regiment's 3rd Battalion and the 57th Field Artillery arrived later in the day, it established its positions between Hill 1221 and the inlet's southern shore.

The 31st Tank Company, commanded by Captain Robert Drake, was four road miles farther south, in the abandoned village of Hudong-ni, where it had stopped to rest and refuel. Drake said that he would lead the tanks to the main task force on the 28th.[11]

By late November 27, RCT-31 was strung out along ten miles of road, occupying seven positions – and expecting no major enemy action that night.

However, civilians questioned by the 1st Battalion intelligence officer through an interpreter reported that Chinese soldiers boasted that they were going to take back Chosin Reservoir. The intelligence was considered farcical.[12]

Later, a report reached MacLean that several hundred Chinese troops had been seen in a village east of the inlet. He sent the 42-man Intelligence & Reconnaissance Platoon, commanded by Lieutenant Richard Coke Jr, to investigate.

The platoon set out in jeeps equipped with mounted machine guns. It neither reported back by radio nor returned. Indeed, the platoon was never heard from again.

It was later learned that five of the men survived a clash with Chinese troops; at least two became war prisoners. Another survivor was found by Army medics and treated. He had a bullet wound to the head and shrapnel wounds, and had probably been left for dead. He died 42 years later.[13]

The Chinese had originally planned for the 80th Division to march south down the east side of Chosin Reservoir to Hagaru-ri and there join the 58th Division in attacking the vital 1st Marine Division hub during the night of November 27.

However, the 80th and one regiment from the 81st Division found their way unexpectedly blocked by RCT-31.

The 58th Division delayed its assault on Hagaru-ri for one day, and the plan changed. Instead of attempting to push through to Hagaru-ri, forthwith, the 80th and 81st Division regiments now planned to surround and attack Task Force MacLean that night.

The Chinese regiments were rich in manpower with 14,334 officers and men, but lacked heavy weapons and, of course, air support.

They, like other CCF units, were essentially a "pre-industrial" army armed with "archaic and mixed ordnance" but, through fast marches with light loads, capable of impressive feats of mobility, although hampered by poor communications and medical care.[14]

The three 80th Division regiments – the 238th, 239th, and 240th – planned to attack RCT-31 from the north and east. Attacking from the south, the 81st Division's 242nd Regiment was to cut off MacLean's escape route to Hudong-ni. The plan was ambitious: isolate MacLean's various units, and annihilate them one by one.[15]

However, the Chinese were operating under a huge misconception due to poor intelligence-gathering. The regimental commanders believed they would each be attacking an American company of about 200 men, when in fact the targets were battalion-size-plus – more than three times larger than anticipated, and supported by heavy arms.[16]

Moreover, the Chinese were using outdated World War II-era Japanese maps that delayed the assault. Two battalions of the 238th Regiment went to the wrong staging sites, four miles from their target. The 3rd Battalion was reassigned as the attacking unit, and the entire operation was paused at midnight while the battalion got into position.

In the meantime, men froze to death while lying in the snow and waiting for the attack signal.

Song Xieseng, assistant captain of the 238th's 7th Company, was aware that the Security Company had had to wait hours in the snow while its battalion returned from the wrong location.

When the attack order came and Song sent some men to contact the Security Company, they returned with the astonishing news that everyone in the Security Company had frozen to death. "Are you sure?" Song asked incredulously. His men said they had checked closely for signs of life, but there were no survivors.

After repeated requests for the attack to begin – not only were men freezing to death, but many had eaten nothing in two days – the 80th Division issued the attack order.[17]

Kong Qingsan's artillery squad was setting up its 92mm gun and discovered that it had nothing to support the gun's left leg. Kong used his body as the support. When he ordered his men to fire, the gun's recoil killed him.[18]

Marine Captain Edward Stamford, the forward air controller assigned to the 32nd Infantry's 1st Battalion after Inchon, was sent by Lieutenant Colonel Faith late November 27 to Company A, the northernmost of Faith's three companies.

Faith wanted Stamford and the four enlisted men in his Tactical Air Control Party to be in the lead company and summon close-air support if needed during the next day's advance to Chosin Reservoir's northern dam.[19]

Stamford was a sergeant in a Marine engineering unit when World War II broke out. He, like many enlisted men, went to aviation school, received an officer's commission, and was sent to the Pacific, where he was a dive-bomber pilot during the Battle of Bougainville in the Solomon Islands, and on other battlegrounds.

The Pacific War was a laboratory for the continued evolution of Marine close-air support – a necessary improvisation given the Marines' lack of the heavy artillery that the Army possessed. Strike aircraft became the Marines' "flying artillery," operating 50 to 200 yards in front of friendly troops.[20]

Stamford got in on the ground floor. In 1944, he attended a 13-week course at the Marine Air-Infantry School in Quantico, Virginia, that qualified him as a trained infantry officer and taught him to appreciate the infantry's problems. Acquiring the skills both of an aviator and an infantryman was a step toward becoming a forward air observer in the Air Naval Gunfire Liaison Company – ANGLICO for short.

After years of further training, assignments as an aerial observer, and a multitude of rehearsals, Stamford was sent to Korea with the Eighth Army's Fifth Cavalry Regiment during the summer of 1950. He joined the 7th Division when it landed at Inchon on September 18, and the next day became the first ANGLICO man to call in an air strike during the Korean War.

The plane knocked out a North Korean observation post. Witnessing the strike were Faith and Generals David Barr and Henry Hodes, the 7th Division's assistant commander. They were suitably impressed that a Marine on the ground with a radio could direct a pilot to a target by using visual landmarks.[21]

During Stamford's six weeks with the 7th Division, two problems became apparent to him: the troops were not well-trained, and the language barrier between the Americans and the South Korean troops was highly problematic.

Faith's battalion consisted of 745 American soldiers and about 300 South Korean recruits. The South Korean soldiers were known as KATUSA, the acronym for "Korean Augmentees of the United States Army" – fill-ins for men that had been detached from the 7th Division earlier in the war and sent to the 24th and 25th Divisions.

The South Koreans had not received even basic training. Their effectiveness was further impaired by their inability to understand or speak English, while their American counterparts were at a similar disadvantage regarding the Korean language.[22]

The coming crises and emergencies would only be exacerbated by the problems identified by Stamford.[23]

There had been no warning of Chinese forces in the area, and MacLean's task force was unprepared.

Just after midnight, Chinese troops marching straight down the road from the north crashed into Faith's "A" Company. The enemy troops killed men in their tents and in their sleeping bags.

Captain Ed Scullion, the "A" Company commander, was among the victims, and the battalion assistant operations officer sent by Faith to take his place was shot dead before he could take command.

Awakened by gunfire and Captain Scullion's shouting, Captain Stamford heard "chattering outside our bunker, the poncho was pulled aside ... I saw a fur-rimmed face in the moonlight and fired at it from a sitting position." The Chinese soldier had dropped a grenade, and the explosion wounded one man inside the bunker.

Stamford gathered up a handful of enlisted men and led them to the "A" command post to help organize a defense.[24]

The enemy had overrun the company's 60mm mortars, and they fell into Chinese hands. Lieutenant Carlos Ortenzi, the mortar officer, rallied his men and they counterattacked, recapturing their position after a bitter battle.

Ortenzi approached Stamford and said, "Well, captain, you are the next senior man. I guess you have the company."

Stamford withdrew the mostly intact 2nd Platoon from the line and sent it to sweep the rear of infiltrators that had slipped past soldiers asleep in their foxholes.

He found the company executive officer, Lieutenant Cecil Smith, inside the command bunker and placed him in charge of the 1st Platoon, whose commander had been wounded. Stamford set up two machine guns to cover a draw that the Chinese were using to gain entry into the company perimeter.

By these actions, Stamford stabilized the "A" Company position, fending off subsequent attempts to overrun the CP, and cleared the area of infiltrators.[25]

The attack from the north on the 32nd Regiment included a North Korean tank and a self-propelled gun. Corporal James Godfrey, a "C" Company 75mm recoilless rifleman, destroyed them both.

Godfrey's quick defensive action called attention to himself, and he was assailed by scores of enemy soldiers, whom he wiped out with his recoilless rifle, then helped repel the repeated attacks that followed.[26]

It began snowing before dawn and the cold deepened. With daylight, the 1st Battalion executive officer relieved Stamford of temporary command of "A" Company and placed Lieutenant Smith in charge. Faith wanted Stamford to concentrate on his forward air control duties.

Stamford's ANGRC-9 radio, his primary means of calling in air strikes by Corsairs from Yonpo airfield and carriers offshore, had been "holed" and was useless. Yet he was still able to communicate via a backup radio working off a vehicle battery.[27]

His first order of business was to clear the Chinese-occupied hills overlooking the 1st Battalion perimeter.

Four Marine Corsairs arrived overhead at sunrise, and Stamford directed them to a ridge 300 yards from "A" Company where Chinese troops had taken cover.

The Corsairs hit them with napalm, driving them into the open where they were shot down by machine guns and small-arms fire. The gull-winged aircraft followed up with rocket and 20mm gunfire. The airstrikes broke the back of the Chinese attacks on Faith's battalion.[28]

South of the inlet four miles away, the 239th's 2nd Battalion attacked Task Force MacLean from the east. The attacks surprised the 31st Infantry's 3rd Battalion and the 57th Field Artillery, and the enemy found Americans sleeping in their tents on Hill 1200.

The Chinese riddled the tents before the soldiers could get out. They then overran Hill 1100 and charged west toward the 57th's guns, following the communications wire strung along the ground.

The Chinese battalion's 4th Company, led by Captain Li Changyan, overran the 31st Infantry command post in a farmhouse between the inlet and the 32nd Regiment to the north. Enemy soldiers shot several officers, among them Lieutenant Colonel William Reilly, the 3rd Battalion commander, during a furious gun battle fought among a cluster of houses. The attackers set fire to trucks in the area, and the conflagration blazed brightly in the night.

Reilly, shot four times, attempted to assist a Lieutenant Anderson, who was frantically attempting to draw his pistol from its holster. Reilly discovered that the problem was that Anderson's right arm had been blown off by a grenade and he didn't know it.

Reilly placed the pistol in Anderson's left hand, and Anderson fired left-handed until he died later that night.[29]

When the Chinese overran the 31st's CP, Zhang Jiqing, a squad leader, snatched a banner hanging outside the farmhouse and used it to gather food and medicine looted by the soldiers.

Zhang's political commissar was astounded when he saw the banner; it was the 31st Infantry's regimental flag. Today the 31st's colors are on display in China's Korean War Museum in Beijing.[30]

Lieutenant John Gray and his "M" Company 81mm mortar team occupied a blocking position southeast of the 3rd Battalion CP. He watched the Chinese nearly overrun the entire battalion perimeter, stopped only by desperate hand-to-hand fighting.

"Had they dislodged us, they would have cut the battalion in two and the battle would have been over that night," he said.

"M" Company's commander, Captain Earl Jordan Jr, "was in tears about what was happening," said Gray, "but he was fighting like a demon. He was some bear of a man, almost out of control."

Jordan's example inspired his company to give no ground to the attackers that night.[31]

Jordan, 33, who had fought in Italy during World War II with the 36th Division's 143rd Infantry Regiment, was wounded that night, but remained in command.

At daybreak, when he inspected his company's positions, he counted more than 60 enemy dead within yards of them, nearly all of them armed with American Thompson submachine guns and .45-caliber pistols.[32]

"K" and "I" companies, which held a ridgeline east of the 31st's perimeter, were hit from the east – lightly at first, but then with intensifying pressure.

"K" Company's South Korean troops bolted for the rear. Captain Robert Kitz briefly stopped the panicked withdrawal, but then the entire company line disintegrated as the Chinese pressed their attack.[33]

The Chinese overran an "I" Company platoon and streamed down the ridge, crashing through an 81mm mortar platoon in front of "M" Company's command post and menacing the 57th Field Artillery "A" Battery.

Learning that the infantrymen that had screened "A" Battery were withdrawing to its rear, its commander, Captain Harold Lodge, roved the gun sections and told his men to fight as long as they could.

Then, the Chinese were upon them. An explosive ignited two 5-gallon cans of gasoline, setting the "M" Company CP ablaze. "Several CCF ran up to where the CP was burning and started warming themselves by the fire," said Lieutenant Thomas Patton of "A" Battery. "Captain Lodge killed one and the others were shot by some of the members of the gun sections."

The "A" Battery gun crews were driven into the "B" Battery perimeter, around which retreating infantrymen from "I," "K," and "L" Companies rallied – "M" being the only company that stood fast during the tornadic attacks.

With daylight, Captain Kitz organized a counterattack that succeeded in retaking "A" Battery and turning the howitzers on the fleeing Chinese.[34]

The Chinese also enveloped the 57th Field Artillery headquarters and the 15th AAA (Antiaircraft Artillery) AW (Automatic Weapons) command post, which was in charge of the fast-firing M-16 and M-19 antiaircraft guns.

Captain James McClymont, the AAA Automatic Weapons Battalion commander, climbed aboard an M-19 and ordered the crew leader to open fire with his dual 40mm guns on enemy soldiers exposed by a flare. The Chinese were approaching the AAA position in marching formation.

"Immediately, the high explosive shells burst in the column of men, and I ordered fire at full automatic [about 240 high-explosive rounds per minute]. In only seconds there was no movement from the column," said McClymont.

Then, a major with the 57th Field Artillery Battery raised McClymont on the phone and informed him to his horror that he had fired on "friendly troops."

Filled with dread, McClymont took three of his men down to the road. To his immense relief, he confirmed that the dead were Chinese – about 80 of them.[35]

At daybreak, the Chinese withdrew from the hilltops surrounding the battleground – because daytime meant air strikes. They pulled back everywhere except from a roadblock on Hill 1221. That chokepoint severed the road between MacLean's task force and Hudong-ni and Hagaru-ri to the south. RCT-31 was surrounded.[36]

Captain Drake's tank battalion had stopped at Hudong-ni to refuel and rest for the night. Drake was unaware of the desperate fighting around the inlet a few miles to the north; perhaps the mass of Hill 1221 muffled the sounds of the battle.

The 31st Medical Company also arrived at Hudong-ni that evening. The medical company commander wished to push on to RCT-31 that same night, although Captain Drake strongly urged him to wait until morning, when he could proceed under the protection of Drake's tanks.

Disregarding Drake's advice, the medical company left Hudong-ni after midnight and drove north toward Hill 1221 and RCT-31.

A little more than a mile north of Hudong-ni on a hairpin turn at Hill 1221, a battalion from the 81st Division's 240th Regiment attacked the medical convoy.

A sergeant who managed to crawl down a drainage ditch and return to Hudong-ni blurted out the news of the ambush. A few other survivors trickled into Hudong-ni overnight.

An unknown number of men managed to push through the ambush and reach RCT-31; no one knew how many because radio communication had broken down.

The next morning, patrols found bodies and wrecked vehicles scattered along the road, with Hill 1221 still firmly in the hands of Chinese troops.[37]

Although the Chinese attacks east of Chosin Reservoir had failed to annihilate RCT-31, enemy troops had succeeded in surrounding it, isolating it from other units in the area, and driving it into a pocket.

However, the cost to the Chinese was high: the 80th Division lost nearly 3,200 men – 30 percent of its manpower. They were either killed outright on the battlefield, or were wounded and froze to death in the arctic cold.[38]

With daylight, Lieutenant Colonel Faith dispatched "B" and "C" companies to retake a knoll captured overnight by the Chinese. Aided by air strikes called in by Captain Stamford, the counterattacks cleared the heights of enemy troops.[39]

The Corsairs from Yonpo airfield and the Task Force 77 carriers in the Sea of Japan also blasted the hilltops around the inlet, from which 80th Division troops had infiltrated the 3rd Battalion's perimeter and set fire to its command post.

Task Force MacLean had survived to fight another day.

During the night's fighting around Chosin Reservoir, in the 2- to 3-foot-deep snow and extreme cold, the 9th Army Group reported the loss of 10,000 men. Moreover, it had failed to annihilate either the 1st Marine Division or RCT-31.[40]

Colonel MacLean had spent the night at Faith's CP north of the inlet. He returned to the 31st Infantry at dawn as heavy snow fell. Radio communication was sketchy and MacLean did not have a full picture of what had happened overnight at the 31st Infantry position, but he was optimistic.

MacLean had seen that the 32nd Regiment was still intact. And although he wasn't fully aware of the 31st Regiment's condition, he believed, without any evidence, that its 2nd Battalion would join him east of the reservoir later that day, vastly improving the task force's situation.

However, clogged roads and changed orders had so hindered the 2nd Battalion it was able only to reach Koto-ri, a dozen miles east of RCT-31. Now that the Chinese had cut the MSR between Koto-ri and Hagaru-ri, the battalion would be unable to assist Task Force MacLean.[41]

Finally, MacLean was confident that Captain Robert Drake's 31st Tank Battalion would join RCT-31 on the 28th.

Indeed, Drake intended to do so, even though he had had no communication with any of the RCT-31 units and was unaware of the Chinese attacks that had occurred overnight. For its part, RCT-31 was unaware that Drake planned to attempt to join it.[42]

At 10am, Drake set out from Hudong-ni with 16 Sherman M4 tanks, ambulances, and a volunteer force consisting of clerks, cooks, and technicians – but no infantrymen. General Hodes, the 7th Division's assistant commander, accompanied the relief convoy, although Drake was in charge.

Hodes had traveled to the area east of the reservoir at the behest of the division commander, General David Barr, to oversee MacLean's operation. Hodes was a combat veteran of World War II, when he had commanded the 112th Infantry Regiment in Europe.

Drake's convoy hadn't gone far when Chinese antitank teams firing American-made rocket launchers knocked out the two lead tanks at the roadblock on Hill 1221.

When the tanks behind them attempted to bypass the disabled tanks, they slid off the frozen road, and got bogged down in the marshy lower ground. Two of them got stuck and were abandoned. The Chinese on Hill 1221 blistered the area with machine-gun fire, and attempted to capture Drake's tanks.

Realizing that he could not get through to RCT-31, Drake ordered the 12 surviving tanks to turn back and return to Hudong-ni, intending to return the next day with infantry and air support.

At Hudong-ni, Hodes got into a jeep that took him to Hagaru-ri, where he sought help from General Smith. Hodes never returned to Hudong-ni.[43]

Chapter 10

Out on a Limb

November 28–29

We're still attacking and we're going all the way to the Yalu ... Don't let a bunch of Chinese laundrymen stop you.

General Ned Almond, X Corps commander.[1]

It was as though a whole field got on its feet and moved forward.

Lieutenant Colonel Thomas Ridge describing the white-clad enemy troops that attacked Hagaru-ri.[2]

The Chinese forces are committed in North Korea in great and ever-increasing strength ... We face an entirely new war.

General Douglas MacArthur's bitter news to the Joint Chiefs of Staff on November 28.[3]

In Yudam-ni, the dawning of November 28 revealed a gruesome tableaux of bloodstained snow, frozen human viscera and detached limbs.

The bodies of Chinese soldiers were frozen in grotesque attitudes, death having caught them in the acts of fighting, killing, and breathing their last. Enemy corpses lay in heaps before the American heavy machine guns. Some lay in neat rows where they had been mowed down.

Under a clear blue sky, it was more than 20 below zero with a brisk wind out of Siberia that made the temperature feel much colder. Steam and smoke billowed from idling trucks and cook fires built to warm men and their rations. Clouds of condensation rose into the air above each living man.

Thousands of men had died or had been wounded during the long night of attacks by three Chinese divisions, but the Marines' lines had held where it counted. Yudam-ni remained in American hands.

For how long was anyone's guess.

Despite the bleak arctic panorama and the many uncertainties that the new day presented, daytime was welcomed by the Marines after the desperate fighting throughout the seemingly endless night. Daytime meant close-air support and pinpoint artillery fire.

Yet orders still stood for the Fifth Marines to resume their attack to the west that morning, despite Yudam-ni being undeniably surrounded by tens of thousands of Chinese soldiers. X Corps and the 1st Marine Division had not changed the plan.

Nonetheless, Lieutenant Colonel Ray Murray, the Fifth Marines' commander, at 5:45am issued the first order recognizing the drastically changed situation; he directed his men to withdraw from their exposed positions on Southwest Ridge, and for all of his units to prepare defensive positions.

Standing orders notwithstanding, there would be no drive west to Mupyong-ni.

"I personally felt in a state of shock, the kind of shock one gets from some great personal tragedy, the sudden loss of someone close," said Murray of his state of mind after the night's distressing developments.

The new day had brought bad news from nearly every front: three Chinese divisions surrounded Yudam-ni; the road from Yudam-ni to Hagaru-ri was severed; and Hagaru-ri and Koto-ri were encircled by enemy troops.[4]

In the absence of General Smith and other ranking division officers, Murray and Colonel Homer Litzenberg, the Seventh Marines' commander, took the unusual step of sharing the command of the two regiments.[5]

Although Litzenberg was 46 and had more than a decade of seniority over the 36-year-old Murray, he consented to the arrangement. They set up side-by-side command posts, and their staff officers worked alongside their opposite numbers.

Besides suspending the Fifth Marines' march to Mupyong-ni and instead going on the defensive, they agreed the day's priority should be securing the ridges looming over Yudam-ni.[6]

Under the new defensive alignment conceived by Litzenberg's operations officer, Major Hank Woessner, the Fifth Marines would man the northern half of the Yudam-ni perimeter. The Seventh Marines, more badly battered by the Chinese attacks than the Fifth, was responsible for the southern lines.

The severe losses suffered by the Seventh's Easy and Dog Companies on Hills 1282 and 1240 on North Ridge led to the consolidation of the companies' remnants into the "2nd Provisional Battalion" under Major Hal Roach, Litzenberg's logistics officer. The understrength provisional battalion was fleshed out with men from the regimental headquarters, artillerymen, and Marines from other units.[7]

The Chinese attacks ended most of what passed for amenities in North Korea's brutal cold: "After the Chinese attacked, you were in cold 24/7. No more warming tents, or hot chow," said Warren Wiedhahn, a rifleman in the Fifth Marines' 2nd Battalion.[8]

With Yudam-ni momentarily secure, a rescue mission was mounted at 8am to relieve the Seventh Marines' Charlie Company, pinned down in a draw bordering the northwestern slope of Turkey Hill, formally known as Hill 1419.

Lieutenant Colonel Ray Davis's 1st Battalion was sent down the MSR toward Toktong Pass. After relieving Charlie Company, Davis's men would, if possible, continue to push on to Fox Hill. Whatever happened, the battalion must return to the Yudam-ni perimeter before nightfall to help repel the anticipated enemy attacks.

Davis's Able and Baker Companies, familiar with the area after hard fights there during the two previous days, would approach Turkey Hill from west of the MSR, then converge on it from the south. With luck, they would smash the very Chinese force that had mauled them earlier.[9]

The Chinese had struck Charlie at 2:50am on the 28th and continued their assault past sunrise. The company radio was disabled, but the forward artillery observer's radio linked to George Battery in Yudam-ni was operational.

Lieutenant Joe Glasgow was able to request concentrations of 105mm fire on enemy staging areas around Charlie. But the company mortars made more of a difference than the big guns, whose firing was hampered by the extreme cold.

Captain John Morris had reinforced his Charlie riflemen with headquarters men and spare troops from the machine-gun and mortar sections. But all of his headquarters men were dead or wounded, along with several gunners, when the fighting began to ebb with daylight. Nonetheless, Morris's perimeter had held.[10]

In need of ammunition, Morris's dwindling force braced for more attacks after losing 15 men killed and more than 50 wounded.

By 10am on November 28, enemy troops were again closing in on Charlie Company. Lacking an operable radio, the frustrated company forward air controller could contact neither tactical air coordinators nor the fighter-bombers circling overhead to request an air strike. Help was so close, but maddingly out of reach.

As it set out to relieve Charlie Company, Able Company came under fire in a gorge 300 yards south of the Yudam-ni perimeter. Five hours later, it was still a mile away from Turkey Hill. After Baker Company joined the attack, the two companies reached Charlie at 3pm.

Davis was able to reach tactical air coordinators in Hagaru-ri, and they dispatched four Australian P-51s to the Charlie Company battleground. The P-51s dove down and napalmed a farmhouse compound where the Chinese were massing for another attack and then flailed the enemy-held heights above Turkey Hill with rockets, bombs, and 20mm shells. The Chinese fled down the hill toward the MSR – and into a curtain of gunfire from Charlie's sister companies, Able and Baker.

Pausing before a narrow, enemy-held ridge separating Able from Charlie, two Able rifle platoons supported by mortar fire attacked the height.

A black giant of a man in a parka led one of the assault squads, swinging a large, double-headed axe in wide arcs that severed limbs and crushed skulls. He was known as "Ivan the Terrible." The few Chinese that attempted to make a stand fled.

"I'd run, too, if I had that ugly monster coming at me with an axe," exclaimed a Baker Company mortarman who watched the spectacle through binoculars.[11]

More close-air support arrived overhead, blasting the Chinese with machine guns and rockets. A Corsair planted a napalm canister amid a group of enemy soldiers fleeing into a wooded area, killing 40 of them.

Able's 60mm mortars pried enemy soldiers loose from another finger ridge and Marine riflemen riddled them before darkness fell, with the aid of Corsair rockets, machine guns, and napalm.

Able and Baker cleared out pockets of Chinese around the ravine occupied by Charlie as the company's many wounded were loaded in trucks that transported them back to Yudam-ni. Just 15 of the Charlie defenders were able to walk away from the battleground without assistance.[12]

All three of Davis's companies returned that night to the Yudam-ni perimeter.

Paul Robinson, a Charlie infantryman, had taken over as corpsman when the regular company corpsman was killed. Back at Yudam-ni, Robinson took a Marine to the medical tent and the doctor informed the injured Marine that he would lose both feet to frostbite. After receiving that diagnosis, the Marine impetuously attacked a Chinese machine-gun nest and was killed. He was posthumously awarded the Bronze Star.[13]

The day after the Chinese assaults at Yudam-ni and east of Chosin Reservoir, General Smith, accompanied by some members of his staff, traveled by helicopter from Hamhung to Hagaru-ri and opened his division headquarters in a two-room former Japanese bungalow on the northern edge of town.

A large poster of Joseph Stalin hung on one wall. Leave it there, Smith told his staff. "It might inspire us," he said.

The rest of his staff, which had left Hamhung four days earlier with most of Smith's personal effects, were stranded at Koto-ri when the road north was blocked by the Chinese.[14]

Upon learning of the situation in the farthest reach of his division's advance, Yudam-ni, Smith upheld Murray's and Litzenberg's decision to temporarily halt the attack to the west.

"It was manifest that we were up against a massive force out there," said Smith.

He also approved their shared command arrangement at Yudam-ni, since Smith's assistant division commander, General Eddie Craig – who ordinarily would have been sent to take command – was Stateside on emergency leave.[15]

General Ned Almond flew to Hagaru-ri in an L-17 reconnaissance plane with his 26-year-old junior aide, Lieutenant Alexander Haig Jr, to discuss the situation with Smith.

After conferring with Smith, Almond declined to change his order for the Marines to resume their attack west from Yudam-ni, despite the village's encirclement by tens of thousands of enemy troops.

When Almond departed, Smith's frustration boiled over. As he passed his chief of staff, Colonel Alpha Bowser, Bowser heard Smith say, "That man must be crazy."[16]

Smith's headquarters sent a report every four hours to X Corps describing what the division knew was happening at Yudam-ni. Lacking radio communication with the village, only sketchy details were available.

X Corps provided no direction. "Apparently they were stunned; they just couldn't make up their minds that the Chinese had attacked in force," Smith concluded.

MacArthur and his Far Eastern command had been convinced that the war would be over in weeks, and that the Chinese would not intervene. They had been proved terribly wrong.[17]

After two days passed, an X Corps order to Smith directed him to open the MSR between Yudam-ni and Hagaru-ri, and to send a regiment to Hagaru-ri to rescue RCT-31 east of Chosin Reservoir.

The order must have appeared chimerical to Smith and his staff.

X Corps had not retracted its order for the Marines to attack west from Yudam-ni through the mountains and march 55 miles to Mupyong-ni to link up with the Eighth Army.

Besides being contradictory, the orders appeared nonsensical amid the current crisis.

"My God, we were being attacked by three CCF divisions ourselves," Smith said, and the Chinese had cut the MSR in two places between Yudam-ni and Hagaru-ri. He would be hard-pressed to merely extricate his regiments from Yudam-ni.[18]

Colonel Alpha Bowser's assistant division operations officer, Lieutenant Colonel Joseph "Buzz" Winecoff, was dispatched from Hagaru-ri by helicopter to Yudam-ni. Winecoff was instructed to deliver the astounding order for the march west to resume, but more importantly to make an on-the-ground assessment of the actual situation in the remote village.

Major Hank Woessner, Litzenberg's operations officer, was flabbergasted when Winecoff told him that X Corps, and presumably the 1st Division, expected the Yudam-ni Marines to follow orders to march west into the Taebaek Mountains.

Look around you, Woessner told Winecoff in disbelief. Report to Smith and Bowser what you see. Immediate evacuation from Yudam-ni was the only reasonable course if the Marines there were to get out alive, he said.

Indeed, Winecoff, an experienced combat officer, had a good look around at the precarious situation in Yudam-ni, before reboarding the helicopter that had brought him there.

At Hagaru-ri, he delivered an electrifying report to Bowser and Smith. They now knew that matters were much worse at Yudam-ni than they had imagined. They began drafting a plan to withdraw the regiments to Hagaru-ri.[19]

But until X Corps issued an order for a withdrawal from Yudam-ni, the Marines could only defend their fragile perimeter against the legions of enemy troops. They could not withdraw from Yudam-ni without X Corps's permission.

For two days, X Corps trod water while MacArthur continued to digest the news of the Chinese attack. Almond's deputy chief of staff, Bill McCaffrey, said, "General Almond was not about to protest an order from General MacArthur. After all, everyone said Inchon wouldn't work."[20]

On the 28th, MacArthur cabled the Joint Chiefs of Staff with the bitter news from the Korean front: "The Chinese forces are committed in North Korea in great and ever-increasing strength. ... We face an entirely new war." That last sentence would reverberate throughout the Pentagon and White House.[21]

"A terrible message has come from General MacArthur," JCS chairman General Omar Bradley told President Harry Truman. "The Chinese have come in with both feet," Truman glumly observed to his staff.[22]

At an emergency session of the National Security Council on November 28, Averell Harriman noted that Pravda was quoting anti-Truman administration newspapers that were vilifying Truman's conduct of the Korean War.

After the president vented his pent-up anger at the opposition party, Truman proposed *more* defense spending for the war.

On December 1, a $16.8 billion supplemental spending bill was submitted to Congress, on top of $15 billion in defense spending already approved for the year. The spending supplement was followed by another $11.6 billion supplemental defense spending proposal.[23]

Zhan Da'nan, the 27th Army's assistant commander, had succeeded in encircling the US 7th Division units east of Chosin Reservoir during the night of November 27–28 with four regiments of his 80th and 81st Divisions. Now, he intended to wipe them out piecemeal.

The Chinese troops were looking forward to looting the Americans' warm winter clothing and food, for the men lacked adequate clothing and had not eaten in two days.

During the first night's attacks, after surprising the Americans in their sleep, shooting them, and taking an "additional shot" at Americans lying on the ground or under trucks, the enemy troops had pillaged their tents.[24]

Zhan might have felt victorious after these attacks, which resulted in the encirclement of RCT-31. But thousands of Zhan's dead, either killed outright or wounded and now blocks of ice, littered the battleground in their yellow uniforms.[25]

Lieutenant John Gray, the 25-year-old 81mm mortar platoon leader with the 31st Infantry's "M" Company, was a Cleveland, North Carolina, native who had fought as a Marine in five Pacific War campaigns. As a Marine reservist after the war, he returned to college, graduating with a second lieutenant's commission in the Army. From Inchon to Chosin, Gray led a 31st Regiment mortar platoon.

His World War II combat experience enabled Gray to react coolly when the Chinese were overrunning the 3rd Battalion. His platoon stood fast, knowing that if it were swept away, the battalion would be cut in two and possibly destroyed. When November 28 dawned,

Gray was alive and unwounded, and his mortar platoon was relatively intact.[26]

Fighting continued sporadically throughout November 28 around Lieutenant Colonel Faith's perimeter. The Chinese persisted in attacking the boundary between B and C Companies and held a knoll that they had seized during the night. The vantage point enabled them to fire downhill at the Americans.

Repeated air strikes called in by Captain Stamford failed to clear the knoll, as did C Company's counterattacks.

Stamford asked Faith to permit him to go to the point of the counterattack to call in the strikes, but Faith did not want him to leave the battalion CP, fearing that he would become a casualty and Faith would then be without a forward air controller.[27]

That afternoon, Faith's men observed long columns of Chinese troops, some riding Mongolian ponies, moving south along the eastern skyline, beyond the range of the American guns.

Clearly Zhan's 80th Division was preparing for nightfall, when it would resume its effort to wipe out RCT-31.

Although air strikes directed by Stamford killed hundreds of the enemy troops and their ponies, Corsair pilots reported there were 500 additional mounted Chinese troops in the same area.[28]

Around sundown, 300 to 400 Chinese troops appeared from the north on the road east of the reservoir with a tank and two self-propelled guns. From Faith's battalion CP, Stamford called in an air strike that wiped out the entire column.[29]

Faith's 1st Battalion had gone out on a limb in its eagerness to launch its offensive to the north and reach the Yalu River, despite the Marines' warnings. Faith's men were nearly four miles north of RCT-31's 3rd Battalion.

After General Almond conferred with General Smith in Hagaru-ri on the 28th, he flew by helicopter to RCT-31, touching down in a frozen rice paddy near the 32nd Regiment CP.

Despite the alarming reports that were beginning to reach X Corps headquarters, Almond appeared blithely unaware of the severity of the situation at Chosin Reservoir. He remained buoyantly optimistic.

Around Lieutenant Colonel Faith's perimeter, frozen American and Chinese corpses from the previous night's fighting lay on the ground.

Almond told Faith that his 1st Battalion must recapture the ground lost to the enemy the previous night. When Faith told Almond that his battalion had been attacked by elements of two Chinese divisions, Almond scoffed at the very idea.

"That's impossible," he said. "There aren't two Chinese Communist divisions in the whole of North Korea."

Faith's men were attacked, Almond said, by remnants of the 42nd Army's three divisions – the ones that had struck X Corps on November 2 – as they fled to the north.

He concluded his lecture by exhorting Faith: "We're still attacking and we're going all the way to the Yalu ... Don't let a bunch of Chinese laundrymen stop you."[30]

With that, Almond distributed three Silver Stars – he customarily brought medals with him on his visits to the front lines. He awarded one to Faith, and the others went to men of Faith's choosing. Faith selected wounded Lieutenant Everett Smalley, who was seated nearby, and a mess sergeant who happened to be walking by.

Almond gave a brief pep talk and departed. Faith tore off his Silver Star in disgust and flung it into the snow.[31]

The X Corps commander helicoptered to Colonel MacLean's CP four miles to the south, where he pinned medals on Lieutenant Colonel Bill Reilly, the wounded commander of the 31st Infantry's 3rd Battalion, and others.

Almond gave MacLean the same instructions that he had given Faith: resume the march north to the Yalu River, undeterred by any remnant 42nd Army elements – which in fact at that time were with the 13th Army in western Korea. Almond was operating on erroneous intelligence.

After his session with MacLean, Almond reboarded his helicopter and flew to Yonpo airfield to catch a plane to Tokyo. He was due at a conference at the Far Eastern Command headquarters.[32]

At Yudam-ni, the weather turned colder, with temperatures dropping to between 30 and 40 degrees below zero.

The 59th Division's 177th Regiment, which had been ordered to break through Yudam-ni's southern defenses with battalion-size attacks, had suffered the same fate as the 79th Division. The 79th's losses were in the thousands after its futile attempt to capture Hills 1282 and 1240 on North Ridge.

An officer of the 177th Regiment acknowledged, "The Marines were indeed the toughest fighting unit among the UNF [United Nations Forces] troops."[33]

Despite the enemy's heavy losses, the Fifth and Seventh Marines still faced enormous numbers of Chinese troops on all sides of the Yudam-ni valley, and enemy on the MSR south to Toktong Pass and Hagaru-ri.

Few if any of the starving, poorly clad Chinese soldiers that attacked the Marines at Yudam-ni had succeeded in obtaining food or warm clothing – and food was the principal reason many of them had joined the CPVF in the first place.

By November 28, starvation had set in. It was remarkable that the peasant army was capable of fighting at all. Its resilience might have even been considered praiseworthy had the Chinese soldiers not been trying so hard to annihilate the American troops around Chosin Reservoir.

The Chinese suffered intensely from North Korea's excruciatingly cold weather. While attempting to sleep in a fetal position on the snow-covered ground, their hands, feet, and socks often froze together into one icy clump.

Their numb, club-like hands were unable to unscrew the caps on their hand grenades. It often did not matter when the fuses refused to ignite anyway. Bare hands stuck to mortars and mortar shells. The below-zero temperatures caused mortar tubes to shrink and become unusable.[34]

The Chinese 79th, 89th, and 59th Divisions had isolated the Fifth, Seventh, and Eleventh Marine Regiments. Now it was a matter of drawing the noose tight and fulfilling Mao's order to destroy the American units.

Despite staggering losses that suggested a change in tactics was in order, the Chinese remained committed to frontal attacks against the Marines' lines, still believing overwhelming manpower could counteract the Marines' annihilating firepower advantage.

The 27th Army's leader, Peng Deqing, had demanded that his officers "make a daring attack with your troops, and fight the battle absolutely to the end." They had done that, but without success, and with staggering losses.[35]

Meanwhile, hundreds of Marine casualties had flooded Yudam-ni's spartan medical facilities. The 450 battle and 175 non-battle casualties quickly filled the field hospital tents, and many of the wounded were left out of doors in the arctic cold. In an effort to alleviate the acute discomfort of the wounded being treated outdoors, hay was collected from haystacks scattered throughout the area. It was spread in the courtyards of the native homes in Yudam-ni.

The wounded were placed feet-to-feet on the hay and covered with large tarpaulins. The 4th Battalion of the Marines' Eleventh Artillery supplied enough tentage to shelter 500 men.[36]

Navy doctors and hospital corpsmen cared for the wounded. The corpsmen accompanied Marine infantrymen into combat and treated their wounds. They received special training at US naval hospitals in emergency care, basic life support, anatomy, and physiology.

At first, they wore Red Cross helmets, but stopped doing so when their helmets made them the targets of Chinese snipers.[37]

The cold complicated treating the wounded. "Everything was frozen," Lieutenant Commander Chester Lessenden, the Fifth Regiment's surgeon, said. "Plasma froze and the bottles broke. We couldn't use plasma because it wouldn't go into solution and the tubes would clog up with particles."

Medical personnel had difficulty changing battle dressings with gloves on; if they worked bare-handed, their hands would freeze. They would not cut a man's clothing off to get at a wound because the man would freeze to death. "Actually, a man was often better off if we left him alone," Lessenden said.[38]

The Marines dug in and tightened their perimeter around Yudam-ni in anticipation of another night of frontal attacks.

But the fighting was at a lower intensity around Yudam-ni during the night of November 28–29 because of the Chinese losses during the previous night. So severe were they that their senior officers were forced to combine and reorganize units with the survivors.[39]

Chapter 11

Fox Hill Surrounded

November 28–30

Marines, tonight you die! Marines, tonight you die!

CHINESE SOLDIER SHOUTING IN ENGLISH BEFORE AN ATTACK AT FOX HILL.[1]

They came at us in a mass formation ... They came up the same way essentially for three nights. A smarter commander instead of hitting us in the same place, approaching the same route ... would have figured maybe I should go around.

CAPTAIN WILLIAM BARBER, FOX HILL.[2]

By this time some of us began to think this was probably our grave that we were sitting on.

PFC JAMES KANOUSE, FOX COMPANY.[3]

Captain Barber's Fox Company Marines had repulsed a Chinese regiment during the first night's assaults at Toktong Pass at a cost of 20 killed, 54 wounded, and three missing. Marines who suffered relatively minor wounds remained at their posts along the icy perimeter.

After daylight on November 28, Chinese forces still ringed Barber's perimeter in the snow and bitter cold, despite the loss of 450 men.[4]

Barber had arranged for two Navy corpsmen to care full-time for the wounded in heated tents. During daylight hours, Barber rotated his combat Marines through heated tents inside the perimeter, where they could get warm and have a cup of coffee.

Although Fox's prospects looked bleak, Barber was confident that his company, whose marksmanship and military comportment had improved during his brief tenure, could hold back the Chinese.

"The Chinese weren't very effective or very well led" on Fox Hill, Barber said. He said they would routinely approach from the northwest, following a draw that concealed them until they were 100 to 150 yards from the Marine lines, and then charge across open ground.

"They came at us in a mass formation ... They came up the same way essentially for three nights."

He praised the Chinese troops' discipline and their willingness to follow orders, no matter how seemingly impossible. But Barber said that "a smarter commander instead of hitting us in the same place, approaching the same route ... would have figured maybe I should go around."[5]

The day following the first Chinese attacks, General Smith sent Lieutenant Colonel Randolph Lockwood and a rescue column from Hagaru-ri to relieve Fox Company.

Lockwood commanded the Seventh Marines' 2nd Battalion, but had remained in Hagaru-ri – temporarily, he had believed – with his headquarters and weapons companies while Fox, Easy, and Dog Companies had marched to Toktong Pass and Yudam-ni.

With the MSR now severed and bristling with Chinese units, Lockwood could not now drive over Toktong Pass into Yudam-ni 14 miles away, as he had planned.

Early on November 28, Lockwood set out on foot from Hagaru-ri for Fox Hill with a composite unit of "cooks and bakers" from the 2nd Battalion Headquarters Company.

The relief column was led by three Sherman tanks from the 1st Tank Battalion. Scarcely a mile beyond the Hagaru-ri perimeter, Lockwood crested a hill and saw one of the Sherman tanks lying on its side and on fire. Abandoned gold mines lined the sides of a series of gorges along the road ahead.

Rifle and mortar fire began to rain down on the relief column, and Lockwood realized that it was coming from all sides. More Chinese troops poured out of the abandoned mines and the volume of enemy fire intensified.

Lockwood attempted to maneuver around the roadblock, but failed. He radioed for assistance, and the First Marines' 3rd Battalion, minus George Company and the only infantry unit in Hagaru-ri, came to his aid and escorted Lockwood's cooks and bakers back to Hagaru-ri by late morning.[6]

Apprised by Colonel Homer Litzenberg that help would not be coming that day, Barber said to his executive officer, Lieutenant Clark Wright, "We're on our own."[7]

An R4FD cargo plane made a supply drop to Fox Hill later in the day, but the parachutes landed in no-man's-land. The airdropped ammunition being desperately needed, the Fox Marines wasted no time in attempting to retrieve it.

Chinese snipers shot supply Sergeant David Smith in the leg when he made the first attempt. Four men ran to Smith's aid with a stretcher, and one of them was shot in the leg, too. A four-man detail dispatched the sniper.

Then, machine gunners laid down covering fire that permitted the retrieval of both the wounded men and the supplies, which included grenades, blankets, stretchers, .30-caliber ammunition, and mortar shells.[8]

With nightfall on Fox Hill came the expectation of another Chinese attack.

About 10pm, an amplified British-accented voice called out from the Chinese lines: "Fox Company! You are completely surrounded! You are greatly outnumbered!" The only recourse was surrender. "Otherwise, you will be slaughtered!" The harangue was followed by a recording of Bing Crosby singing "White Christmas," and a Chinese man shouting in English, "Marines, tonight you die! Marines, tonight you die!"[9]

The moment before the assault began, a lone Chinese bugler stood in front of the enemy lines, motionless, and pressed the horn to his lips. Robert Leckie described him in *The March to Glory* as a "heroic figure out of an antiquity when Mongol horses trod the earth of Europe."

A Marine who did not share Leckie's romantic image of the bugler cried, "Lemme fix that bastard!" He hurled a grenade that landed at the bugler's feet; the bugler did not budge and continued to blow a bugle call. There was a flash, and the horn gave a discordant bleat and was heard no more. The sound of gunfire drowned out everything else.[10]

Enemy mortar fire preceded groups of 40 to 50 Chinese infantrymen that began storming the Marine positions. Some of them infiltrated behind Peterson's platoon and inexplicably then stood in a tight group, arguing loudly. Peterson and another officer cut them down with machine guns.[11]

Lieutenant Don Campbell, Fox's forward artillery observer, guided 105mm howitzer fire from the How battery in Hagaru-ri onto a saddle where the Chinese were assembling above the perimeter. The cannon fire was followed by a crescendo of Marine 60mm and 81mm mortar fire.

Earlier that day, Pfc Ken Benson, having recovered his eyesight after shards from his shattered eyeglasses temporarily blinded him, returned to his squad, which he discovered had just four of its original 14 men left. It dawned on him that his squad's diminishment was a microcosm of what Fox Company had suffered.

"Now we were scared," Benson said. "The realization was sinking in. This is for real. The shock was beginning to wear off, and the very real feelings of fright came."[12]

"By this time some of us began to think this was probably our grave that we were sitting on," said Pfc James Kanouse.[13]

Benson revisited the place where he and Hector Cafferata had fought the previous night. He was looking for personal effects the two had left behind. Their sleeping bags had been bayoneted, and feathers were everywhere.

The bayoneted sleeping bags gave Benson an idea for luring the Chinese to their deaths. He stuffed several sleeping bags with snow to make them appear occupied by Marines. The decoys, he hoped, would delay the enemy and draw their fire, making them good targets for the Marines.

As the battle raged around them, Benson and his mates on the perimeter waited for the Chinese to fall for the ruse. They watched an enemy squad ascend the hill, stop before the sleeping bags and fire at them from pointblank range. Benson and his comrades cut down the enemy soldiers in a blaze of gunfire.[14]

However, Chinese machine-gun fire shattered Captain Barber's pelvis and wounded Lieutenant Bob McCarthy in the leg.

Barber plugged the bullet hole in his hip with a wadded handkerchief. Corpsmen splinted his cracked pelvis with pine boughs and treated it with sulfa powder and bandages.

Still very much in charge, Barber hobbled around the perimeter on a makeshift crutch, continuing to issue orders.[15]

The Marines threw grenades at the Chinese buglers, believing that putting them out of action would sow confusion. They blew whistles to distract the enemy from their attack plans, sometimes with success.[16]

Against a battalion-strength Chinese attack, Fox Company had held for a second night. Five Marines died and 29 were wounded. The Chinese 59th Division lost an estimated 200 men killed; their wounded froze to death where they fell.

Supplies were airdropped at mid-morning of the 29th, and a helicopter brought fresh radio batteries for the company's ANGRC-9 radio, nicknamed the "Angry 9."

Barber had requested it after he discovered that the SCR-300 radio that he had been issued could not reach either Hagaru-ri or Yudam-ni. The ANGRC-9, normally used for naval gunfire coordination and by forward air controllers, had a better range.[17]

A second airdrop during the afternoon of November 29 by C-54s of the Far East Cargo Command landed 500 yards west of the perimeter. Lieutenant Peterson, although twice wounded, led some of his men to retrieve the supplies, but enemy gunfire pinned them down.

After dark, as the temperature dropped to 20 degrees below zero, Captain Barber sent another detail to the airdrop site under mortar and artillery covering fire. The men brought back critically needed mortar shells and grenades, wool blankets, stretchers, and other supplies.

That day, Barber was informed by radio not to expect immediate relief from either Yudam-ni or Hagaru-ri, which were both surrounded, besieged, and their defenders outnumbered.[18]

Litzenberg and Murray continued to try to reach Fox Company, however. On November 29, they organized a composite battalion and sent it south on the MSR toward Toktong Pass to relieve Fox Company, with orders to then proceed to Hagaru-ri.

The battalion, led by Major Warren Morris, a veteran of Guadalcanal and Tarawa, consisted of Baker and George Companies from the Seventh Marines, and the Fifth Marines' Able Company. The relief column was armed with 81mm mortars and 75mm recoilless antitank rifles.

Morris's battalion ran into trouble two and a half miles south of Yudam-ni as Baker Company advanced along the left side of the MSR, with George on its right.

Lieutenant Woody Taylor's Baker platoon topped a ridge and saw that the valley below was teeming with enemy troops – at least a battalion. An observation plane pilot dropped two messages to the Marines warning that strong Chinese forces were entrenched ahead on both sides of the MSR.

As Morris's men began exchanging fire with large Chinese formations, Litzenberg ordered the composite battalion to return to Yudam-ni.[19]

The fierce Chinese attacks to break Fox Company's grip on Toktong Pass, and the losses the enemy continued to suffer nightly, underscored the high value placed by the enemy on seizing the gateway between Yudam-ni and Hagaru-ri.

Conversely, Barber and his Marines were prepared to fight to the last man to defend the critical mountain pass.

Chapter 12

Hagaru-ri

November 28–29

It was as though a whole field got on its feet and moved forward.

LIEUTENANT COLONEL THOMAS RIDGE DESCRIBING THE ATTACK ON HAGARU-RI BY THE WHITE-CLAD ENEMY TROOPS.[1]

We were stacking up dead Chinese in front of us and using them as shields to fire behind. We'd work in relays.

SERGEANT JOE QUICK ON EAST HILL.[2]

While the Marines at Yudam-ni and Fox Hill and the RCT-31 soldiers east of Chosin Reservoir had fought feverishly through the dark, bitter-cold hours of November 27–28, the more than 3,000 Marines and soldiers at Hagaru-ri, the critical hub for all operations around Chosin, had enjoyed a remarkably quiet night. The respite was short-lived.

Soldiers from the 20th Army's 58th Division and a 59th Division regiment had quietly encircled Hagaru-ri. The village lay in a bowl several miles in diameter, surrounded by hills. A knot of tall ridges that overlooked the town from the east became known collectively as East Hill, or Hill 1071.

Lieutenant Colonel Tom Ridge was placed in charge of Hagaru-ri's defense by Colonel Alpha Bowser, General Smith's operations officer.

Ridge's 3rd Battalion of the First Marines – How and Item Companies, George Company having remained at regimental headquarters in Koto-ri – was the only exclusively infantry component of Hagaru-ri's defense force.

Upon Ridge's arrival on the 27th, he ordered his operations officer and weapons company commander to walk Hagaru-ri's four-mile perimeter and make a plan for defending the base with two-thirds of a rifle battalion and assorted other troops.[3]

Also in Hagaru-ri, besides Ridge's two companies, were three companies of Marine engineers and a company of Army engineers that was sent to Hagaru-ri to build a forward base for X Corps. One of the Marine engineer companies was working around-the-clock to scrape an airstrip from the frozen ground south of the hamlet before the arrival of deep winter, and another was tearing down a sawmill complex to salvage its lumber.

Fifty-eight Marine, Army, Navy, and South Korean units in all were in Hagaru-ri, by one count. They had arrived piecemeal during the preceding days in small groups and set up bivouacs. By the 28th, Hagaru-ri had become crowded, with yet more Korean refugees arriving daily.[4]

There was a detachment from the 1st Marine Service Battalion; the headquarters company of the Eleventh Marine Artillery Regiment, and that regiment's How and Dog batteries; the Weapons Company of the Seventh Marines' 2nd Battalion; the 1st Motor Transport Battalion; and the 1st Marine Tank Battalion's Pershing and Sherman tanks.

It was a motley force, but most of the men were Marines who had undergone infantry training and knew how to care for and fire a rifle.

East Hill rose just 500 yards from General Smith's headquarters in a Japanese pagoda on the north edge of town. At such close proximity to East Hill, Smith would witness some of the fiercest battles at Hagaru-ri in the days ahead.

When Korean refugees reported large numbers of Chinese troops in the vicinity on the 28th, Ridge sent two Counter Intelligence Corps agents attached to the 1st Marine Division to reconnoiter the area.

The agents, who were Korean, made a circuit of the perimeter, mingling with Chinese troops to assay their strength and intentions.

Chinese officers boasted to the agents that they would occupy Hagaru-ri that very night. The attack would come at 9:30pm, they said. The Chinese 58th Division, just five miles away, planned to hit the southwestern side of the perimeter.[5]

Ridge had already determined that the southwest perimeter was the probable point of attack, and he had positioned How and Item companies to defend the likeliest approaches from that direction.

After their perambulation of the four-mile Hagaru-ri perimeter on the 27th, Ridge's officers had concluded that two regiments – not two companies – would be needed to defend it.

Ridge was compelled to improvise. He formed provisional detachments of service and support troops and posted them north of town to guard the northern perimeter.

Gaps in the perimeter would be protected by supporting fire from Dog Battery's six 105mm guns and, if needed, by cooks and bakers and whomever else was available. How Battery on Hagaru-ri's northwestern edge was dedicated to supporting Fox Hill's defenders. It was not an ideal situation.[6]

"One has to know when to throw away the book and depend upon all appropriate variations of military history as thought provokers when facing unusual situations," Ridge said.[7]

This was one of those unusual situations. Hagaru-ri was surrounded by 16,000 Chinese troops – 12,000 from the 58th Division, reputed to be the best division in the 20th Army, and a regiment of 4,000 men from the 59th Division. The Chinese were targeting both Hagaru-ri's southwest perimeter and East Hill.[8]

It took hours for the assault troops to reach their attack positions in the dark and extreme cold, without local guides, accurate maps, or even radio communication between the two battalions that were to occupy East Hill.

Somehow, the Chinese soldiers were able to approach the perimeter largely undetected.

On Hagaru-ri's southwestern perimeter, How and Item Companies had had hours to prepare for the attack that they were assured was coming at 9:30pm.

The Marines had used Composition C-3 plastic explosives obtained from the engineers to blast holes in the frozen ground to build entrenchments. They had filled sandbags supplied by the engineers with the dirt that the explosions yielded.

Barbed wire was threaded between bricks and drenched with water that, when frozen, cemented it in place. Five-gallon gasoline cans were rigged with white phosphorus grenades that could be detonated by pulling strings; the explosions would ignite the gasoline.

Three ravines that led into the sector were boobytrapped with anti-personnel mines. Tanks were positioned at each end of the two rifle companies to throw out crossfire.

Hot food was served to the men before dark, as light snow began to fall.[9]

Probing attacks by small groups came first. Then there began the heaviest Chinese mortar barrage of the Chosin campaign – 18 82mm mortars fired 90 shells apiece, and 54 60mm mortars each lofted 120 shells at East Hill for 30 minutes.

The main attack did not come at 9:30pm, but an hour later in a snowstorm.

Three shrill whistle blasts, three red flares, and white phosphorus shells announced its commencement.

Lieutenant Colonel Ridge watched in wonder as the attack began. "It was as though a whole field got on its feet and moved forward," he said of the white-clad enemy troops.[10]

They came in waves.

"You could hear them chattering to each other, keeping up their spirits," Pfc Charles McCaren of Item Company said of the Chinese. "Behind us, Lieutenant Fisher yelled, 'Open fire!' and that's how it began. A hell of a lot of Chinese went down, but a hell of a lot more kept coming. You got the impression the waves were endless, like surf lapping on a beach."[11]

The Chinese appeared suddenly before Captain Clarence Corley's How Company, hurling grenades – shocking because it seemed incredible that they had gotten so close to Corley's lines undetected. They focused their attack on an 800-yard-wide section of the southwest perimeter.

When Lieutenant Wendell Endsley, How's 3rd Platoon commander, was killed, enemy troops poured through the middle of the line, and ran along the airstrip and behind the tents. The starving attackers paused at How's mobile kitchen to eat – and to be shot down by defenders. Subsequent waves carried the Chinese deeper into the perimeter.[12]

During the initial assault from the south, the 173rd Regiment's 6th Company was wiped out by a hurricane of machine-gun, mortar, and artillery fire. The 7th Company took its place, and with the 5th and 9th Companies broke through the perimeter to the airstrip.

Under floodlights, work continued on the airstrip 500 yards south of the village even as the battle raged along the perimeter.

But when the fighting neared the airfield and the construction workers came under fire, engineers from Dog Company of the 1st Engineer Battalion got down from their bulldozers and snatched up their rifles. They formed a scratch rifle squad that drove off the intruders. Then they returned to their earth-moving equipment and resumed work.[13]

Driven away from the airstrip, the infiltrators stormed into the village. It was bedlam, said Lieutenant Roscoe L. Barrett, who commanded How Company's 1st Platoon.

Enemy troops ran amok everywhere – along the airstrip, behind the tents.

There was house-to-house fighting as the starving, freezing Chinese soldiers sought food and warmer clothing, with the thermometer plummeting to 30 degrees below zero and 2 inches of snow coming down.

Surgeons did not pause in their life-saving work at the 1st Medical Battalion's clearing station despite the machine-gun bullets crashing through the plywood walls.[14]

"Tracers were so thick that they lighted up the darkness like a Christmas tree," said Sergeant Keith Davis.[15]

Chinese light artillery opened up from the heights above town, with one round hitting a fuel dump. Dog Battery gunners immediately engaged them, aware of the mortal threat they posed to Hagaru-ri. If unchallenged, the enemy guns could pour fire into the tight perimeter and ignite the fuel and ammunition dumps.

The Dog Battery commander, Captain Andy Strohmenger, came up with an imaginative solution to the problem of locating and neutralizing the Chinese battery. He advanced one of his six 105s 150 yards in front of the line while silencing the other five.

After it had fired several rounds, Chinese gunners took Strohmenger's decoy under fire.

The enemy gun flashes enabled Strohmenger to quickly calculate their azimuth and range – and place accurate counterbattery fire on them.

Two 76mm mountain guns were destroyed, and two others were withdrawn.[16]

After they broke through the southwestern perimeter, the Chinese appeared to lose momentum and succumbed to their craving for warm clothing and food – not having eaten in two or three days.

They stopped to snatch food from the galley and clothing from the supply tents, but not weapons or ammunition. Chinese commanders refrained from shelling the supply depots so that their troops might loot them.

The pause in the Chinese attack gave the Marines an opportunity to reorganize and rush in reinforcements from Ridge's battalion command post.

Lieutenant Grady Mitchell, Ridge's assistant operations officer, led 25 X Corps signalmen and engineers to plug the breaches in the perimeter. Mitchell was killed and there were several other casualties, but the scratch force sealed off the penetrations.

"If the enemy had decided to effect a major breakthrough at this time, he would have experienced practically no difficulty," said Captain Corley. "However, he seemed content to wander in and around the 3rd Platoon, [and the] galley and hut areas."[17]

As mortar fire rained down on the Chinese, the Marines held their ground. The badly mauled attackers limped away before dawn when they ran out of ammunition.

"You could note the dead lying in windrows in front of the machine guns [where they had] ... come as far as they could before being shot down," said Lieutenant Colonel Joseph Winecoff, a division operations officer.

At daybreak, 750 Chinese bodies, their uniforms still smoldering from tracer rounds, were counted along Hagaru-ri's southwest perimeter.

But not all of them were dead. One of them abruptly sat up and began rooting around in his clothing.

"At first I thought he was trying to put out the fire in the cotton, but he was just getting out his cigarettes," said Pfc Charles McCarren.

"We watched him extract one from the pack with his numb fingers and light up." A Marine shot him in the chest.[18]

Li Bin, the 173rd Regiment's commander, attempted to organize his men for another attack that morning, but his ranks had been sapped by casualties and hunger. His men implored him: "Give us one potato since we have eaten nothing in two or three days."

Li wept; he had no potatoes to give. His 2nd Battalion attacked anyway, but did not achieve a breakthrough.[19]

The 173rd Regiment's losses from the attacks on Hagaru-ri's southern perimeter reportedly left it with just 1,000 combat-capable men of the regiment's former 4,000. About 500 of Hagaru-ri's defenders became casualties during the attacks on the southern perimeter, including 300 infantrymen and 200 men belonging to headquarters and service units.[20]

Shortly after the 173rd Regiment attacked the southwestern perimeter, the 2nd and 3rd Battalions of the 172nd Regiment stormed East Hill. The Chinese rightly saw it as a great prize, for it rose 300 feet above the village and dominated the MSR where it entered Hagaru-ri from Koto-ri.

Unable to coordinate an attack with the 2nd Battalion because of lack of communications, the 3rd Battalion alone managed to overrun East Hill, but at a cost of nearly all of its three companies.

Captain Wang Xuedong's company of the 2nd Battalion fought for four hours and withdrew when nearly all of his men were killed. "Our battalion ran out of ammunition, and we received no food supply at all," he said. "In addition, the temperature dropped to 30 degrees below zero." When Wang withdrew his company, just 18 men remained able to fight.[21]

Marine counterattacks during the morning of November 29th, aided by close-air support and accurate artillery fire, greatly thinned the enemy ranks, but did not reclaim East Hill for the Americans.

Over the next two days, the Marines and Chinese engaged in a death struggle for control of East Hill. American firepower exacted terrible casualties, yet the Chinese somehow clung to the hillcrest.[22]

Before the November 28–29 attacks, Lieutenant Colonel Ridge had quickly grasped East Hill's importance to Hagaru-ri's defense. He assigned Dog Company of the Army 10th Engineer Combat Battalion, commanded by Captain Philip Kulbes, to seize the complex of ridges, saddles, and rock formations and hold it.

The company of 77 Americans and 90 South Korean conscripts had reached Hagaru-ri early November 28 to build a forward command post for X Corps. Besides expropriating the Army engineers, Ridge also took command of men from the Army's 4th Signal Battalion, which was to establish the forward command post's communications. He assigned the signalmen to help defend the perimeter.

Kulbes protested to Ridge that his company was at Hagaru-ri to build the command post and that his men had no combat infantry training.

But he agreed to accept tactical advice from a Marine officer. Captain John Shelnut, the 3rd Battalion's Weapons Company executive officer, was appointed Kulbes's advisor, accompanied by Pfc Bruno Podolak, a radioman.

Kulbes's men were issued four .50-caliber machine guns; five light .30-caliber machine guns; and six 3.5-inch rocket launchers, and sent to East Hill.[23]

Burdened with their weapons and gear, the engineers toiled up the steep hill in the dark. It was literally a sheet of ice, and the difficult ascent was slowly accomplished by taking two steps forward, while sliding one step backward. The men had trouble just remaining on their feet.

They had reached the south end of a spur ridge protecting the MSR approach to Hagaru-ri from Koto-ri when the Chinese attack began.

In their customary bands of 40 to 50 men, four Chinese companies assaulted East Hill from two sides, beginning at 2am. They overran the Army engineers and South Koreans, who streamed down the hill until Army officers held them in a defensive line 250 yards below the hillcrest.

The enemy dug in without pressing the attack into the perimeter, and the nearby division CP and supply dumps. The attackers had suffered numbing losses.[24]

The provisional company of Army engineers and laborers had fared badly, too. When Major Edwin Simmons, the 3rd Battalion's Weapons Company commander, attempted to contact them by radio, Pfc Podolak said that Captain Shelnut was dead, and there were no Army officers present. "There's nobody up here except me and a couple of doggies [Army enlisted men]," Podolak said.

Simmons told him that it was his duty as a Marine to take charge. When Simmons attempted to reach Podolak again, his radio was dead.[25]

Hagaru-ri's night of peril had become a day of peril. The fraught situation required unorthodox measures, such as sending into combat men who had received training as Marine infantrymen but occupied non-combat positions, or Army units such as Kulbes's engineers who had no combat training. Everyone would have to pitch in to preserve Hagaru-ri as the 1st Division's essential operations hub.

At 5:30am, Major Reginald Myers volunteered to mount a counterattack on East Hill's southern slope with a band of service troops – clerks, typists, and truck drivers – and stragglers scraped up from inside the perimeter. He formed them into a 315-man provisional company consisting mostly of Marines but with a few soldiers. Myers was the 3rd Battalion's executive officer and had fought on Okinawa with the Fifth Marines.

Ridge delayed launching the counterattack until 9:30am, when the morning mists were expected to lift, permitting Corsairs from VMF-312 to provide close-air support.[26]

It took 45 minutes for Myers's men to crawl up the icy slope to the line of departure while 105mm howitzers prepared the ground ahead of them.

Then, the Corsairs rocketed and napalmed Chinese positions as the provisional company launched its frontal attack – the only tactic Myers dared to employ with such a mixed force.

The Chinese were ready for them, however. They channeled Myers's men into "kill zones" where many of them were cut down and others were turned back. But a stubborn core of attackers pushed on.

Seventy-five of the 315 men that began the attack nearly reached the hill crest, where they were stopped by intensive machine-gun and rifle fire and grenades.

Along the way, the scratch force picked up Pfc Podolak, the orphaned radioman who had directed the morning's 105mm preparatory fire while concealed in a hole. Podolak joined the attack, taking a round in the radio pack strapped to his back.

High on East Hill, Myers's shockingly diminished assault force relieved Kulbes's engineers and repeatedly counterattacked, but without driving the Chinese from the hilltop. Myers's men dug in and fought a close-quarter seesaw battle with the 172nd Regiment's 2nd and 3rd Battalions.

It ground on for 14 hours without a resolution, although Myers's men made small inroads while awaiting reinforcements.[27]

Marine Sergeant Joe Quick said the Chinese "would come at us like fire ants, wave after wave ... You'd burn the rifling out of your M-1 firing at them. Our machine guns would overheat from all the firing ... We were stacking up dead Chinese in front of us and using them as shields to fire behind. We'd work in relays."[28]

Yet the summit remained out of reach on November 29. Enemy gunners firing from rocky crevasse foiled the Marine attacks.[29]

The Chinese reinforced their East Hill defenders with a platoon from the 172nd Regiment's 3rd Company. Captain Yang Gensi's 50 men had eaten nothing in two days, so a basket of yams was sent to the 57 men on the hill. They were grateful to receive three yams apiece.

Yang and his men then fought until they were down to three effectives and ran out of ammunition. Clutching a 20-pound satchel charge, Yang hurled himself into a group of Marines.[30]

Captain George King, commander of Able Company of the 1st Engineers Battalion, launched a supporting attack at noon, but was pulled back and sent up the north face to meet Myers's men on the hillcrest.

The meeting did not take place; the engineers and Myers's provisional company spent the night 500 yards apart, under attack by tenacious 172nd Regiment units that during the night managed to regain some of their previous positions.[31]

Chinese officers were impressed by the Marines' determined attacks and steady advancement toward the hilltop. When stopped, they would dig in before then resuming their push.

"I never saw anything like the American Marines' combat moves," said Captain Wang Xuedong of the 172nd Regiment's 1st Company.[32]

The 58th Division had nearly overrun Hagaru-ri, but the assault forces were hampered by their inability to communicate with one another and coordinate their attacks on East Hill and the southwestern perimeter. Chinese division officers were sent to each regiment amid the fighting in an ultimately futile attempt to coordinate the attacks.

The enemy's communications breakdown proved to be a blessing for the Hagaru-ri defenders.

"We began to realize that Chinese communication was so bad they never really knew how well off they were, or how bad off they were," said Colonel Alpha Bowser, the 1st Division operations officer. "Had they known this and been able to react to it, there were several cases in which they could have cut us to ribbons."[33]

Moreover, when the Chinese did manage to infiltrate the Marine lines, they too often succumbed to their intense hunger and their craving for warm clothing. Unit discipline broke down, and the troops indulged in mass looting.

The Chinese attacks on Hagaru-ri failed. The Chinese 80th Division, which had been expected to join the 58th Division assaults, never arrived.

Indeed, the 80th was embroiled in a finish fight with the 7th Infantry Division's RCT-31 east of Chosin Reservoir.

Chapter 13

Surrounded, Losing Hope

East of Chosin

We knew we were trapped and couldn't expect help ... It looked like Custer's Last Stand was going to be re-enacted.

Pfc James Ransom Jr, east of Chosin Reservoir.[1]

Unless someone can help us, I don't have much hope that anybody's going to get out of this.

Lieutenant Colonel Don Faith's message to the 1st Marine Division from RCT-31.[2]

It was pitiful. Some of these men were dragging themselves on the ice, some had gone crazy and were walking in circles.

Lieutenant Colonel Olin Beall describing the Task Force Faith survivors.[3]

During the night of November 28–29, Chinese officers re-formed the freezing, starving soldiers of the 80th and 81st Divisions for another attempt to crush the two elements of Colonel MacLean's RCT-31, separated by four miles.

Temperatures fell to between minus 20 and minus 30, and a blustery wind from the north whipped the light snow that was falling into sheets of stinging ice pellets.

The soldiers of the 80th Division's 238th and 239th Regiments reached their attack positions stealthily by crawling through ravines and defiles from both the east and the west.

About 10pm, they assaulted the 31st Regiment's 3rd Battalion lines near Pungnyuri Inlet.

Lieutenant John Gray, the mortar platoon leader, was surprised that the Chinese had gotten so close without being seen. He and his men lit into the enemy with their .30-caliber machine gun and M-1 carbines.

Too late, Gray realized that some of the enemy had gotten behind his position. He was preparing to shoot a Chinese soldier when a burst of automatic weapons fire sent him tumbling downhill head over heels. Seeing stars, he came to rest against the wall of a ruined hut.

Enemy soldiers were approaching, bayoneting American soldiers that had fallen. Gray discovered that his right hand was broken and his right arm was useless. The trigger of his carbine was dangling from his bloody finger; the barrel and receiver group were all that was left.

Left-handed, Gray grasped his .45-caliber pistol. As three enemy soldiers stood over him, he shot them all and dragged himself away.[4]

Chinese assault troops broke through the 31st's perimeter, and died in a fusillade of anti-aircraft 40mm gunfire from one of the M-19 self-propelled guns. At the same time, Chinese white phosphorus mortar shells struck down some of the American soldiers, who died in agony.[5]

"We were told that the enemy force was a paper tiger," said Song Xiesheng, assistant captain of the 7th Company of the 80th Division's 238th Regiment. "Hundreds and hundreds of soldiers charged the enemy without artillery coverage and firepower protection. Then, we found out the enemy was not a paper tiger, but a real tiger with strong firepower and combat effectiveness."[6]

MacLean's perimeter held, greatly aided by the M-19 Bofors and the M-16 half-tracks with quad .50-caliber guns placed around the inlet.

As daylight crept into the sky on November 29, hundreds of Chinese bodies could be seen strewn along the perimeter – and inside of it where they had broken through.[7]

Along the 32nd Regiment perimeter four miles to the north, the tense anticipation of a renewed attack ended at 1am on the 29th.

Chinese troops came down the road from the north, nearly enveloping "A" Company on the left and once more attempting to break through the boundary between "B" and "C" companies on the right. Faith rushed headquarters troops to seal the gap in the line.

At 2am, as the fighting continued, Colonel MacLean ordered Faith to prepare to withdraw his battalion and join MacLean's 3rd Battalion to the south.

Faith immediately had his men unload the 60 trucks inside the perimeter and fill them with his battalion's wounded and dead.

"There were a lot of dead," said 1st Sergeant Richard Luna. "I saw them being drug in, frozen stiff already, and a lot of casualties also that had already been loaded on the trucks ... Some had frostbite, frozen hands, frozen feet."[8]

At 4:30am, Faith's convoy began moving out amid a heavy snowfall, with "B" and "C" Companies providing flank security on the high ground on both sides of the road. "A" Company was the rearguard.[9]

Five Marine squadrons covered Faith's four-mile march to join the 31st Regiment's 3rd Battalion south of the Chosin inlet. Guided to targets by Stamford, the squadrons killed Chinese troops on the road and in the ridges to the east. Stamford also directed an airdrop of supplies by the Air Force Combat Cargo Command.

MacLean had planned for the consolidation to be completed by daylight, but the Chinese blocked the bridge over Pungnyuri Inlet with logs.

Faith led ten men in an attack on the enemy troops defending the roadblock and cleared the logs from the road.

Then, Chinese soldiers appeared on the road to stop the convoy. The rearguard, "A" Company, moved onto the ice away from the road, circled behind the advancing Chinese and wiped them out. About 130 enemy soldiers died.[10]

The men at the head of Faith's column were stunned by the appearance of MacLean's perimeter when they arrived at 12:30pm, eight hours after setting out – "a scene of total devastation," according to Lieutenant James Campbell, a Weapons Company platoon commander.

At that moment, MacLean's men were battling a major Chinese assault on their perimeter. Enemy troops were "pouring down the surrounding hill," but the 57th Field Artillery's quad .50-caliber machine guns and the 40mm antiaircraft weapons took a terrific toll.[11]

Then, on the road along the inlet, MacLean saw a column approaching – from the south. "Those are my boys!" he exclaimed, believing they were his much-delayed 2nd Battalion, coming up from Hagaru-ri.

But the troops on the road were firing on his perimeter, and his men were firing back.

Believing the groups were sister battalions, MacLean impulsively darted onto the ice in an attempt to stop the exchange of gunfire.

However, the approaching column was Chinese, and the enemy soldiers began firing at MacLean.

"He was hit several times and staggered, fell, and finally was led off the ice by what appeared to be Chinese soldiers," said Edward Magill of the 57th Field Artillery, who witnessed MacLean's wounding and capture.

MacLean reportedly died during the fourth day of his captivity and was buried near the road.[12]

Faith formed a skirmish line and attacked the Chinese across the inlet ice, striking the enemy's rear as it prepared to attack the 57th Field Artillery. The assault scattered the Chinese, who left behind 60 dead.[13]

With Colonel MacLean gone, command of RCT-31 automatically fell to the next senior office – the 3rd Battalion commander, Lieutenant Colonel William Reilly.

Reilly had been badly wounded, though, during the first night's attacks, when his CP was overrun. Because of his incapacitating wounds, Reilly said that Faith should take charge of the combined command. Task Force MacLean became Task Force Faith.[14]

Inside the 3rd Battalion perimeter, an area of 600 yards by 2,000 yards, Faith's men found a "ghastly mass" of frozen American and Chinese corpses.

Captain Erwin Bigger of the 32nd Regiment's "D" Company said that the Chinese had killed many of MacLean's men in their bedrolls.

The Chinese now held the surrounding ridges. Rations were nearly gone, and ammunition and gasoline supplies were dwindling fast.[15]

The situation at the inlet being dire, Faith appealed by radio to Hagaru-ri for help.

"Unless someone can help us, I don't have much hope that anybody's going to get out of this," Faith told the Marines.

The reply from Hagaru-ri was disheartening: "We are bringing in a lot of air support, but that's all we can give you. We just don't have enough people to risk losing our hold on the foot of the reservoir."

"I understand," Faith replied. The new task force leader formed a strong, tight perimeter with the men still able to fight and weighed his few options.[16]

At Hagaru-ri on the 30th, Almond named General Smith commander of all of the Chosin Reservoir-area units. Almond ordered Smith and General Barr to prepare a plan to extricate RCT-31 from east of the Reservoir. He suggested redeploying a regiment from Yudam-ni to rescue RCT-31 – laughably unrealistic, with Yudam-ni surrounded and the MSR to Hagaru-ri severed.

Almond said that once the isolated Marine and Army units were united at Hagaru-ri, the Chosin Reservoir area must then be abandoned, and the troops withdrawn south toward Hungnam.

Almond authorized Smith to destroy any equipment that might slow his withdrawal and promised to airdrop supplies to his division.

Smith replied that his top priority was the evacuation of his wounded. Moreover, he could not afford to abandon his heavy equipment, which would be needed during the withdrawal.

After Almond departed, Smith, Barr, and Barr's assistant commander, General Henry Hodes, agreed that the Marines could do nothing to help RCT-31 until the two regiments in Yudam-ni reached Hagaru-ri.

None of Hagaru-ri's defenders could be spared until then.[17]

"General Hodes was quite embarrassed about asking us for help in extricating the Army troops," said Colonel Alpha Bowser, the 1st Division's operations officer.

"He recognized that what he was asking was impossible. Any Marine force from Hagaru-ri strong enough to blast its way through to the GIs would have left our perimeter dangerously vulnerable."[18]

Smith pointed out that Task Force Faith's 3,200 combat troops were more numerous than the three understrength rifle companies that Smith might send from Hagaru-ri.

He simply could not jeopardize the hub of the entire Chosin operation by stripping its defenses to rescue RCT-31.

If Hagaru-ri fell, the entire enterprise might be doomed, he said, including his Fifth and Seventh Regiments 14 miles away at Yudam-ni.

In his new capacity as commander of all Chosin Reservoir-area forces, Smith ordered RCT-31 to fight its way south to Hagaru-ri, along with the 31st Tank Company and the headquarters troops from Hudong-ni.

He pledged to give top priority to air support for RCT-31, but said that he could not spare any troops until the Fifth and Seventh Marines reached Yudam-ni.[19]

Much as they wanted the Marines' assistance, Barr and Hodes saw the sense of Smith's argument and reluctantly accepted it.

Barr helicoptered to Faith's CP at the inlet and, with "a tear in his eye," told him that the Marines would not be coming to his rescue. RCT-31 would have to save itself. Faith stoically replied that the effort would begin December 1.[20]

Later that day, Smith wrote in his log, "The [RCT-31] are about five miles north of us and I do not see why they cannot do something. They want to be rescued. I have nothing now to help, just a battalion at Hagaru-ri which has its hands full. When I get more troops I will have to help them out."[21]

Another discouraging development occurred during the afternoon of the 29th, when the 40mm ammunition that Faith had requested for the M19 Bofors was mistakenly airdropped to Captain Robert Drake's 31st Tank Company at Hudong-ni.

Drake's tanks could not use the 40mm ammunition – and they did not receive the 105mm shells that Drake had requested.

Drake's company, which had lost four tanks during its first attempt to reach RCT-31 on the 28th, tried again on the 29th with its remaining 12 tanks.

Unlike the first attempt when the tanks advanced without any infantry protection, this time 50 to 75 infantrymen were sent to provide security.

It was not enough. Lacking artillery support and with just one mortar, the tanks could not climb the slippery road to Hill 1221 anyway.

When Corsairs arrived, there was no forward observer to direct them to targets.

Drake's four-hour advance stalled just a mile from the RCT-31 perimeter before having to turn back, with 20 men lost.[22]

On the 30th, Drake's company, foiled from joining Task Force Faith by the Chinese battalion occupying Hill 1221, was recalled to Hagaru-ri to help defend its perimeter.

The 31st Tank Company and the 31st's rear command post decamped from Hudong-ni, initially towing two inoperable tanks and then abandoning them before proceeding to Hagaru-ri with ten of its original 16 tanks.

Drake's tank column had been the last, best hope to reinforce Task Force Faith, and now it had gone.

Because of RCT-31's abysmal communications, Faith and his officers were unaware that the tanks had departed.[23]

Morale was "real bad" inside RCT-31's perimeter, said Pfc James Ransom Jr. "We knew we were trapped and couldn't expect help ... It looked like Custer's Last Stand was going to be re-enacted."[24]

Chinese losses, too, were staggering. After two nights of attacks on the three Army battalions, 56 percent to 68 percent of the four enemy regiments' combat troops had been lost.[25]

Captain Edward Stamford, the Marine forward air controller for Faith's 1st Battalion, had become solely responsible for calling in close-air support for Task Force Faith. Colonel MacLean's Air Force forward air controller had been killed, and his radios were badly damaged during the first night's attack.

Stamford's team cannibalized the Air Force team's equipment and pieced together a usable communications system after laboring under fire for four hours.[26]

Marine Air Wing close-air support enabled RCT-31 to repulse the heavy Chinese attacks launched against it on the 30th. Captain Stamford called in 38 strikes against the attacking Chinese.

Over a period of 12 hours, the fighter-bombers dropped 21 napalm tanks, 16 500-pound bombs, and 21 fragmentation bombs, and fired 190 rockets.[27]

The Chinese attacked again during the night of November 30–December 1. Aided by heavy mortar fire, they nearly overran the perimeter. However, the Americans held on, partly due to the poor condition of the starving, half-frozen attackers.

The 5th Company of the 80th Division's 240th Regiment had lain in the snow, awaiting the signal to attack while Chinese artillerymen shelled the perimeter. When a bugle call summoned the 5th Company to attack, none of its 120 men stood up; they were all dead, frozen to the ground.[28]

By dawn, the medical supplies of Faith's 1st Battalion were exhausted, and a Chinese mortar round scored a direct hit on the aid station, wounding all of the medical personnel, including the battalion surgeon. Medics were forced to clean wounds with disinfectant, and to use handkerchiefs, undershirts, and towels for bandages.[29]

Inside the perimeter, the situation was catastrophic.

"The dead, concentrated in central collection points, had to be used as a source for all supplies, including clothing, weapons, and ammunition," said Major Wesley Curtis. "Everyone seemed wounded in one fashion or another and to varying degrees of severity. Frozen feet and hands were common. The wounded who were unable to move about froze to death."

The American dead, frozen through and through, were stacked 4 feet high because the frozen ground made it impossible to dig graves.[30]

A 3rd Battalion infantryman, James Sellers, said that ammunition was in such short supply that he and his comrades attacked hills with fewer than three banana clips for their carbines – and naked bayonets. Moreover, practically everyone had dysentery; Sellers' own weight dropped from 154 pounds to 118 pounds.[31]

With ammunition and rations nearly depleted, Faith decided that the beleaguered battalions' only hope for survival was to try to fight their way south to Hagaru-ri. The subzero weather was deepening, RCT-31 had been under attack for 80 hours, and it was doubtful that Faith's men could last another night.

Faith believed that if the task force could reach Hudong-ni, four miles to the south, it would be reinforced by the 325 men of the 31st's rear CP and Captain Drake's tank battalion.

But Drake and the rear CP troops were gone, and Chinese units now occupied Hudong-ni.

Faith's task force was completely isolated, with no friendly troops between it and Hagaru-ri.[32]

Stamford radioed the breakout plan to the 7th Division headquarters, which approved it. Then, the FAC summoned squadrons of Corsairs and Skyraiders for an air strike at 1pm on December 1 for the breakout's commencement.[33]

It was a calculated act of desperation.

Song Shihun, the Chinese 9th Army Group commander, had overreached. Rather than massing the eight divisions of his 20th and 27th Armies to destroy the Fifth and Seventh Marines as his superior, Peng Dehuai, had ordered, Song had chosen to envelop the entire 1st Marine Division, and the units of the Army's 7th Division east of Chosin Reservoir.

Song had never faced US firepower, which he had believed to be equivalent to that of the Nationalists that he had faced throughout the civil war. Peng, however, had seen American firepower firsthand in western Korea during the First Offensive in late October and early November, and he was wary of it.

Song's overly ambitious strategy had so far failed.[34]

The 80th Division's deep losses during two nights of attacks on RCT-31 had rendered it unable to launch a major attack during the night of November 29–30.

Zhan Da'nan's division had suffered 6,150 casualties, or 60 percent of its combat strength. Frostbite had incapacitated even more men. Zhan asked Song to send reinforcements.[35]

On the 30th, Song called a conference to discuss the 9th Army Group's failure to destroy the Marines west of Chosin and its staggering casualties.

Representative of the losses suffered, the 238th Regiment's 3,600 troops had been winnowed by combat wounds and cold to just 300 combat-capable men. Other units had suffered comparable losses.[36]

Peng Deqing, the 27th Army's commander, proposed that instead of continuing to seek the annihilation of the Fifth and Seventh Marines at Yudam-ni, Song's army change its priorities. Peng and Zhang Yixiang of the 20th Army advocated destroying X Corps's weak link: RCT-31 east of Chosin Reservoir.

Peng's proposal was adopted, and the 27th Army combined its 80th and 81st Divisions at Sinhung-ni, north of the inlet, with the 94th Division in reserve. Additional roadblocks were erected between

Hagaru-ri and Sinhung-ni to block reinforcements from Hagaru-ri, and to bar Faith's withdrawal.

Tao Yong, deputy commander of the 9th Army Group, and Zhan Da'nan, the 27th Army's deputy commander, led the new annihilation force of about 25,000 men.[37]

West and south of Chosin, the 27th Army's 79th Division and the 20th Army's 58th and 59th Divisions were ordered to contain the Marines at Yudam-ni and Hagaru-ri, preventing them from coming to the aid of RCT-31. But Chinese leaders no longer believed that they could wipe out the Marines. The 9th Army Group would instead concentrate on destroying Task Force Faith.[38]

The Marines' upcountry march to Chosin Reservoir. (USMC)

General O.P. Smith (left) confers with General Ned Almond, commander of X Corps. (USMC)

The 41 Commando joined X Corps in northeast Korea in November 1950 and marched north to Koto-ri on its way to the Chosin Reservoir area. (Getty Images)

Marines carve a Thanksgiving Day turkey during the calm before the storm. (USMC)

General Douglas MacArthur watching the Inchon landing from the USS *Mount McKinley*. (US Navy)

Marines in defensive positions near Yudam-ni. (Alamy)

Marines carry out their wounded. As well as battle casualties, both sides had to contend with serious frostbite and cold-weather injuries. (USMC)

Marine dead at Yudam-ni. This was one of the unthinkable occasions where the dead had to be left behind. (USMC)

Marines break out of Yudam-ni on the MSR. (Getty Images)

General Song Shihun, commander of the Chinese 9th Army Group. (USMC)

Don Faith commanded Task Force Faith during its doomed attempted breakout from east of Chosin Reservoir. Faith was killed and was posthumously honored with the Congressional Medal of Honor. (US Army)

Corsairs use napalm to clear the way for Marines during their breakout from Hagaru-ri. (USMC)

The MSR near Hagaru-ri during the Marines' breakout. (Getty Images)

Chinese prisoners of war. (USMC)

Delays in the breakout to the sea resulted in traffic jams on the MSR, and an opportunity for the exhausted Marines to snatch a short nap. (USMC)

With room needed in the convoy for freshly wounded men, the Marines prepare to bury 117 of their dead comrades at Koto-ri. (USMC)

This iconic photograph taken by *Life* magazine photojournalist David Douglas Duncan shows a cold, weather-beaten Marine during the breakout, trying to loose a single, frost-coated bean from the others in his can. When asked what he would have wanted if he could have had any wish, he raised his eyes to the gray sky. “Give me tomorrow,” he said. (David Douglas Duncan Papers and Photography Collection, © Harry Ransom Center, The University of Texas at Austin)

The bridge blown by the Chinese over the 2,200-feet-deep chasm at Funchilin Pass. Bridge spans were parachuted to engineers, who built a new bridge, enabling the convoy to proceed. (USMC)

North Korean refugees crowd the waterfront at Hungnam. About 98,000 civilians were evacuated along with X Corps. (DOD)

Chapter 14

Hellfire Valley

Very well then, we'll give them a show.
REPLY OF LIEUTENANT COLONEL DOUGLAS DRYSDALE OF 41 COMMANDO TO BEING ORDERED TO PUSH ON TO HAGARU-RI DESPITE HEAVY CASUALTIES.[1]

The task force made a significant contribution to the holding of Hagaru-ri, which was vital to the division.
GENERAL O.P. SMITH AFTER TASK FORCE DRYSDALE'S ARRIVAL IN HAGARU-RI.[2]

Amid the many crises confronting X Corps in the Chosin Reservoir area, General Smith remained convinced that Hagaru-ri's preservation was absolutely essential to the survival of the two Marine regiments at Yudam-ni and to RCT-31 east of the Reservoir.

Hagaru-ri's capture by the Chinese would exponentially increase the difficulty of extricating the dispersed units, if not make it impossible.

For that reason, Smith took the risky step on November 28 of ordering Colonel "Chesty" Puller to send a relief column to Hagaru-ri from Puller's own beleaguered First Marines outpost at Koto-ri 11 miles to the south on the MSR.

That day also marked the arrival at Koto-ri of Captain Carl Sitter's George Company of the First Marines; the spit-and-polish, clean-shaven, green-bereted 41st Independent Commando, British Royal Marines; and Baker Company of the Army's 31st Regiment.

Puller designated the three infantry companies and their 630 men as the bones of the relief column, which also included 300 transient troops, and vehicles and tanks. They were ordered to fight through the enemy roadblocks to Hagaru-ri.

Led by Lieutenant Colonel Douglas Drysdale, the 41st Commando commander and the senior combat officer in the convoy, it became known as Task Force Drysdale.

Drysdale, 44, had distinguished himself in Burma during World War II and had become commander of 41 Commando at the onset of the Korean War.[3]

It was the first time since the 1900 Boxer Rebellion that British Royal Marines fought alongside US Marines. Weeks earlier, Smith was asked whether he could use the services of the 41 Commando, which was then in Japan.

The commandos were "anxious to serve with the 1st Marine Division," said Smith, "but did not want to be attached to an Army unit." Smith replied that "we would be very glad" to receive the vaunted reconnaissance company.[4]

Task Force Drysdale began marching north on the MSR at 9:30am on November 29 with 925 men, 141 vehicles, and two tank platoons with 29 tanks – 17 in the vanguard and 12 in the rearguard. Drysdale had requested that the tanks be dispersed throughout the column, but his request was rejected.[5]

Lieutenant Paul Sanders's five-tank platoon from the 1st Tank Battalion's Dog Company led the way, followed by Sitter's company and the commandos.

The tanks and infantrymen met well-entrenched enemy troops at Hill 1236 a mile and a half north of Koto-ri.

The Chinese 20th Army's 60th Division had set up roadblocks to stop the convoy, and its 179th Regiment held Hill 1236.

For four hours, it bitterly resisted the convoy's advance, with explosives teams sprinting toward the tanks and attempting to blow themselves up beneath them. They disabled two tanks, blocking the road.[6]

Master Sergeant Rocco Zullo of Sitter's George Company broke up one roadblock by firing several 3.5 rocket launcher rounds at it from a distance of 200 yards. The fusillade drove the Chinese from their positions and the Marines seized Hill 1236.

Later, seeing several wounded Marines exposed to enemy fire, Zullo climbed aboard a truck, where he manned and fired a .50-caliber machine gun, drawing enemy fire away from the wounded until he was shot in the stomach.

Believed dead, Zullo was later placed in the improvised morgue at Hagaru-ri. When a corpsman passing Zullo's body heard a cough, a quick check revealed that he was still alive.[7]

The 179th Regiment set up more roadblocks. Held up a mile farther on the MSR at Hill 1182 by Chinese mortar and machine-gun fire, the task force briefly paused so that eight more tanks from Koto-ri could work their way to the scene of the fighting.

Peng Fi, the 60th Division's commander, ordered the 179th Regiment to attack. After setting fire to barrels of gasoline in the middle of the MSR, 20 men armed with satchel charges and grenades descended on the tanks. Five men blew themselves up beneath some of them, blocking the road.

The vanguard of tanks, US and British Marines, and assorted Army infantrymen was able to push on toward Hagaru-ri. Its progress was slowed by enemy units, which the tanks and infantrymen destroyed piecemeal.[8]

At 4:15pm the column halted, having traveled just four miles north from Koto-ri, less than halfway to Hagaru-ri.

Tank officers told Drysdale and Sitter that they believed the armor could get through to Hagaru-ri, but advised against proceeding with the unarmored trucks because of the shell-pitted road and intensifying Chinese gunfire.

Should they even resume the advance? Drysdale asked Puller, who radioed General Smith in Hagaru-ri for a decision.

Smith ordered the task force to "press on at all costs." As Smith later told historian S.L.A. Marshall, "War leaves no soft options."

The previous night's powerful attacks at Hagaru-ri had alarmed the defenders, now unsure whether they could continue to hold out without reinforcements.

Drysdale replied, "Very well then, we'll give them a show." The fighting intensified. "When the going got tough, we just bashed on," said a Royal Marine.[9]

Halfway to Hagaru-ri, intensive mortar, machine-gun, and rifle fire again stopped the column. A mortar round hit an ammunition truck and set it ablaze, temporarily blocking the MSR.

Behind Drysdale's vanguard, the rest of the convoy entered a long, narrow valley and found itself barricaded by roaring gasoline fires in the road to the north and south.

From the high ground to the right, the Chinese poured sheets of fire into the column, forcing the men to take cover behind their vehicles or in the roadside ditches.

It was a perfect ambush along the one-mile stretch of the MSR that would become known as Hellfire Valley.

"The bright lights from their flashing gunfire lit up the sky," said Commando Mick O'Brien. "The next day, we could see dead Chinese everywhere and plenty of our own fallen."[10]

Prevented by enemy gunfire from clearing the blazing vehicles blocking the road to the north and south, the column behind the vanguard began to disintegrate.

Trapped were 61 of Drysdale's commandos, most of the 31st Infantry's Baker Company, and nearly all of the headquarters and service troops.[11]

Marine air strikes kept the Chinese at bay until it got dark, when enemy soldiers were emboldened to approach the trapped allied troops. They formed one large and three smaller pods spanning 1,200 yards, north to south.

The Chinese further divided the trapped men so that the larger group of 130 to 140 men, led by Major John N. McLaughlin, was isolated from the three smaller ones to the south.[12]

Drysdale's leading echelon pressed on with no one behind it, accompanied by Lieutenant Sanders's five tanks.

Because of an atmospheric anomaly, Koto-ri and Hagaru-ri could not radio one another, but Sanders's tank radio could communicate with both bases. Sanders's radio became the medium for relaying messages back and forth, and he was privy to Hagaru-ri's urgent pleas for reinforcements.

About a mile and a half south of Hagaru-ri, Drysdale's group was fired upon by enemy occupying the high ground. Drysdale was wounded in the arm by a grenade fragment.

When a tank slid off the road, Lieutenant Sanders, with tracers flickering around him, stood in the open to get his bearings until the tank regained the road. At nightfall, two enemy soldiers tried to creep up on Sanders from behind, and he shot them both with his .45.

With Drysdale wounded, Captain Sitter took command of the task force.

Sitter was 27 years old and had been a Marine since enlisting in 1940. During the Pacific War, he was twice wounded, at Eniwetok and Guam, and won a field commission and a Silver Star.

As the Chinese prepared to attack, Sitter quickly formed a perimeter, and using tanks as covering fire, his men repulsed the Chinese assault. Pfc William Baugh threw himself on a Chinese grenade that sailed into the perimeter, and was killed protecting his comrades. Baugh was posthumously awarded the Congressional Medal of Honor.[13]

On the outskirts of Hagaru-ri's perimeter, General Almond's advance team had erected pyramidical tents for X Corps's forward base. During the first night's attacks, the advance team was deployed to stem the Chinese assault at East Hill, and the Chinese had jammed into the tents to get warm.

They spilled out of the tents when the Drysdale task force appeared. The Chinese destroyed two tanks and inflicted several casualties before they were cut down.

The Dog Company tanks and Sitter's George Company began entering the Hagaru-ri perimeter around 7pm.

Sitter reported to his battalion commander, Lieutenant Colonel Ridge, who was in charge of the perimeter defense. Ridge sent George Company to East Hill to relieve Major Reginald Myers' mixed force.[14]

Drysdale's elite commandos, trailing the tanks and Sitter's company as they entered Hagaru-ri, were surrounded by the Chinese outside of the village. There, amid seven trucks set ablaze by the Chinese, the foes waged a ferocious battle, as engineers on bulldozers and under floodlights continued building the airfield nearby.[15]

The commandos repelled the enemy's attempts to infiltrate their hastily formed moving perimeter. Casualties were heavy, especially among the officers, as the British inched their way toward Hagaru-ri. They reached the perimeter after midnight.

Drysdale reported to Ridge with a snappy salute as blood dripped from his wounded arm. "41 Commando, present for duty," Drysdale said.

Half of the commandos' original complement of 235 men was still available to fight; the others had been killed or wounded, or were trapped in Hellfire Valley.[16]

Ridge sent the commandos to aid Captain Sitter's company on East Hill.[17]

With most of the vanguard's 17 tanks, 400 of the 925 men who had set out from Koto-ri that morning reached Hagaru-ri that night.

The Chinese had successfully ambushed the unlucky troops mousetrapped by the 179th Regiment between burning vehicles to their north and south in the mile-long confines of Hellfire Valley.

From the 30-foot-high plateau to the east of the MSR, Chinese troops with machine guns and mortars rained a murderous fire down on them.

The road back to Koto-ri offered a glimmer of hope for those at the rear of the convoy. Some trucks in that part of the column managed to slip away and reach Koto-ri at 2:30am on the 30th with dozens of other vehicles.

For others that had been cut off, Major Henry Seeley, a Marine motor transport officer, organized a fighting withdrawal on foot to Koto-ri for the willing and able.

Three of the smaller trapped groups joined together west of the MSR at 3:30am, crossed the Changjin River, and reached the nearby wooded hills. The group hiked back to Koto-ri without meeting any opposition, reaching the base along with the motor transport troops and others that had gotten away.[18]

However, the Marines, soldiers, and trucks pinned down in Hellfire Valley were quickly surrounded by Chinese soldiers approaching in the dark. With little hope of getting out of the trap, Major John McLaughlin's group fought the Chinese from ditches alongside the road.

"They came at us single file from a number of directions," said Sergeant James Nash. "We just kept knocking them down like shooting ducks, but they just kept pouring in. The bugles, whistles, shouting – it never stopped."[19]

They ran out of grenades, and a 75mm recoilless rifle that had done such good service was disabled.

At 4:30am, the 60th Division's chief political officer, Xu Fang, sent a captured American officer down to the road with a surrender demand.[20]

McLaughlin and a British commando went out to parley, hoping to stall until help could arrive, or until some of the trapped men could slip away. McLaughlin began the negotiations by brashly demanding that the Chinese surrender.

"But it made little impression," he said.

The Chinese instead gave McLaughlin ten minutes to discuss surrender with his officers. If the truce expired with no agreement, the Chinese promised an all-out attack.[21]

With just 40 men remaining who were capable of fighting and little or no ammunition, McLaughlin agreed to surrender, if the seriously wounded could be evacuated.

When the Chinese consented to the stipulation, the fighting stopped. One hundred thirty men became Chinese prisoners; counting other captives taken during the battle, more than 200 men were marched to POW camps in the north.[22]

Among them was Sergeant Nash. He and other POWs were force-marched through Hellfire Valley for a mile on their way to captivity in Manchuria.

"That was a sight I'll never forget," Nash said of the aftermath of the Hellfire Valley battle. "It had been snowing all night. Bodies were everywhere. Arms and legs were frozen in mid-air. It was pretty grim. Depressing."[23]

The losses had been grievous: 162 dead or missing. The 31st Infantry's Baker Company alone had lost 119 men, with 100 of them either dead or missing; 70 managed to make their way back to Koto-ri.[24]

Seventy-eight vehicles and one tank were lost in the Hellfire Valley inferno, including General Smith's van, with his clothing, records, and personal papers.[25]

Dozens of Marines, soldiers, and British commandos avoided capture and went to ground in the hills, cut off from friendly forces at Koto-ri and Hagaru-ri. They intended to hide until they could be rescued.

The Chinese did not keep their promise to allow the wounded to be evacuated, but permitted some of the seriously wounded to be taken to a Korean hut, where their wounds were bandaged, and where they were fed potatoes and dried beans.

When the Chinese soldiers withdrew into the hills the next morning, the American troops took the wounded to Koto-ri. They were among the 159 wounded men who were repatriated by various means.[26]

Forced to abandon his vehicle, Lieutenant Alfred Catania of the 377th Transportation Truck Company took cover in a ditch. While there, he was wounded in the back by a shell fragment and in the shoulder by a .45-caliber slug that snapped his collarbone.

After getting a shot of morphine, Catania continued to command his small unit, eventually leading his men back to Koto-ri, after the Chinese let his party pass.[27]

Left behind was red-haired Corporal C.V. Irwin, a reservist who was the 1st Marine Division's diarist.

Wounded in the thigh in Hellfire Valley, Irwin dragged himself into a hut near the MSR. After the Chinese left the area, a North Korean boy cared for him for a week, until a Marine patrol discovered him.

Evacuated to a hospital in Japan, Irwin lost both legs to amputation. He was later fitted with prostheses, married, and had two children.[28]

About 100 tank company Marines and 300 other seasoned infantrymen had reached Hagaru-ri. General Smith was grateful. Even with Task Force Drysdale's heavy casualties, the relief convoy had been a partial success.

"The task force made a significant contribution to the holding of Hagaru-ri, which was vital to the division," said Smith.[29]

The vanguard of Task Force Drysdale arrived in Hagaru-ri during an unexpectedly quiet period, aside from scattered harassing fire.

During the previous night of November 28–29, the Chinese 58th Division had struck hard at the southwest perimeter and East Hill, but did not achieve a major breakthrough.

The 80th and 81st Divisions, which were to have joined the 58th in assaulting Hagaru-ri, had unexpectedly encountered RCT-31's three battalions northeast of Hagaru-ri, and were fully occupied with trying to annihilate that force.

The battered 58th Division had to continue the attacks on Hagaru-ri alone, but it first needed to regroup.

At 8am on November 30, Captain Carl Sitter's understrength George Company, having survived its close call in Hellfire Valley, attacked East Hill. It assaulted both sides of the ridgeline, with a platoon ascending each side. The icy slopes and long-range automatic weapons fire slowed the attack.

When it bogged down, Sitter tried to hit the CCF right flank with his third platoon and two reserve engineer company platoons. Both attacks failed, despite 25 air strikes and daylong artillery fire. George Company had to settle for establishing defensive positions high on the hill.

On the southwestern perimeter, Item and How Companies reinforced their sandbagged foxholes, registered their mortars and artillery, and laid their booby traps in anticipation of large-scale attacks that night, November 30–December 1.

Units of the Chinese 58th and 59th Divisions assaulted the Item and How positions just before midnight on the 30th, charging into a firestorm of Marine mortar, heavy machine-gun, artillery, and tank fire.

They struck the same place repeatedly. Momentum sometimes carried the Chinese as far as the Marine foxholes, where they died. When the attack ended, between 500 and 750 enemy soldiers lay dead in the snow, at a cost to the Marines of two killed and ten wounded.[30]

At the same time, a Chinese regiment attacked the Marines' reverse slope lines on East Hill, shouting "Abraham Lincoln! Abraham Lincoln!" as they careered downhill –a weird concatenation of a Marine engineer platoon's sign and countersign, "Abraham" and "Lincoln."[31]

Defended by George Company, three engineering company platoons, and service battalion troops, the Marines' lines crumbled. They were driven to the foot of the hill by the flood tide of Chinese troops, some led by officers on horseback, amid a cacophony of bugle calls and whistles.

Enemy bullets "zinged and snapped" over the Marines' heads. The ghastly tableau was bathed in an other-worldly shade of green from the Chinese illumination grenades and tracers, a vivid contrast to the snow stained red with blood.[32]

Army and Marine service troops stemmed the attack at a secondary defensive line, and the Eleventh Marines' How Battery homed in on the momentarily jubilant Chinese, pulverizing them with 105mm shells.[33]

In the midst of the crisis, Lieutenant Richard Carey drafted "all available hands" from Hagaru-ri, including headquarters clerks and typists, cooks and bakers, to reinforce the embattled defensive lines, where the Marines fought at close quarters with bayonets and rifle butts.

The reserve infantry company, the 41 Commando, was sent to regain lost ground on George Company's left flank; its furious counterattack drove the Chinese back to the hill crest by morning.

Hundreds of Chinese were killed, with 120 piled in front of one machine-gun position. The weary defenders reported 60 killed and wounded. Enemy mortar fire nearly annihilated George Company's 1st Platoon, and its 3rd platoon lost half of its 28 men when it was pushed off the hill.

Captain Sitter was wounded by grenade fragments in the face, arms, and chest, but he refused evacuation. Despite his wounds, he visited each foxhole and gun position in his company throughout the night to boost morale.

"What are you going to do?" Sitter asked his men. "You're going to fight, dammit. You must fight or we aren't getting out of here. It's that simple."[34]

Sitter was awarded the Congressional Medal of Honor for his actions that night.

The melee on East Hill ended in a stalemate, with the Chinese retaining possession of the hill crest.

Daylight illuminated a gruesome scene: a hillside littered with frozen Chinese corpses.

The Chinese 172nd Regiment's 2nd Battalion, which began the night's attacks with 1,200 men, counted just 100 when the night ended. It was replaced by the 4th Battalion.[35]

Captain Wang Xuedong, the commander of the 2nd Battalion's 1st Company, said that he had never seen anything like the American Marines' tactics.

"They stayed where they were stopped, waited for reinforcements, and then charged again," he said. "With each charge they came closer to our positions, until they were no more than two dozen meters away."

Wang withdrew his shattered company, reduced to just 18 men, but that night the Chinese recovered some of the positions lost to the Marines.[36]

The two Chinese attacks on the nights of November 28–29 and November 30–December 1 had sapped the 58th Division, which had sustained more than 8,000 casualties of its original force of 12,000 and had just 1,500 men still able to fight by December 1. The 20th Army ordered the 58th Division to suspend its attacks.[37]

After three days of being ultimately responsible for fending off the massive Chinese attacks on Hagaru-ri, Lieutenant Colonel Ridge "was pretty low and almost incoherent" from lack of sleep when he met during the morning of December 1 with General Smith, according to Smith's log.

Ridge told Smith, who had watched the fighting on East Hill from the doorway of his command post two-thirds of a mile away, that he could not hold the airstrip and East Hill with his current forces.

"I told him he would have to hold both and would have to do it with what we had," Smith wrote.[38]

Chapter 15

The Airfield

December 1, 1950

To General Smith's proposal two weeks earlier to build an airfield at Hagaru-ri to evacuate casualties, General Ned Almond, X Corps's commander, clearly perplexed, had asked, "What casualties?"

Certain that the war would quickly end with United Nations forces reaching the Yalu River, Almond had not seen the point of an airstrip at Hagaru-ri. At Smith's insistence, however, Almond permitted the Marine general to proceed, but without X Corps resources; the Marines would have to build the airstrip themselves. Excavation began November 19.[1]

By December 1, with 600 wounded men at the division field hospital in Hagaru-ri, Almond's reaction to Smith's idea seemed absurd. Moreover, another 500 casualties were expected from Yudam-ni, and 400 from RCT-31 east of the Reservoir.

In his partial defense, Almond did not then know that massive numbers of Chinese troops would attempt to annihilate his X Corps.[2]

After laboring nonstop for 12 days and nights, Delta Company of the 1st Engineer Battalion, frequently interrupted while working under floodlights at night by Chinese small-arms fire, had carved a very bumpy 2,900-foot northwest-to-southeast landing strip from the frozen black loam. Disappointingly, it was just 40 percent of the prescribed length for a high-altitude landing strip.[3]

It did not appear to be long enough to accommodate the workhorse C-47s that would bring supplies from Japan and fly out the wounded.

Engineering manuals stated that at 4,000-feet elevation and with below-zero temperatures, Hagaru-ri would require a runway at least 7,600 feet long for C-47s to land and take off.

During the morning of December 1, the division surgeon, Navy Dr Eugene Herring Jr, told General Smith that his medical facilities were severely stressed by the 600 casualties in Hagaru-ri.

With an estimated 900 more wounded men soon to arrive from Yudam-ni and east of the Reservoir, they would be quickly overwhelmed. Alarming as they were, Herring's projections were low compared with the actual number of men that would pass through his medical tents.[4]

Smith now realized that he could not wait for engineers to extend the runway to the manual's specifications.

He authorized a trial run.

At 2:30pm on December 1, as parka-clad Marines tensely watched, an Air Force C-47 cargo plane from the Far East Air Force landed on the primitive airstrip and braked to a stop. Thirty minutes later, the two-engine aircraft raced down the short runway with 26 wounded men, getting just enough lift in the thin, freezing air to become airborne.[5]

One of the first men to leave Hagaru-ri was Lieutenant Colonel Bill Reilly, the badly wounded commander of the 31st Regiment's 3rd Battalion. He had been airlifted from the inlet to Hagaru-ri two days earlier on General David Barr's helicopter.[6]

Three more C-47s arrived that afternoon, and 60 men were evacuated to Yonpo airfield and thence taken to hospitals in Hamhung and Hungnam. Critical cases were flown to hospitals in Japan.

The day's evacuations ended when the landing gear of an incoming plane laden with ammunition collapsed, and the plane had to be unloaded before it could be moved and destroyed. By then, darkness had fallen.[7]

It was now a certainty that Hagaru-ri would serve as the focal point for X Corps's withdrawal down the MSR to the northeastern Korean coast.

At a Far East Command conference in Tokyo on the day of the first Hagaru-ri airlifts, the decision was made to devote every C-119

Flying Boxcar in the theater to airdropping supplies and ammunition to units in the Chosin Reservoir area. C-119s had already parachuted tons of supplies to the surrounded Marines at Yudam-ni – 64 tons on November 29, and 87 tons on November 30.

Unlike the C-47s, the Flying Boxcars were considered too large to land at the Hagaru-ri airstrip, but they could airdrop six tons of cargo in one pass. The C-47s had just a two-ton capacity, and required multiple passes to discharge it.

General William Tunner's Far East Combat Cargo Command would dedicate itself to resupplying X Corps's troops during their breakout from the Chosin Reservoir area.

Tunner was the man best suited for the job, having overseen some of history's most successful cargo airlifts: resupplying China's Nationalist armies over the Himalayas during World War II, and the 1948 Berlin airlift.[8]

One time, the code name routinely used to request an airdrop of 60mm mortar shells, "Tootsie Rolls," went through untranslated because the radio operator did not have the code sheet at hand. Consequently, boxes of Tootsie Rolls were what was airdropped to the Marines.

The mortar men were highly displeased with the mix-up, but everyone else appreciated the airdropped chocolate treat, which provided quick energy and was also used, after being warmed in the mouth, to plug bullet holes in gas tanks, radiators, and fuel lines. Thereafter, the Tootsie Roll became the Chosin campaign's culinary icon.[9]

Chapter 16

The Chinese Destroy a Regiment

East of Chosin Reservoir

If you are going to die, do it in the attack. Let's get moving and secure this hill.

Captain Erwin Bigger, wounded and hobbling on two canes before an assault east of Chosin Reservoir.[1]

It was heartrending, like a bad dream ... I could see the Army guys, all strung out, cut off, overwhelmed. I could see what was going to happen down there, and I was helpless to stop it.

Pilot Sam Folsom, who witnessed the end of Task Force Faith.[2]

There was no resistance left in the column. Motors in the trucks were not running – drivers were not in the cabs of the trucks. The only sound was the moaning of the wounded and dying.

Major Wesley Curtis describing the death throes of Task Force Faith.[3]

Under attack for 80 hours in subzero weather, Task Force Faith was past desperation. As November 30 drew to a close, it was doubtful whether the three Army battalions east of Chosin Reservoir would survive another night.

Although Lieutenant Colonel Faith's 32nd Infantry battalion had succeeded in joining the 31st Infantry's 3rd Battalion at the inlet, both units were sapped by three nights of determined Chinese attacks that had left hundreds of Americans either dead or wounded. The survivors hadn't slept in days.

The aid station tents were at capacity, and many other wounded men lay outside under tarpaulins. There were no more bandages or morphine, and medics were forced to treat wounds with disinfectant, and to use cloth wrappings in lieu of bandages.[4]

Moreover, the weather was worsening, if that were possible: temperatures reached 30 below zero with snow.

Three regiments from the Chinese 81st Division – the 241st, 242nd, and 243rd – had arrived overnight to shore up the decimated 80th Division and the 81st's 242nd Regiment.

The intensive cold and the US Army's infantry battalions and anti-aircraft artillery and automatic weapons units had thinned the ranks of the exhausted 80th and 81st by 60 percent or more.[5]

Nonetheless, at daybreak December 1, rather than withdraw into the hills to avoid the Marine close-air support squadrons, the now reinforced Chinese chose to go for the jugular. They fought the Americans hand-to-hand, making close-air support extremely difficult.[6]

Task Force Faith was intact but in poor shape overall. With his men nearly out of ammunition, Faith knew that they could not endure another night of fighting and that he must act now before it was too late.

With low skies foreclosing the possibility of close-air support that morning, Faith decided to make a run for Hagaru-ri in the early afternoon. He scheduled an air strike coinciding with the beginning of the breakout.

Task Force Faith would take only those trucks in the best operating order – 22 of the two-and-a-half-ton trucks were deemed so – and drain the gasoline from the rest and destroy them. Artillery and heavy mortar crews were ordered to fire all of their heavy ordnance and smash their weapons.

The operable trucks were emptied, and several hundred badly wounded men were placed in them, two deep.

The 32nd Infantry battalion, with Lieutenant James Mortrude's Charlie Company on point with an M-19 dual 40mm halftrack to help clear the way, was chosen to lead the convoy on the first leg of the breakout – the two-mile journey to Hudong-ni. Faith was counting on joining Captain Drake's 31st Tank Company and RCT-31's rear command post there.[7]

Out of radio contact with those units for days, Faith was unaware that the situation in Hudong-ni had radically changed, and that no help awaited him there.

Light snow fell and temperatures were below zero when the convoy set out at 1pm on December 1. On schedule, a flight of Corsairs appeared overhead to provide close-air support for the column.

They needed it badly, for ammunition was now precious: the 40mm antiaircraft ammo for the M-19s was nearly gone, the quad-.50s could only be used sparingly, and some of the infantrymen were down to one clip apiece. The edges of Faith's moving perimeter were marked by colored panels so that they were clearly visible from the air.[8]

Just as the column began its march to the south, it was met by gusts of Chinese gunfire from the hills ahead and to the east – and then the four Corsairs attacked.

In a tragic miscalculation, a napalm canister struck the head of the convoy, and some nearby Chinese troops.

The ensuing scene of horror and chaos was unforgettable.

Major Hugh Robbins, lying wounded in a truck, said flames immediately engulfed more than a dozen American soldiers. "I could see the terrible sight of men ablaze from head to foot, staggering back or rolling on the ground screaming."

"It was terrible," said Private James Ransome. "Where the napalm had burned the skin to a crisp, it could be peeled back from the face, arms, legs. It looked as though the skin were curled like potato chips."

Their comrades tried to extinguish the burning petroleum, which bore through their clothes and skin, by rolling the men in the snow, but it did no good. In their agony, the victims begged to be shot.[9]

"They were miserable. The quicker they died, the better off they were," said Harrison Ager, an Army truck driver.

The napalm splashed the left leg of mortarman Daniel Fritz's fatigue pants, which began burning along with his leg. "The mind shuts out pain after a while," he said. "I felt warm, and I thought, gee this is the best I've felt in weeks."[10]

An officer who had been burned black asked for a cigarette, and walked toward the frozen hills held by the Chinese, never to be seen again.[11]

Nineteen US soldiers perished in the "friendly fire" incident.[12]

It was a terrible psychological blow for men who had not slept in days and had already seen comrades killed all around them.

Fearful of a second napalm strike, the soldiers scattered in every direction. Lieutenant Colonel Faith, however, somehow managed to restore order and get the column moving again. Enemy gunfire raked it from the high ground east of the road – in a bitter irony, from positions dug ten days earlier by the Fifth Marines.

Faith moved his Baker Company to the point, replacing the shaken men of Charlie and Able Companies, which had borne the brunt of the napalm strike.[13]

The withdrawal to Hudong-ni and Hagaru-ri became a running fight, with the massive Hill 1221, still held by the Chinese, looming in the convoy's path.

Captain Edward Stamford, the Marine forward air observer whose call sign was "Boyhood 14," directed air strikes that drove the Chinese away from the road as the convoy lumbered on. Spotting Chinese throwing grenades from a culvert, Stamford called in a strike just 50 yards in front of him; a rocket destroyed the culvert.[14]

Two miles from the perimeter, the radio in the artillery observer's jeep received this message: "To Colonel Faith: Secure your own exit to Hagaru-ri. Unable to assist you. Signed Smith CG 1st Marine Division."

General Hodes, the 7th Division's assistant commander, had written the message, and Smith had signed it. It told Faith what he already knew.

The Chinese had blown apart a 20-foot bridge span over a broad stream that emptied into the reservoir. The infantrymen were able to get over it, but when the trucks attempted to cross the iced-over stream, they broke through the ice. As the wounded shrieked in agony, a tracked M-19 winched the trucks over rough ground and up the embankment.

The Chinese riddled the trucks laden with seriously wounded men, re-wounding the wounded. Once again, Stamford called in air strikes against the enemy positions.[15]

In order to destroy the Chinese roadblock at the base of Hill 1221, the hill itself had to be seized, or else enemy troops would be able to fire down on the convoy. As nighttime approached, Faith and some of his officers tried to organize an assault to clear the hill.

Unit integrity had disintegrated, and many men had lost the will to fight as Chinese bullets sang around them, inflicting wounds and adding to the pain of the wounded in the trucks.

Soldiers hid under the stalled trucks, some of them refusing to fight, others unable to, and some already resigned to captivity.

Faith strode up and down his column with his .45-caliber pistol in his hand, exhorting his men to leave the ditch alongside the road and assault Hill 1221 and threatening to shoot deserters. Each time he passed his jeep he stopped to fire a burst from the jeep's mounted .30-caliber machine gun.

Faith discovered two frightened ROK soldiers who had lashed themselves to the undercarriage of a truck. When they refused to come out, he shot them both.

The willing among Faith's men assaulted Hill 1221 piecemeal, in small groups organized by his officers, some of them consisting of just three or four men.

A group of nearly 100 men was led by wounded Captain Erwin Bigger, who commanded Faith's Weapons Company and had fought at Anzio in World War II. Bigger, hit in the legs earlier in the day by a mortar round, used two aiming stakes as canes to propel himself.

"If you are going to die, do it in the attack," Bigger said, brandishing his canes at his men. "Let's get moving and secure this hill."

Bigger's party captured part of the hilltop, and after his men were strafed by friendly aircraft, they slid down the hill's west side and onto the ice of Chosin Reservoir, heading for Hagaru-ri.

As they neared the operations base, Marines led them in through the mine fields that they had sown along Hagaru-ri's northern shoreline.[16]

Charlie Company's commander, Lieutenant James Mortrude, led some of his men in an assault on 1221. "We just moved up the hill firing, screaming," he said. South Korean soldiers joined in that attack.[17]

Captain James McClymont, who had commanded a battery of M19s and was a veteran of the ill-fated *Market Garden* operation in Holland in 1944, led another assault group up the hill. It began with his two sergeants and several other men.

But when McClymont reached the hillcrest, only his two sergeants remained with him. They fought entrenched enemy troops in foxholes until, realizing that many more dug-in Chinese troops were on the hill, they slid down the slope toward the road to Hagaru-ri.

Faith managed to round up about 350 men, most of them walking wounded, and advanced toward the roadblock at Hill 1221's base. As he approached it, he saw that it consisted of three of Captain Drake's immobilized tanks from the failed relief effort days earlier.

With each of them leading about 100 men, Faith and his adjutant, Major Robert Jones, attacked the roadblock.

At the same time, Captain Jordan, commander of the 31st Infantry's "M" Company, also assaulted the roadblock with a shouting group that included Lieutenant John Gray, wounded days earlier. Gray had gotten out of a truck to join the attack.[18]

After the roadblock was cleared, an enemy soldier hiding in the brush flung a grenade at Faith. Wounded by steel fragments, one penetrating just above his heart, he fell, badly wounded. He was wrapped in a blanket and placed in the lead truck's passenger seat.

"I felt a great loss," said Major Jones. "He was the leader. I had been with him all the way. We had made the top of that hill and gotten into a situation where we could move the troops."[19]

With Faith out of action, Jones watched all semblance of unit cohesion dissolve before his eyes. The men had been through too much with no sleep, and now the chain of command was gone.

"At this stage of affairs, with no organization, no crew-served weapons, no communications, no NCO and officer leaders to look to, the fighting units came apart, and left individuals who were in the main looking for ... medical care and safety," said Jones.

Task Force Faith had ceased to exist.[20]

"After Colonel Faith was killed, it was everyone for himself. The chain of command disappeared," said Sergeant Chester Blair. "Some men sat down and refused to move."[21]

The coming of nighttime emboldened the Chinese in the hills to close in on the convoy. Unable to stop them, Corsair pilots saw enemy soldiers fire at close range into the truck column, and bayonet wounded men.

A pilot who witnessed the chaotic scene, Sam Folsom, said, "It was heartrending, like a bad dream ... I could see the Army guys, all strung out, cut off, overwhelmed. I could see what was going to happen down there, and I was helpless to stop it." Moreover, his Corsair was unarmed; he was an observer that day.[22]

Marine pilots Thomas Mulvihill and Edward Montague heard Captain Stamford come onto the radio to say, "It's all over." Stamford then continued, "This is Boyhood One-Four. I am destroying my radio."[23]

The lead convoy remnant led by Captain Jones pushed on toward Hudong-ni with several trucks. As they approached the village, the Chinese soldiers who now occupied it opened fire, killing the drivers of the three lead trucks.

The driver of a fourth truck tried to push through the stalled vehicles, and the four trucks all plunged down an embankment, spilling screaming men onto the ground and crushing them, "like the world gone mad," said Lieutenant James Campbell.

After briefly hiding in a culvert, Campbell led a group of 17 men along the Reservoir shoreline until they reached the Marine lines.[24]

After Faith was wounded, Stamford took charge of one group. He, along with Captain Jones, convinced some of the walking wounded to help clear the road ahead of two inoperable trucks.

They unloaded the wounded from the trucks, placed them in the beds of other trucks and on their hoods and bumpers, and pushed the two disabled trucks off the road. The strenuous effort reopened the wounds of the walking wounded who had pitched in.[25]

When the convoy was moving again, Stamford hiked ahead to the lead truck, now 400 yards past the Hill 1221 roadblock. In the dark, he ran into a couple of officers "standing around in some kind of fog or daze."[26]

Upon reaching the lead truck where Faith lay semiconscious in the passenger seat, Stamford asked him whether he still wished to continue to Hagaru-ri. Faith murmured, "Yes." Stamford walked ahead of the column, reaching another blown bridge.

He found a path leading to a nearby railroad crossing that he believed would support the trucks. Entering a small building by the side of the road, Stamford proposed to survivors gathered there that they continue advancing to Hagaru-ri on the railroad tracks.

Looking around, Stamford "saw a lieutenant colonel and a few other officers and none made any attempt to take over command. I became peeved and started out to lead the convoy."[27]

A reconnaissance plane appeared over the column as daylight ebbed and dropped containers on the road. They were full of leaflets that warned: "Enemy on all sides. Don't stay on trucks. Cross ice to our troops south end of reservoir."[28]

Leading the convoy over the railroad tracks and then back to the road, Stamford and a few other men were captured. When their captor became distracted, they escaped and ran toward the reservoir.

Limping on a sprained ankle, Stamford reached Hagaru-ri at 2:25am December 2.[29]

The last act of the tragedy unfolded that night among the stalled trucks outside of Hudong-ni.[30]

At nightfall, about 250 men remained in the convoy. Combat patrols ranged ahead to the outskirts of Hudong-ni, where they came under fire from the Chinese that now occupied the village. Burned-out tanks blocked the road.

The convoy's rearguard troops began to drift away in groups, intent on reaching the frozen reservoir. The seriously wounded remained in the truck beds.[31]

"We were out of ammunition, we were out of everything," said Lieutenant Gray. "We got the convoy down to Hudong, where we thought our regimental headquarters might be. But the 31st Tank Company had been withdrawn back to Hagaru to help defend it."

With Hudong-ni now in Chinese hands, "we had no choice but to surrender or retreat across the reservoir," Gray said.[32]

Major Wesley Curtis, the 1st Battalion's operations officer, limped past the silent vehicles and saw Faith, dying or dead, in the cab of a disabled truck beside the dead driver.

"There was no resistance left in the column," Curtis said. "Motors in the trucks were not running – drivers were not in the cabs of the trucks. The only sound was the moaning of the wounded and dying."[33]

As the thermometer dove to minus 30 degrees, enemy troops closed in on the 15 stalled trucks and hurled white phosphorus grenades into them, evoking a fresh cacophony of anguished cries.[34]

Roving the stalled convoy, the Chinese looted the wounded and made prisoners of those who could walk. Those who could not were either shot or left to die in the arctic cold.[35]

James DeLong of King Company was taken prisoner. His hands were tied behind his back and he was marched away from the convoy. When a soldier in his group began limping, DeLong said, "A Chinaman ran up behind him and shot him."

Louis Grappo had lain unconscious for hours in one of the silent trucks. When Grappo was awakened by the throbbing of his wounded leg, he saw that the man next to him was dead from a bullet wound to the head.

He heard Chinese soldiers moving around the stalled convoy and pulled a body over him for protection, and gripped a grenade. "If they come for me, I'll pull the pin," Grappo told himself.

The trucks were silent and the Chinese were gone when Grappo regained consciousness again. He crawled out of the truck and somehow managed to reach the reservoir ice.[36]

North Korean civilians passing on the road bowed slowly to the wounded GIs, and melted snow for them to drink.[37]

By midnight, only the dead and seriously wounded remained at Hudong-ni.[38]

Private Hubert "Ed" Reeves, who had been wounded by an antitank round three days earlier, was in one of the stalled trucks, unable to walk. "The driver said they're burning the trucks," he said. Reeves took out his Gideon New Testament and began reading Psalm 23.[39]

Chinese soldiers were unable to burn his truck because the gas tank was shot up and the fuel had leaked out. Instead of burning the truck, they began shooting the wounded men one by one.

After they shot the man next to Reeves, it was Reeves's turn. "I said Jesus here I come." The muzzle blast stunned him, but the bullet did not penetrate his skull; he had received a superficial scalp wound.

When another group of Chinese soldiers discovered that he was still alive, "they worked me over good with rifle butts and bayonets" and threw him onto a pile of bodies.

He could not stand, and he could not use his hands, which were broken. He crawled away on his elbows and knees toward the reservoir. It took a long time to reach the ice.

A Chinese soldier with a burp gun approached Reeves. Believing that after all that he had been through, he would be shot anyway, Reeves cried, "Ahhh, no!" and the enemy soldier ran away.

By dawn, Reeves had covered nearly three miles and was still crawling. A wounded GI joined him on the ice as three Marine Corsairs appeared overhead. Reeves shouted at the GI to write "HELP" in the snow that covered the ice. The GI spelled out the word by dragging a foot in the snow.

One of the Corsairs dropped low and signaled "OK," and the planes then flew in a protective circle until a jeep appeared.

Lieutenant Colonel Olin Beall, commander of the Marine 1st Motor Transport Battalion, and his driver were looking for survivors.

Beall helped the wounded GI into the jeep, and then he took off his parka, wrapped Reeves in it, and lifted him into the jeep.

They drove straight to the Hagaru-ri airstrip, and Beall helped carry Reeves on a stretcher to a C-47 that was about to take off from the airfield.

Reeves was flown to Yonpo airfield and treated at a military hospital for his shrapnel and scalp wounds, then flown to Tokyo, where he was hospitalized.

During Reeves's passage through a series of military hospitals, doctors believed that he probably would not survive. Yet, against all odds, he lived, although his frostbitten feet and all of his fingers were amputated. He was just 18 years old.

Reeves was fitted with prostheses to replace his feet. He earned a college degree, married, and became a computer programmer for the Department of Defense. He and his wife reared seven children.[40]

As traumatized survivors of doomed Task Force Faith continued to trickle into Hagaru-ri over the reservoir ice on December 2, a company-size Army task force was organized in Hagaru-ri to rescue whatever remained of Faith's convoy.

Led by Lieutenant Colonel Barry Anderson, the Army infantrymen and a few tanks got on the road to Hudong-ni. Strong Chinese resistance prevented the soldiers from advancing far.

Anderson's men were recalled after it became evident that there were no longer any organized elements of Faith's task force east of Chosin, only stragglers.[41]

Fifty-two-year-old Olin Beall, with more than 30 years in the Marine Corps, had led the last supply convoy from Hagaru-ri to Yudam-ni on November 27, returning that evening with a truckload of wounded Marines. They had gotten out just before the Chinese sprang their trap on the two Marine regiments in the Yudam-ni valley.

When pilots had first spotted men on the reservoir ice during the late afternoon of December 1, Beall had sent a squad to guide them through the minefield in front of his perimeter.

As groups of RCT-31 survivors continued to appear on the reservoir ice, Beall organized a rescue operation to collect men who had managed to walk or crawl away from the destroyed convoy.[42]

"It was pitiful. Some of these men were dragging themselves on the ice, some had gone crazy and were walking in circles," Beall said.[43]

On December 2, Beall and five other men gathered up wounded men six or seven at a time in Beall's jeep over a 12-hour period in 24-below-zero temperatures. They used parkas as sleds to drag the wounded men to the jeep.

The strong northern wind made it difficult to even stand on the ice. At times, they were fired on by Chinese snipers and machine guns, but no one was hit.[44]

At the end of the day, Beall and his team brought 319 survivors into the Hagaru-ri aid stations.[45]

The next day, Beall returned to the ice with two men after an observation plane reported seeing more wounded men. As they advanced toward the reservoir's eastern shore, Beall and his men came under heavy enemy fire.

The aerial observer called in close-air support that drove off the enemy, and Beall was able to go ashore near Hudong-ni. Reaching the main road, he saw the line of silent vehicles.

Peering into each truck, jeep, and trailer, Beall saw that they were all full of corpses, more than 300 total. Amid the two-deep stretchers he saw men frozen in the act of trying to pull themselves out from beneath the stretcher above them.

"I saw this and shall never forget it," Beall said.[46]

When Beall returned to where his driver, Pfc Ralph Milton, had stopped his jeep on the reservoir ice, he told Milton, "They're all dead."

Before nightfall that day, a flight of Corsairs dropped napalm pods along the length of the column, incinerating the trucks, jeeps, and trailers, and cremating the corpses inside them.[47]

More than 1,000 of the 3,200 troops in the three battalions of the Army's 31st and 32nd Infantry were killed or captured east of Chosin Reservoir. Just 385 of the survivors that managed to reach Hagaru-ri were able to fight again.

Had RCT-31 withdrawn to Hagaru-ri immediately after the attacks on November 27–28, it would not have undergone the horrors of the next few days. More of the men surely would have survived.

That did not happen. General Almond, obediently prosecuting MacArthur's battle plan, instead disparaged the Chinese forces facing Lieutenant Colonel Faith as "a bunch of Chinese laundrymen," and ordered Faith to recapture the ground the unit had lost during the first night's assaults.[48]

Aided immensely by the incredible firepower of its self-propelled M-16 and M-19 antiaircraft gun carriages, RCT-31 stood its ground for five days against the main strength of three 27th Army divisions: the 80th, 81st, and 94th.

Although not an elite force like the Marines – some soldiers had received virtually no training at all – they accounted for thousands of casualties and bought precious time for the 1st Marine Division defenders at Hagaru-ri.

RCT-31 prevented the 27th Army's divisions from reaching the 1st Division hub at Hagaru-ri and reinforcing the 20th Army's 58th Division.

Task Force Faith's actions prevented Hagaru-ri from being overrun by the 80th and 81st Divisions. Had Hagaru-ri fallen, the Fifth and Seventh Marines would have had nowhere to regroup upon breaking out from Yudam-ni.[49]

Yet RCT-31's demise was unquestionably ugly and tragic.

General Hodes, the 7th Division's assistant commander, reported that RCT-31 "was completely overrun." An aerial survey of the disaster showed that "there are many bodies around the trucks. Apparently, these bodies were the wounded who were left on the trucks and the people who stayed to protect the trucks."[50]

Crippled by poor communication equipment, RCT-31 never enjoyed reliable radio links with the 7th Infantry Division or the 1st Marine Division at Hagaru-ri. Consequently, higher command never fully grasped RCT-31's dire situation.[51]

After RCT-31 had ceased to exist, Song reported to his superiors on December 3: "The 27th Army has completely annihilated the retreating enemy from Sinhung-ni, at the Hudong-ni line, capturing 150 enemy soldiers and most trucks and vehicles."

Peng Dehuai and Mao congratulated Song on having destroyed an entire American regiment – the only instance that this occurred during the Korean War.[52]

Not knowing the full story of what had happened to RCT-31, the Marines were largely unsympathetic to the bedraggled, wounded, frostbitten soldiers arriving in small groups in Hagaru-ri.

General O.P. Smith wrote in his daily log: "The story of these battalions is a pitiful one and not a credit to many of the personnel of the battalions. As far as I can determine, they left their wounded to shift for themselves."

In a letter to a friend, Smith granted that while the battalions might have fought gallantly, "after their breakup they straggled into Hagaru-ri over a period of three or four days with no semblance of organization. We know also that the able-bodied men came in first."[53]

RCT-31's last stand broke the 80th Division, which was unable to take the field again until spring 1951.

Nonetheless, Task Force Faith was excluded from the Navy Presidential Unit Citation awarded in 1950 to the 1st Marine Division for its actions in northeast Korea.

Edward Magill of the 57th Field Artillery wrote that "it has always angered me that Generals Almond and Barr did nothing to secure recognition for the soldiers who fought and died on the east side of Chosin Reservoir."

Most of the officers and NCOs had been killed or incapacitated, and their men were suffering from "hunger, dehydration, lack of sleep, long exposure to severe cold, and the physiological effects of prolonged combat," said Magill.[54]

For decades, Task Force Faith was maligned as incompetent, even cowardly. Finally, after re-examining RCT-31's actions, the Navy belatedly awarded Task Force Faith the Presidential Unit Citation in 2000, 50 years after its last stand.[55]

Chapter 17

Yudam-ni and Fox Hill

November 30–December 3, 1950

It all seemed so hopeless ... What was our little chopped up battalion going to do against such a huge force? We were agonizingly aware that the Chinese could swallow us in a single bite.

DR HENRY LITVIN, A BATTALION SURGEON WATCHING CHINESE TROOPS CONVERGE ON THE LAST MARINES WITHDRAWING FROM YUDAM-NI.[1]

No one ever doubted the troops from Yudam-ni would make it, but there was always a question of how many would.

LIEUTENANT PATRICK ROE, SEVENTH MARINES INTELLIGENCE OFFICER.[2]

Back-to-back nights of relentless Chinese attacks had failed to crush beleaguered Fox Company on Toktong Pass. Every assault had been bloodily repulsed. Yet Captain William Barber had to gloomily concede that his men, surrounded by the Chinese 59th Division, were on their own for now.

From Yudam-ni, seven miles to the north, a relief battalion of Marines from the Fifth and Seventh Regiments had set out November 29 with the object of reaching Fox Company. It was stopped just 300 yards south of Yudam-ni by Chinese troops that occupied the hills and draws on both sides of the MSR. The composite battalion was recalled to Yudam-ni.[3]

Although no relief came to Barber's men overland, some aid arrived from the sky. C-119 Flying Boxcars from the Far East Combat Cargo Command in Japan parachuted supplies and ammunition to Fox Hill. Although most of the materiel landed west of the perimeter and had to be retrieved through enemy fire, it was welcome nonetheless.[4]

Airdropped supplies were critically needed by the far-flung Marine and Army units in the Chosin Reservoir area. The American base in Ashiya, Japan, became the hub for dispatching supply planes; extra workers were added to handle the increased workload.

The parachuted rations, ammunition, blankets, and medical supplies provided the margin between hunger and starvation, ammunition rationing and running out.

Private Robert Foelske was aboard a C-119 and overseeing the provisions near the rear open hatch when two guidance ropes snapped. Foelske was knocked unconscious and blown out of the plane.

Fortunately for Foelske, he was wearing a parachute and the cold air brought him around in time for him to pull the ripcord. Foelske landed in a tree without suffering a major injury. He walked all night, evading Chinese forces, until reaching friendly lines.

Two days later, he was ferried back to Ashiya air base in Japan, where his crewmates were astounded to see him alive. He joined them as they boarded a C-119 preparing to leave on a new mission.[5]

A Chinese machine-gun bullet had shattered Barber's pelvis the previous night, but the tough captain remained fully in command, although in pain. He stumped around his perimeter with a stout stick serving as a crutch.[6]

As night approached, the Marines witnessed the astonishing sight of three companies of Chinese troops marching down the MSR in parade formation – each company five abreast and 25 rows deep. They disappeared into a grove of fir trees west of the Fox perimeter. Then, two more columns joined them, making a full battalion.

Lieutenant Elmo Peterson, who commanded the 2nd Platoon, radioed the coordinates to Lieutenant Don Campbell, the forward artillery observer, at Barber's CP.

Campbell promptly relayed the information to How Company's 105mm batteries in Hagaru-ri. Minutes later, anti-personnel rounds began exploding above the grove into which the Chinese had disappeared, raining shrapnel on the enemy troops, and causing an unknown number of casualties.[7]

At 2am on November 30, the Chinese broadcast a surrender appeal made by a Marine artilleryman, Lieutenant Robert Messman of King Battery, who had been captured two days earlier near Yudam-ni.

"Men of Fox Company, if you surrender now the Chinese will treat you according to the Geneva Convention," he said, evidently reading from a script. "They will feed you. They will provide warm clothing. They will treat your wounds."

In response, Fox machine gunners defiantly fired a few rounds into the freezing night.[8]

Then a Chinese squad crept down the MSR and began moving through the brush toward the Marine lines.

Earlier, the Marines had left their holes and concealed themselves under white blankets in the snow. When the enemy troops reached the empty foxholes, the Marines opened fire, killing them all.[9]

Lieutenant Peterson's squad laid another trap for infiltrators. They had stuffed the sleeping bags of some of the dead Americans with snow and pine boughs, and arranged five frozen American corpses in sitting positions near the sleeping bags.

Other enemy soldiers that had followed a ravine to the perimeter from the northwest split into two groups: one going for the sleeping bags, and the other attacking the figures seated nearby.

With bayonets, they ran through the sleeping bags several times, and fell upon the corpses with knives and bayonets. When their weapons failed to penetrate the frozen flesh, they realized they had fallen for a ruse – an instant before they were cut to pieces by Marine rifle and Browning Automatic Rifle (BAR) fire.[10]

Before the main Chinese assault, the Marines watched the roughly 500 men assemble in front of the woods at the base of a hill and begin jogging in place in an attempt to stay warm in the arctic cold. They vigorously pumped their arms and legs as political commissars delivered fiery pep talks.

Then, three Chinese companies armed with grenades, satchel charges, and fixed bayonets launched the main assault from south of the MSR.

Illumination rounds exposed the attackers to the Marines inside the perimeter.

Advancing at a fast jog, they formed five lines 75 yards long and crossed the MSR.

Then, the Marines hit them with a hurricane of heavy machine-gun fire, mortars, rifle fire, and 105mm shell fire from Hagaru-ri.

The battle, if it could be called that, was over in ten minutes. When the shooting stopped, about 400 Chinese soldiers lay dead in the neatly aligned rows in which they had attacked.[11]

"My God, it was a slaughter!" exclaimed Barber. "The Chinese didn't have a chance ... It was a big turkey shoot for us."[12]

Enemy sniper fire suddenly erupted from the nearby hills as the Chinese sought retribution. How Battery in Hagaru-ri flayed West Hill, Rocky Knoll, and Rocky Ridge (Hill 1653) with the anti-personnel ordnance that had been so effective earlier. The eight-minute barrage drove the enemy to the reverse slopes of the three hills.

In the morning, three Corsairs appeared overhead, and rocketed, bombed, and napalmed Rocky Knoll and Rocky Ridge. After three runs, they waggled their wings and headed back to their base as the Fox Company Marines cheered.[13]

Before nightfall, Flying Boxcars airdropped more supplies and ammunition. Three inches of snow fell that night as the temperature fell to 20-below-zero arctic cold.[14]

As snow steadily fell, the Chinese moved four machine guns into firing positions on Rocky Ridge, and began directing harassing fire at the Marine perimeter.

Barber decided to put a stop to it.

Lieutenant Campbell, the forward artillery observer, radioed Rocky Ridge's coordinates to Captain Benjamin Read at How Battery in Hagaru-ri.

After the howitzers had fired on the ridge, the heavy mortar section discharged two illumination rounds to enable Campbell to adjust the howitzer fire.

No adjustment was necessary. To everyone's amazement and delight, the initial strike was perfect; it wiped out the four machine guns.

After that stunningly precise piece of artillery work – so rarely accomplished in combat, much less at the extreme range of effectiveness – the Chinese attempted no further organized offensive action that night, aside from sniping at the Marine perimeter from the nearby hills and ridges.[15]

On December 1, Barber's men gathered all of their dead up to that point and laid them under ponchos near the MSR embankment. C-119 Flying Boxcars airdropped more supplies.

On the fifth night of the siege, December 1–2, the 59th Division did not launch any large-scale attacks against Fox Company, contenting itself with long-range sniper fire. Chinese casualties, the intensive cold, and the enemy's ration shortages discouraged offensive action.

But another factor was the 59th's prodigious efforts on the other side of Toktong Pass to stop the Marine breakout from Yudam-ni.

Barber had learned earlier on December 1 that the Seventh Marines were pushing south on the MSR toward Fox Hill against strong resistance, while the Fifth Marines' 2nd Battalion continued to occupy Yudam-ni, acting as the rearguard for the Seventh.

The Chinese attacks on X Corps that began November 27 had temporarily paralyzed Generals Almond and MacArthur, who had anticipated a triumphant drive to the Yalu River that would end the war quickly. The troops might be home as early as Christmas, they had confidently predicted.

After the massive Chinese offensive began, Almond was summoned to an emergency meeting at MacArthur's headquarters in Tokyo to re-assess the situation.

During these dark days of uncertainty, Colonel Alpha Bowser, Smith's operations officer, acknowledged, "I really thought we'd had it ... I would not have given a nickel for our chances of making it."

Fortunately, most of the Marines did not share Bowser's pessimism, believing that they would fight their way out of the Yudam-ni valley.[16]

At the Tokyo meeting, Almond declared that he still expected the Marines and the 7th Division to continue attacking north and west. They would cut the Chinese supply lines from Manchuria into North

Korea – what might generously be construed as a fantasy under the circumstances.

"For two days we received no orders from X Corps to withdraw from Yudam-ni," said General Smith. "Apparently they were stunned, just couldn't believe the Chinese had attacked in force."[17]

Smith and his staff were not idle. On the 29th, having heard nothing from X Corps, they ordered the Seventh Marines to clear the MSR to Hagaru-ri, while the Fifth Marines were directed to continue to hold Yudam-ni.

In Tokyo, it was MacArthur who finally injected reality into the crisis. X Corps must go on the defensive, he said. The troops in the Chosin Reservoir area must withdraw down the MSR to the Hamhung–Hungnam area along the Sea of Japan, MacArthur concluded.[18]

During the night of November 29, an X Corps preliminary order arrived in Hagaru-ri for the Marines to redeploy a regiment from Yudam-ni to Hagaru-ri – exactly what Smith had anticipated earlier.

The next day, Almond brought to Smith's headquarters a new order, No. 8, which superseded the previous night's directive. The order authorized Smith to withdraw his units from Yudam-ni to Hagaru-ri.

X Corps Order No. 8 said in part: "1stMarDiv: Operate against enemy in zone: withdraw elements north and northwest of Hagaru-ri ... to Hagaru-ri area; secure Sudong–Hagaru-ri main supply route in zone."[19]

Even when the Chinese resumed their attacks during the night of November 29–30, a feeling had begun to spread among the embattled Marines on Fox Hill and at Yudam-ni that the Chinese had shot their bolt.

They had failed to destroy the Marines in the farthest valley of the Chosin Reservoir area, or even to achieve a significant breakthrough.

On the 29th, Marine squadrons had attacked enemy troop concentrations around Yudam-ni and east of Chosin that threatened the isolated Marine and Army units.

At Hagaru-ri, which had stood off strong enemy attacks during the previous night, four VMF-312 Corsairs struck 300 Chinese troops on

East Hill with fragmentation bombs, rockets, and 20mm shells, killing 75 of them and wounding many others. The attacks helped preserve the perimeter from enemy infiltrations.

Outside Yudam-ni on the 29th, pilots observed 2,000 Chinese massing for a daytime attack on the Fifth Marines' Baker Company, which was guarding the village's northern approaches.

Air strikes eviscerated the enemy troops, and the enemy attack became "a piecemeal venture," with about 500 Chinese racing downhill amid bugle calls, whistles, and shouts.

Swooping down from an altitude of 5,000 feet, the Corsairs doused the attacking waves with four napalm tanks, followed by strafing runs. Marine infantrymen plastered the attackers with small-arms, automatic weapons, and 4.2-inch mortar fire. Three hundred Chinese soldiers died.

Pfc Francis Killeen said that his Seventh Marines' Able Company was on a hilltop when Corsairs made a diving close-air support attack south of Yudam-ni.

"We'd be on top of this cloud, and one of these nuts would fly over trying to get a bearing. He'd be so close you could reach up and touch his wings."

Afterward, as Killeen and his comrades walked through the scene of carnage wrought by the flyers, "One Marine said, with a twinkle in his eye, 'Here we get these guys all corralled in one place where we can get them, and this flyboy comes along and messes everything up.'"[20]

During the morning of November 30 after a bitter-cold night, rumors circulated among the Yudam-ni Marines that they were at last going to retake the initiative.

This, and the fact that three nights of massed enemy attacks had cost the Chinese thousands of dead without causing any significant breach in the perimeter, almost felt like "a moral turning point," according to a Marine Corps record of the campaign.[21]

By 6am, the Fifth and Seventh Marines staffs, working through the night, had completed a joint operating plan that put into action the scheme that Smith and his staff had sketched out the previous day for the two regiments.[22]

Preparations for the breakout from Yudam-ni began before the sun had risen very far above the horizon.

Close-air support by fighter-bombers from Yonpo airfield and carriers in the Sea of Japan leveled the playing field against an enemy that enjoyed decisive numerical superiority.

At dawn of November 30, night fighters of VMF(N)-513 struck in support of the Fifth Marines' Baker Company at Yudam-ni after ground troops marked their front lines with phosphorus grenades. The planes were able to come in close to the Baker lines to strafe and bomb approaching enemy soldiers.

Around noon on the 30th, the Chinese attempted another daytime assault, just as they had on the 29th.

Pilots from the *Leyte* and *Philippine Sea* reported several hundred enemy troops staging north of Yudam-ni. The Corsairs struck with devastating power with bombs, rockets, and napalm.

As hundreds of survivors ran downhill toward the Marine lines, the Corsairs returned and hit them again with napalm pods and 20mm gunfire, smashing the attack. About 200 survivors fled, leaving the hillside and hilltop carpeted with enemy bodies.[23]

The Yudam-ni FACs were so confident in the precision of the pilots that they sometimes called in air support 30 yards in front of the Marine lines, laying down colored markers to denote the front lines' boundary.

"At Yudam-ni it was not unusual for us to be on one side of a mountain and the Chinese 20 or 30 yards away on the other," said Lieutenant Colonel Frederick Dowsett, the Seventh Marines' executive officer.

In the late afternoon of November 30, Corsairs from VMF-212 were recalled by a forward air controller to strike Chinese troops attacking the Fifth's 3rd Battalion for the second time that day. They struck with fragmentation bombs, napalm, and rockets, thwarting the attack.

The Chinese soldiers initially remained in their positions during air attacks.

"They would freeze in their tracks and stand erect with their arms outstretched to resemble a tree, or squat to appear as a bush," said

Captain Donald Conroy of VMF-214. But after they had experienced the terror and agony of napalm drops, the enemy troops scattered and took cover.

Under the cover of air strikes and artillery fire, the Fifth Marines disengaged from their positions north and northwest of the village to form a tighter perimeter around Yudam-ni. The tactical move freed the Seventh Marines' 3rd Battalion to begin leading the march south on the MSR toward Hagaru-ri on December 1.

South of Yudam-ni, the half-frozen, starving soldiers of the Chinese 59th Division prepared to stop any attempted Marine breakout. Lacking heavy equipment, they could build only the simplest defensive works in the intensive cold. They waited for the Marines to come.[24]

Danger lay on all sides for the Marines: the Chinese manned three formidable roadblocks and held high ground on both sides of the MSR.[25]

Amid the rapid preparations for the breakout, General Almond's Blue Goose L-5, a single-engine wing-over-the-fuselage plane, made a daring landing under fire at Yudam-ni on a frozen streambed. After taking aboard several wounded men, it took off again under fire. "I was afraid our Goose was cooked that time," quipped Captain Charles Keleman, the pilot.[26]

Before the Marines began their withdrawal from Yudam-ni, other steps were taken to reorganize, pare, and otherwise prepare the regiments. The remnants of the Seventh Marines' two badly diminished rifle companies, Easy and Dog, were combined into a single unit of 75 men. It was reinforced by the 1st Battalion's Weapons Company and 115 men from the 4th Artillery Battalion.[27]

The mongrel unit adopted the nickname "Damnation Battalion," also its radio call sign. Major Hal Roach, the Seventh Marines logistics officer, was its commander. The men proudly wore green neckerchiefs made from shredded parachute silk as badges of distinction.[28]

Dog and Easy Companies' 2nd Battalion commander and his headquarters company were marooned in Hagaru-ri and their sister Fox Company was still fighting for its life on Toktong Pass.

The two companies, provisionally attached to Lieutenant Colonel Ray Davis's 1st Battalion, had grittily defended Hills 1282 and 1240 on North Ridge during the first night's attacks. Although reduced to platoon size, the survivors had prevented the Chinese from overrunning the Eleventh Marines' artillery batteries in the valley below, which would have been possibly a mortal blow to the regiments' survival.

The rifle companies were joined by artillerymen whose mission had ended. The Eleventh Marines' 4th Battalion had fired off its ammunition and discarded most of its gear. Its 105mm guns were tethered to their tractors and put on the road, and any remaining ammunition was destroyed.[29]

Also converted into infantry reinforcements were men assigned to headquarters and service units.[30]

Recognizing that the convoy rolling out of Yudam-ni would need space for the wounded – and for those who would be wounded during the fighting ahead – Colonel Litzenberg and Lieutenant Colonel Murray reluctantly conceded that some dead Marines would have to be buried in a field south of Yudam-ni.

"Marines do not leave their wounded or dead behind," wrote General Victor Krulak, "not so much because it is uncivilized but simply because the casualties, living or dead, are still their buddy and to forsake them would be unthinkable."[31]

This was one of those unthinkable occasions, though.

After truck cargo areas were filled with wounded men and supplies, no room remained for the dead.

Frozen Marine corpses were gathered and taken to collection points. Many of them had fallen and then had become frozen in grotesque positions. Men on the collection detail had to snap arms and legs so that they could be loaded like cordwood onto the trucks.[32]

Work parties loaded 85 bodies, wrapped them in parachute cloth, and took them to a 6-foot-deep trench carved by bulldozers. Navy chaplains performed the burial rite. Then, two bulldozers pushed frozen dirt over the corpses.

"It was hard duty," said Pfc Robert Pruett, one of the bulldozer drivers. "All we could do was push them into the pit ... and try to spread them out evenly."

When the corpses were in the ground, Pruett and the other driver guided their bulldozers over the burial site to tamp it down.[33]

The Fifth Marines had the sticky job of disengaging in the face of the enemy from Hill 1426 southwest of Yudam-ni, and from Hills 1282 and 1240 on North Ridge – the hills that were so tenaciously defended November 27–28 by the Seventh's Easy and Dog Companies. George Company was the last to break contact with the Chinese on Hill 1282, where Easy Company had been nearly destroyed.

Close-air support made it possible. Dispatched to provide it were 96 fighter-bombers from Yonpo airfield and another 184 carrier-based planes from Task Force 77 in the Sea of Japan.[34]

Low-flying Corsairs pinned down enemy soldiers on Hill 1282 – first with dummy runs and then with live ones – enabling the Fifth's George Company to withdraw without any casualties and join the rest of Lieutenant Colonel Robert Taplett's 3rd Battalion.[35]

Lieutenant Colonel Harold Roise's 2nd Battalion manned the regiments' "rear wall" while the other units began moving south down the MSR. It had relieved Lieutenant Colonel William Harris's battalion of the Seventh Marines on the perimeter.[36]

Left behind as the Chinese began converging on Yudam-ni from the surrounding hilltops, Roise's men burned supplies and gear that had not been loaded onto the convoy, but could not be permitted to fall into the enemy's hands. They began to feel isolated and some of them despaired, fearing that they were to be sacrificed.[37]

The Chinese grew bolder. They entered the village outskirts and began to dig through the smoldering debris for food and warm clothing.

Captain Franklin Mayer, Roise's headquarters commander, nervously watched Roise chain-smoking in his jeep, hoping at any moment to get the word to pull out.

"We were all pretty rattled by this time," Mayer said. They feared that the Chinese might interpose themselves between Roise's battalion and the tail end of the column already marching down the MSR.

VMO-6 conducted an emergency medical evacuation from Yudam-ni at dusk on December 1; the HO3s-1 helicopter's landing and takeoff were illuminated by jeep headlights.[38]

"By the time dusk fell, all of us in the aid station were beginning to act like men who were doomed," said Dr Henry Litvin, the battalion surgeon. "It all seemed so hopeless ... What was our little chopped up battalion going to do against such a huge force? We were agonizingly aware that the Chinese could swallow us in a single bite."[39]

Harris's 3rd Battalion of the Seventh made the first moves during the withdrawal. Three miles south of the village, it attacked Hill 1419 east of the MSR, also known as Turkey Hill. It was to be the jumping off point for a bold overland attempt by Lieutenant Colonel Ray Davis to relieve Fox Hill.

Harris's men also assaulted Hill 1542, on the west side of the MSR. It and Turkey Hill comprised the so-called "gateway" to Toktong Pass and Hagaru-ri.[40]

Taplett's 3rd Battalion of the Fifth Marines and Davis's battalion would carry out a two-faceted tactical move southward toward Toktong Pass.

Taplett's "Dark Horse" battalion – another radio call sign nickname – and Davis's battalion would be enshrined in the 1st Division's Chosin Reservoir annals after the events in the days ahead.

If all went according to plan, they would meet atop Toktong Pass, breaking the siege of Fox Company.

At 3pm on December 1, Taplett's battalion marched out of Yudam-ni after a three-day standoff with the Chinese on Hill 1282, where the Marines held one side of the ridge, and the Chinese held the other. Until Taplett's men pulled out, the enemies, who could not see one another, exchanged mortar fire and volleys of grenades.[41]

Several thousand Marines streamed out of Yudam-ni, either afoot or, if wounded or frostbitten, aboard some of the several hundred assorted vehicles in the convoy, some of them pitted by bullets.

"The troops felt badly about pulling out," said Major Hank Woessner of Litzenberg's staff. "The general attitude was that we should stay where we were and inflict more death and destruction on the enemy."[42]

Sleepless, bearded, haggard, clad in filthy clothes, and many of them limping from frostbite, the Marines slogged along at a tortoise's pace toward Toktong Pass and Hagaru-ri.

There would be no stopping, except when fighting forced the column to halt, sometimes for long periods. During those interludes, whenever possible the men slept on their feet or slumped against the convoy's vehicles.

They were battered but unbeaten. Captain Milton Hull, Dog Company's commander, "was bloody, limping, but walking ... He had a patch over one eye," said Woessner.

Dense columns of smoke rose from Yudam-ni into the sullen gray sky as engineers burned what had been left behind. The Chinese moved in as soon as the Marines pulled back.[43]

Corsairs and Skyraiders hovered overhead, providing close-air support for the breakout to Hagaru-ri. They were guided by forward air observers traveling in the column and accompanying the flanking units assigned to clear the hills.

The pilots followed the MSR's serpentine path through a series of narrow canyons and circled over the column, sometimes 40 to 60 planes at once.

VMO-6 directed 13 air strikes; reported sightings of five Chinese platoons, two companies, and three battalions; and evacuated 23 casualties.

Enemy snipers targeted the truck drivers, and replacement drivers were in great demand.[44]

Lieutenant Patrick Roe, an intelligence officer with the Seventh Marines' 3rd Battalion, later wrote, "No one ever doubted the troops from Yudam-ni would make it, but there was always a question of how many would."[45]

General Smith's *Aide Memoirs* declared that it was essential that a mobile column, such as now trod the MSR south of Yudam-ni, occupy the "shoulders" of a corridor flanked by mountainous terrain.

This solution, wrote Smith, was similar to that used by the French in the North African Riff Campaign of 1925.

The French mobile column had consisted of four infantry battalions supported by artillery, service troops, and supply trains. They traveled in a diamond formation, self-supporting and screened by mounted partisans.

The Marines of 1950 substituted infantry companies augmented by artillery and close-air support for the mounted French partisans.[46]

Taplett's men passed through Harris's battalion at Turkey Hill to take the lead on the MSR with Yudam-ni's lone tank, Pershing No. D-23. Harris's battalion waged a fierce battle to capture Hill 1542 and Turkey Hill (Hill 1419) on either side of the MSR, screening the advance of Taplett's battalion.

By nightfall, however, Harris's Item and George Companies were stalled on the eastern slope of Hill 1542. How Company managed to capture Turkey Hill, with the aid of Able and Baker Companies of Lieutenant Colonel Davis's 1st Battalion.

During the night, three Chinese companies that were under orders "to annihilate the defending enemy before daylight," assaulted Item and George Companies.

The relentless attacks culminated in a Chinese "inverted wedge" attack at 4:30am on December 2 that produced large numbers of casualties on both sides.

George Company was on high ground south of Yudam-ni when the Chinese struck. Pfc Fred Davidson had just made himself comfortable in his sleeping bag when he heard shouting and shooting.

"I saw white blurs running past on the right. I raised the rifle but it wouldn't fire," he said. An enemy soldier ran straight at him, and Davidson struck him in the head with the rifle, breaking the stock in two.

Davidson discovered that the Chinese soldier had bayoneted him in the side. Upon further investigation, Davidson saw why: his attacker was out of ammunition.[47]

By morning, George and Item Companies mustered fewer than 200 men between them.[48]

East of the MSR and halfway to Toktong Pass, Item Company fought a grim battle to capture Hill 1520 – actually a mountain that was nearly a mile high.

The desperate Chinese attacks on the hill inspired furious Marine counterattacks. After one enemy assault, platoon Sergeant William

Windrich of Item Company, leading a squad, counterattacked a knob held by grenade-throwing enemy troops.

Despite a serious head injury received while fighting hand-to-hand, and with seven of his 12 men also wounded, Windrich organized a second counterattack and pulled to safety wounded and dying men. Hit again, this time in the legs, Windrich refused evacuation and continued to lead his men in repulsing repeated enemy attacks.

Then, weakened by blood loss, Windrich collapsed in the snow and died a short time later. Windrich was posthumously awarded the Congressional Medal of Honor.[49]

Because of Item Company's severe losses, Sergeant James Johnson, an artilleryman fighting as an infantryman, took over as a platoon leader.

When his platoon was ordered to withdraw, Johnson ably supervised the withdrawal, providing covering fire. He was last seen alive while embroiled in a close-combat grenade exchange. Johnson, like Windrich, was awarded the Congressional Medal of Honor posthumously.[50]

Item Company paid a frightful cost on Hill 1520, losing all of its officers except for Lieutenant Willard Peterson, who became the company commander. Item claimed that it inflicted enemy losses of 342 men.

Reduced to platoon size by daylight December 2, Item was sent to reinforce George Company, which by then was in even worse shape, with fewer than 20 able-bodied men.

The beat-up remnants were placed in reserve with a provisional platoon composed of communications, mess, and staff personnel. Taplett's two spent companies were replaced by the "Damnation Battalion," itself a composite of two depleted rifle companies, artillerymen, and a weapons company.[51]

The grinding advance proceeded hill by hill, scarcely covering a few miles during the first day. The "Damnation Battalion" encountered a blown bridge over a ravine teeming with enemy troops armed with machine guns. The column stopped.

Marine close-air support came to the aid of the stalled convoy. Twelve Corsairs circling above swooped down on the ravine, wiping out the Chinese.

The bridge was repaired, and the column moved on.[52]

"It was a ragtag-looking bunch," said Major Woessner, describing the filthy, bearded Marines streaming south from Yudam-ni. "It looked like the Spirit of '76."

Two miles from the MSR, 1,000 or more Chinese were spotted in the hills. Corsairs plastered them with napalm, bombs, and rockets.[53]

Captain Lyle Bradley, a Corsair pilot with VMF-214, acted as Major Ken Reusser's wing man as they flew in low visibility and falling snow beneath a 400-foot ceiling.

Bradley and Reusser were the only pilots in their squadron who were able to start their planes in the extreme cold that gripped Yonpo airfield that morning. They did it by first draining all of the oil from their engines, and then putting it back in.

Once they were airborne in the hills bracketing the MSR, which was shrouded by falling snow, they spotted a group of Chinese troops in white quilt uniforms.

Forward air controller Dunkirk 1-4 directed Bradley to an enemy mortar position behind one of the hills. Bradley flew so low that "it seemed that I was skimming the treetops."

Seeing footprints in the snow and men in the forest below, Bradley was cleared to drop his bombs in an area paralleling the road. Because of the low cloud ceiling, the drop would have to be made from 300 feet.

"The blast was so loud with the canopy open that I couldn't tell whether or the not the plane was being hit," Bradley said.

Dunkirk 1-4 radioed Bradley, "Looks like a perfect hit ... we love you Corsair people."[54]

In the middle of the convoy was the 100-vehicle medical train. The wounded, most of whom had received only rudimentary treatment and little food, were layered three deep in the truck beds, separated by cut timber slotted through the sides of the trucks.

They were unable to get out to urinate, and relieving themselves was an ordeal anyway, with having to sort through multiple clothing layers. Empty plasma bottles were passed around in the trucks for use as human waste receptacles.[55]

The walking wounded guarded the convoy, fending off any enemy soldiers who managed to draw too close to the column. Only serious cases were permitted to ride: men with gut wounds, the blind, those with critical leg wounds, and those with severe frostbite that would require amputation. Many of the truck-bound asked to be armed for the trip.

Navy Commander Horace Epes, who led *Leyte*-based VF-33, said his squadron sometimes caught the Chinese in the open.

"I vividly recall catching a couple of Red soldiers hot-footing it down the road carrying a long pole with a big kettle of what looked like soup – that no one ever drank."[56]

The Chinese sent reinforcements to Turkey Hill overnight December 1–2, and recaptured it at 3am. However, they were driven off it after the Seventh Marines' 1st Battalion joined the two-day battle begun by How of the Seventh's 3rd Battalion.

It was imperative that the 1st Battalion secure Turkey Hill before mounting an overland march to relieve Fox Company on Toktong Pass.

The three Chinese companies that had held the hill were wiped out. "There were only 20 men left when we walked down the hill," said Major Zhou Weajiang.[57]

That night, the convoy stopped for no apparent reason amid a heavy snowfall. Lieutenant Colonel Ray Murray, the Fifth Marines' commander, tried to radio someone at the head of the convoy but could not raise anyone.

He got out of his jeep and walked down the MSR until he came to a truck that had stopped. No vehicles were in front of it.

"I got up on the running board of this truck and the driver was sound asleep and so was the man riding beside him ... So, I shook him and woke him up and I never saw a more frightened person in my life. I told him, 'Let's get going down the road.'" The truck quickly caught up with the slow-moving convoy.[58]

When a bridge collapsed under the weight of a truck filled with wounded men, the truck overturned and 20 men were flung into freezing creek water from the truck bed. Lieutenant Morton Silver and his assistant, Paul Swinn, crawled under the truck through the frigid water, freed the trapped men from the tangled chutes and primer cord that had served as their bedding, and pulled them to safety.[59]

Meanwhile, D-23 became stuck in a ditch while trying to back up, but a diesel tractor with a chain extricated the tank.[60]

As the convoy crept through the hills, the Chinese 59th Division stoutly resisted with machine-gun and mortar fire. The Marines smashed through the 59th Division's roadblocks between Yudam-ni and Toktong Pass, one by one.

The weather did not help either. It snowed and that night, temperatures fell to 25 degrees below zero, with the shrieking winds from the north creating a wind chill of minus 50 degrees in the hills.

Chapter 18

The Relief of Fox Company

December 1–2

If this force bogged down, the fate of the Fifth and Seventh remained in doubt. The chances of mishap were everywhere.

Major Fox Parry on Davis's relief effort.[1]

When the troops were told to hold where they were, they fell over like frozen flies. They just couldn't stay on their feet.

Lieutenant Colonel Davis describing the overnight relief march to Fox Company.[2]

Tears came to the eyes of raggedy Marines who had endured bitter cold and savage battle to reach this place of suffering and courage.

Lieutenant Joe Owen, describing the relief column's reaction upon reaching Fox Company.[3]

The Yudam-ni Marines had failed to break through the Chinese roadblocks on the MSR and relieve Barber's Fox Company – besieged by an enemy regiment for four days on Toktong Pass. Reinforcing Fox Company was essential if the convoy were to cross the mountain pass and reach Hagaru-ri.

The failures of the Marines to bludgeon their way to the pass on the MSR prompted Colonel Litzenberg to seek outside-the-box ideas on how to relieve Fox Company.

In his usual blunt way, he ordered his best battalion commander, 35-year-old Lieutenant Colonel Ray Davis of the 1st Battalion, to come up with a plan.

"Nothing works," Litzenberg told Davis. "You have to get to them. The Chinese think we're road-bound. They think we'll stick with our vehicles. And they won't expect us to attack at night."[4]

He ordered Davis to return in 20 minutes with a plan.

Davis returned to Litzenberg's CP with a plan for a cross-country dash over the ridges to the high ground overlooking Fox Hill from the north.

Leaving behind his wounded and cold-injury disabled, all of his vehicles, and the supplies and equipment they could not carry with them, Davis's Marines would bring two 81mm mortars, six .30-caliber machine guns, ammunition strapped to litters, and extra mortar and rocket rounds in their parka pockets.

For sustenance, they would take with them fruit cocktail, peaches in syrup, and chocolate bars – all to provide quick energy. They brought one hand-cranked ANGRC-9 radio because the battery-powered sets were dead.[5]

"Plan approved! Go!" Litzenberg told Davis.

Major Fox Parry, the artillery battery commander, witnessed the meeting of Litzenberg and Davis. He described the plan to reach Fox Company as "a dramatic play fraught with danger. The risks were enormous."[6]

Risky, indeed. "He was sending Davis off into the frigid gloom away from the main body, thus splitting up the undermanned, tired-out force that was already heavily burdened with wounded," said Parry. "If this force bogged down, the fate of the Fifth and Seventh remained in doubt. The chances of mishap were everywhere."[7]

Yet, neither Litzenberg nor Davis betrayed "a hint of passion," said Parry. "They were just two men going about their business."

Davis was a taciturn Georgian who was 12 years into a Marine Corps career that would span three wars. During World War II, he had fought on Guadalcanal, Cape Gloucester, and Peleliu.

Wounded during the first hour of the bloody battle for Peleliu in September 1944, Davis refused evacuation and continued to lead the First Marines' 1st Battalion. It sustained 71 percent casualties in 12 days. Davis was awarded a Navy Cross for having rallied his men to repulse a Japanese penetration of his lines.

Everyone knew that the mission, if successful, could ensure the survival of hundreds of Marines, said Davis.

"Some fellow Marines were in trouble. We were going to rescue them, and nothing was going to stand in our way. Everyone knew this was an important mission. By seizing the pass we would unlock the gate and hold it open for the rest of the Marines in Yudam-ni."

Although exhausted, cold, and underfed, his men were elated to be participating in a scheme upon which rested the fates of the Fifth and Seventh Marines.[8]

Davis would have only a primitive map, the guidance of a star in the southern sky, and star shells fired every three minutes to point the way to Toktong Pass.[9]

He assembled his company officers and, with a stick in the snow, traced the route they would follow.

The launch point for the audacious mission was Turkey Hill. Possession of the massive hill had been hotly contested earlier by Charlie Company and the Chinese, until Charlie was withdrawn.

How Company tried to capture it, but could not do it alone. After Davis reinforced How with his Able and Baker Companies, by 7:30pm on December 1 it was secured.

A blizzard struck as the battalion formed at Turkey Hill for the overland march.

The troops were tired, having all been up since dawn. They were largely unshaven, their skin caked with soot from their fires, and their eyes sunken from lack of sleep. The urine frozen on their pants legs attested to their difficulty in peeling back six layers of clothing to relieve themselves.[10]

Before they moved out, Davis ordered his men to run in place to check for noisy gear. Then every weapon in the Yudam-ni perimeter was fired to divert attention from what Davis's men were daring to attempt.[11]

Davis wanted Lieutenant Chew-Een Lee and his 2nd Platoon of Baker Company to break trail through the knee-high snow drifts.

Although his right arm was still in a cast because of a gunshot wound that he had received a month earlier, the gritty Lee would lead the way over the three ridges that stood between the MSR and Fox Hill, eight miles distant.

Lee, a 24-year-old California native, joined the Marine Corps at the end of World War II, and became the first Chinese-American officer in Corps history. Fluent in Mandarin Chinese, earlier, during the fighting at Sudong, Lee had hurled insults at the enemy in their native tongue, momentarily confusing them.

A wiry 118 pounds and 5 foot 6 inches tall, Lee had incredible stamina and was a natural combat leader. He was a stern officer who did everything by the book, and demanded perfection of his men in all things.

When he had time for it, Lee would boil rice, mix it with condensed milk, and sometimes share it with his men. "It was incredibly delicious, given the circumstances," said Corpsman William Davis.[12]

He set the highest standard for himself. Lee later said, "I was never in my sleeping bag myself. Whenever there's an attack, I expect the officers to be on their feet and move from position to position, and influence the action."[13]

On November 2, Lee was wounded in the right elbow during the Sudong fight, when he single-handedly knocked out a Chinese bunker.

After being evacuated to an Army field hospital in Hungnam, Lee and a wounded Marine sergeant broke out of the hospital, intending to rejoin their units.

They stole a jeep from the motor pool at gunpoint, and drove it up the MSR until it veered off the road, landing on its wheels. An Army ambulance drove Lee and the sergeant the rest of the way up the MSR to Baker Company.[14]

Guided by the bright star on the southern horizon, Davis's column moved out from Turkey Hill at 9pm December 1 on its mission to relieve Fox Company.

It was windier and colder up in the hills than it was at Yudam-ni, where the recorded temperature was minus 26 degrees. Davis believed that the wind chill might have made the temperature feel as cold as 75 below in the ridges.[15]

Carrying 80 pounds of gear, two-thirds of his body weight, Lee led the half-mile-long file of 500 men that included Davis's battalion and How Company into the snow-covered highlands.

Baker Company was on point, followed by Davis's command post, and then Able, Charlie, and How companies. How, which had sustained heavy casualties that day at Turkey Hill, was a last-minute addition; this came as an unpleasant surprise to How's survivors, who had thought they were to be relieved.[16]

To make himself visible to his men, the diminutive Lee wore two electric-pink target panels.

Behind Lee trudged Davis's battalion, described by one Marine as "a chain-gang of zombies, blindly following the man in front."

On the ridges' steep slopes, the footing was not too bad for the men breaking trail through snow that in places was waist-deep, and for those immediately behind them.

But after their feet had tamped down the snow, the path became a sheet of ice. Men slipped and fell, to the accompaniment of angry curses and groans.[17]

The Marines climbed steep finger ridges on their hands and knees, only to tumble down the icy slopes on the other side.

The star on the southern horizon and star shells fired from Yudam-ni were supposed to help keep the column on course as it pushed deeper into the hills. Snow, darkness, and intervening hills, however, often concealed both the lodestar and the star shells from view.

"Time had no meaning," wrote Lieutenant Joe Owen, who commanded a mortar platoon. "We labored through infinite darkness in ghostly clouds of snow over an icy path that rose and fell but seemed to lead nowhere. We saw only the back of the man ahead, a hunched figure in a long, shapeless parka, whose every tortured step was an act of will."[18]

Early in the march, Davis mingled with Able Company, where he found "men already completely exhausted and in a state of collapse. I asked them what outfit they were from and they could not even answer. I'd shake them bodily to try and arouse them."[19]

Trudging through the valleys without the anticipated visual guides, the column veered off-course, and began drifting to the southwest, toward the MSR.

Having destroyed the three Army battalions east of Chosin Reservoir, the Chinese 9th Army Group redoubled its efforts to annihilate the 1st Marine Division at Yudam-ni, Hagaru-ri, and Koto-ri.

In a telegram sent December 2, Mao Tse-Tung wrote that he "really hope[s] Song and Tao [Song Shilum and Tao Yong, the 9th's commander and assistant commander] should pay all their attention to the great advantage of wiping out the encircled US 1st Marine Division through tonight and tomorrow night."

The 9th's 26th Army, held in reserve, had been sent from the Yalu River to relieve the 20th and 27th Armies. It was expected to arrive on December 3. Until that time, the 20th and 27th were to continue their encirclement of the Marine division.[20]

Three Chinese divisions, gutted by casualties sustained during five days of contact with the Marines, remained in action in the Yudam-ni area: the 20th Army's 59th and 89th Divisions, and the 27th Army's 79th Division.

The 20th Army's 58th Division was besieging Hagaru-ri, while its 60th Division, which had mauled Task Force Drysdale in Hellfire Valley, continued to man roadblocks between Hagaru-ri and Koto-ri.[21]

Lieutenant Lee's view of the star shells was obstructed by the terrain, and he stopped to get a compass bearing. This inadvertently triggered an "accordion effect" in the file behind him, where Marines collided with one another, some of them falling on the icy trail.

For the men in the column, it was an exhausting slog through the snow-covered hills. Snow fell steadily, and it was so pitch-black in the valleys that many of the Marines plodded on with one hand on the man's shoulder in front of him.

"Ray Davis went up and down the line. 'Don't sit down, don't go to sleep,' he would say," said Pfc Harold St John.[22]

"Not a distinguished terrain feature was to be seen" with snow pelting down in the stygian darkness, said Lieutenant Joe Owen.[23]

"It is pretty difficult to read a compass at night," Lee acknowledged. "I veered off to the right."[24]

Concerned about the column's drift that he thought he detected, Davis "got down into a Chinese gun pit with a map, compass, and flashlight, under a poncho, to plot our route.

"Getting up out of the hole, I lost my bearings and could not reconstruct what I had done while I was in the hole. It was that numbing cold."

He made another attempt, this time with a staff officer close by, to whom he relayed the bearings before he could forget them.[25]

Now certain that his column had strayed off-course and risked walking into their own artillery fire, Davis attempted to relay a warning to Lee at the head of the column.

The message did not reach Lee. The Marines' sound-muffling parka hoods, the terrain, and the bitter cold winds foiled the attempt.

Davis decided to charge to the head of the column with his radioman and runner, and to remedy the potentially dangerous situation in person. It took him an hour to get there, beating along a path parallel to the column. On the way, he was berated and cursed for making too much noise, and told to "pipe down."[26]

"I was in good shape and I was dying," said Lieutenant William Davis of Able Company. "All the 18-year-old kids were moaning and groaning. And here was Davis humping up and down. He was phenomenal ... He was a very unassuming man. He wasn't a runner, he wasn't an athlete, he was just a doer ..."[27]

Davis sent his runner ahead, but a non-commissioned officer collared him for being too noisy.

Owen was moving beside the column, taking a message from Lee to Lieutenant Joe Kurcaba behind him, when "I collided with a Marine churning forward through the snow. As we both recovered our balance, I recognized Colonel Davis. He had run forward, concerned that we had veered off our azimuth. The men, not recognizing the colonel in the darkness, hissed at him to keep down the noise."[28]

"What's the holdup, lieutenant?" Davis asked Owen as he continued to the head of the column.

Reaching Lee on point, Davis ordered a halt while he took a compass reading and made a course correction.[29]

When they heard Chinese soldiers conversing nearby and smelled cooking food, the prospect of contact with the enemy had "an adrenalin effect," said Owen. "The men became sure-footed, alert."[30]

After crossing the next ridge and entering a meadow with rock outcroppings, the Marines came under fire. As Owen's mortarmen and the machine gunners set up on an outcropping, riflemen passed through in two columns, each man dropping off the 81mm round that he carried in his voluminous parka pocket. The mortars were fired one after the other.

Hurling grenades, the riflemen overran the enemy position, driving away the defenders – all but those who chose to stay and fight, and they were all killed.[31]

"We had to keep moving," said Davis. "If you paused at all, the troops would kind of fall out. If they stayed down in that snow very long, they would be gone."

Nearby enemy soldiers wounded several Marines with long-range rifle fire. Davis believed they might have been firing merely to keep up their morale, and had not really seen the Marines.

Pfc St John was shot in the arm, suffering nerve damage. A corpsman put a battle dressing on the wound, removed an ampule of morphine from his mouth, where he had kept it thawed, and gave him a shot. St John was able to continue the trek to Fox Company.[32]

Davis did not understand why the Chinese did not hear his men, though, "with our assorted moans and groans, and crying out from occasional rifle rounds that hit into Marine parkas and soft Marine flesh."

That almost included Davis, who took a round through his parka hood that grazed his forehead and knocked him to the ground.[33]

The column rearguard, How Company, which was carrying the wounded, came under attack, and two platoons were dispatched from Baker and Charlie Companies to bail it out.

After they escorted How to the main column, the Marines took an overdue rest break a mile north of Fox Company and awaited daybreak there. The men had been in action for 20 hours straight.[34]

"When the troops were told to hold where they were, they fell over like frozen flies," said Davis. "They just couldn't stay on their feet."

Davis's officers and NCOs organized small patrols to maintain a state of vigilance. Each company had teams of NCOs that kept some of the men alert until sunrise.[35]

Davis contacted Litzenberg's CP with his hand-cranked radio, requesting that it notify Fox Company that Davis's men would attempt to establish contact at first light. Davis did not want to risk an exchange of "friendly fire" in the dark.[36]

The two-hour break gave the men "newfound strength," said Davis.

The Chinese suffered grievously in the severe cold and wind. One of Davis's sergeants led him to an enemy foxhole and pulled out what appeared to be a block of ice, but which was a Chinese soldier.

"Is he dead?" Davis asked. The sergeant said that the man's eyes were moving. Nearby, they found an enemy outpost, with a half-dozen soldiers frozen in their holes, all dead.[37]

The deep arctic cold affected the men's ability to speak and even think.

"My mind was so numbed that when I did get my commanders together for a talk ... I made them repeat to me what I had said to them," said Davis.[38]

When the march resumed at daybreak, Lieutenant Harrol Kiser's 1st Platoon took the lead from Lee and his 2nd Platoon.[39]

The head of the column was fired upon as it approached Hill 1653, known as Rocky Ridge, en route to the Fox perimeter. Mortars plastered the ridge, and Captain Barber called in an air strike. Kiser's platoon overran the Chinese entrenchments, closely followed by Lee's men.

"In that battle I felt absolutely exhilarated," said Lee. "By the time we got to the top of the hill, I could not move my legs, [which were] like lead. If an enemy solder had stood up and poked a finger at me, I thought I would have fallen over. I was 24 and thought it was my age."[40]

It wasn't Lee's age, it was the 4,000-foot elevation and the fact that he hadn't slept in more than a day.

Davis reached Captain Barber on the radio. Barber "brought tears to my eyes," Davis said, when he offered to send a patrol to lead Davis's men into Fox Company's lines.

"We knew where he was, and we would fight our way in, I told him," Davis said.

To ease Davis's entry into the Fox perimeter, Barber's forward artillery observer, Lieutenant Don Campbell, ordered How Battery in Hagaru-ri to fire 105mm rounds all along Fox's perimeter – except at Davis's entry point – while Fox's forward air controller summoned close-air support.[41]

Davis ordered Baker Company to lead the way into Fox Company's perimeter.

The Baker Marines forgot their exhaustion in their excitement at having accomplished their perilous mission. They *ran* the last yards to Fox Hill. It was 11:25am on December 2, the morning after the fifth night of Fox's encirclement.

With "a wild cheer, we broke forward in a jubilant run," Lieutenant Owen said. The Fox Company Marines also cheered, waving blue, yellow, and red parachute fabric from the supply airdrops.[42]

"They sprinted through the snow with a speed that seemed to mock the awful night that had passed, and they burst into Fox Company's lines with shouts and grins," Robert Leckie wrote in *The March to Glory*.[43]

"We were astonished by our first view of Fox Hill," wrote Owen. Blood, trash, and hundreds of Chinese corpses and body parts covered the hillside, the result of the nights of intensive fighting.

Davis's men now saw the toll exacted by Fox Company in its desperate defense against 10-to-1 odds. "Thick bands" of dead Chinese lay before the Marine guns.

"Many of them seemed asleep under blankets of drifted snow, but their bodies were frozen in spasms of pain," Owen said.

"A white-clad column had fallen in the formation that had attracted the attention of Fox Company's machine gunners," he said. "Craters of dirt and snow made by the big guns at Hagaru-ri were rimmed with bodies and parts of men."

Along the perimeter, the enemy dead were stacked four or five high to protect the Marines' foxholes

"We stood in wonder" before the scene of death and slaughter, said Owen. "Men bowed their heads in prayer. Some fell to their knees. Others breathed quiet oaths of disbelief. Tears came to the eyes of raggedy Marines who had endured bitter cold and savage battle to reach this place of suffering and courage."[44]

Many of the living wore arm slings and blood-soaked compresses; others hobbled around on makeshift leg splints. The recently killed, wrapped in parachute cloth, were stacked outside the aid tents.[45]

Fox Company had suffered 118 casualties: 26 killed, 89 wounded, three missing. Six of its seven officers were wounded. Just 82 of Fox's original 246 men remained able to fight.[46]

An 18-year-old Texan in the relief column had categorically refused to go further after the column's rest break. When persuasion didn't work, he was put in a makeshift straitjacket and his comrades carried him the last mile on a stretcher.

His condition worsened throughout the morning, but there were no visible signs of an injury. Navy doctor Lieutenant Peter Ariola, who had accompanied Davis's column from Yudam-ni, was baffled.

A few hours later, to everyone's amazement, the Marine died. His body was added to the dead Marines outside the aid tent.

Ariola was the first Navy doctor on Fox Hill. Until his arrival, the many wounded had been treated by Fox Company's competent Navy corpsmen.

Ariola was just getting to work when a Chinese sniper shot him in the back when Ariola poked his head out of the aid tent to speak to someone. The bullet killed him instantly.

Marines carried Ariola's body to the place where the dead were laid and set it down beside the young Texan's corpse.[47]

Chapter 19

Entering Hagaru-ri

Look at those bastards! Those magnificent bastards!

A Navy surgeon was heard to say when the Marines marched into Hagaru-ri.[1]

Some were without hats, their ears blue in the frost. A few walked to the doctor's tent barefoot because they couldn't get their frostbitten feet into their frozen shoe pacs.

Correspondent Marguerite Higgins's description of the Yudam-ni Marines after they arrived in Hagaru-ri.[2]

Our troubles are over. We've got it made. The Chinese don't stand a chance.

Colonel Alpha Bowser, 1st Division operations officer, as the Yudam-ni Marines reached Hagaru-ri.[3]

Davis's battalion was now behind the Chinese divisions intent on destroying the convoy from Yudam-ni that was marching south on the MSR.

The convoy's progress had been painstakingly slow throughout December 2 as the Marines cleared the high ground of enemy soldiers on both sides of the road. The column pushed on until 2am December 3, when it stopped 1,000 yards from Fox Hill.[4]

Aboard the Task Force 77 carriers and at Yonpo airfield, ice and snow greatly complicated the task of dispatching squadrons to the battle zone and retrieving the fighter-bombers when they returned.

Snow and extreme cold beset Yonpo. Sea squalls and ice slowed air operations on the carriers and escort carriers.

On the *Baedoeng Strait*, flight deck crews scraped off 3 inches of ice three mornings in a row. The *Sicily* was compelled to stop flight operations one day because of 75mph winds and green seas over-washing the ship's bow.

Planes were lost. Pilots that ditched at sea had just 20 minutes before fatal hypothermia set in.[5]

As the division emerged from the Yudam-ni valley, 10,000 enemy troops were spotted west of Hagaru-ri, and another large body of Chinese to the southwest.

Air strikes hammered the formations with napalm, rockets, and machine-gun fire, inflicting an estimated 70 percent to 80 percent casualties on the enemy troops. The air strikes were just some of the 255 sorties flown that day.[6]

The Chinese especially feared napalm. "When we used napalm, packs went one way, rifles another, and the enemy took off," said Lieutenant Daniel Green, a forward air controller with the Fifth Marines.[7]

At daylight on December 3, a large number of Chinese troops approached on the skyline, poised to strike the column. Hundreds more were spotted two miles away, also marching toward the MSR.

Eight Corsairs shot through a hole in the heavy overcast and with machine-gun fire drove the enemy soldiers over the hill crest. There, pilots observed gun emplacements with interconnecting trenchworks.

They napalmed the Chinese that were caught in the open and, when they took shelter in some woods, the pilots napalmed the woods.

"We were cleared to hit everything up there," said VMF-214 pilot Bill Witt. "We were loaded with rockets and machine guns. It was a slaughter – they were bailing out and skiing down the mountain to surrender. The division was begging us to shoot them before they could get down to them – they just could not handle them."[8]

At least 500 enemy soldiers died in the bloodbath that became known as "The Great Slaughter."[9]

On Fox Hill during the morning of December 3, Davis reorganized his four companies into two attack forces consisting of Companies "A" and "B," and Companies "C" and "H." They expanded Fox Company's perimeter and cleared both sides of Toktong Pass and the finger ridges pointing toward Hagaru-ri.

The adjustments were made to ease the passage of the convoy approaching from Yudam-ni. Davis ordered small fires built inside the perimeter to attract fire from enemy soldiers, whose positions could then be pinpointed and wiped out.[10]

The patrols sent to clear the pass flushed the last intact battalion of the Chinese 59th Division. It blundered into the path of the column approaching from Yudam-ni.

When Colonel Litzenberg was informed, he turned to Lieutenant Colonel Murray and said, "Ray, notify your 3rd Battalion commander that the Chinese are running southwest into his arms."[11]

Trapped between Major Tom Tighe's Companies "A" and "B" of Davis's battalion, and Lieutenant Colonel Robert Taplett's 3rd Battalion of the Fifth Marines, the Chinese stopped in their tracks and looked around in confusion.

With the enemy battalion pinioned between the two battalions, Lieutenant Campbell, the Fox Company forward artillery observer, and Taplett's FAC summoned artillery fire from Hagaru-ri and from the rear of the convoy.

The barrage decimated the Chinese battalion. Taplett then called in an air strike that wiped out the survivors with rockets and napalm.[12]

By 10:30am on the 3rd, the 59th Division battalion ceased to exist as a result of what was described as "probably the greatest slaughter of the breakout."

It was, in the vernacular of the Chosin Marines, a "turkey shoot." More than 500 Chinese soldiers died.[13]

While the Chinese were being annihilated northwest of Fox Hill, Davis personally led Charlie and How Companies in a sweep of the hills east and northeast of the pass. The attack cleared the way for the convoy to proceed to Hagaru-ri.[14]

That morning, a two-seat helicopter approached Fox Hill to evacuate a wounded Marine. It suddenly began gyrating in the sky, and crashed in flames against a hillside. The pilot, Lieutenant Robert Longstaff, was killed.[15]

The union of Davis's 1st Battalion and Taplett's 3rd Battalion was complete by 1pm. The Marines made preparations for the final segment of the march to Hagaru-ri, with Davis's men leading the column.[16]

The badly wounded and the frostbitten from the Fox Hill battles were squeezed into trucks in the convoy that were already filled with the seriously wounded from Yudam-ni and the breakout battles. The ambulatory wounded walked.

Among the latter was twice-wounded Lieutenant Elmo Peterson, shot the first time in the shoulder and later in the back, with the bullet lodging in his abdominal cavity. Peterson and another lieutenant – the only two Fox Company officers still on their feet – took charge of the 100 or so Fox Marines still able to walk.[17]

That left the problem of disposing of Fox Company's dead. The bodies were first checked for signs of life by holding a mirror to their mouths to determine whether they were still breathing.

Some of them were buried on Fox Hill or beside the MSR in a "hasty field burial" after identification and personal effects were collected. The rest were secured to vehicles in the convoy.[18]

Davis's battalion, with the lone Pershing tank at its head, led the seven-mile march down Toktong Pass to Hagaru-ri.

Colonel Litzenberg walked beside his jeep, which was full of wounded Marines. The Fifth Marines came next, with the Seventh Marines' 3rd Battalion bringing up the rear. Two VMO-6 observation planes circled overhead to warn of any enemy ahead.[19]

Prime movers – tracked vehicles used to move field pieces –were towing eight 155mm howitzers when they ran out of fuel around 2am on December 4. It was 25 below zero.

"The cold was excruciating to all personnel who had no way to seek relief from it," the Fifth Marines special action report said.

The hulking prime movers had to be pushed off the road so that the rest of the convoy could proceed to Hagaru-ri; an air strike later destroyed them.

Ironically, just one-half mile farther down the MSR there was a cache of airdropped diesel fuel that would have enabled the prime movers to refuel and reach Hagaru-ri.[20]

The delay gave the Chinese an opportunity to throw up a new roadblock and blow a bridge. They raked the convoy with gunfire, and an intensive firefight erupted, lasting until daylight, when close-air support arrived overhead.

The combination of pointblank fire from a 105mm howitzer and a 75mm recoilless rifle, air strikes, and a ground attack by a Marine rifle platoon from Hagaru-ri crushed enemy resistance. When the gunfire ended, 150 Chinese soldiers lay dead.[21]

The 41 Commando and a tank platoon accompanied by Marine riflemen were sent from Hagaru-ri at 4:30pm to drive Chinese troops from a hill near the village's first checkpoint.

The Commandos trotted out "in perfect order." "They looked so neat and clean and militarily ship-shape," said Lieutenant Patrick Roe. "We were all filthy, with ripped parkas that had lard all over the front from spilled C-rations. Our hair was all matted, our faces bearded and grimy, our lips cracked."

A clean-shaven, crisply attired British Commando lieutenant stiffly saluted Lieutenant Joe Owen and asked him where to set up his machine guns. With the Commando lieutenant was a mustachioed sergeant "whose proper military bearing could have come straight from the pages of Kipling."

Before Owen could reply to the lieutenant's query, Corpsman Ed Toppel, who had been limping for two days from a bullet in his leg, snapped back, "We don't give a goddamn where you set up your goddamn machine guns. Just do it so we can go someplace and get warm!"[22]

Six hundred yards from the Hagaru-ri perimeter, Davis's men stopped. Some of the ambulatory wounded in the trucks joined the walking wounded on the road.

Davis formed them into a route column, and they dressed ranks and threw back their shoulders. They resumed their approach to the perimeter, their feet pounding the frozen ground in unison.

"Thinking of everything these Marines had done," Davis began singing the "Marines Hymn." It was picked up by the men near him, and soon the entire battalion was singing it at the tops of their lungs.

"It sounds corny as hell, but I cried," Davis said. "I was never so proud to be a Marine in my life as I was right then, to be there with those men."[23]

From still contested East Hill on the northeast edge of Hagaru-ri, the men in Captain Carl Sitter's George Company of the First Marines saw the spectacle unfold below them.

The Seventh and Fifth Marines were coming in, Sitter's men shouted back and forth. When the strains of the "Marines Hymn" reached their ears, they began singing along from East Hill.[24]

General Smith said the sight of his regiments marching toward Hagaru-ri was "quite an emotional experience for both those in the column and for those who met the column at the road block on the perimeter ... The trucks and jeeps were peppered with bullet holes and gashed with shrapnel. Wounded men were stuffed in layers in the backs of the trucks; other were lashed across the hoods of jeeps or tied to the fenders."[25]

Smith and Colonel Alpha Bowser, Smith's operations officer, heaved sighs of relief. "Our troubles are over. We've got it made," Bowser said. "The Chinese don't stand a chance."

Smith replied, "Bowser, those Chinese never did stand a chance."[26]

Smith believed that when the Fifth and Seventh Marines marched into Hagaru-ri, "the critical part of the operation had been completed ... We would fight our way down to Koro-ri, where we would gain additional strength."

Although the two regiments were battered, "this was a very powerful force," Smith said. "It was well-supplied with ammunition, fuel, and rations; was powerfully supported by Marine and carrier-based air; possessed organically artillery, tanks, and the wide gamut of infantry weapons."[27]

As the haggard, bearded, filthy Marines entered Hagaru-ri, it was indeed an emotional moment. The Marines inside the perimeter greeted them warmly with tears in their eyes

A Navy surgeon, Dr Robert Harvey, was heard to say, "Look at those bastards! Those magnificent bastards!"[28]

"Our parkas were all stained with blood, food, gun oil, and dirt," said Lieutenant Joe Owen. "Our filthy faces were matted with bristly beards that bore icicles of mucous and spittle."[29]

Nineteen-year-old Pfc Win Scott of the Fifth Marines' Charlie Company, wounded on North Ridge outside Yudam-ni during the first night of the Chinese attacks, rode into Hagaru-ri on a litter atop a trailer pulled by a jeep.

During the second day of the breakout from Yudam-ni, the man next to Scott died. Dead men that were frozen stiff lay all around Scott during his three days in the truck convoy.

"Bodies were strapped on the barrels of artillery, on the sides of trucks, across hoods, anywhere there was space," he said.[30]

Lieutenant Elmo Peterson led a group of 30 or more Fox Company Marines to the front of the line of vehicles, intending to intercept any Chinese troops that tried to interfere with the column as it neared Hagaru-ri. When they were yards away, Peterson warned the Marines inside the perimeter of their approach so that they would not get shot.

Peterson went straight to sick bay to have his wounded shoulder examined. It was badly infected, and Peterson was flown out of Hagaru-ri.[31]

The convoy's vanguard slogged the dangerous 14 miles from Yudam-ni to Hagaru-ri in 59 hours; Davis's battalion entered the perimeter at 7pm on December 3.

The column continued to pass into the perimeter for 20 hours, all night and into the next day. The last of them, the Seventh's 3rd Battalion, arrived at 2pm on December 4, 79 hours after leaving Yudam-ni.[32]

Leaving Yudam-ni with about 600 wounded men riding in or lashed to the convoy's jeeps and trucks, medical personnel and chaplains collected hundreds of additional wounded along the way from the hill fighting along the MSR and from Fox Company.

They reached Hagaru-ri with more than 1,500 battle casualties, plus another 1,000 non-battle casualties – mostly cold weather injuries.[33]

General Field Harris, the 1st Marine Air Wing commander, wrote to the commander of Task Force 77, Admiral Richard Ewen, of the Marines' escape from Yudam-ni: "They thanked God for the air. I don't think they could have made it as units without air support. The next job is to get them off this hill ... Can use all the help you can give us until they get down. Tell your pilots they are doing a magnificent job."[34]

The 1st Division and X Corps recognized the crucial role played by close-air support in their battles with the Chinese. The "flying artillery" countered the enemy's overwhelming numbers and prevented the breakout from descending into chaos and disaster.

General Smith extolled the aviators. "Never in its history has Marine Aviation given more convincing proof of its indispensable value to the ground Marines."[35]

Capitalizing on close-air support's vital importance, Task Force 77 augmented its presence in the Sea of Japan with the fast carrier *Princeton* and the escort carrier *Sicily*, recalled from Japan. They joined the escort carriers *Baedoeng Strait* (code-named "Bing-Ding") and *Bataan*, and the fast carriers *Leyte, Valley Forge*, and *Philippine Sea*.[36]

For the next phase of the withdrawal, planners drew heavily on the close-air support paradigm that was so successful during the Yudam-ni breakout.

They added two airborne tactical air controllers to fly Corsairs ahead of and on each side of the column as it marched south. On the ground, forward air controllers would accompany the convoy and each flanking battalion.

Finally, all day long a four-engine Douglas R5D Skymaster transport with three controllers aboard would float above the entire scene – an airborne Tactical Air Direction Center. It would dispatch all support aircraft that were aloft and assign them to ground-based forward and tactical air controllers. It was a pioneering innovation.[37]

The Marines that marched into Hagaru-ri from Yudam-ni stood in line for up to four hours for pancakes, bacon, and powdered eggs, while their comrades were receiving treatment for their wounds in the hospital tents. Blood streaked the ground between the medical facilities and the airstrip's evacuation site.[38]

"There was a pile of cardboard cartons. We ripped off a couple of chunks of cardboard. We took out our spoons and started eating pancakes," said Corporal Robert Kennedy, a BAR man with the Fifth Marines' Dog Company. But not every man had managed to keep his mess kit spoon.[39]

Lieutenant Roscoe Barrett was stunned while visiting the Marnes' bivouacs when he saw "long lines of bleary-eyed men, half frozen and dazed, eating off pieces of cardboard with their fingers because they had no mess gear."

Others wandered around or slept on the frozen ground. Those with battle wounds or frostbite waited in the cold to enter the aid stations.[40]

Kennedy said that his platoon went into a house, lay down on the floor, and went to sleep. "We slept that day, that night, out of the wind and out of the cold, a bug pile of people."[41]

Soon after the arrival of the Fifth and Seventh Marines news correspondents from US, French, and British publications appeared in Hagaru-ri. When word reached them of the Marines' predicament, the reporters boarded transport planes sent to Hagaru-ri to evacuate the seriously wounded to hospitals in Hungnam and Tokyo.[42]

Keyes Beech of the *Chicago Daily News*, who during World War II had been a Marine combat correspondent on Tarawa and Iwo Jima, described the freezing, sleepless Marines who poured into Hagaru-ri from Yudam-ni: "Seldom has the human frame been so savagely punished and continued to function. Many men discovered reserves of strength they never knew they possessed. Some survived and fought on willpower alone."[43]

Beech was shocked by the aged countenance of Dr Eugene Herring, whom he had known during the fighting in Seoul. Herring had treated wounded Marines at Yudam-ni.

"By God, we brought out our wounded," Herring declared to Beech. "We had some of the wounded driving jeeps. We had others strapped across radiators and tied to prime movers ... Some of them lay there in the cold for as long as 72 hours without moving. When we got to Hagaru, the only way you could tell the dead from the living was whether their eyes moved. They were all frozen stiff as boards."[44]

Beech wrote that Lieutenant Colonel Ray Murray, the Fifth Marines commander, appeared to have also aged since Beech had last seen him in Seoul – he was thinner and his cheekbones were more prominent. Murray poured each of them some bourbon in a canteen cup.

"You should have been with us at Yudam-ni. You'd have gotten a story there!" He said that he was certain that the Marines would be able to march from Hagaru-ri to the sea. "We got out of Yudam-ni, didn't we? If we got out of there, we can get out of here."

Murray told Beech that he had not believed that they could break out of Yudam-ni. "I never told anyone," Murray said, wiping away tears with his dirty parka sleeve. When he tried again to talk about Yudam-ni, he found that he could not.[45]

Another new arrival at Hagaru-ri was David Douglas Duncan with two Leica cameras. The *Life* magazine correspondent's photographs of the Marines' breakout would become iconic.[46]

Marguerite Higgins of the *New York Herald Tribune* was the only woman among the 131 correspondents accredited to cover the Korean War. An attractive 30-year-old blonde who wore tennis shoes and baggie fatigues and was known as a fearless, aggressive reporter, Higgins had been in Korea since the Pusan Perimeter battles. Later, she landed at Inchon with the Fifth Marines.

At Hagaru-ri, she mingled with the men who had just arrived after the long breakout from Yudam-ni.

"The men were ragged, their faces swollen and bleeding from the sting of the icy wind," she wrote. "Some were without hats, their ears blue in the frost. A few walked to the doctor's tent barefoot because they couldn't get their frostbitten feet into their frozen shoe pacs."

She described the men as "exhausted, and the tension among them was all-pervasive. They had the dazed air of men who accepted death and then found themselves alive after all," she wrote. "They talked in unfinished phrases. They would start to say something and then stop, as if the meaning was beyond any words at their command."[47]

Lieutenant Colonel Murray, acquainted with Higgins from the fighting at Inchon and Seoul, told her that "those five days and nights fighting our way out of nightmare alley were the worst thing that ever happened to the Marines ... Night after night near Yudam-ni I thought I'd never see daylight again." He said the Chinese blundered by dispersing their strength, instead of concentrating it. If they had done so, "we could never have gotten out of the trap."[48]

Higgins intended to march from Hagaru-ri to the sea with the Marines after being invited to accompany a Fifth Marines company.

General Smith nixed the plan, telling Higgins that "there are a lot of good Marines who are getting frostbite, and if you march down with these Marines you probably will get frostbitten, and then somebody is going to have to take care of you. I am sure these Marines will see that you are taken care of, and we haven't got men for that kind of business."[49]

Higgins wrote with asperity that Smith "had a strong seizure of chivalry ... and insisted that the walkout was too dangerous." Her editors watered down her first draft about Smith's decision.

She was flown to Koto-ri, where Colonel "Chesty" Puller, the First Marines commander, put her on a plane with General Lemuel Shepherd, commander of the Fleet Marine Force, Pacific. Shepherd, too, had wanted to march out with the Marines, but Smith wouldn't allow it.

When Higgins implored Shepherd to let her stay, Puller shook his head and took one of her arms and twined it with one of Shepherd's. "Please, Maggie, go with General Shepherd," Puller said.

Shepherd later said, "O.P. should have let her stay with the troops. She would have been a Joan of Arc to those Marines on the way down."

Higgins left on the last plane out of Koto-ri. After it landed at Hungnam, she got a ride to Chinhung-ni and began walking back up the mountain to join the Marines as they marched down.[50]

From Peking, Mao Tse-Tung inflated the achievements of the Second Offensive. He pronounced it an unqualified success in northeast Korea, where Chinese troops had surrounded the 1st Marine Division and the Army's 7th Division.

"Most of those enemy forces have been destroyed," Mao said. "The remnants are under continuous attack ... The enemy forces on both the eastern and western fronts are running for their life with extreme anxiety and panic."[51]

For all of Mao's hyperbole, it was an undeniable fact that the Chinese intervention in the undeclared war was driving the United Nations forces out of North Korea.

PART IV

The March to the Sea

Chapter 20

Readying the Breakout

December 4–5

There were bodies all over the place. ... They were stacked up, quilted uniforms smoking.

Lieutenant Harold Dawe describing the East Hill fighting.[1]

What I saw turned my heart to ice, a wall of Chinese soldiers in white, creeping across the snow in total silence.

Lieutenant Harold Trapnell describing the East Hill attacks.[2]

There can be no retreat when there's no rear. You can't retreat, or even withdraw, when you're surrounded. The only thing you can do is break out, and in order to do that you have to attack, and that is what we're about to do. It will be an attack in another direction.

General O.P. Smith on the breakout to Koto-ri.[3]

The Chinese 9th Army Group's reserve, Zhang Renchu's 50,000-man 26th Army, began marching to Hagaru-ri from the Yalu River area on December 1 to relieve the 20th and 27th Armies, which had been depleted by shockingly high casualties, frostbite and lack of food.

The two armies' 100,000 troops had encircled the 1st Marine Division, but had failed to destroy it. That job now fell to the 26th Army.

Peng Dehuai, the CPVF's commander, approved of 9th Group commander Song Shilun's decision to send in the 26th Army's four divisions – the 76th, 77th, 78th, and 88th.

But he urged Song to continue pressing the Americans with the 20th and 27th Armies until the 26th reached Hagaru-ri for what Peng fervently hoped would be the final battle.

"The encircled enemy at your [eastern] front has been cut by half with heavy casualties," Peng wrote. "Hope you will go all out to wipe out the surrounded enemy troops."

Mao Tse-Tung, too, was closely monitoring events at Chosin Reservoir. On December 2, he exhorted Song and his assistant commander, Tao Yong, to "pay all their attention to the great advantage of wiping out the encircled US 1st Marine Division through tonight and tomorrow night."[4]

Song had believed that the 26th could march through the 100 miles of forested mountains in three days, and be ready to attack on December 3. Based on that assumption, the relief force was supplied with just three days' rations, consisting largely of buns sliced into cracker-like wafers.[5]

But Zhang's men were unfamiliar with the mountain footpaths leading them to the Chosin Reservoir, and they had neither trucks, reliable operational maps, nor good local guides to lead the way. They were compelled to send reconnaissance companies ahead to find the paths. One division, the 88th, still clad in summer-weight clothing, got lost.

Instead of taking three days, the relief expedition's overland trek took five days, even with forced marches. The men ran out of food as they marched day and night through the deep snow and dense forests, harried by American air raids and freezing in temperatures of 20 below zero and lower. They were delayed one day while reconnaissance units tried to find the paths to Chosin Reservoir.

"Somehow, before we reached Hagaru-ri six days later [on December 6], our food had long gone since the men were very hungry through the forced march for six days," said Ma Rixiang, an assistant political instructor with the 77th Division.

Exhausted and starving, some men sank into the snow and did not get up again.[6]

The 76th and 77th Divisions arrived at assembly areas outside Hagaru-ri on December 5; the 88th and 78th Divisions got there later. Nearly every man in the 3rd Battalion of the 76th's 227th Regiment froze to death one night after getting lost in the mountains.[7]

Fearing that the 26th Army was going to arrive too late to destroy the Marines, General Song raged at his 9th Army Group staff. "Where is the second echelon?" he shouted. "Where is the 26th Army?" Song was so upset that he flung his teacup to the ground.[8]

The 1st Marine Division planned to begin withdrawing from Hagaru-ri early December 6.

Hill 1419, or East Hill, the large hill mass looming 500 feet above Hagaru-ri's northeastern quadrant – and the MSR extending south from the village – was Hagaru-ri's Achilles heel.

The 27th Army's 58th Division had controlled East Hill's crest since November 29, while just below the crest were allied defensive positions that consisted of a medley of Army and Marine service and headquarters troops; Captain Carl Sitter's George Company of the First Marines; and Lieutenant Colonel Drysdale's 41 Commando, supported by tanks and artillery.

Until December 3, the fear had been that a massive Chinese attack might overwhelm the thin defensive line, enabling the enemy to seize Hagaru-ri and the crucial airfield. Or if enemy artillery were manhandled to East Hill's summit, Hagaru-ri, its medical facilities, and ammunition depots would be at the mercy of the Chinese.

Whatever the case, a breakout to the sea on the MSR would be problematic if not impossible if Chinese troops continued to hold East Hill. From its crest, the Chinese could riddle any convoy attempting to leave Hagaru-ri for Koto-ri.

But the situation had radically changed with the arrival of the Fifth and Seventh Marines from Yudam-ni. The first order of business was for Lieutenant Colonel Ray Murray's Fifth Marines to seize and hold East

Hill while Colonel Homer Litzenberg's Seventh Marines prepared to lead the breakout to the south early December 6.

Lieutenant Colonel Hal Roise's 2nd Battalion climbed East Hill during the afternoon of December 5. It was a treacherous ascent. East Hill was nearly perpendicular in places and the snow had been beaten down to slick ice by days of foot traffic. It was devoid of vegetation.

Without the ropes that were in place, it would have been nearly impossible for the men to go up and down East Hill. In places, the ascent consisted of two steps forward, one step backward. Men fell hard on the ice, cursing.

After Roise's battalion relieved Captain Sitter's George Company on December 5, Lieutenant Colonel Murray ordered Roise to seize the high ground above his position so that the Seventh Marines could begin marching south to Koto-ri, 11 miles away.[9]

Sitter's men moved to positions along the western side of the airstrip. They were exhausted and haggard from their nights of staving off Chinese attacks. A machine-gun section that once had consisted of 14 men now had three.

"We were in absolutely terrible shape," said Pfc Bruce Farr of George Company. Many men were afflicted with diarrhea, and had to shed multiple layers of clothing in order to relieve themselves.

At dawn on the 6th, the Chinese assaulted George Company. It repulsed the attackers with heavy casualties, and took more than 20 prisoners.

"Several of them had feet that were elephantine and deformed ... They looked like blocks of ice. We were poorly equipped, but they were a hell of a lot worse," said Private Steve Olmstead.[10]

The Fifth Marines' attack began at 7am December 6 with a 15-minute mortar barrage of East Hill.

Shaped like a horseshoe, East Hill featured a 500-yard-wide saddle between its two high sides. The southeastern side fell off to a spur overlooking the critical MSR escape route to the south – along which the Seventh Marines were to begin the march to the sea that very day.

Dog Company led the attack, and Chinese resistance was initially fierce and stubborn, even in the face of air strikes by 76 fighter-bombers that lasted an hour and a half and that plastered the high ground with rockets, bombs, and machine-gun fire.

Then, the enemy fire suddenly ceased, and at 11am Captain Samuel Smith's company seized the western crest of the spur. It was deserted, except for 30 enemy corpses sprawled on the ground.

Roise sent Captain Uel Peter's Fox Company to replace Smith's men, so that Dog Company could seize the high ground on the other side of the broad saddle.

After two hours of fighting, Dog Company was atop the horseshoe's southeastern rim.

In the saddle between Dog and Fox Companies, enemy troops massed for an attack. The Marines shredded them with every weapon at hand, while Corsairs bombed, strafed, and rocketed them. They were sitting ducks.

Terrified and demoralized by the hurricane of gunfire, 220 enemy soldiers surrendered en masse – the largest number of Chinese soldiers captured at one time during the Chosin Reservoir campaign.[11]

By early afternoon, the Fifth Marines held East Hill and its knob overlooking the MSR.[12]

But the battle for East Hill was far from over.

Two divisions of the Chinese 26th Army had finally reached the Hagaru-ri area. Without food or rest, the 76th and 77th Divisions' exhausted, starving survivors of the 100-mile forced march from the Yalu River were thrown into the fight for East Hill.[13]

After the 26th Army's arrival, the pitched battle went on for 22 hours before the Marines completely secured the hill.[14]

In this new iteration of the East Hill fighting, the 26th Army did not face the polyglot Army, British, and Marine combat, service, and headquarters units that for days had barely withstood the attacks of the 20th Army's 58th Division.

Their adversary was the Fifth Marines, X Corps's most veteran, battle-hardened unit. The Fifth had comprised the core of the Marine Provisional Brigade that stood fast at the Pusan Perimeter in August and led the UN counterattack across the Naktong River. It was the first to land at Inchon, seizing the small, outlying island of Wolmi-do. The Fifth had fought through the debris-filled streets of Seoul.

In World War I, its exploits at Belleau Wood and St Mihiel, and during the Meuse–Argonne offensive, earned the regiment three Croix de Guerre citations and the right to wear the *Fourragère* on their uniforms' left shoulder. In February 1941, the Fifth Marines formed the nucleus of the 1st Marine Division at its creation.[15]

Soldiers from the 26th Army's 76th Division appeared at nightfall on the MSR in columns of four abreast, carrying ammunition on stretchers. They immediately began climbing East Hill.

Beginning at 9pm, the reinforcements began a series of counterattacks to recapture East Hill that lasted until midnight.

Dog Company alone, down to 80 effectives, killed 175 enemy troops. There was a two-hour lull, and then the assaults resumed with greater intensity, continuing until dawn, in what was described as the most intensive battle of the Chosin campaign.

The Marine Corps historical record said the Chinese flung themselves at the Marines' positions with a "dogged fatalism" that commanded the Fifth's grudging respect, even as the Marines cut down the enemy attackers.

Lieutenant Karle Seydel, a machine-gun officer, was the only unwounded Dog Company officer to emerge from the fighting in the hills northwest of Seoul three months earlier.

On East Hill, luck ran out for the officer with a reputation of taking good care of his men. Sergeant William Gerichten, a machine-gun section leader, was nearby when Seydel was killed.

"He took a step sideways and fell in the snow. It was so slippery up there that people were falling all the time, but it was clear he was dead and had died instantly, which is the best way," he said.

Seydel's body was trundled down the hill, but the truck taking away the dead left without him. His comrades performed a hasty roadside field burial.[16]

The struggle for East Hill against the 26th Army surpassed anything that even veterans of the Yudam-ni fighting had seen.

"Never before had they seen the Chinese come on in such numbers or return to the attack with such persistence," the Marine Corps official record said. The enemy soldiers fell before a tornado of gunfire from tanks, artillery, mortars, rockets, and machine guns.[17]

Dr Henry Litvin, treating the wounded at the aid center down the hill, lifted the helmet of a wounded man and watched his brains pour out. Litvin "stepped back, overwhelmed by the waste and horror of it, knowing I couldn't do a darn thing to help him."

At the base of the hill, Roise's Easy Company was slammed by a furious attack, but accounted for 300 enemy dead. The Fifth's Able and Charlie Companies of the 1st Battalion, aided by tanks from the Army's 31st Tank Battalion, cut down 560 Chinese. Many of them were killed while crossing open ground under pre-registered US mortar fire.

Lieutenant Harold Dawe's Charlie Company, in positions near an ammunition dump, said when the fighting ended, "there were bodies all over the place ... They were stacked up, quilted uniforms smoking."[18]

A tightly packed wall of Chinese attacked Able Company, after having crept noiselessly to nearby assault positions. Lieutenant Nicholas Trapnell said that an Able gunner fired a short burst of tracers so that they could see what faced them.

"What I saw turned my heart to ice," he said, "a wall of Chinese soldiers in white, creeping across the snow in total silence."[19]

Furious close-in fighting and massive Chinese casualties caused the next few hours to pass in a gory blur.

Although supported by mortar and artillery fire, the Chinese failed to break through Able Company and were annihilated. When the attack ebbed, the Able Marines found themselves covered with picric acid dust from the Chinese grenades.

Some of the enemy soldiers, freezing and starving, ran to the huge supply dumps near the base of East Hill, in search of food and warm clothing.[20]

With daylight, the return of close-air support compelled the eviscerated enemy units to withdraw.

Lieutenant Colonel Murray's 1st and 2nd Battalions claimed more than 1,000 enemy killed during the long night. Many of the bodies were charred by white phosphorus.

Dog Company, which had borne the brunt of the attacks, suffered losses of 13 killed and 50 wounded.[21]

While the Yudam-ni Marines were marching into Hagaru-ri on December 4, one of the most dramatic narratives of the Chosin Reservoir campaign was unfolding 17 miles to the north.

Ensign Jesse Brown, the first black US Navy fighter pilot, was on a reconnaissance mission from the USS *Leyte* with his VF-32 wingman Lieutenant Thomas Hudner Jr.

Soaring over the snowy hills north of Chosin Reservoir, Brown's Corsair was hit by ground fire that severed an oil line.

Flying too low to use his parachute, Brown crash-landed his plane in a pasture covered in deep snow. Upon impact, the plane's instrument panel crushed Brown's right knee, and he was pinned in the cockpit wreckage, unable to get out. Then, the wreckage caught fire.

Unwilling to abandon his friend, Hudner, who had trained with Brown, crash-landed his Corsair near Brown's aircraft, defying Navy rules and risking court martial. Hudner injured his back during the crash-landing, and hobbled painfully on foot to Brown's smoking plane.

Try as he might, Hudner could not free Brown from the wreckage. Working bare-handed in the bitter cold, Hudner packed snow around the fuselage to prevent the flames from reaching his friend.

His squadron mates, circling above, strafed 100 Chinese troops that were racing to the crash site, and radioed for a rescue helicopter. Bring an axe and a fire extinguisher, Hudner added.

As the afternoon hours wore on, the time came for VF-32 to return to the *Leyte*. The Corsairs circling overhead said their goodbyes by buzzing Brown and Hudner and waggling their wings.

A short time later, Lieutenant Charles Ward of VMO-6 landed his Sikorsky helicopter at the crash site. He had brought the axe and fire extinguisher requested by Hudner.

By now, Brown was barely semiconscious. His lips were blue and he was shivering violently from the cold. Hudner removed his stocking cap and slipped it over Brown's head. He wrapped Brown's hands in a scarf.

For an hour, as daylight began to fade, Hudner and Ward took turns flailing with the axe at the instrument panel in a desperate attempt to free Brown. Their efforts failed.

Brown became unresponsive in the subzero cold and stopped breathing.

As darkness descended, Hudner and Ward lost hope that they would be able to free Brown from the plane.

They reluctantly concluded that they had no choice but to leave him in the smoldering Corsair. They flew away in Ward's helicopter and went to Koto-ri, from where Hudner returned to the *Leyte*.

The next morning, the pilot of a reconnaissance plane that flew over the crash site reported that Brown's body had been stripped of its jacket and gear.

VF-32 returned to conduct what pilots called a "funeral flight." Brown's squadron mates napalmed the crash site so that nothing salvageable remained.[22]

Hudner was never court-martialed, but was instead awarded the Congressional Medal of Honor; Ward received the Silver Star.

Before the cargo planes began landing at the Hagaru-ri airstrip on December 1 and taking the wounded to hospitals in Hungnam and on to Tokyo, 152 wounded soldiers and Marines were evacuated from Hagaru-ri, Yudam-ni, and Koto-ri in small planes and helicopters like the one flown by Lieutenant Ward.[23]

The test flights on December 1 had determined that C-47s could land and take off from Hagaru-ri's 2,900-foot airstrip, despite specifications that a 7,600-foot runway was required at 4,000-feet elevation. All-out evacuation of the wounded from Hagaru-ri began the next day, when 919 men were flown out in Marine R4Ds and Air Force Combat Cargo Command C-47s.

The arrival of the Fifth and Seventh Marines from Yudam-ni with their wounded put an additional strain on the medical teams, and two surgical teams from the 1st Medical Battalion were flown in by helicopter.

Over a 48-hour period, medical personnel treated and processed 1,500 soldiers from Task Force Faith and 1,000 Marines, ticketing many of them for evacuation.[24]

Between December 1 and 6, a total of 4,312 casualties were flown from Hagaru-ri: 3,150 Marines; 1,137 Army; and 25 British Marines. Just two planes were lost during this operation.[25]

Besides the wounded being evacuated from Hagaru-ri, 537 replacements were flown in for the planned breakout from Hagaru-ri to Koto-ri. Many of them had been wounded in September during the Inchon–Seoul operation, and had recovered. Equipped with cold weather gear, they were assigned to the three Marine regiments.

Moreover, 138 bodies were flown out. "We didn't want to bury them in that God-forsaken place. We had a good cemetery at Hungnam," General Smith wrote.[26]

The evacuation policy for wounded men being flown out of Hagaru-ri stipulated that except for the most critical cases – which were sent directly to Tokyo – the wounded were first sent to either the 1st Marine Division hospital in Hungnam; the Army's 121st Evacuation Hospital in Hamhung; or the USS *Consolation* in Hungnam Harbor. Those cases requiring more than 30 days of hospitalization were sent on from Yonpo airfield to Tokyo.[27]

Wounded Marines who were evacuated to Japan often ended up at Yokosuka Naval Hospital, where "we were treated like royalty," said Private George Crotts, "with officers' wives handing out coffee and doughnuts from welcome wagons. They gave each of us a [sleeping] rack in a huge auditorium that had been turned into a hospital ward."[28]

As December 2 ended, Division surgeon Dr Eugene Herring stared in alarm at the list of men that he had cleared for evacuation that day. All of his seriously wounded men were not being evacuated, he discovered.

At the beginning of the day, Herring had 450 men ready for evacuation; at day's end, 260 remained in his care. Yet, 919 men had been flown out of Hagaru-ri.

The numbers did not add up.

Herring took his concerns to General Smith. In his log that day, Smith wrote, "Unfortunately, there are a good many Army men, not casualties, that got on planes ... Men got on stretchers, pulled a blanket over themselves and did a little groaning, passing as casualties."[29]

Smith and his staff had wrongly assumed that Air Force evacuation officers would screen the men boarding the flights. They did not. The Air Force officers determined only whether there were sufficient planes for the men lined up to board them, and not whether their injuries warranted evacuation.[30]

Smith immediately established a screening process. He posted military police outside the cargo planes, allowing no one to board without a doctor-issued evacuation ticket. Frostbite cases were screened three times – by a battalion surgeon, a team of division and regimental surgeons, plus a line officer from each regiment.[31]

Keyes Beech, the *Chicago Daily News* correspondent, joined Dr Herring as he examined a line of walking wounded. Herring determined whether each man was able to walk down the MSR to the sea, or should be flown to a military hospital.

Beech said the animated man that he had known in Seoul was a snappish "dry husk" of his former self – gaunt in appearance, with sunken eyes and a white stubble of beard that made him look older than his years.

After examining one Marine's purple feet, Herring told him, "OK, son, you walk out."

The Marine strenuously objected. "For Jesus H. Christ's sake, look at my feet," he told Herring.

"You can walk, can't you?" Herring shot back. "Now get out of here and walk."

After the man had left, Herring confided to Beech that deciding who walked and who boarded an evacuation flight was "the hardest thing I ever had to do in my life. They all want to fly out. Who the hell doesn't want to fly out? I'd like to fly out myself."[32]

Captain Paul Fritz, an Air Force pilot, described "lines of wounded men ... motley bandages and compresses covering their wounds, makeshift arm and leg splints, crutches made from tree limbs."

After they boarded, a powerful stench filled the plane, said Fritz: "the smell of fresh and dried blood, filthy combat dungarees, unwashed bodies, spent gunpowder, and vehicle exhaust fumes."[33]

Air Force General William Tunner, commander of the Combat Cargo Command, flew to Hagaru-ri to tell Smith that he was willing to send all the planes needed to evacuate the entire division if Smith wished.

Smith replied, "Look, nobody's going to get out of here [by air] that's able-bodied. Do you realize we've just flown in 600 replacements [537 actually]?" Smith said Tunner's "jaw dropped."[34]

December 6 was the final day that wounded men were evacuated from Hagaru-ri – mostly men from the Seventh Marines who were wounded that morning during the beginning of the breakout to Koto-ri. Late in the afternoon, the last two C-47s departed Hagaru-ri for Yonpo airfield.[35]

General Almond had flown to Hagaru-ri after the ragged, exhausted Yudam-ni Marines entered the perimeter. As was his custom, Almond brought medals to bestow.

He awarded Distinguished Service Crosses to General Smith, Murray, Litzenberg, and Lieutenant Colonel Olin Beall, who had rescued the Army RCT-31 survivors from the Chosin Reservoir ice.

Because Almond had with him just one actual medal, Smith, Murray, and Litzenberg urged him to give it to Beall.

Almond appeared to be moved by the scene that met him in Hagaru-ri. Perhaps it was the large number of wounded men, or the sight of the gaunt, disheveled survivors of the march from Yudam-ni to Hagaru-ri.

"I never could figure whether it was the cold or his emotions, but he was weeping when he came to see me," Smith wrote.[36]

The 1st Marine Division's Order 25-50, written by Colonel Alpha Bowser, the division operations officer, was the blueprint for the breakout from Hagaru-ri to Koto-ri, 11 miles to the south.

Assembling all of his unit commanders the day before the operation began, Smith provided them with the details: the Seventh Marines would lead the breakout at first light on December 6, while the Fifth held the Hagaru-ri perimeter until all of the units had marched out, when it would then follow, serving as the rearguard.

Attached to the rearguard were Lieutenant Colonel Douglas Drysdale's 41 Commando and Lieutenant Colonel Thomas Ridge's 3rd Battalion of the First Marines.

A 490-man provisional Army battalion made up of the 385 able-bodied survivors of Task Force Faith as well as soldiers who had helped defend Hagaru-ri was attached to the Seventh Marines. It was designated as the 31/7, led by Lieutenant Colonel Barry Anderson, the 31st's operations officer. The soldiers were divided into four small companies to help clear the ridges of enemy troops.

The assorted Marine headquarters and service troops and engineers were assigned to walk beside the 1,000 vehicles in the two vehicle trains: Train 1, accompanying the Seventh Marines, and Train 2, which would travel with the Fifth.[37]

"All personnel except drivers, relief drivers, radio operators, casualties, and personnel specifically designated by RCT commanders will march on foot to [protect the] flanks of motor serials," the orders said.

The division command post was placed in the middle of the convoy so that it could quickly direct the action if necessary.[38]

The column's configuration was described as a "moving hedgehog," with the infantry leading the convoy and guarding its flanks and rear, protecting the vehicles, men, and equipment in the middle.

Like a hedgehog, it bristled with guns and could fire in every direction. Infantry units would clear the hills and ridges on both sides of the MSR ahead of the main column. Keeping men active would have the added benefit of reducing frostbite casualties, it was believed.[39]

They would be aided by close-air support from land-based fighter-bomber squadrons and those operating from the half-dozen aircraft carriers and carrier escorts in the Sea of Japan.

Smith ordered that "no vehicle should be left behind that would roll, and that no materiel would be left behind which could be carried."

Meticulous instructions were issued for the burning, crushing, and disabling of everything not carried out. Wooden stocks of rifles were to be broken or burned, the barrels bent; machine guns, mutilated and smashed; mortars and rocket launchers, "smash entire weapon."

The destruction of vehicles required cutting all tires and tubes; puncturing radiators; smashing carburettors and distributors; cutting wires and fuel links; and then burning the vehicle if gasoline remained in the tanks.[40]

It would be an orderly withdrawal, and there would be no running of enemy troop gauntlets as some Eighth Army units had so disastrously attempted in western Korea at the end of November.[41]

The 1st Division's encirclement did not become a major story in US newspapers until the Fifth and Seventh Marines reached Hagaru-ri on December 3. By coincidence, that was when newspaper correspondents began arriving at the airstrip on C-47s that were then loaded with wounded men and flown to Hungnam.[42]

When they learned that the division planned to march down the MSR to the sea, the reporters bombarded General O.P. Smith with questions about the planned withdrawal. Were the Marines in fact retreating? Marines had never retreated.

"Certainly not," Smith calmly replied. "There can be no retreat when there's no rear. You can't retreat, or even withdraw, when you're surrounded. The only thing you can do is break out, and in order to do that you have to attack, and that is what we're about to do. It will be an attack in another direction."

Smith's explanation was amended by newspaper headline writers in the United States to the pugnacious, "Retreat, Hell! We're attacking in another direction!" Yet it would have been uncharacteristic of Smith the Christian Scientist to use the word "hell."[43]

The general thought it was strange that the press viewed the impending march to the sea as "the crisis of the operation. This simply was not the case," he wrote. "The advance of the two regiments to Yudam-ni and their subsequent return to Hagaru-ri were the real crisis hours."[44]

Captain Michael Capraro, who was a 1st Marine Division public information officer, said the division had proven that it was "the strongest division in the world. I thought of it as a Doberman, a dangerous hound straining at the leash, wanting nothing more than to sink its fangs into the master's enemy."[45]

In a frozen field at Hagaru-ri as wind-driven snow pelted down, Lieutenant Colonel Ray Murray, the Fifth Marines' commander, spoke to his battalion commanders and a knot of reporters about the forthcoming march to the sea.

Some of the officers took the news hard, according to correspondent Marguerite Higgins. "Their expressions were of deeply hurt pride."

Echoing General Smith's words, Murray told them, "This is no retreat. This is an assault in another direction. There are more Chinese blocking our path to the sea than there are ahead of us. But we're going to get out of here."

They were going to come out in good order, "as Marines, not as stragglers. We're going to bring out our wounded and our equipment. We're coming out, I tell you, as Marines or not at all."[46]

All night long, the Eleventh Marines' artillery batteries shelled the area between Hagaru-ri and Koto-ri to prepare the way for the march to the sea.[47]

Before Smith boarded a helicopter to fly to Koto-ri – only after being discouraged by his staff from traveling with the convoy – he witnessed a final inspection of the 41 Commando, now at just 50 percent strength after the fighting in Hellfire Valley and on East Hill.

"British imperturbability was at its best when Lieutenant Colonel Drysdale held an inspection shortly before departing from Hagaru-ri," Smith wrote.

"Disdainful of the scattered shots which were still being heard, the officers moved up and down the rigid lines of the Commandos, and men whose gear was not in the best-possible shape were reprimanded."[48]

Chapter 21

Hagaru-ri to Koto-ri

December 6

We just want all the air you can give us. The only thing we don't want [is] the Air Force mixed up in this; we don't want to get involved with them, because they don't have our control system.

General O.P. Smith to General Field Harris of the 1st Marine Air Wing.[1]

Personal effects were thrown everywhere. All this, frozen in time. There was no gore, it had all frozen. There was nothing but death.

Pfc Doug Michaud, while marching through Hellfire Valley a week after the Chinese ambush.[2]

At daybreak on December 6, silvery fog shrouded Hagaru-ri as the 2,200-man Seventh Marines led the convoy out of Hagaru-ri. The regiment was functioning at about half of its original strength.

Fox Company, rebuilt after its five-day ordeal on Toktong Pass, was on the point, supported by tanks. Lieutenant Ralph Abell had succeeded the wounded Captain William Barber as Fox's commander.[3]

Until the fog burned off, the column was without close-air support, although General Ned Almond had in place for the breakout one of the greatest concentrations of air power of the Korean War, using every squadron available to X Corps.

They included 1st Marine Air Wing squadrons VMF-312 and VMF-214 based at Yonpo airfield; Task Force 77's Navy and Marine squadrons operating from the aircraft carriers *Leyte*, *Valley Forge*, *Princeton*, and *Philippine Sea*; Marine fighters from the escort carrier *Badoeng Strait*; US Fifth Air Force and Australian Air Force fighter-bombers; and medium and heavy bombers.

The plan was for 24 close-support aircraft to circle above the convoy at all times during daylight hours. After dark, "heckler" night-fighter planes would take over, for the convoy would continue to advance around-the-clock until it reached Koto-ri, 11 miles distant.[4]

General Smith told General Field Harris, commander of the 1st Marine Air Wing, "We just want all the air you can give us. The only thing we don't want [is] the Air Force mixed up in this; we don't want to get involved with them, because they don't have our control system."

Smith said the Air Force did not believe that close-air support was worth the effort. "Their main objection was philosophical; they did not want anybody on the ground telling a plane what to do."

The Marines, he pointed out, addressed that issue by requiring their forward air observers to be pilots as well as trained infantry officers.[5]

Moreover, it might take 45 minutes for the Air Force to act on a request for support; by that time, the mission was likely outdated. The 1st Marine Air Wing usually acted within five or ten minutes.

Smith and Harris worked out an arrangement for the Marine and Navy squadrons from Yonpo and the carriers to cover an area five miles on either side of the road, "and then the Air Force could drop anything they wanted anyplace else, as long as they left this corridor five miles on either side of the road."[6]

Chinese troops hid in the huts of North Korean civilians during the daytime and moved at night. Some of the North Koreans urged that the huts be burned down, and so Harris instructed his pilots to napalm all of the huts within five miles of either side of the MSR.

After those missions were carried out, "the poor devils had no shelter; they were just out in the open then," wrote Smith.[7]

Harris told Admiral Edward Coyle Ewen of TF-77, "I want to be able to cover their flanks and rear one hundred percent, and to blast any major resistance to their front. Can use all the help you can give me until they get down. Tell your pilots they are doing a magnificent job."[8]

Twenty-two planes from the *Leyte* and VMF-214 were on station overhead when the convoy left Hagaru-ri for Koto-ri. When it came under fire from enemy gun positions 75 yards from the MSR, the trucks and infantry escort stopped.

VMF-214 Corsairs attacked the Chinese emplacements with rockets and proximity-fused 500-pound bombs. Ensuing strikes alternated between dummy runs and live ones to conserve ammunition.

As the attacks continued, Colonel Litzenberg ordered the column forward, although the air strike targets were just 100 yards from the MSR. There was no margin for error.

Commander Horace Epes of *Leyte*'s VF-33 said his squadron Corsairs were fully loaded, and it was "cold as hell" in the planes, but colder on the ground – 25 below zero, with a foot of snow.

A forward air controller directed Epes's flight to dive above him and carry out its attack perpendicular to the column. "Our empty cases fell among the Marines, our bullets and light bombs landed on the Chinese 50 yards ahead of them," said Epes.

The FAC then instructed Epes to make another pass – this time with napalm, and even closer.

"We were afraid we would burn up our own troops, but we complied," he said. "We dropped napalm bombs on the sides of the hills, with Marines all along the road directly beneath. If the temperature hadn't been 25 degrees below, I don't believe the Marines could have stood the heat. Maybe it felt good."

During VF-33's attacks, Marine mortars were homing in on the same targets, with their shell trajectories arcing higher than the low-flying planes. The mortar men aimed for the planes' tails, getting their projectiles into the air before the next plane arrived.

The combined mortar and air attack drove the Chinese gunners to cover and the column was able to pass unmolested.[9]

During the march to Koto-ri, more than 200 aircraft operated daily. On December 6 and 7, the 1st MAW flew 240 sorties; 240 more originated from the Task Force 77 carriers; and the Fifth Air Force accounted for an additional 83 sorties.[10]

With four tanks comprising the spearhead, the Seventh's 1st Battalion attacked its first objective, enemy-occupied high ground a mile south of Hagaru-ri. Baker Company surprised 24 Chinese soldiers asleep in their foxholes, killing 17 of them.

As the Seventh Marines marched toward Koto-ri, the Fifth Marines continued to hold onto Hagaru-ri until the convoy was well on its way.

Pack Train No. 1 did not get on the road until 4pm of the 6th, and it was the morning of the 7th before the Fifth marched out of Hagaru-ri. Its 2nd Battalion was the division rearguard behind Pack Train No. 2.[11]

Nine Chinese roadblocks barred the way to Koto-ri. While each of them would be eliminated, their dogged defenders would add 600 American casualties to the campaign's bloody toll.[12]

At the beginning of the breakout, Lieutenant Colonel Randolph Lockwood was relieved of command of the Seventh Marines' 2nd Battalion.

In November, Lockwood had remained in Hagaru-ri with his Headquarters Company while his Dog, Easy, and Fox Companies had gone north toward Yudam-ni. When Lockwood was unable to join them after the Chinese cut the road, his spirits noticeably declined.

By December 6, Lockwood had grown apathetic and did little except sit in his jeep and brood. Alarmed by Lockwood's behavior, a subordinate officer asked the battalion surgeon and assistant surgeon to examine him.

They concluded that Lockwood was neurotic and unfit for command. Major James Lawrence Jr became the 2nd Battalion's acting commander.[13]

Nothing was left behind in Hagaru-ri that could be useful to the enemy. Airdrops had created stockpiles of food, ammunition, and petroleum for the breakout, but when the trucks were loaded and the convoy pulled out of Hagaru-ri, a surplus remained.

It was left to Able Company of the 1st Engineers Battalion and the Explosive Ordinance Section of the Headquarters Company engineers to destroy the clothing, equipment, rations, and ammunition that remained.

Bulldozers crushed the rations, which were then soaked with gasoline and burned. Explosives destroyed the surplus ammunition.[14]

About 200 Chinese soldiers captured during the fighting on East Hill were left behind in Hagaru-ri when the Marines withdrew.

"A lot of them were in such bad shape that we left them there, left some medical supplies and left them there for the Chinese to come along and take care of them after we left," said the Fifth Marines' commander, Lieutenant Colonel Ray Murray.

The worst Chinese frostbite victims hobbled on feet that were "huge globs." "I know that if they lived, their legs would have had to be amputated," said Murray. "The most stoic people you ever saw in your life. I really felt sorry for them ..."

During the Fifth Marines' last night on East Hill, a platoon of tanks fired all night, while 3.6-inch rocket launchers fired phosphorus shells, and machine guns blazed away nearly nonstop, burning out the barrels, requiring their replacement.

In the morning, from the edge of the perimeter, Murray and some of his staff officers surveyed the gruesome scene: nearly a regiment of dead Chinese soldiers carpeted the area around East Hill – more than 800 Chinese killed, mainly troops from the tardy 26th Army. There were "just windrows of dead Chinese out there," said Murray. "You couldn't walk without stepping on a body."

The cotton batting of their quilted uniforms had caught fire when they were hit with phosphorus shells. "The poor bastards had burned to death," said Murray.[15]

Lieutenant Colonel Hal Roise's 2nd Battalion held its position on East Hill until Pack Train No. 2 withdrew from Hagaru-ri under the protection of the 1st and 3rd Battalions, and the Seventh's 3rd Battalion.

Roise's men descended East Hill and marched out of Hagaru-ri with the Marine engineers amid plumes of dense black smoke.

The Army's 31st Tank Company, led by Captain Robert Drake, was the rearguard. Chinese soldiers swarmed the burning dumps, braving the flames in the hope of snatching food or warm clothing.[16]

Marching out of Hagaru-ri in the fog, the Fifth Marines passed a mound of Chinese bodies – men who had been killed earlier that day when they attacked the Seventh Marines. Inspect each body, the men were told, and if a man happened to be still breathing, finish him off.

Major Thomas Durham, the 3rd Battalion operations officer, discovered an enemy soldier that was still breathing and "sent him to join his ancestors with a .45 slug through the temple. This was the first man I ever killed at close range."[17]

The convoy passed a napalmed Chinese machine-gun crew. The gunner still clutched the gun handles, his eyes open but black and hollowed out. Someone stuck a lit cigarette in the corpse's mouth.[18]

Chinese soldiers roved the high ground east of the MSR, shooting at the troops marching beside the convoy and picking off truck drivers. Shortly after the commencement of the march, three rounds from a Chinese 3.5-inch bazooka smashed into the lead bulldozer-tank, igniting an hours-long struggle.

Bereft of close-air support due to the morning fog, a coordinated attack of troops and tanks, supported by artillery fire, attempted to clear the high ground. When visibility finally permitted, air strikes and 81mm mortars joined in.

The coordinated assault drove off a large enemy force, permitting the convoy to proceed again at noon.[19]

It was the first of many delays that beset the convoy during its slog to Koto-ri.

Elements of at least six Chinese divisions were converging on the MSR to stop the breakout and fulfill Mao Tse-Tung's vow to annihilate the 1st Marine Division.[20]

By nightfall, the column's vanguard, led by the Seventh's Fox Company, had advanced two and a half miles down the MSR, while the 1st Battalion cleared the high ground on one side of the road and the Provisional 31st Army Battalion assaulted the heights on the MSR's other side.

Survivors of the Task Force Faith disaster and some Hagaru-ri service troops comprised the Army battalion, led by Lieutenant Colonel Barry Anderson. Its assignment, clearing the MSR's eastern ridges, began well. More than 100 Chinese soldiers surrendered without a shot fired.

But when a Chinese sniper opened up, Anderson's men withdrew down the ridge to the MSR.

Lieutenant Ralph Abell, who was in charge of Fox Company, asked an Army captain what he was doing.

"My men are freezing in the wind up there," he told Abell. "They need a little break."

When Abell told the captain to get his men back to the ridgetop, the captain replied that Abell, a lieutenant, couldn't tell the captain what to do.

At that moment, Colonel Litzenberg pulled up in his jeep. When he learned what the officers were arguing about, Litzenberg told the Army captain, "When a Marine lieutenant tells you what to do, you *will* follow his command, since he represents *me*."

The captain sent his men back up the ridge, but when the enemy again opened fire, they came running back down to the MSR, and passed through the convoy to the other side.

Lieutenant Colonel Frederick Dowsett, the Seventh Marines' executive officer, was exasperated by the Army battalion's failure.

"The Army officers said they didn't have control of their troops and couldn't get them to move," he said.

Dowsett ordered his 3rd Battalion to secure the high ground and for the provisional brigade to "get the hell out of the way."[21]

General Smith said the soldiers in the provisional battalion "had no spirit. We helped them as best we could. We even flew in weapons for them, as they had thrown theirs away. They expected us to take care of them, feed them, put up their tents. We disabused them of this idea."[22]

Aware from reconnaissance reports that Chinese reinforcements were arriving hourly – they could be seen on the eastern skyline – the column pushed on in the darkness.

The breakout was a stop-and-go crawl because of fierce resistance by a regiment of the 26th Army's 76th Division. The column was stopped every 1,000 to 1,500 yards by enemy gunfire, roadblocks, and blown bridges.

At a massive roadblock, enemy soldiers killed several truck drivers and set eight trucks on fire. The roadblock was cleared, and the column moved on.[23]

A new problem arose: the Chinese soldiers were frequently seen wearing the same parkas as the Marines. From a distance, it was difficult to tell them apart.

"We had lost so many men by this time that the Chinese all seemed to have on our parkas," said Lieutenant Harrol Kiser of the Seventh Marines.[24]

During the night of December 6–7, Chinese troops destroyed two bridges and raked the convoy with machine-gun and rifle fire. They riddled the Seventh Marines' command post, which was brightly illuminated by a house burning nearby. Vehicles stalled on the road. Swept by gunfire, the vehicles caught fire and blazed in the night.

Master Sergeant William McClung, who had been a Japanese prisoner for more than three years after being captured on Bataan in World War II, dragged two wounded Marines from a burning ammunition truck. He was shot dead while attempting to rescue a third man.[25]

During the furious Chinese attack on the command post, Lieutenant Colonel Dowsett was wounded; Captain Donald France, the Seventh's intelligence officer, and Lieutenant Clarence McGuinness were killed.

Lieutenant Cornelius Griffin, a Catholic chaplain, was wounded in the jaw when enemy gunfire peppered the ambulance in which Griffin was administering last rites to a dying Marine.

Griffin's clerk, Sergeant Matt Caruso, died when he flung himself between Griffin and the dying man, absorbing most of the enemy bullets.[26]

Griffin was known and liked for sharing with wounded men the small bottles of whiskey that he carried in his voluminous parka pockets.

"This is not the way I had expected to be doing His work," Griffith said, although he also pitched in often to treat battle wounds when his assistance was needed.[27]

Colonel Litzenberg sorted out the confused situation at his shot-up command post by loudly yelling orders. "It was always such a comfort to hear him," said Sergeant Robert Gault of Graves Registration.[28]

After the Seventh Marines's rifle companies had passed, the Chinese attacked the Division Headquarters Company and ahead of it, the Military Police Company, which was guarding 160 Chinese prisoners released from the Hagaru-ri town brig.

Headquarters Marines deployed in the ditches, with two machine guns manned by bandsmen. Night-fighting Corsairs came to the Marines' aid when the clouds cleared.

The POWs were ordered to lie flat on the road, but the attackers appeared to aim at them while shouting at them in Chinese.

Pandemonium ensued. Some of the prisoners attempted to flee and were caught in a crossfire between the Marines and the Chinese. One hundred thirty-seven of them were killed before the Marines repelled the attack.[29]

A company-size enemy force penetrated to within 30 yards of the convoy. The enemy troops were repulsed during a bitter fight that saw Lieutenant Charles Sullivan, 6 foot 4 inches tall and 240 pounds, empty his bayoneted carbine and throw it 15 feet like a javelin into the chest of an enemy soldier.[30]

The column then entered Hellfire Valley, where Task Force Drysdale was ambushed on November 29.[31]

Mounds of frozen corpses and smashed, gutted vehicles presented a ghastly spectacle.

Corporal Jerry Maill, a Royal Marine Commando with an 81mm mortar platoon, said returning to Hellfire Valley was nearly as unnerving for those who had fought there earlier as was the original battle.

"We found our dead where they had fallen in the snow, preserved in gruesome positions," said Maill. "It was a terrible sight."[32]

"It seemed there were hundreds of [disabled or destroyed trucks] of all descriptions, all with a light coat of snow covering them," said Captain George Rasula of the 31st Infantry.

In many of the trucks, the drivers, dead for a week and frozen stiff, still sat rigidly behind the steering wheels.

The Marines found a man still alive in an overturned truck; he had somehow survived a week in the subzero cold. Moreover, when quizzed, the man was able to display his knowledge of Americana by correctly answering a question about Stan Musial (the great St Louis Cardinals outfielder).[33]

Half an hour before midnight, Chinese on the heights above Hellfire Valley ambushed the column with machine-gun, rifle, and mortar fire, and rockets fired from a 2.36-inch launcher inside a sandbagged culvert.

Sergeant Alan Gearing of the Fifth Marines' George Company described it as "a rainstorm of lead ... Guys kept dropping in the road, and the corpsmen could hardly keep up. I felt like a walking dead man."[34]

The gunfire riddled the trucks in the column. Gas tanks exploded, and flames crackled in the subzero night.

Amid the debris and the ice-encrusted bodies of Chinese and American soldiers – some frozen in firing positions – were Christmas parcels looted from the trucks by enemy soldiers and ripped open.

Bright wrappers and colorful ribbons were incongruously strewn for a quarter mile through the wreckage, along with letters ransacked from mail bags and scattered like confetti.

The Marines gathered up some of the mail, which had been ripped apart by explosives and blown about in the wind.[35]

"We couldn't help ourselves; we bent down and looked at names and addresses," said Pfc Doug Michaud. "Personal effects were thrown everywhere. All this, frozen in time. There was no gore, it had all frozen. There was nothing but death."[36]

Amazingly, amid the debris Lieutenant Herc Kelly found a Christmas parcel addressed to him. Inside were chocolate chip cookie crumbs, a note from his wife, and a pedometer – which he promptly strapped to one of his ankles.

In an officer's footlocker in the wreckage Kelly found a Marine major's blue and white dress uniforms and four bottles of Canadian Club. Kelly passed around two of the bottles and kept the other two.[37]

Between two bodies under a truck lay a puppy, also dead, with its head on its paws.[38]

Fresh Chinese attacks struck the convoy.

About 800 Chinese soldiers assaulted the area where the George and How artillery batteries were located. Their nine howitzers were quickly deployed on the road under heavy fire. The gunners thrust the guns' muzzles between the trucks as the enemy massed 70 yards away behind a railroad embankment.

With no time to dig the howitzer's trails into the thick ice that coated the road, the gunners braced their bodies behind the gun shields against the recoil.

Firing pointblank across the railroad embankment, they shredded the troops seeking protection behind it with shrapnel. Every round heaved off the ammunition trucks went into the gun breeches indiscriminately.

"There was no time to sort the ammunition; the men threw the rounds into the breeches and fired away," said Major Fox Parry, the 3rd Artillery Battalion commander. "High explosive, white phosphorus, and armor-piercing rounds bombarded the railroad embankment at the treeline, spraying deadly fragments on the Chinese."

More than 600 rounds were loaded and fired as rapidly as possible so that the Chinese would have no time to scale the embankment and attack.

The Chinese replied with machine guns and mortars from both sides of the road, killing and wounding gunners and other men in the truck column. A five-gallon gasoline can strapped to the side of an ammunition truck caught fire; the men smothered the flames with sleeping bags before they could ignite the ammunition.

"This was no textbook battle," Parry wrote. "It was a life-or-death struggle between nine howitzers and the men who manned them and an enemy infantry battalion."

After every fourth or fifth round fired, the crews pushed the guns back into position.

The desperate battle went on for an hour and a half, with the gunners continuing to load and fire even when wounded, until daylight crept into the eastern sky. Then, 40 or 50 Chinese soldiers were seen fleeing from behind the railroad embankment.

The firing stopped. A Marine patrol counted between 500 and 800 dead or dying enemy soldiers behind the embankment. Parry's artillerymen reported three men killed and 34 wounded.[39]

The column's rearguard, the Fifth Marines, spotted a large group of Chinese in the open moving down a snow-covered hill on its flank and called in an air strike. The overwhelming power of close-air support was emphatically displayed.

Lieutenant Colonel Murray said that when several aircraft began shooting at the enemy soldiers, "it was like a school of fish that something's after ... These Chinese would dart one way and back, and all of them running, trying to get back over the hill, and these planes, one after another coming in and firing at them, and finally a few did get over the top, but there were hardly any of them left."[40]

Around daybreak on the 7th, Lieutenant Colonel William Harris, commander of the Seventh Marines' 3rd Battalion, vanished. He was the son of General Field Harris, the 1st Marine Air Wing commander. Lieutenant Colonel Harris had been acting peculiarly recently – among other things, giving away personal items and wandering off alone without an escort.

At the beginning of World War II, the Japanese had captured Harris in the Philippines and he spent years as a war prisoner. He had vowed to never be captured again.

Harris was last seen standing alone a few hundred feet up a ravine on the east side of the MSR. Colonel Litzenberg sent a platoon to try to find Harris, but it returned empty-handed.

Harris's executive officer, Major Lefty Morris, had taken on many of Harris's duties as his behavior had grown odder. Morris was given command of the 3rd Battalion.[41]

At 5:30am on December 7, the Seventh Marines' Easy Company reached the First Marines' perimeter at Koto-ri after 22 hours on the MSR.

The Seventh's other units entered Koto-ri by 7am. They had broken through the roadblocks and the ambushes laid for them by Chinese 26th Army's 76th Division. After surmounting these obstacles, the Marines fought a running battle with the 77th Division the rest of the way to Koto-ri.[42]

Upon the Seventh's arrival, it was immediately sent back to the MSR to keep it open for the Fifth Marines and Pack Train No. 2.

During its retrograde march, the Marines found 22 British Royal Marines from 41 Commando alive in Hellfire Valley.

They had been marooned in enemy-held territory since the night of November 29–30.

Food and medical supplies had been airdropped to them on December 4 after an observation plane spotted the word "HELP" stamped in the snow three miles north of Koto-ri. Nine of the commandos were carried out on stretchers.[43]

On December 7, the Seventh's Fox Company was sent to a rendezvous site two miles north of Koto-ri to retrieve American prisoners being released by the Chinese.

As soon as they left the MSR, the Fox Marines' foreboding increased. Were they walking into an ambush?

The Fox Marines followed a streambed to a one-story house. As enemy troops watched from the skyline, the Marines found several Army captives and two Commandos lying on the floor of the house, one of them clutching a mailbag.

They were Hellfire Valley survivors. The Marines carried them on stretchers back to the MSR.[44]

The last of the Marines in the column entered Koto-ri at 9:30pm on December 7 – 38 hours after the withdrawal from Hagaru-ri began.[45]

"I was in Koto when they came in," wrote Associated Press correspondent Jack Macbeth. "It was a gruesome sight: wounded men with their blood frozen to their skins; their clothes stiff with ice; grotesque dead men lying across trailers and stretchers; live men stumbling along, grimacing from frostbite, using their rifles as crutches."[46]

The Marines reported 616 casualties during the withdrawal from Hagaru-ri to Koto-ri, and estimated that they had killed more than 2,000 Chinese troops.[47]

Chapter 22

Koto-ri

December 8

It may have appeared to some that there was considerable cause for apprehension over an enemy attack at Koto-ri. For my own part, upon arrival at Koto-ri, my feeling was that we were in.

General O.P. Smith after his division marched from Hagaru-ri to Koto-ri on December 6–7.[1]

Colonel Lewis B. "Chesty" Puller and his 2,600 First Marines had defended Koto-ri from repeated Chinese attacks since the 2nd Battalion established a rudimentary perimeter defense on November 24.

It was refined over the next several days, with a special effort put into the defense of the northern perimeter, the most likely avenue for a Chinese attack.

During the night of November 29–30, Easy Company, which was defending the northern sector, repulsed a battalion-size Chinese attack, killing 123 enemy troops and wounding 47 at a cost of 24 casualties.

The Chinese attackers encountered what one historian described as "a curtain of fire"; just 17 got inside the perimeter, and they were all killed in hand-to-hand fighting.[2]

Other units and supporting arms had streamed into the perimeter during the push to the Yalu River, and then became stranded when the Chinese 60th Division severed the MSR to Hagaru-ri.

Besides Puller's 2nd Battalion, there were 1,500 Army troops from the 7th Division; a number of 105mm howitzers from the Eleventh Marines; 4.2-inch mortars; an antitank unit; and a 1st Medical Battalion company.[3]

When he led the First Marines north to Koto-ri in November, Puller prioritized tents over ammunition. "I'll take care of my men first. Frozen troops can't fight. If we run out of ammunition, we'll go to the bayonet."[4]

Puller was a genuine Marine Corps legend, having earned four Navy Crosses before the Korean War.

His 32 years in the Corps began with service in Haiti and Nicaragua during the 1920s and 1930s, and he was a member of the "Horse Marines" in China. Two Navy Crosses were awarded for his service in Nicaragua.

The ramrod-straight Virginian was known for his aggressiveness and leading from the front. During World War II, he commanded Marines on Guadalcanal and Cape Gloucester, earning a Navy Cross for his leadership during each of those campaigns.

On Peleliu, Puller's First Regiment was decimated in just one week. General William Rupertus, the 1st Marine Division commander, repeatedly ordered Puller to send his battalions against well-entrenched Japanese in Peleliu's highlands.

The First Marines' losses in one week surpassed anything previously seen by a Marine regiment. Shocked by Puller's casualties, General Roy Geiger ordered Rupertus to withdraw the First Regiment, overriding Rupertus's and Puller's vehement objections.

General O.P. Smith, who was the 1st Division's assistant commander on Peleliu, said of Puller's actions there, "There was no finesse about it, but there was gallantry and there was determination."

Some senior Marine officers believed Puller lacked the ability to command a regiment and had displayed "callous disregard" for his men's lives on Peleliu. Puller arrived in Korea while still under the cloud of Peleliu.[5]

The Koto-ri perimeter became overcrowded after the arrival from Hagaru-ri of roughly 10,000 Marines, Royal Marine commandos, and soldiers. The 14,229 troops were jammed into the perimeter plus a full complement of artillery and 50 tanks, requiring food and shelter, medical care and ammunition.[6]

Yet General Smith was supremely confident that even with tens of thousands of enemy troops in the area – the 26th Army and elements of the 20th and 27th Armies – the Chinese could not stop the breakout to the Sea of Japan.

"It may have appeared to some that there was considerable cause for apprehension over an enemy attack at Koto-ri," Smith wrote. "For my own part, upon arrival at Koto-ri, my feeling was that we were in."[7]

After Pfc Jack Wright of the Fifth Marines' George Company and some of his comrades had obtained a tent and moved into it, there was a tap on the canvas. A British Commando captain asked if he could billet 12 of his men there. Wright and his comrades readily agreed.

"The Brits looked like they had come right off a parade," said Wright. "The first thing they did was clean the place up. They tore the stove apart and cleaned it, then gathered up the litter and threw it out."

Wright and an Army corporal picked up their gear and left the tent, "ashamed because we looked so cruddy."[8]

The 185th Engineer Combat Battalion had begun building Koto-ri's airstrip on the northern perimeter, the best place for an airfield. Unfortunately, it was half in and half out of the perimeter – problematic because it meant that construction work could be done only during the daytime, when enemy activity was low, and not at night when crews could be attacked.

Despite these drawbacks, during the first 20 hours of work, the engineers were able to grade enough of a runway to accommodate light reconnaissance and spotter planes and helicopters. These aircraft were able to fly out two wounded men at a time.

After that runway was extended by 300 feet, converted World War II-era Grumman TBM torpedo bombers began landing and taking off on December 7, evacuating up to nine men at once. An aircraft carrier signal officer stationed at the airstrip used paddles to guide the planes to safe landings.

Desk-bound wing and staff officers volunteered to fly out some of the wounded in the stripped-down Avengers, which were unheated and uncomfortable, but served the purpose.

"Not only are the people seriously wounded, they are frozen, too," said a VMF-214 mechanic who helped unload wounded men from the torpedo bombers in Hungnam. He described a Marine whose breath escaping from between his purple lips "was the only sign of life."

"Between [the] fingers on his right hand was a cold cigarette that had burned down between his fingers before going out. The flesh had burned, but he had not noticed."[9]

Two hundred casualties were flown out of Koto-ri December 7 on TBMs, light aircraft, and helicopters.

Pilots told Smith that if the runway were extended another 400 feet to 1,750 feet, the roomier C-47s, able to transport up to 40 men at once, could land and take off. Evacuations would increase exponentially.

During the night of December 7–8, engineers graded another 400 feet of runway so that C-47s could land.[10]

Heavy snow on December 8 caused flights to be suspended at the airstrip, with the exception of a lone C-47 that risked crashing, yet managed to land and take off with 19 casualties.

The next day, when the storm had passed, Koto-ri's hospital tents were cleared and 225 serious cases were flown out.[11]

The airstrip extension and the wholesale casualty evacuations might not have occurred without the determined efforts of 46-year-old Lieutenant Colonel John Upshur Dennis Page.

Page had spent World War II training troops at Fort Sill, Oklahoma, a job at which he had been highly successful. When the war ended, however, Page regretted not having been in combat. He arrived at X Corps headquarters in Hamhung on November 27, 1950, eager to see action.

His job ostensibly was to place communication teams along the MSR. However, Page did much more than that.

He variously acted as a bombardier on a light plane, a tank commander, a one-man army flushing Chinese snipers, and a guardian of the engineers extending the runway.[12]

Page's adventures began November 29, when he led a nine-jeep communications convoy out of Hamhung on the MSR toward Chosin Reservoir. Five inches of newly fallen snow covered the road, where he stationed his teams at key points.

Approaching a blown-out bridge at dusk, Page's driver, Corporal David Klepsig, drove their jeep down an embankment, where they were fired upon and forced to run for cover.

Page instructed Klepsig to drive the jeep back to the road while Page covered him with his carbine. When Klepsig reached the road, he found Page standing in the middle of the MSR, boldly spraying the enemy positions with his carbine. The stunned Chinese did not fire back, and the men drove on to Koto-ri.

The next morning, discovering that Koto-ri was surrounded and might be overrun, Page began rounding up Army artillerymen, military policemen, engineers, medics, and truck drivers who had been separated from their units. Page organized then into a reserve force for Puller's Marines.

Puller's small hospital was full, and he directed Page to supervise the extension of the airstrip so that more men could be evacuated. At that time, the airfield could accommodate just reconnaissance planes and helicopters.

Page saw that the airstrip must be extended so that larger planes could land and take off, but that enemy snipers in the ridges were picking off construction workers.

Page armed himself with his carbine, extra ammunition, and grenades, and asked the pilot of a reconnaissance plane, Lieutenant Charles Kieffer, to fly him over a nearby mountain pass occupied by Chinese soldiers.

As they flew over the mountain, Page pulled the pins from three grenades and threw them onto a large tent, destroying it. Observing that foxholes stippled the ridge, Page instructed Kieffer to make another pass, and he bombed the entrenchments with more grenades. On yet another pass, he shot up the occupied foxholes with his carbine.

Back in Koto-ri, Page was checking on the progress of the runway extension when he saw a grader driver fall from his seat, shot through the neck by a sniper. The other workers scattered.

Page leaped atop a tank, manned the .50-caliber machine gun and ordered the crew to drive to the edge of a sniper-infested hill. With short bursts, he killed the snipers.

Back at the airstrip, Chinese troops poured out of gullies nearby to overrun the runway. When Marines stopped them and they fled, Page leaped atop another tank. Blazing away with the tank's machine gun, he helped chase off the enemy soldiers.

After those skirmishes, the Chinese stopped trying to interfere with the runway work.[13]

There was no room for the dead on the planes flying out hundreds of wounded men from Koto-ri before the breakout planned on December 8. More casualties were expected after the truck convoy got under way; space on the trucks was reserved for them.

The remaining option pleased no one, but necessity required it: with little time before the breakout from Koto-ri, the dead would have to buried in a mass grave there.

It would be exceedingly difficult. Temperatures below minus 30 degrees on the 4,000-foot plateau, exacerbated by the howling winds out of Manchuria, had made the ground as hard as concrete.

The burial site chosen for the interment of the 117 Marines, soldiers, and sailors was a former artillery command post that had been dug earlier. Engineers with explosives hollowed out a pit, aided by two bulldozers that carved out a ramp for the trucks laden with the bodies, each wrapped in a sleeping bag or parachute.

A brief service was held in a driving snowstorm in the bitter cold after the dead were laid in rows in the large hole, and then covered with ponchos. Protestant and Catholic chaplains read selections from Scripture as General Smith and his battalion commanders looked on.

"As soon as each chaplain had said his little bit for the fellows, we would cover them up and close them in," wrote Robert Gault of Graves Registration. "Everyone was given a very fine burial, I think, under the circumstances."

Smith briefly noted in his log: "A mound was bulldozed over the bodies. It was not a pleasant sight."[14]

A Graves Registration officer later made a map of the site in the event that the Marines returned to disinter them. The bodies are still there.[15]

At home, Americans were learning to their dismay of the 1st Marine Division's plight from newspaper stories, under headlines such as: "Battered U.S. Marines Stage Fightingest Retreat"; "1st Division Marines Walk Out of Icy Hell"; "Marines, Outnumbered and Frozen, Fought in Best Tradition of Proud Service"; and "One of the Bloodiest Chapters in Marine History."

In a radio broadcast, Walter Winchell said, "If you have a father, brother, or son in the 1st Marine Division ... pray for him tonight."[16]

Syndicated columnist Drew Pearson weighed in with a sharp critique of the decision-making that led to the entrapment of the Marines. The headline read: "Marines Trapped in Korea Were Victims of Bad Military Errors."[17]

New York Times columnist James Reston described the grim mood in Washington: "Every official movement in the capital today, every official report from Tokyo, and every private estimate of the situation by well-informed men reflected a sense of emergency and even of alarm about the state of the United Nations army in Korea."[18]

General Walter Bidell Smith, director of the Central Intelligence Agency, said, "Only diplomacy can save MacArthur's right flank."

Time magazine reported that at the Chosin Reservoir campaign's nadir, the trapped troops were written off as "The Lost Legion," and their escape was touted as "The Christmas Miracle."

Miracle or not, Americans' support for the Korean War dropped sharply between July, when 66 percent favored intervention, to 39 percent in December.[19]

In his book *The Coldest Winter*, the late author David Halberstam wrote that as the news reached the American public about the crisis of the 1st Marine Division, "seemingly cut off and surrounded by a giant force of Chinese, there was widespread fear that the division might be lost. Omar Bradley himself [the chairman of the Joint Chiefs of Staff] was almost certain they were lost."

Halberstam described the breakout as "a masterpiece of leadership on the part of their officers and of simple, relentless, abiding courage on the part of the ordinary fighting men – fighting a larger force in the worst kind of mountainous terrain and unbearable cold that sometimes reached down to minus forty."[20]

At Koto-ri, General Smith sensed his men's growing confidence that they would reach the sea. "The men instinctively felt that we were over the hump," he wrote.

Inside the hospital tent where he and Colonel Alpha Bowser were planning the breakout's next stage, Smith heard singing coming from a nearby tent. It was snowing outside.

"I do not know who was doing the singing, but I know it gave me quite a lift. Here was confidence," Smith wrote.[21]

Smith and Bowser decided to stick with the same plan that they had followed during their march from Hagaru-ri to Koto-ri. Infantrymen would capture the high ground with close-air support so that the convoy could advance.

At the same time, the 1st Battalion of the First Marines, which Puller had left to protect the MSR at Chinghung-ni, 12 miles south of Koto-ri, would attack northward and seize Hill 1081. The large prominence was the vital terrain feature that overlooked Funchilin Pass.[22]

Chapter 23

The Bridge

Complete despair was my reaction when I looked down from the high ground and saw that chasm between us and Chinhung-ni.

LIEUTENANT WILLIAM DAVIS DESCRIBING THE 2,000-FOOT CANYON WHERE THE CHINESE HAD BLOWN THE BRIDGE AT FUNCHILIN PASS.[1]

Dammit, sir! I got you across the Han River at Seoul and I got you an airfield at Hagaru – and I'll get you a goddamn bridge at Koto!

LIEUTENANT COLONEL JOHN PARTRIDGE TO GENERAL O.P. SMITH ABOUT BUILDING A BRIDGE OVER THE GORGE AT FUNCHILIN PASS.[2]

One huge problem remained: four miles south of Koto-ri, the Chinese had blown the concrete bridge at Funchilin Pass. The bridge was on the most dangerous stretch of the MSR between the coast and Yudam-ni.

It passed over four huge pipes called penstocks that funneled water flowing subterraneanly from Chosin Reservoir to hydroelectric power plants in the valley below.

The bridge, which was adjacent to Changjin Power Plant No. 1, was undamaged when the Marines marched up the MSR to Koto-ri, Hagaru-ri, and Yudam-ni. At the time, General Smith suspected that the enemy had deliberately let it remain intact, not wanting to impede the Marines' advance. He believed that the Chinese intended to destroy it and isolate the division after it had passed over the bridge.

"It was shrewd of Smith to understand that, but it's hard to think of any other capable officer who was paying attention not coming up with much the same scenario," wrote Major James Lawrence, commander of the Seventh Marines' 2nd Battalion. "[General Ned] Almond seemed to have so little respect for the Chinese as fighting men that it was as if he didn't care."[3]

Only when most of the division was north of the bridge did the Chinese blow it up on December 1, evidently to prevent reinforcements from reaching the Chosin Reservoir area from Hungnam, and to sever the avenue of retreat.

Army engineers from Chinhung-ni replaced the blown section with a wooden span.

When it, too, was blown by the Chinese, the engineers installed a steel span.

On December 4, the Chinese destroyed the third bridge, leaving a 29-foot gap above a heart-stopping chasm 2,000 feet deep.

Smith and his engineers had to find a sturdy replacement that could support the Marine convoy's trucks and tanks.

Otherwise, the vehicles would have to be left behind on the northern side of the canyon.[4]

Marines on foot might bypass the bridge site on trails that went down into the canyon and up the other side, but the truck-bound wounded would have to be carried out. "To leave them was unthinkable," said Lieutenant William Davis of the Seventh's Able Company.[5]

After surveying Funchilin Pass from a reconnaissance plane, Lieutenant Colonel John Partridge, the gifted leader of the 1st Engineer Battalion, conceived a risky plan for replacing the bridge span.

On December 6, Partridge described his plan to General Smith.

Smith had a multitude of questions, and after attempting to answer many of them, the normally reserved Partridge became exasperated with the general.

"Dammit, sir! I got you across the Han River at Seoul and I got you an airfield at Hagaru – and I'll get you a goddamn bridge at Koto!"

Smith quietly enjoyed Partridge's outburst and had no further questions.[6]

Partridge's plan called for parachuting to Koto-ri 22-foot steel Treadway bridge sections, each weighing 2,500 pounds. This had never been attempted before.

By a stroke of luck, in Koto-ri there happened to be a platoon of the Army 58th Engineer Treadway Company and four Brockway trucks, two of them operable. The Treadway company had installed bridges in Italy during World War II. If the sections could be air-delivered intact, Partridge's plan might work.[7]

A test-drop of one span near Yonpo airfield went badly; the span landed too hard, and was damaged and unusable.

A special detail of Air Force parachute-riggers tackled the problem. They tried airdropping a span with two larger, 48-foot parachutes, hoping for a softer landing. The experiment worked.

During the morning of December 7, eight C-119 Flying Boxcars took off from Yonpo airfield carrying one bridge section apiece. Twice the number needed, this allowed for breakage; if four landed at Koto-ri intact, the bridge could be constructed.

One bridge section landed outside of the Koto-ri perimeter and was recovered by Chinese troops, while a second one landed hard on the frozen ground and was badly damaged.

Six spans, however, fell inside the perimeter. Brockway truck crews recovered them and deemed them usable. Precut plywood for flooring arrived in a subsequent airdrop.[8]

The material needed to install the bridge sections was readied by late afternoon on the 7th.

Heavy snow fell during the morning of the 8th, so close-air support was unavailable. But that afternoon the Brockway trucks left Koto-ri to attempt to bridge the chasm. Enemy artillery and mortar fire, snowfall, and extreme cold forced the Brockway crews to return to Koto-ri for the night.

"The enemy could not have picked a better spot to give us trouble," wrote General Smith.[9]

While the Brockway trucks returned to Koto-ri, the Seventh's 1st and 2nd Battalions pushed ahead on the high ground toward the bridge site.

The wind-blown snow fell so thickly that the Marines could barely see their way forward, and the temperature was nearly 30 below zero. The 1st Battalion scrambled to the high ground east of the MSR, while the 2nd Battalion began to clear the heights west of the road.[10]

It was fitting that the 1st Battalion was again in the vanguard of the 14,229-man column, paired with the 2nd Battalion.

The 1st Battalion had led the march to Chosin Reservoir and had done much of the fighting at Sudong in early November. Now, the division was returning, with the 1st Battalion once more out in front, thinned by battle casualties and severe frostbite.[11]

The Funchilin Pass chokepoint was the last, best chance for the Chinese to thwart the escape from the trap in which they had snared the Americans.

The late-arriving 26th Army hastened to block the breakout. On December 6, its 226th, 227th, and 228th Regiments and their 54 infantry companies totaled 14,000 men. On paper, this was a powerful force.

In reality, the subzero cold and starvation had sapped the 26th's fighting strength. When the 227th's 3rd Battalion got lost in the mountains, most of its 1,000 men froze to death overnight.[12]

After reaching Hagaru-ri, the 26th Army had raced through the icy hills for three days without rest to stop the Marines' breakout.

The 20th and 27th Armies were mere shadows of their former selves. The 20th was able to send just 200 men, the survivors of its 58th and 60th Divisions, to Funchilin Pass. Just 2,000 men of the 27th Army's 50,000 men that had begun the Second Offensive two weeks earlier remained able to fight.[13]

Enemy soldiers churning through the snowbound hills to Koto-ri and Funchilin Pass were determined to stop the breakout at all costs – with a bloody finish fight if necessary.

On the high ground east of the MSR, enemy gunfire lashed Able Company, which led the assault, inflicting heavy casualties. Baker Company was ordered to take the point from Able.

"The tracers were weird streaks of orange that flew at us out of the blinding snow clouds. Our new corpsman was quickly put to work," wrote Lieutenant Joe Owen, Baker's mortar officer. Owen was given command of a rifle platoon after its commander became too ill to continue.[14]

Lieutenant Joe Kurcaba, Baker's commander, summoned Owen to the MSR and, pointing to a map, told him to take out the Chinese guns firing at them from a hill to the left.

At that moment, a sniper's bullet drilled Kurcaba through the forehead, and he slumped into Owen's arms, dead. "This beautiful Pollack with his broad Slavic face, he was like a big brother to us," said Owen.

Owen took the map to Lieutenant Chew-Een Lee and informed him that he was the new Baker Company commander.

Minutes later, machine-gun fire stitched Lee's face and right arm.

The tough, diminutive lieutenant, already twice wounded during the campaign, was able to walk down the hill. He was strapped to a stretcher and blankets were piled on him as his body temperature plummeted due to shock and extreme fatigue. Lee survived.[15]

Minutes later, Chinese soldiers in a hillside bunker obscured by the blowing snow shot Owen in the left shoulder and right elbow as he led an attack, putting him out of action as well.

Now, Lieutenant Woody Taylor, Baker's only unwounded officer, took charge of what was left of the company – 27 men of the original complement of 180. Aided by a tank, Taylor's men neutralized the bunker.[16]

Arriving with Major Webb Sawyer, the 1st Battalion commander who had succeeded Lieutenant Colonel Ray Davis, at Taylor's tiny command post, Colonel Litzenberg ordered Taylor to send a platoon along the ridgeline to make contact with Marine units ahead of him.

Taylor replied, "Hell, Colonel, I haven't got a platoon left in the whole damned company."

Sawyer told Taylor to send whatever was available.[17]

Taylor reconstituted his company into two pitifully undersized platoons. They pushed along the ridgeline until they reached the top of Funchilin Pass in a howling windstorm, in temperatures of minus 30 degrees with an added wind chill.[18]

The Chinese 58th Division's 173rd and 174th Regiments, which were rushed ahead to defend Hills 1304 and 1350 below Koto-ri and block the Marines, were in even worse condition than the Marines. During the blizzard on December 8, Marine tanks shredded the defenders at a roadblock on the MSR, forcing them to withdraw.

The Marine rifle companies fought the Chinese well into the night so that the convoy could slip down the MSR the next day.

During the morning of December 9, the skies cleared and an American air raid plastered Hills 1304 and 1350 with bombs and napalm.

Hu Qianxiu, the 58th Division's chief of staff, was killed in the raid, along with division and regimental staff officers with him at the division command post. Qianxiu was the highest-ranking Chinese officer killed during the Chosin Reservoir campaign.[19]

The Marines who reached the high ground above the blown bridge were met with a daunting sight.

"Complete despair was my reaction when I looked down from the high ground and saw that chasm between us and Chinhung-ni," said Lieutenant William Davis of Able Company. "Here was the great divide, the Korean mini-Grand Canyon that could cancel everything the Marines had achieved up to this point."[20]

When Colonel Litzenberg urged Major Warren Morris, the 3rd Battalion commander, to move faster and to commit his reserve company. Morris told Litzenberg, "All three companies are up there – 50 men from George Company, 50 men from How, 30 men from Item. That's it." Each company was no bigger than a platoon.

Litzenberg sent his regimental reserve, the 2nd Battalion, to aid Morris.[21]

Near the broken bridge, one of the Baker Company platoons found 50 Chinese troops frozen stiff in their foxholes.

"They were so badly frozen that the men simply lifted them from the holes and sat them on the road where Marines from Charlie Company took them over," said Major Sawyer, the 1st Battalion commander.

Their feet swollen to the size of footballs, the Chinese were dazed by fatigue, and their hands were frozen to their weapons.

"Some of them had to have their fingers broken in order for us to take the rifles from their frozen hands," said Sergeant Lee Burgee.

Days of bitter cold with little food or rest had taken an exorbitant toll on the Chinese, incapacitating many of them and killing others.

On a ridge that day, Burgee encountered a Chinese soldier sitting on his haunches with his rifle leveled at Burgee. "I almost fired, then I saw he was dead – frozen stiff in that position."[22]

Lieutenant Taylor, Baker Company's commander, said the enemy troops the Marines took prisoner on the ridges "were half dead, their hands and feet frozen."

Taylor said that his men could neither provide them with medical care, take them along with them, nor leave them in their rear. They must be "put ... out of their misery," he said. "My men took twenty or twenty-five of them out of this world, and frankly I've never regretted giving that order."

Sergeant Sherman Richter said that the battalion CP on the road had ordered Baker Company to send down the prisoners for interrogation.

"It was snowing, there was no air cover, we were out of food, we climbed hill after hill ... We said, 'Fine.' The Chinese prisoners were lined up and shot. A message was sent back to battalion: 'The prisoners tried to escape and we shot them.'"[23]

At the valve control building of Changjin Power Plant No. 1, the Marines killed a large number of enemy soldiers inside. Outside the building, they were surrounded by unarmed Chinese troops that wanted to surrender.[24]

One of them said that he belonged to a 1,000-man battalion that had run through the mountains the previous night to take positions defending the power plant. After a sudden temperature drop, the soldiers had frozen in their own sweat, he said.[25]

On the MSR south of Koto-ri, *Life* magazine photojournalist David Douglas Duncan photographed a Marine during a rest break. Duncan's photograph soon became iconic – symbolizing the Marines' breakout to the sea.

"... the cold had cut into his face and eyes until even the look of animal survival was gone," Duncan wrote. The Marine poked at his rations with a spoon and raised a frozen bean to his lips, thawing it in his mouth.

Duncan posed a question: what would the Marine ask for if he could have anything that he wanted.

The Marine raised his eyes to the gray sky.

"Give me tomorrow," he said.[26]

With clearing weather and the resistance mostly suppressed on the heights around the bridge site, the Brockway trucks could now lumber down the MSR from Koto-ri and lay the steel bridge sections over the chasm.

But would Lieutenant Colonel Partridge's outside-the-box solution actually work?

The first problem was that the Treadway sections were too short: 22-foot-long sections to span a 29-foot gap.

Enemy gunfire spattered down from the heights as the engineers pondered the problem.

Adding to the challenge were the subzero temperature and winds howling out of the north – not ideal conditions for puzzling out a solution for getting 14,000 men and their vehicles across a 2,000-foot-deep canyon.

Colonel Litzenberg sent 50-ton trucks to shield the doughty engineers, who had built the Hagaru-ri airfield under fire. As before, they worked under Partridge's supervision.

Aided by 100 men that included Chinese prisoners, they constructed a "crib" from bridging timbers that had been stored near the bridge by Korea's Japanese occupiers years earlier.

The crib extended over a ledge that was 8 feet below the former bridge. The timbers were stacked in crisscross layers so that they resembled a latticework. Frozen Chinese bodies were used to fill the holes.[27]

The Brockway trucks laid the steel Treadway sections, and the thick plywood bed was placed between them.

It was no less than "a high-wire act," in the words of some onlookers, and it took three and a half hours to complete. The engineers held their breath as a jeep became the first vehicle to attempt a crossing.

The bridge creaked and groaned but held, and the jeep reached the other side safely.

Partridge jubilantly returned to the head of the division convoy of 1,400 vehicles queued all the way back to Koto-ri and told the drivers that they could now proceed over the Treadway bridge.

Around 6pm, after the first dozen vehicles had gotten over the bridge, a loud snap was heard. A large bulldozer had crashed partway through the bridge's thick plywood centerpiece and had become stuck there.

The bulldozer driver quickly got off the machine and jogged to the bridge's north side.

The column could not move with the bulldozer blocking the way.

Up stepped Tech Sergeant Wilfred Prosser, widely regarded as the division's best heavy equipment operator. Guided by flashlights, Prosser gingerly backed the big machine to the north side of the bridge.

Partridge and his engineers huddled around the bridge, brainstorming how to fix the problem. They decided to discard the plywood bed and re-lay the steel Treadways as far apart as possible – at 11 feet, 4 inches.

After being re-spaced by bulldozers, the Treadways were able to accommodate vehicles of all axle widths, but with no margin for error. Each crossing would have to be made slowly, because both the wide-tracked tanks and the narrow-axle jeeps would have just inches to spare.[28]

Guided by men with flashlights, the bridge traffic resumed, and continued all night long. The drivers and the thousands of men on foot crossed the chasm while trying not to peer into the inky-black void beneath them, lest they become disoriented and plunge to their deaths. No one did.

Partridge described the night crossing as "extremely eerie. There seemed to be a glow over everything. There was no illumination and yet you seemed to see quite well; there was artillery fire; there was the crunching of many feet and many vehicles on the crisp snow. There were many North Korean refugees on one side of the column and Marines on the other. Every once in a while there would be a baby wailing. There were cattle on the road. Everything added to the general sensation of relief, or expected relief."[29]

Just south of the bridge, the engineers were concerned about another obstacle that lay across the MSR. Blown by the Chinese, a massive concrete trestle that had supported a mountain tramway blocked the MSR. Engineers believed only explosives could remove it.

The solution was far easier than anyone anticipated. There was no need for explosives. Because the trestle lay on a sheet of ice, a single bulldozer was able to push it off the road and over the lip of the canyon.[30]

For eight hours, vehicles, troops, and North Korean civilians crossed the bridge, braving whistling sub-arctic winds, drifting snow, and 30-below-zero temperatures.

The vehicle traffic included 50-ton tanks and towed artillery, all of them first descending the road from the 4,000-foot Koto-ri plateau with its hairpin turns in the dark before reaching the bridge.

Enemy resistance was nearly nonexistent because the Seventh Marines had cleared the nearby heights.[31]

At the rear of the column, a serious problem developed. Thousands of refugees, infiltrated by enemy troops, were pressing against the rearguard.

Up to this point, a roadblock north of Koto-ri had restrained the homeless refugees. During the snowstorm of December 8, they had huddled together in an attempt to get warm, emitting "a low-pitched wail of misery." Navy corpsmen attended to a pair of refugee women who gave birth that bitter-cold night.[32]

As the last units withdrew from Koto-ri, Army 155mm howitzers ten miles away at Chinhung-ni laid down interdiction fire to prevent Chinese troops from closing in on the column's rear. The last units left Koto-ri under harassing small-arms fire.

About 50 wounded enemy prisoners were left behind at Koto-ri in a heated house. Medical personnel had treated their wounds and their frostbite, and food and water were left with them.

The Americans placed a Red Cross panel on the side of the house so that the Chinese would not destroy it. It was reciprocity for the care given by the Chinese to UN captives two weeks earlier in Hellfire Valley.[33]

Thousands of North Korean refugees, with Chinese soldiers lurking in their midst, shadowed the column when it left Koto-ri.

The civilians' homes had been ransacked and burned, they were hungry and cold. Nothing remained for them in their homeland.

They hitched their hopes for survival to the American troops, wherever they were going, and not to the capricious mercies of the Chinese and North Korean soldiers.

At the bridge, the tanks brought up the column's rear. The division's skeletal reconnaissance company, just 28 men led by Major Walter Gall, was the only infantry unit protecting the last ten tanks in the convoy. They were stopped behind a tank that experienced "brake lock" and stalled. The 30 tanks ahead of the stall had continued to roll toward the bridge.

As the refugees drew closer, the Marines fired warning shots over their heads to keep them at a distance. The shots were answered by gunfire from behind the refugees. The Chinese infiltrators were using them as shields.

"We weren't worried about the Chinese," said Gall, "but we were worried about those civilians. If they had overrun us we would have been finished."

Gall ordered a machine gun set up in the middle of the road behind the tanks. Pfc Glenn Kasdorf, the gunner, could not find any ammunition for it. After going to retrieve a belt, he returned to find four Chinese soldiers around the gun, one of them armed with a Thompson submachine gun.

After a tug-of-war over the machine gun, Kasdorf left with the ammunition belt, and the enemy soldiers got the weapon; Kasdorf was later able to retrieve it, too.[34]

Out of the milling crowd stepped five Chinese soldiers; someone called out that they wished to surrender.

Lieutenant Ernest Hargett, the Reconnaissance Company's operations officer, went to meet them, carbine at the ready. As Hargett drew nearer, the lead man stepped aside, revealing four Chinese troops with burp guns.

Hargett's carbine failed to fire, and he charged the lead Chinese soldier, striking him with the carbine. A grenade detonated, spraying Hargett with steel fragments.

Corporal Gene Anyotte opened fire with a BAR and killed the enemy soldiers.

The foes fought at close quarters with fists, bayonets, and rifle butts as more Chinese troops descended from the adjacent hills, throwing grenades and satchel charges.

A grenade blast flung Pfc Robert DeMott over the edge of the chasm, but by an incredible stroke of luck he landed, unconscious, on a ledge below the rim and did not plunge 2,000 feet to his death. After he regained consciousness, DeMott was able to rejoin his unit.

The situation deteriorated further. Chinese troops attacked Hargett's men from the rear and the high ground. The besieged reconnaissance company pulled back to the tanks as enemy soldiers set up machine guns in the road and the civilians lay flat to avoid getting shot.

Enemy soldiers swarmed the last tank in line, and it was lost. With their rifle butts, the Marines rapped on the second-to-last tank to warn the crew of the imminent danger, but no one emerged.

Five of the tanks in front of it were abandoned, but two others managed to maneuver around the brake-locked tank and cross the bridge.[35]

It shouldn't have happened, said General Smith.

"We had taken the precaution of putting the tanks at the rear of the column, because we were afraid if something happened to a tank it would block the road, and it'd be so heavy you couldn't move it," Smith said.

"So, the tanks were the last elements in the column, and Lewie [Colonel Chesty Puller] just assumed the tanks would take care of the rear, and he let Sutter [Lieutenant Colonel Allan Sutter, the 2nd Battalion commander] go on down the road. Then the Chinese came down the slopes over the road and they began intermingling with the refugees – there were about 3,000 refugees who were following us out – and the refugees kept coming forward."[36]

Puller's error left the tanks' protection in the hands of Hargett's 28 men. This was a too-thin barrier indeed between the rear of the convoy and the thousands of desperate refugees with enemy troops in their midst.

During the chaotic last hour of the bridge crossing, the reconnaissance company lost two men killed, 12 wounded, and one missing.

The toll would surely have been higher had it not been for the experimental, lightweight body armor worn by some of the reconnaissance Marines. The tough fiberglass plates in the Marines' utility jackets evolved from the World War II Army Air Corps flak jackets, and effectively stopped most shell and grenade fragments.

The flak jackets were eventually issued to all of the front-line troops in Korea.[37]

Puller had walked most of the way from Koto-ri, shouting at each unit that he passed, "Don't forget you're 1st Marines! Not all the communists in hell can overrun you!"[38]

He waited at the bridge until all of the reconnaissance Marines had crossed, and only then went over the Treadway. Lashed to his jeep bumper was the body of a tank crewman. Two other bodies were tied to the jeep hood, their faces waxen with cold. Several wounded men were crowded in the jeep's rear.[39]

At 2am on December 11, after the last vehicle had gotten over the bridge, Lieutenant Colonel Partridge ordered the bridge blown with 300 pounds of Composition C. Chief Warrant Officer Willie Harrison set off the charge.[40]

"I had a sense of well-being after all had gone across and I'd blown the bridge," Partridge said.[41]

Chapter 24

The Last Furlong

Some of my boys came up this hill knowing full well they had but minutes to live. They assaulted. It's a miracle anyone got up this hill at all.

CAPTAIN ROBERT BARROW OF THE FIGHT FOR HILL 1081.[1]

Seen from the air, [the] march held both magnificence and pathos. There was a Biblical pageantry about it. Everything seemed frozen – grey clouds ... the evergreen mountains, the hills, the yellow roads ... the dusty battle cars ... the white-clad groups of refugees wading the rivers or huddling together in the hills ... the endless columns of troops in olive drab.

ASSOCIATED PRESS CORRESPONDENT HAL BOYLE, WHO VIEWED IT FROM A PLANE.[2]

Never in its history has Marine aviation given more convincing proof of its indispensable value to the ground Marine ... A bond of understanding has been established that will never be broken.

GENERAL O.P. SMITH.[3]

Two days before the Treadway bridge crossing, Lieutenant Colonel Donald Schmuck had led his 1st Marines Battalion north from Chinhung-ni to secure the heights south of Funchilin Pass. Hill 1081 was the dominant terrain feature between the bridge and the railhead leading to the lowlands.

The ice-covered hill was defended by the 180th Regiment of the Chinese 60th Division, entrenched in sandbagged bunkers.

Until now, Schmuck's battalion had not engaged in any large-scale fighting during the campaign, but had patrolled aggressively. Ten days earlier, harassed by probing nighttime attacks by enemy troops that hid by day in houses in a nearby mountain valley, Schmuck went after them.

With Able Company, part of Baker Company, and his mortars, Schmuck's men drove the Chinese out of the valley and burned down the houses that had sheltered them. They killed 56 enemy soldiers. The rest had fled, some on shaggy Mongolian ponies, and were harried by Corsairs from VMF-312.[4]

Earlier, a Schmuck patrol had scouted Funchilin Pass, encouraging the Marines at Koto-ri to believe that soon they would reach the Sea of Japan.

"We discounted the danger because we knew that Schmuck had already been over the ground," said General Smith.[5]

Now, ordered by General Smith to secure Hill 1081 and the six-mile stretch of road between Chinhung-ni and Funchilin Pass, Schmuck's 1st Battalion at last had an important part to play in the breakout to the Sea of Japan. The Marines were eager to go into action.

Moreover, Hill 1081 was the enemy's last chance to stop the Marine withdrawal.[6]

Heavy snow fell as the Marines began marching north at 2am on November 8 toward Hill 1081, planning to be in position to attack at 8am.

Schmuck's men were equipped with heavy weapons: 18 Army self-propelled quad .50s and twin 40mm Bofor guns, and 81mm and 4.2-inch mortars. Two ambulances and a jeep also accompanied the battalion.

Units from the Army's 3rd Infantry Division were combined into a provisional force designated Task Force Dog, which took the place of the 1st Battalion in Chinhung-ni. Dog was given responsibility for security on the MSR south of Chinhung-ni.[7]

The snowstorm reduced visibility to 20 feet and screened the Marines' approach. Although outnumbered 3-to-1, Schmuck's battalion enjoyed the advantage of surprise as it began climbing the steep, icy slopes of Hill 1081.

"We were crawling up the incline, sometimes on all fours, sometimes using the butt of our weapons as climbing clubs," said Pfc Gordon Greene. "Occasionally a man would lose his footing and make a clean sweep of an entire fire team as he plummeted downhill like a human toboggan."[8]

Bursting into a bunker complex, Baker Company found a kettle of rice cooking and killed or drove out all of the bunker's occupants.

The snowstorm deepened into a blizzard. Yelling loudly, Able Company Marines attacked another sandbagged bunker complex, but were riddled by a lone enemy machine gun.

It was neutralized after a roaring firefight that left ten Marines dead and 11 wounded. Sixty Chinese bodies were counted in the bunker complex area.[9]

When the Chinese counterattacked, they were repulsed with 18 men killed.

Because of the steep, slippery terrain, it took several hours for the Marines to carry casualties the 700 yards to the battalion aid station at the foot of Hill 1081.[10]

To compound the misery, it was one of the Chosin campaign's coldest nights. Temperatures dove below minus 40 degrees as strong winds howled down from Funchilin Pass.

Captain Robert Barrow, the commander of the company nicknamed "Able Able-Hot to Go," spent the night roaming his lines, making sure that his men changed socks to ward off frostbite.

Putting on a fresh pair of socks was a laborious endeavor; it required the Marines to take off their gloves to unlace their boots, and then remove the boots, change socks, put everything back on, and walk around to restore circulation.

Despite Barrow's careful attention, 67 of his men were lost to frostbite, with seven of them becoming amputees.[11]

Clear weather on December 9 gave Schmuck and his Marines a better picture of what they faced: three layers of hills and a 400-yard-long ridge ending in a mountain peak, the summit of Hill 1081.

The previous day's strong winds had intensified into a gale so strong that at times the men were unable to stay upright.

However, the improved visibility meant that the battalion could rely on its supporting arms, especially close-air support.[12]

Pilots reported that the hill was alive with enemy soldiers.

The Marines attacked that morning. Fighting raged for hours around the bunkers, with Schmuck's men assaulting the sandbagged defenses from two sides.

Although outnumbered 2-to-1, Able Company, attacking in a column of platoons, finally reached the crest at 3pm. There lay the bodies of more than 100 enemy soldiers who had frozen to death. The others had fled down the hill's other side – into the arms of Baker Company at the foot of the hill.

Fighting nearly to the last man, the Chinese lost 530 men killed, while Able-Able was reduced to 111 combat-capable men from its original strength of 223.[13]

"Some of my boys came up this hill knowing full well they had but minutes to live," Barrow said. "They assaulted. It's a miracle anyone got up this hill at all."[14]

The timing of Hill 1081's capture couldn't have been better. Soon after, Schmuck's men spotted the vanguard of the convoy marching down the MSR from the Treadway bridge. The road was now open to Hamhung, Hungnam, and the Sea of Japan. It was 1am on December 10.

The Chinese, however, had not given up their pursuit. Three hundred fifty enemy troops attacked the First Marines' George Company as it held open the MSR from a hill west of the road. Despite the severe cold with 65-knot winds adding to the misery, the assault was waged with determined ferocity. Most of the attackers died.[15]

"They [the convoy] traveled on the road while we [the 20th Army] stalked them on the hills and high grounds along both sides of the road," said Captain Wang Xuedong.

Dense formations of Chinese troops were observed east of the MSR, moving southward with the apparent object of heading off the convoy. Battered by air strikes and concentrations of mortar and self-propelled weapons fire, the Chinese were slaughtered in droves.

Wang's men kept up the chase despite the severe cold, steadily mounting casualties, lack of food, and no new winter clothing. To aid his frostbitten men, Wang cut his blanket into strips in which they wrapped their hands and feet.

The 20th Army's 173rd Regiment was also following the ridgelines and awaiting a chance to pounce on the Marines on the road. Stalking the Marines was deadly for Zhu Wenbin's infantry company; it lost half of its men to tank fire.

When Zhu's starving men, having eaten nothing in three days, saw that the Marines had set up tents for the night, the Chinese prepared to launch an attack.

Zhu's men animatedly discussed the prizes that they hoped to find in the Marines' tents: canned meat, Tootsie Rolls, and Marlboro cigarettes.

"We were excited about the night attack since we may be able to get into the Americans' tents and find some food," Zhu said.

But the Marines drove the attackers away before they could enter a single tent. Afterward, Zhu's company had just eight men left who could fight; it was ordered to withdraw to Koto-ri.[16]

The Chinese pursuit was nearing its end, and the 9th Army Group had become a shadow of what it had been on November 27.

The 27th Army, which had attacked at Yudam-ni and joined the pursuit of the Marines down the MSR, was nearly extinct. Its 79th Division, at one time more than 10,000 strong, was reduced to just 300 men.[17]

The column's vanguard, the Seventh Marines' 1st Battalion, reached Chinhung-ni at 2:45am on December 10. After a traffic station was established, the first vehicles rolled into the village at 8:30am.[18]

The convoy continued south to Sudong, where Chinese forces had first attacked the 1st Division in early November during its march north to Chosin Reservoir. The Seventh Marines had so badly bloodied the Chinese 124th Division that it was withdrawn from the battle zone.

Chinese troops had reoccupied the village. Shortly after midnight of December 10, when the convoy reached Sudong, enemy soldiers burst out of their hiding places inside the village's houses, firing burp guns and hurling grenades. The convoy came to an abrupt halt as a wild melee engulfed the village.

Army Lieutenant Colonel John U.D. Page, whose forays against the Chinese in a plane and on a tank at Koto-ri had played such an important role in its airstrip expansion, happened to be present when the fighting erupted.

As aggressively combative as he had been at Koto-ri, Page organized and led the initial effort to repulse the attackers – a machine-gun company of the 26th Army's 77th Division.

Partnering with Marine Pfc Marvin Wasson, Page charged to the head of the vehicle column, flipping the selector on his carbine to full automatic. Firing as he ran, Page attacked a group of 30 Chinese soldiers. The enemy soldiers fled.

Wasson was wounded, and Page continued ahead alone. He was last seen alive shooting at the Chinese in the flickering light of burning convoy trucks.

When Page did not return, Lieutenant Colonel Walton Winston, commander of the Army's 52nd Transportation Truck Battalion, took over and organized a successful counterattack.

Eight Americans were killed and 21 were wounded in the firefight. Enemy troops destroyed nine trucks and personnel carriers.[19]

The Chinese machine-gun company had gone into action with 204 men. It withdrew from Sudong with just 12 soldiers still able to fight.[20]

The column resumed its march south from Sudong and found Page's body outside the village in the middle of the MSR, amid 16 enemy corpses. Page was posthumously awarded the Congressional Medal of Honor and the Navy Cross for his deeds.[21]

The surviving units of the 9th Army Group converged on Hamhung as cold weather and starvation continued to thin its ranks. The 26th Army's 76th Division began its pursuit of the American column with more than 14,000 troops. By December 12, fewer than 5,000 remained.

Of the 58th Division's 173rd Regiment – 4,500 strong upon launching its attacks on Hagaru-ri on November 28 – just over 320 men remained combat-capable.

The enemy's pursuit operations ended December 15. By then, the Chinese were incapable of mounting even a company-size attack around Hamhung.[22]

In a letter to his wife, Lieutenant Colonel James Polk, a staff officer at General Douglas MacArthur's Far East Command in Tokyo, described the bleak atmosphere at the Dai Ichi after the Chinese intervention: "The whole of DHQ ... has a bad case of the blues ... The old man, MacA I mean, is really one hell of a gambler ... Well, this time he gambled it a little too hard and really pressed his luck a bit too far and the whole house fell in on him. He just didn't believe that the whole CCF would be thrown against him." Just days earlier, the feeling was that "the whole thing was going to end in a victorious flourish and now no one can see the end."[23]

Secretary of State Dean Acheson wrote in *Present at the Creation* that MacArthur fell into a "blue funk, sorry for himself ... and sending what we call posterity papers to the Press and Pentagon."[24]

The crumbling of expectations from "home for Christmas" to contemplating the wholesale withdrawal of UN forces from the Korean peninsula began November 25 with the attacks on the Eighth Army in western Korea. Even then, however, MacArthur believed that X Corps could still fulfill its mission of reaching the Yalu River and cutting off the Chinese forces inside Korea from their supply bases in Manchuria.

The attacks on the 1st Marine Division and RCT-31 at Chosin Reservoir on November 27–28 cast a pall of disbelief over the Dai Ichi.

After delivering the shocking news to the Joint Chiefs of Staff on November 28 that "we face an entirely new war," MacArthur further alarmed the Chiefs by describing enemy troops pouring into Korea, with "several hundred thousand reinforcements" close at hand. They intended "the complete destruction of United Nations forces and the securing of all Korea."[25]

General "Lightning Joe" Collins, the Army chief of staff, embarked on a field visit to Korea, and returned with a bleak assessment of the situation.

Senior military leaders considered several courses of action – up to the evacuation of the Korean peninsula.

General Edwin Wright, the operations officer of the Far East Command, presented MacArthur with the range of options.

MacArthur ordered General Almond on December 8 to redeploy X Corps from northeast Korea to South Korea, where it would join the Eighth Army.[26]

Truman kindled apprehension around the world when he pointedly refused to rule out using nuclear weapons to counter the Chinese attacks. The president suggested that their deployment would be up to the military – in other words, MacArthur.

Meanwhile, MacArthur was chafing at the constraints placed on his use of air strikes in Manchuria and was demanding "reinforcements of the greatest magnitude."[27]

MacArthur's popularity had plummeted worldwide since the halcyon days of Inchon and Seoul. The British blamed his "home-for-Christmas" offensive for the Chinese intervention, and believed that his arrogant impetuosity made him a dangerous man.[28]

MacArthur lobbied Washington to give him authority to bomb Chinese sanctuaries in Manchuria, but was rebuffed at every turn.

After Air Force Chief of Staff Hoyt Vandenburg toured the Korean battlefronts, he concluded that such a bombing campaign was unneeded, but MacArthur continued to press for it.

The Truman administration, however, was loath to risk starting a major war with China and was unwilling to even commit additional troops, fearing that this would incite a wider war.[29]

After ordering his generals in Korea to go on the defensive and canceling the 1st Marine Division's attack to the west from Yudam-ni, MacArthur began crafting a counternarrative for posterity.

In his *Reminiscences*, he wrote that the drive into North Korea was no less than a reconnaissance in force whose intent was to "upset the enemy's timetable, causing him to move prematurely, and to reveal the surreptitious massing of his armies. He had hoped to quietly assemble a massive force till spring, and destroy us with one mighty blow ... Had I not acted when I did, we would have been a 'sitting duck' doomed to eventual annihilation." Having sprung "the Red trap," MacArthur's armies escaped it, in his revisionary account.[30]

Incredibly, MacArthur went on to absolve himself of all responsibility for the disaster by asserting, "it is historically inaccurate to attribute any degree of responsibility for the onslaught of the Chinese ... to the strategic course of the campaign itself."[31]

Ten miles south of Koto-ri at Chinhung-ni, some of the troops were put aboard trucks that carried them to Hamhung. There being too few trucks to carry all of the men, many continued on foot for another 13 miles to Majon-dong, where more trucks were available.

Farther down the mountain, the temperature was warmer but still below zero.

"The wind was intensely cold and strong, making progress extremely difficult," the Fifth Marines' 2nd Battalion report said. "The temperature dropped to -10 degrees F. These factors plus the fact that all the men were tired, cold and many suffering from frostbitten feet, made the trek to the railhead an extreme hardship for those walking."[32]

At Sontang, two miles below Majon-dong, X Corps had assembled all of its available railroad equipment. There was an eight-car hospital train as well as scores of rail cars to transport the troops the rest of the way to Hamhung and Hungnam.

The Army's 3rd Infantry Division now assumed permanent responsibility for the security of the lower MSR.[33]

During the last leg of the Marines' journey to Hungnam, the Sea of Japan came into view.

The thrilling sight recalled the reaction of ancient historian Xenophon's celebrated "Ten Thousand," related in his *Anabasis*, when the Greek mercenaries reached the Black Sea in 401 BCE after months of marching, fighting, and privation.* "The sea! The sea!" the Greeks cried, embracing one another and weeping with joy, before erecting a cairn and sacrificing to their gods.[34]

The spectacle of the final part of the Marines' march to the sea might have been best viewed from above.

Associated Press correspondent Hal Boyle wrote, "Seen from the air, [the] march held both magnificence and pathos. There was a Biblical

*Xenophon's Greek mercenaries used tactics that resembled those of the Marines – controlling the heights above their avenue of retreat. Recruited to help Cyrus the Younger overthrow his brother the king, the Greeks were forced to withdraw after Cyrus was killed at the Battle of Cunaxa in Babylon. The Persians then lured the Greek senior officers to a tent where they slaughtered most of them. Xenophon, an Athenian scholar and historian who had studied under Socrates, then took charge. He led the mercenaries 1,000 miles over desolate mountains, and across rivers and plains to the Black Sea.

pageantry about it. In a plane at 4,000 feet the great retreat looked like a scene from a silent movie epic. ... Everything seemed frozen – grey clouds ... the evergreen mountains, the hills, the yellow roads ... the dusty battle cars ... the white-clad groups of refugees wading the rivers or huddling together in the hills ... the endless columns of troops in olive drab. But as the plane came lower, the tableau surged with warming life."[35]

One of General Smith's regimental commanders summed up the breakout in a conversation with the general by concluding that while he was not a religious man, "he felt that we had walked in the hand of God."[36]

On the way down the mountain, the Marines sang an Australian marching song, "Bless 'Em All," which mocked practically the entire world and its institutions. It was said that an obscene variation of the refrain was actually sung.

Bless 'em all, Bless 'em all,
The Commies, the UN and all
Them slant-eyed Chink soldiers hit Hagaru-ri
And now know the meaning of USMC.
So, we're saying good-by to them all
As home through the mountains we crawl.
The snow is ass-deep to a man in a jeep
But who's got a jeep?
Bless 'em all.
Bless 'em all, Bless 'em all,
The long and the short and the tall.
We landed at Inchon and old Wolmi-do
Crossed the Han River and took Yongdong-po.
But we're saying good-bye to it all,
To Hamhung and Hungnam and Seoul.
There'll be no gum-beatin', we're glad we're retreatin'
So cheer up me lads
Bless 'em all!
Bless 'em all, Bless 'em all,

The admirals an' commodores all
Bless General MacArthur and bless Harry, too
Bless the whole brass-hatted Tokyo crew,
For we're saying good-bye to it all.
We're Truman's "police force" on call,
So put your pack on, the next stop is Saigon
An' cheer up me lads
Bless 'em all![37]

In a letter to Commandant Clifton Cates, Smith said that he was proud of his 1st Division. "The officers and men were magnificent. They came down off the mountain bearded, footsore, and physically exhausted, but their spirits were high. They were still a fighting division."[38]

General Victor Krulak later wrote in his book, *First to Fight*, that "an unusual, and generally unheralded, aspect of the Marines' quality as fighters" was their "adaptability, initiative, and improvisation."

At Chosin Reservoir, this was demonstrated by their perfection of close-air support, and their use of helicopters to ferry men to difficult-to-reach battlefields and to evacuate the seriously wounded.[39]

Belying their reputation as battle-hardened warriors, the Marines showed great solicitude for their wounded comrades.

"Cold chills still go up my spine," wrote Master Sergeant Thomas Britt of the Army's 3rd Division, "as I recall watching Marines, themselves frozen from head to foot, meticulously caring for their wounded and bringing back the dead bodies of their comrades. The Marines were battle-scarred, but still looked as if they could do battle."[40]

During its 57 days of operation from October 26 to December 11, the 1st Marine Air Wing flew 3,703 sorties while carrying out 1,053 missions in support of the 1st Marine Division. VMO-6 helicopters and observation planes completed 837 missions.

The Chinese onslaught of November 27–28 inspired a sharp increase in VMO-6 activity at Yudam-ni and Hagaru-ri. All available aircraft flew from dawn to dark daily – on the 28th alone, 73 helicopter and 68 observation plane missions, with 50 casualties evacuated.

The 29th and 30th saw no slackening of effort. On December 1, when the first C-47s landed at the newly completed Hagaru-ri airstrip, VMO-6's main mission gradually shifted back to being the "eye in the sky" – spotting enemy troop concentrations and directing air strikes.

During the Chosin Reservoir air war, eight pilots were killed or died of their wounds; three were wounded; and four were listed as missing in action.

On December 3, Lieutenant Robert Longstaff of VMO-6, on his way to evacuate a wounded Marine from the Fifth Regiment, was shot down over Sinhung-ni, and then killed by enemy small-arms fire. A Fifth Marines patrol recovered Longstaff's body.[41]

General Smith was effusive in his praise for the squadrons' hugely successful close-air support. He credited repeated missions in the same areas for the pilots' familiarity with the difficult terrain and the companies operating there.

"Without your support our task would have been infinitely more difficult and more costly. During the long reaches of the night and in the snow storms, many a Marine prayed for the coming of day or clearing weather when he would again hear the welcome roar of your planes as they dealt out destruction to the enemy," Smith wrote to General Field Harris, the 1st MAW's commander.

"Never in its history has Marine aviation given more convincing proof of its indispensable value to the ground Marine ... A bond of understanding has been established that will never be broken."[42]

Until December 9, General Smith had understood that his division would occupy defensive positions southwest of Hungnam, possibly through the winter. He anticipated a fresh campaign in the spring.

But the plan changed. On December 10, new orders directed the division and the 3rd ROK Division to embark immediately by sea to South Korea.

The Army's 7th and 3rd Infantry Divisions would defend the Hungnam perimeter during this first phase of X Corps's evacuation from northeastern Korea. Naval aircraft from seven carriers and gunfire from 13 ships would support the withdrawal.[43]

The Seventh Marines marched directly to the docks at Hungnam and began boarding the troop ships on December 11.

The Fifth Marines went aboard ship on the 12th, and the First Marines on the 13th. It was the division's fourth embarkation in five months.

The troops were filthy; most of them had not taken off their clothes for nearly two months, and it was said that they smelled like "a herd of wet water buffaloes." Sergeant Lowell Lein of the Seventh Marines' Baker Company said he "never put water to my face for six weeks except to drink it. We looked like a lot of coal miners."

After the 22,215 Marines had gotten on the four transports, 16 landing craft, an assault cargo ship, and seven merchant ships with their gear, the Navy doctors and corpsmen went to work.

"They cut our boots off," said Sergeant Sherman Richter of the Seventh Marines' Baker Company. "A doctor walked down the line looking at frostbitten toes. 'Treatment. Treatment. Amputate. Treatment. Amputate ...' Everyone held his breath. If your toes were black, it was bad for you."[44]

On December 15, the ships bearing the Marines weighed anchor and sailed out of Hungnam harbor. Their destination was Pusan.

Upon reaching Pusan, the Marines traveled 40 miles west by road and rail to Masan and a large field on its northern outskirts, which they nicknamed "the bean patch." There, the weary division rested and began receiving replacements and new equipment.

The two-week respite provided an opportunity, too, for the men to regain some of the weight that they had lost during the grueling campaign, the result of largely subsisting on frozen, inedible rations; little or no sleep; and ceaseless physical exertion.

Paul Robinson, a Charlie Company infantryman with the Seventh Marines, arrived in Korea weighing 210 pounds, but weighed just 146 when he went home. His weight loss was not unusual.[45]

The 3rd Division of the North Korean People's Army launched strong attacks on the shrinking Hungnam perimeter during the first six hours of December 19, but was repulsed.

The US 7th Division departed on December 20, leaving the Army's 3rd Division to defend the Hungnam perimeter; it left on December 24.

The Marine 1st Amphibious Amtrac Battalion was the last unit to leave the Hungnam beach, at 2:36pm on the 24th.[46]

Besides the 105,000 troops evacuated from Hungnam, the ships carried off 350,000 tons of material and 17,500 vehicles.

North Korean refugees were a growing challenge for X Corps, which had not anticipated a massive exodus of civilians during the wintertime. Many of the refugees had no homes to return to, and others simply did not wish to live under either the oppressive North Korean government, or the Communist Chinese.

Carrying babies and their meager worldly goods on A-frames and in bundles on their backs, thousands of them crowded the perimeters of Hamhung, Hungnam, and the smaller evacuation ports. Hamhung and Hungnam residents also wanted out, and gathered at the docks to board ships going south.[47]

Ninety-eight thousand North Korean civilians were evacuated from northeastern Korea, and more would have left if they could have found room on the transports.

In an interview in Hungnam with newspaper correspondent Marguerite Higgins, Admiral James Doyle, the commander of Task Force 90, said, "My personal observation is that if the lift were available, we could denude North Korea of its civilian population. Almost all of them want to go to South Korea."[48]

Engineers had placed 500 1,000-pound bombs and other ordnance around Hungnam's docks and industrial facilities to detonate when the evacuation ended.

When set off, the explosives produced a spectacular pyrotechnic display, followed by dense clouds of black smoke that darkened the skies over Hungnam.[49]

Mao Tse-Tung and General Peng Dehuai, commander of the Chinese Volunteer Forces, congratulated the 9th Army Group on December 15 for its accomplishments during the Second Offensive.

"You have fought a tough battle in a frozen and snow-covered battleground for almost a month and defeated the American invading forces of the 1st Marine Division and the [US Army] 7th Division ... and achieved a great victory of the campaign."

Two days later, Mao cabled Song Shilun and Peng with more praise, and also with condolences for their losses in northeastern Korea. "The CCP [Central Committee] cherishes the memory of those lost."[50]

After three weeks of fighting at Chosin Reservoir and on the MSR, official Chinese figures showed that the 9th Army Group had lost 48,156 soldiers: 19,202 combat casualties and 28,954 frostbite victims. The total included more than 4,000 men who had died of cold weather injuries.

The 9th Army Group settled into winter quarters in the Hamhung area. The encampment resembled "a giant field hospital," in the words of someone who was there.[51]

Later, Song performed the communist party's ritual confession of errors that he had made during the Chosin Reservoir campaign.

He admitted to serious tactical mistakes – and to a critical strategic one. "It proves that the campaign result could be totally different, if the 26th had followed the 27th Army to move into the front, then the 20th Army had concentrated its attacks on the enemy at Yudam-ni and the 26th and 27th Armies had concentrated their attacks on the enemy at Hagaru-ri."

Had that happened, Hagaru-ri might well have fallen, and the Yudam-ni Marines in the farthest valley would have had no clear escape path.[52]

Instead, the 27th Army divided its four divisions between Yudam-ni and Hagaru-ri, and failed to destroy the Marines at either place.

"If the Chinese had concentrated their troops at the point of exit [from the Yudam-ni valley] we could never have gotten out of the trap," Lieutenant Colonel Ray Murray told Marguerite Higgins. "By trying to keep us consistently encircled, they dispersed their strength."[53]

After X Corps evacuated northeastern Korea in December, Colonel Wong Lichan, a Chinese liaison officer, was en route from Pyongyang to deliver papers to the new North Korean III Corps in Hamhung.

Beside the road, Wong spotted snowy, human-shaped mounds between Kanggye and Chinhung-ni. An air raid alert compelled Wong and his North Korean driver to stop and get out of their car.

Approaching the mysterious snow-covered figures, Wong was astonished to discover that they were Chinese soldiers who had frozen to death.

"There's hundreds like this, maybe thousands," Wong's driver said. "Some of them [were] coolies, most of them soldiers ... There'll be a dreadful stink round here next spring."

The driver tapped one of the corpses, and the snow slid off him to reveal a gaunt, unshaven man with a gaping mouth.

As Wong and his driver continued to travel south, the snowmen became more numerous. They saw entire platoons, squatting with rifles on their shoulder, kitbags on their backs. There were gangs of coolies who died while carrying A-frames, and civilian refugees frozen in heaps in the act of vainly attempting to warm themselves with the body heat of others.[54]

Wong stopped in Chinhung-ni to meet Song at the 9th Army Group headquarters in the town schoolhouse.

During their conversation, Song turned to the map on the wall and jabbed his finger at the image of the Sea of Japan.

"They're gone," Song said. "We could not stop them."[55]

Epilogue

One of the greatest fighting retreats that ever was.
PRESIDENT HARRY TRUMAN.[1]

These textbook precautions [by General O.P. Smith] were all that enabled this magnificent fighting force to battle its way out of the entrapment in one of the most successful retrograde movements in American military history. If it wasn't for his tremendous leadership, we would have lost the bulk of that division up north. His leadership was the principal reason it came out the way it did.
GENERAL MATTHEW RIDGWAY.[2]

Air support provided by the United States Marine Force and Naval Aircraft in this beleaguered area, described as magnificent by the ground force commanders, represented one of the greatest concentrations of tactical air operations in history.
GENERAL DOUGLAS MACARTHUR.[3]

The 1st Marine Division's march to Chosin Reservoir was beyond the scope of the Marine Corps's mission as an amphibious assault force. The Marines were trained to capture beachheads and island strongholds – not to conduct campaigns deep in enemy country.

"This operation bore little resemblance to anything in the past experience of the Marine Corps," concluded an Eleventh Marines after-action report. "The weather, terrain, distances, rapidity of movement, and modes of fighting were new."[4]

The Chosin Reservoir campaign ordinarily would have been an exclusively Army operation.

But the Marines rose to the challenge.

Thrust into mountainous terrain 70 miles from the Sea of Japan in subzero weather, the Marines fought skillfully and tenaciously, performing brilliantly in their unaccustomed role.

With the indispensable aid of close-air support by Marine and Navy fighter-bombers, they employed tactics that they had never practiced, burnishing their reputation for improvisation under fire.

The result was a classic withdrawal in the face of enormous enemy pressure, unmatched in modern times.[5]

During nearly three weeks of combat, Marines together with British and US Army troops inflicted crippling losses on the Chinese 9th Army Group.

The army group reported that 40 percent or more of its combat casualties were caused by Marine and Navy aircraft.[6]

From the onset of the Chinese Second Offensive in northeast Korea on November 27 until its end on December 15, the 1st Marine Division reported 604 men killed, and 3,508 wounded. Another 114 died of their wounds, and 192 were listed as missing in action, for a total of 4,418 combat casualties.

A total of 7,313 additional casualties were classified as non-battle – mainly frostbite and shock, but also "indigestion cases" from eating frozen rations. Non-battle casualties soared during November and December, mainly from frostbite, with 2,408 cases reported in November, and 4,882 in December.

More than half of the division's combat troops were killed or became frostbitten during the campaign. Even the 1st Marine Engineer Battalion that built the Hagaru-ri and Koto-ri airfields and the Treadway bridge at Funchilin Pass sustained 60 percent losses.

For their actions during the campaign, Marines earned 14 Congressional Medals of Honor – seven of them posthumously. Seventeen Medals of Honor were awarded in all, with three of them honoring Army Lieutenant Colonels Don Faith and John Upshur Dennis Page and Navy Lieutenant Thomas Hudner.[7]

General Douglas MacArthur depicted the Marines' breakout to the Sea of Japan as "epic," and President Harry Truman called it "one of the greatest fighting retreats that ever was."

Truman rated General O.P. Smith as one of the three generals that he most respected, the other two being Confederate generals – Robert E. Lee and Stonewall Jackson.

Army historian S.L.A. Marshall said of Smith: "His greatest campaign is a classic which will inspire more perfect leadership by all who read and understand that out of great faith can come a miracle."[8]

Yet, for all of the praise of Smith and his Marines, the Chosin Reservoir campaign was a strategic defeat. By Christmas, rather than X Corps standing on the banks of the Yalu River as a conquering army, it had been driven out of North Korea.

The massive Chinese attacks constituted the first phase of the final partition of the Korean peninsula into a democratic republic and a dictatorship.

MacArthur had made the same mistake that Kim Il-Sung did when Sung's North Korean army overran South Korea: he overextended his supply line and ignored the possibility of a third power's intervention. The gross errors in judgment led to debacles for both MacArthur and Kim.[9]

MacArthur attempted to shift blame for the failure to seize North Korea to the Truman administration. His intemperate words eventually led to his dismissal.

It began on December 1 when MacArthur told *U.S. News & World Report* magazine that the prohibition on striking at enemy forces across the Manchurian border had put his forces under "an enormous handicap without precedent in military history."

Four days after the interview, Truman imposed a moratorium on all government statements to US reporters about foreign or military affairs – and pointedly sent a copy to MacArthur.[10]

On December 30, with the Eighth Army reeling from the Chinese Second Offensive and X Corps now absent from northeast Korea, Truman and his top foreign affairs and military officials asked MacArthur what the United Nations should do if the situation worsened.

He replied that UN forces should blockade China, destroy China's war-making industries, use Chinese Nationalist troops in Korea, and authorize Formosa to launch a counter-invasion of China if necessary. The alternative, he said, was retreating to Pusan and defeat. His recommendations were met in Washington with "consternation."[11]

In February, MacArthur proposed laying a field of radioactive waste along North Korea's border with Manchuria. He recommended also launching airborne and amphibious attacks on both coasts of North Korea to "close a gigantic trap" on the Chinese, forcing them to either "starve or surrender." The Joint Chiefs of Staff rejected the plan.[12]

In March, MacArthur flagrantly violated Truman's ban on statements to the media by accusing higher-ups of undermining the Eighth Army's mission to unite North and South Korea. At the same time, he warned China that it risked military disaster if it did not withdraw from Korea, torpedoing a Truman administration peace initiative before it could be formally extended.[13]

The last straw was MacArthur's letter to House Minority Leader Joe Martin agreeing with Martin's proposal to use Nationalist troops on a second front in Korea. MacArthur's letter asserted that communism must be defeated in Asia or else Europe was doomed. It was front-page news around the world.

On April 11, 1951, Truman fired MacArthur. He was also effectively muzzled: he was denied a farewell address to his troops; forbidden to counsel his successor, General Matthew Ridgway; and prohibited from speaking to the Japanese people, or discussing matters with Japanese officials.

MacArthur returned to the United States, where he was feted with enormous parades – including one with 7 million onlookers in New York City. He addressed a joint session of Congress; his speech was interrupted 30 times by applause.

A Gallup poll showed that 69 percent of voters supported MacArthur, and the White House was inundated by letters protesting his dismissal.[14]

MacArthur prepared a paper on the Korean War for president-elect Dwight Eisenhower in 1952. It proposed that the United States bomb China's military-industrial bases and hold a two-party conference with Soviet President Joseph Stalin with the object of ending the war.

MacArthur's paper said that Stalin should be warned that if no agreement were reached, the United States would deploy atomic bombs and create a radioactive zone south of the Yalu River to prevent China from resupplying its armies. Eisenhower did not act on MacArthur's proposals.[15]

Had MacArthur wished to capitalize on his enormous popularity and seize maximum political power, he might have succeeded. He made no such attempt, though.

The 71-year-old general instead moved into the Waldorf Towers in New York City, where he lived quietly until his death in 1964 at the age of 84. His peaceful exit belied President Franklin Roosevelt's description of MacArthur in 1932 as one of the two most dangerous men in the United States. The other was Louisiana Senator Huey Long, "The Kingfisher."[16]

China's entry into the Korean War, and the Marine Corps's splendid performance at Pusan, Inchon, and the Chosin Reservoir ended the Truman administration's attempts to effectively eliminate the Corps. Its ground and air branches would not be absorbed by the Army and Air Force.

Army General Omar Bradley, the chairman of the Joint Chiefs of Staff, had believed that amphibious operations were obsolete in the nuclear age and that the Navy and Marines were just "fancy dans." Inchon proved Bradley to be wrong.

Rather than being downgraded to a small naval amphibious force – "the Navy's police force," in Truman's intemperate words of June 1950 – the Marine Corps was granted "separate service" status by Congress in 1952, equal to the Chief of Naval Operations with free access to the Navy and Defense Secretaries.

The turnaround began with retired Army General Frank Lowe's tour of the front in October 1950 as Truman's personal representative. Lowe left the war zone highly impressed by the Marines and advised the president to maintain a "ready" force of four Marine divisions with a corresponding number of aviation units, as well as adequate amphibious shipping.[17]

The separate status bill that passed in 1952 was sponsored by Illinois Senator Paul Douglas, a World War II Marine who fought on Peleliu and Okinawa, and Montana Congressman Mike Mansfield, a Marine enlisted man during the 1920s.

The bill guaranteed that the Marine Corps would henceforth consist of a minimum of three combat divisions and three air wings. Whenever the Joint Chiefs of Staff met to discuss Marine Corps matters, the Marine commandant would have a seat at the table. Public Law 416 took effect in June 1952.[18]

After its evacuation from Hungnam, Smith's division bivouacked in the Masan "Bean Patch" from where it had started for Inchon months earlier.

For Corporal Harold Mulhausen of the Seventh Marines' Able Company, it meant shaving and showering for the first time in 50 days. "I hardly recognized myself in the mirror," he said. While he had weighed about 200 pounds when he left Japan, he now weighed 143 pounds fully clothed.[19]

For many Marines, it was a "crushing feeling" to find themselves back in Masan, after having "fought all this hard fight all the way into Inchon and Seoul, and gone all the way up to the reservoir," said Lieutenant Colonel Ray Murray, the Fifth Marines commander.

"It was very depressing and times were very depressing and ... morale was shot. They were making plans for the evacuation of Korea," he said.[20]

And then, on December 23, General Walton Walker, the Eighth Army commander, was killed in a jeep accident, and the war's outlook changed dramatically.

Walker had overseen his army's retreat south of Seoul, and he had appeared overwhelmed and disheartened by the Eighth Army's reversals. MacArthur was already considering replacing him when he died.

The man everyone believed should get Walton's job was 55-year-old General Matthew Ridgway, deputy chief of staff to Army Secretary "Lightning Joe" Collins.

During World War II, Ridgway commanded airborne divisions and corps in Italy, Sicily, and France, and during the invasion of Germany.

Upon being appointed to lead the Eighth Army, Ridgway immediately toured the front lines. He was infuriated by the defeatism that he encountered among his field commanders. And to his dismay, the army was road-bound.

Ridgway announced that, henceforth, his army would patrol constantly, control the high ground, and maintain contact with the enemy.

Lieutenant Colonel Murray, downcast at the prospect of abandoning Korea, attended a meeting with Ridgway at 1st Marine Division headquarters. The general "put his fist on the map and he said, 'I don't know of any reason why we can't hold here and here and here ...'"

Within two months, thanks to Ridgway, the Eighth Army was acting with renewed spirit and confidence.

"He took a thoroughly beaten army and turned it around in an extremely short period of time by sheer force of personality," Murray said, "and believing that they could lick anybody, and I finally concluded I have never, ever met a leader like General Ridgway."[21]

Ridgway's turnaround of the Eighth Army did no less than save South Korea from communist occupation.

The ritual admissions of General Song Shilun to tactical and strategic blunders omitted an equally important factor in his 9th Army Group's failure to destroy the 1st Marine Division – its primitive communications system.

Its telephone lines were cut often by American artillery, forcing commanders to depend on runners to relay orders to units when circumstances changed. The orders often arrived days late, or not at all, if the message bearer was killed or became lost.

Colonel Alpha Bowser, General Smith's intelligence officer, said that if the Chinese had possessed a modern communications system, the Marines might not have escaped from the trap at Chosin Reservoir.[22]

Food shortages, inferior firepower, and an inability to adapt to changing conditions further hampered Chinese operations. And there was North Korea's arctic cold, for which the 9th Army Group was unprepared.

When General Song requested heavy coats, hats, and shoes, the East China Military Region's commissary said that winter clothing had already been issued.

However, it was light winter apparel suited for a campaign in South China's mild climate: quilted cotton uniforms, and light canvas shoes. Heavier clothing arrived as the 9th Army entered Korea, but not in sufficient quantities: 72,000 winter coats, and winter shoes for just 40 percent of the men. No soldiers received gloves.[23]

"The troops were hungry. They ate cold food, and some had only a few potatoes in two days," said Zhang Renchu, the 26th Army commander. "They were unable to maintain the physical strength for combat; the wounded personnel could not be evacuated ... The firepower of our entire army was basically inadequate. When we used our guns there were no shells, and sometimes the shells were duds."[24]

Song said the hardships that his troops suffered were "even worse than those during the [Chinese] Red Army's Long March" in 1934–35.

Song offered to resign. Zhang reportedly threatened suicide.

General Peng Dehuai flew to Peking to confront Mao over the unpreparedness of the Chinese army and to demand better clothing, Soviet equipment, and a logistical system that would deliver food and supplies when they were needed. Mao promised Peng that things would change.[25]

After the battles in North Korea with United Nations forces, the Chinese army adopted new strategies and tactics for fighting a modern war. It now understood that mobility and overwhelming manpower were not enough.

To increase their firepower, the Chinese integrated Soviet heavy arms, tanks, and jets into the Chinese Red Army.

With Soviet assistance, China began modernizing its army and officer corps, and rotating its troops through the Korean War front so that they could gain combat experience. The Korean War became China's "combat laboratory."

From the war emerged a strategy of taking "active defensive military measures" to stop the enemy outside China's borders. The overhaul of China's military began in 1951.[26]

Before the Korean War, General O.P. Smith was the Marine Corps's assistant commandant. He was briefly under consideration as a candidate for commandant, but office politics was never Smith's forte and he was passed over.

Returning to the United States in May 1951, he became commanding general at Camp Pendleton, California, followed by a stint as commander of the Fleet Marine Force, Atlantic. He retired in 1955.

Smith was extremely proud of the Marines he commanded at Chosin Reservoir.

"Probably the American people do not yet understand that we walked out of the Hagaru area and did it in good order with heads up, but they need to understand it if they are ever to appreciate the moral values in this particular operation," he said.[27]

Army General Matthew Ridgway, the man who turned around the fortunes of the Eighth Army in early 1951, praised Smith's meticulous preparations for averting disaster.

He slow-marched his division to the Chosin Reservoir, resisting the insistence of General Ned Almond, the X Corps commander, to move faster. Smith established strongholds and supply depots at Chinghung-ni, Koto-ri, and Hagaru-ri that served him well during the march to the sea.

"These textbook precautions were all that enabled this magnificent fighting force to battle its way out of the entrapment in one of the most successful retrograde movements in American military history," Ridgway wrote. "If it wasn't for his tremendous leadership, we would have lost the bulk of that division up north. His leadership was the principal reason it came out the way it did."[28]

Army historian S.L.A. Marshall wrote: "Final disaster had been averted ... because of the steadiness and wisdom of a Great Marine Commander, Major General Oliver P. Smith. No other operation in the American book of war quite compares with this show by the 1st Marine Division."[29]

A large amount of credit must be given to the aviators who, after taking off from snow-covered Yonpo airstrip or from an icy carrier deck, appeared overhead at first light, shivering in their Corsairs and Skyraiders, whose heaters routinely malfunctioned. Pilots often returned from their missions with no feeling below the waist, needing help to climb out of their cockpits.[30]

Once airborne, the drone of the fighter-bombers' motors buoyed the spirits of Marines who had survived another night of murderous attacks. That sound also sowed fear among the Chinese; their bugles, whistles, and death chants abruptly stopped.

"When [the Chinese] heard those Corsairs, it was just like somebody turned off the noise machine," said rifleman Jon Cole of the Fifth Marines' 1st Battalion.[31]

An aerial spotter for the Eleventh Marines' artillery batteries, Lieutenant Roy Sheil, based at Hagaru-ri, enjoyed a rare view of the close-air support missions and concluded, "The Marine air corps saved the 1st Division from being completely wiped out ... You have never witnessed as many strikes and so much strafing."[32]

In the 1st Division special after-action report, General Smith bluntly asserted that the breakout couldn't have happened without close-air support.

"It is no exaggeration to state that the successful conclusion of this operation would have been nearly impossible without the amount and quality of close air support that was provided," Smith wrote. "It was an ideal combat example of the ultimate perfection of the air-ground team needed to defeat an aggressive, determined enemy."[33]

In his 11th Report of the Operations in Korea of the United Nations Forces, General Douglas MacArthur wrote: "Success was due in no small part to the unprecedented extent and effectiveness of air support. Air support provided by the United States Marine Force and Naval Aircraft in this beleaguered area, described as magnificent by the ground force commanders, represented one of the greatest concentrations of tactical air operations in history."[34]

Time magazine described the Marines' running battle from Yudam-ni and Hagaru-ri to Hungnam as "a battle unparalleled in U.S. military history," containing elements of Xenophon's *Anabasis*, Dunkirk, and Anzio.[35]

Rather than being annihilated by the seven Chinese divisions arrayed against it, the 1st Marine Division inflicted such devastating losses on the Chinese 9th Army Group that it was rendered ineffective for three months.[36]

The Chosin Reservoir campaign rang down the curtain on the second phase of the Korean War, and was the prelude to a larger conflict in which larger armies battled across Korea's mid-section.

By the end of 1950, about 486,000 Chinese and North Korean troops were arrayed against 365,000 United Nations soldiers.

There would be a great deal more bloodletting, a stalemate, and a truce two and a half years later that continues to this day along the 38th Parallel – the same Korea demarcation line agreed upon by the Soviet Union and the United States following Japan's surrender in late 1945.

When the fighting ended, 33,629 of the 1.32 million Americans that served in Korea were dead. An estimated 415,000 South Korean soldiers and civilians were killed, and 1,263 Commonwealth troops.

China sustained 1 million casualties during the war, of which 183,108 were reportedly killed. North Korea's military and civilian casualties numbered 1.5 million.[37]

For those in combat in Korea, it must seem inconceivable that they fought and died in what was technically not a war, but an "armed conflict."

The United States never declared war on North Korea or China and, in fact, has never issued a declaration of war after World War II. The Vietnam War, too, was a so-called "conflict" and not a war.

American troops entered Korea under the auspices of a United Nations Security Council resolution approved in June 1950. Because the UN cannot declare war, this resolution served as the basis for three years of intensive fighting.

Had not the United States led the United Nations intervention, North Korea undoubtedly would have conquered the entire peninsula.

When the fighting ended in 1953, a democratic, dynamic South Korea arose from the war's ashes, uneasily coexisting with its dark twin, authoritarian North Korea.

After the Korean War's dead, wounded, and missing combatants were tabulated, and the tragic loss of Korean civilians was lamented, the Chosin Reservoir campaign stood alone as the conflict's single most dramatic, inspiring battle.

Seldom have men endured worse combat conditions and prevailed – living and fighting in arctic cold for weeks in temperatures reaching 30 below zero or colder, with wind chills surpassing 50 below.

Frostbite was endemic among both the allies and Chinese. It was so cold that weapons malfunctioned; so cold that plasma froze, but so did the blood flow from battle wounds.

Besides battling the shocking cold, US Marines, soldiers, and British commandos faced annihilation by Chinese soldiers that surrounded and outnumbered them 5-to-1 or more in North Korea's glacial mountains, 70 miles from the nearest evacuation port.

They were saved by overwhelming firepower and close-air support, discipline and training, and the steady replenishment of food and ammunition. By contrast, Chinese soldiers suffered and died from the lack of everything except discipline and grit. They froze to death by the thousands.

Although it was a retreat, the Chosin Reservoir campaign will be remembered as a triumph of stubborn courage, determination, and combat efficiency in the worst conditions imaginable.

Acknowledgments

Many thanks to Dr Xiaobing Li, professor of history at the University of Central Oklahoma, and editor-in-chief of *The Chinese Historical Review*.

His book, *Attack at Chosin*, is eye-opening in its depiction of the Chinese army's travails at Chosin Reservoir. Inadequately clothed for below-zero temperatures and without sufficient rations, China's troops suffered from frostbite and even starvation, proportionately more than the Marines and soldiers that they battled in North Korea's bleak, frigid highlands.

Professor Li's insightful research into the Chinese archives produced first-person accounts by foot soldiers and commanders and enumerated the Chinese army's shortcomings, exploited by the 1st Marine Division to escape from the trap at Chosin Reservoir. The Chinese army put the hard lessons learned to good use in the two and a half years remaining in the Korean War.

Megan Harris of the Veterans History Project at the Library of Congress ferreted out interviews with Chosin Reservoir veterans, as she has done for me during the writing of my earlier books about the Pacific War. The audio interviews and transcripts provided rich material that helped humanize this book.

I could not have done justice to the Marines' experiences without the aid of the Marine Corps History Division in Quantico, Virginia. Researcher Nancy Whitfield was of great assistance, sharing with me oral history transcripts and links to the interviews themselves, as well as after-action reports by the embattled regiments.

Tyler Reed aided me in obtaining details on the Marine squadrons that provided close-air support, a major factor in the 1st Division's escape. Marine and Navy aviators continued their pioneering development of close-air support, using the Chosin Reservoir campaign as their laboratory.

Also valuable was Dr Fred Allison's dissertation on the Marine Corps's innovations in close-air support during World War II and through the Korean War, using the famous Black Sheep Squadron as a focal point. Dr Allison is a retired Marine major.

And although many of them are no longer with us, the Marines who spoke with me in 1995 have my sincere gratitude for relating their experiences during the crisis hours at Yudam-ni and on Fox Hill. I interviewed them as I was writing a piece for The Associated Press previewing the dedication of the Korean War Monument in Washington, DC.

Finally, my wife Pat has my gratitude and love for her great patience during the long hours I shut myself away in my study researching and writing this book.

Endnotes

PROLOGUE

1 Jim Wilson, *Retreat Hell! We're Just Attacking in Another Direction* (New York: William Morrow, 1988), 79.
2 Stanley Weintraub, *A Christmas Far From Home* (Boston: Da Capo Press, 2014), 89, 38.
3 Wilson, *Retreat Hell!*, 81.
4 Gen Ray Davis, *The Story of Ray Davis, General of Marines* (Fuquay-Varina, NC: Research Triangle Publishing, 1995), 106–07.
5 Joseph C. Gould, *Korea: The Untold Story of the War* (New York: Times Books, 1982), 345.
6 Seventh Regiment Special Action Report, Folder 7, Marine History Archives; Wilson, *Retreat Hell!*, 66; Thomas McKelvey Cleaver, *The Frozen Chosen. The 1st Marine Division and the Battle of the Chosin Reservoir* (Oxford, UK, New York: Osprey Publishing, 2016), 146–47.
7 Patrick Roe, *The Dragon Strikes. China and the Korean War, June–December 1950* (Novato, CA: Presidio Press, 2000), 404.
8 Dean Acheson, *The Korean War* (New York: W.W. Norton, 1969), 70.
9 Hampton Sides, *On Desperate Ground. The Epic Story of the Chosin Reservoir – The Greatest Battle of the Korean War* (New York: Anchor Books, 2018), 99–100.
10 Bevin Alexander, *Korea: The First War We Lost* (New York: Hippocrene Books, 2004), 259.
11 Roe, *Dragon Strikes*, 265; Xiaobing Li, *Attack at Chosin: The Chinese Second Offensive in Korea* (Norman, OK: University of Oklahoma Press, 2020), 32.
12 Li, *Attack*, 47.

CHAPTER 1: WEST OF CHOSIN RESERVOIR

1 Robert Heinl, *Victory at High Tide: The Inchon-Seoul Campaign* (Baltimore, MD: The Nautical & Aviation Publishing Company of America, 1979), 6–7.
2 Bill Sloan, *The Darkest Summer. Pusan and Inchon 1950: The Battles That Saved South Korea – and the Marines – from Extinction* (New York, London, Toronto, Sydney: Simon & Schuster, 2009), 291.
3 Harry Truman, *Memoirs of Harry S. Truman: Volume Two, Years of Trial and Hope* (Garden City, NY: Doubleday & Company, 1956), 46–51.
4 Heinl, *Victory at High Tide*, 517; Jon T. Hoffman, *Once a Legend: "Red Mike" Edson of the Marine Raiders* (Novato, CA: Presidio, 1994), 363.

5 Hoffman, 388–94; Heinl, *Victory at High Tide*, 517–18.
6 Gail B. Shisler, *For Country and Corps. The Life of General Oliver P. Smith* (Annapolis, MD: Naval Institute Press, 2009), 112; Victor H. Krulak, *First to Fight: An Inside View of the Marine Corps* (New York: Pocket Books, 1991), 134–35, 137; Heinl, *Victory at High Tide*, 6–7, 526–27.
7 Heinl, *Victory at High Tide*, 527, 531.
8 John Toland, *In Mortal Combat: Korea, 1950–1953* (New York: William Morrow and Company, 1991), 28, 30.
9 Lynn Montross and Nicholas A. Canzona, *U.S. Marine Operations in Korea, 1950–1953*, 3 vols. (Washington, DC: Historical Branch, G-3, Headquarters, US Marine Corps, 1954–1957), vol. 3, 15.
10 Stewart Lone and Gavan McCormack, *Korea Since 1850* (Melbourne, Australia: Longman Cheshire, 1993), 96–98, 104; William Stuck, "The Coming of the Cold War to Korea," in Bonnie B.C. Oh, ed., *Korea Under the American Military Government, 1945–1948* (Westport, CN, London: Praeger, 2002), pp. 41–60 (54).
11 BrigGen Edwin Simmons, USMC (Ret)., *Frozen Chosin: U.S. Marines at the Changjin Reservoir* (Washington, DC: History and Museums Divisions, US Marine Corps, 2002), 5; Montross and Canzona, *U.S. Marine Operations in Korea*, vol. 1, 12; Lone and McCormack, *Korea Since 1850*, 109, 66; Joseph C. Gould, *Korea: The Untold Story of the War* (New York: Times Books, 1982), 24–25, 33–35; Allan R. Millett, *The War in Korea, 1945–1950: A House Burning* (Lawrence, KS: University Press of Kansas, 2005), 250–51.
12 Millett, *War in Korea*, 243; Montross and Canzona, *U.S. Marine Operations in Korea*, vol. 3, 33–34; Gould, *Korea*, 32–35.
13 Millett, *War in Korea*, 256–58.
14 Ibid., 188, 244.
15 Marguerite Higgins, *War in Korea: The Report of a Woman Combat Correspondent* (Garden City, NY: Doubleday & Company, Inc, 1951), 25–26; Kevin Mahoney, *Formidable Enemies: The North Korean and Chinese Soldiers in the Korean War* (Novato, CA: Presidio, 2001), 104–05.
16 Max Hastings, *The Korean War* (London, New York, Toronto, Sydney, Tokyo: Simon & Schuster, 1987), 57–58, 60.
17 Lone and McCormack, *Korea Since 1850*, 106.
18 William Manchester, *American Caesar: Douglas MacArthur, 1880–1964* (Boston, Toronto: Little, Brown and Company, 1978), 79–109, 466–97.
19 Shelby L. Stanton, *America's Tenth Legion: X Corps in Korea, 1950* (Novato, CA: Presidio Press, 1989), 35.
20 Sloan, *Darkest Summer*, 87–92.
21 Toland, *In Mortal Combat*, 130.
22 Sloan, *Darkest Summer*, 113–14.
23 Douglas MacArthur, *Reminiscences* (New York, Toronto, London: McGraw-Hill Book Company, 1964), 346; Gould, *Korea*, 95–96.
24 Heinl, *Soldiers of the Sea*, 537–39.
25 John W. Spanier, *The Truman-MacArthur Controversy and the Korean War* (New York: W.W. Norton & Company, 1959), 79–80.
26 Clifton La Bree, *The Gentle Warrior: General Oliver Prince Smith, USMC* (Kent, OH, and London: Kent State University Press, 2001), 107.
27 Shisler, *For Country and Corps*, 134.
28 Krulak, *First to Fight*, 145.
29 La Bree, *Gentle Warrior*, 105.

30 Sloan, *Darkest Summer*, 203.
31 Toland, *In Mortal Combat*, 164–66.
32 Sloan, *Darkest Summer*, 144–57; Toland, *In Mortal Combat*, 160–175.
33 Toland, *In Mortal Combat*, 152.
34 Sloan, *Darkest Summer*, 198–207; Toland, *In Mortal Combat*, 161–67.
35 Sloan, *Darkest Summer*, 209.
36 *The American Presidency Project*. https://www.presidency.ucsb.edu/documents/letters-the-commandant-the-marine-corps-league-and-the-commandant-the-marine-corps
37 Krulak, *First to Fight*, 64–66.
38 Montross and Canzona, *U.S. Marine Operations in Korea*, vol. 2, 33, 146; Stanton, *America's Tenth Legion*, 35.
39 Sloan, *Darkest Summer*, 214.
40 Montross and Canzona, *U.S. Marine Operations in Korea*, vol. 2, 46; National Army Museum, "Battle of Quebec," https://www.nam.ac.uk/explore/battle-quebec.
41 Dean Acheson, *Present at the Creation: My Years in the State Department* (New York: W.W. Norton, 1969), 422; Spanier, *Truman-MacArthur Controversy*, 73–76.
42 Hastings, *Korean War*, 105–06.
43 Montross and Canzona, *U.S. Marine Operations in Korea*, vol. 2, 85–98.
44 Heinl, *Victory at High Tide*, 549–51; Montross and Canzona, *U.S. Marine Operations in Korea*, vol. 2, 103–20.
45 Hastings, *Korean War*, 106; Montross and Canzona, *U.S. Marine Operations in Korea*, vol. 2, 92.
46 Sloan, *Darkest Summer*, 281–83; Montross and Canzona, *U.S. Marine Operations in Korea*, vol. 2, 253.
47 Montross and Canzona, *U.S. Marine Operations in Korea*, vol. 2, 147–50.
48 Ibid., 151–52.
49 Shisler, *For Country and Corps*, 150.
50 Montross and Canzona, *U.S. Marine Operations in Korea*, vol. 2, 152.
51 Montross and Canzona, *U.S. Marine Operations in Korea*, vol. 2, 159–63; Sloan, *Darkest Summer*, 265.
52 Sloan, *Darkest Summer*, 275, 282; Shisler, *For Country and Corps*, 151; Montross and Canzona, *U.S. Marine Operations in Korea*, vol. 2, 195–97, 251.
53 Shisler, *For Country and Corps*, 158–59.
54 Ibid.
55 Hastings, *Korean War*, 110; Gould, *Korea*, 228; Sloan, *Darkest Summer*, 290.
56 Sloan, *Darkest Summer*, 257, 275.
57 Montross and Canzona, *U.S. Marine Operations in Korea*, vol. 2, 271–72, 290.
58 Sloan, *Darkest Summer*, 293.
59 Hastings, *Korean War*, 113; Gould, *Korea*, 228.
60 Sloan, *Darkest Summer*, 291.
61 Montross and Canzona, *U.S. Marine Operations in Korea*, vol. 2, 272–79; Shisler, *For Country and Corps*, 162.
62 Gould, *Korea*, 230–31.
63 Montross and Canzona, *U.S. Marine Operations in Korea*, vol. 2, 284.
64 Stanton, *America's Tenth Legion*, 112.
65 Montross and Canzona, *U.S. Marine Operations in Korea*, vol. 2, 298, 285.
66 Spanier, *Truman-MacArthur Controversy*, 95.
67 Acheson, *Present at the Creation*, 452–53.
68 Ibid., 453; Alexander, *First War We Lost*, 237.
69 Li, *Attack*, 28; Montross and Canzona, *U.S. Marine Operations in Korea*, vol. 3, 6–7.

70 Allen S. Whiting, *China Crosses the Yalu. The Decision to Enter the Korean War* (Stanford, CA: Stanford University Press, 1960), 107–08.
71 Ibid., 94, 111; Spanier, *Truman-MacArthur Controversy*, 100–02.
72 MacArthur, *Reminiscences*, 371–72.
73 La Bree, *Gentle Warrior*, 135.
74 Stanton, *America's Tenth Legion*, 148; Toland, *In Mortal Combat*, 246.
75 Manchester, *American Caesar*, 589, quoting *Time* magazine, October 23, 1950.
76 Spanier, *Truman-MacArthur Controversy*, 104–105; Manchester, *American Caesar*, 585.
77 Stanton, *America's Tenth Legion*, 148.
78 Spanier, *Truman-MacArthur Controversy*, 112.
79 Montross and Canzona, *U.S. Marine Operations in Korea*, vol. 3, 30–31.
80 Ibid., 27–29.
81 Ibid., 30–31.
82 Martin Russ, *Breakout: The Chosin Reservoir Campaign, Korea 1950* (New York: Fromm International, 1999), 12, 14.
83 Wilson, *Retreat Hell!*, 45; Russ, *Breakout*, 14.
84 Russ, *Breakout*, 11–12.
85 Montross and Canzona, *U.S. Marine Operations in Korea*, vol. 3, 3, 34.
86 Russ, *Breakout*, 14–15.
87 Wilson, *Retreat Hell!*, 48–49.
88 Roy E. Appleman, *Escaping the Trap: The U.S. Army X Corps in NE Korea, 1950* (College Station, TX: Texas A&M University Press, 1990), x; Hastings, *Korean War*, 125; Stanton, *America's Tenth Legion*, 175.
89 Sides, *On Desperate Ground*, 75–77.
90 Stanton, *America's Tenth Legion*, 173–74.
91 Ibid., 180–82.

CHAPTER 2: THE CHINESE MENACE

1 Xiaobing Li, Allan Millett, and Bin Yu, *Mao's Generals Remember Korea* (Lawrence, KS: University Press of Kansas, 2001), 33.
2 Montross and Canzona, *U.S. Marine Operations in Korea*, vol. 3, 98; Joseph R. Owen, *Colder Than Hell: A Marine Rifle Company at Chosin Reservoir* (Annapolis, MD: Naval Institute Press, 1996), 113; Russ, *Breakout*, 25; Sides, *On Desperate Ground*, 95, 97.
3 Wilson, *Retreat Hell!*, 55–60; Cleaver, *Frozen Chosen*, 142.
4 Shisler, *For Country and Corps*, 1–15; La Bree, *Gentle Warrior*, 1–4.
5 Thomas E. Ricks, *The Generals: American Military Command from World War II to Today* (New York: Penguin Books, 2012), 150–51; La Bree, *Gentle Warrior*, 10–13.
6 Shisler, *For Country and Corps*, 120–21.
7 La Bree, *Gentle Warrior*, 168.
8 Shisler, *For Country and Corps*, 128–29.
9 Ibid., 155–56.
10 O.P. Smith personal papers, USMC Archives, Box 5, Folder 6.
11 Simmons, *Frozen Chosin*, 5–6; Roe, *Dragon Strikes*, 85.
12 Li, *Attack*, 29.
13 Ibid., 30.
14 Li, Millett, and Yu, *Mao's Generals*, 32.
15 O.P. Smith personal papers, Aide Memoire, USMC Archives, Box 68, File 16.
16 Stanton, *America's Tenth Legion*, 161–62.
17 Korean War, USMC Archives, Box 9, Folder 3, 1stMarDiv SAR.

18 Montross and Canzona, *U.S. Marine Operations in Korea*, vol. 3, 81–82.
19 Ibid., 98; Owen, *Colder Than Hell*, 113; Russ, *Breakout*, 25; Sides, *On Desperate Ground*, 95, 97.
20 Wilson, *Retreat Hell!*, 55–60; Cleaver, *Frozen Chosen*, 142.
21 Montross and Canzona, *U.S. Marine Operations in Korea*, vol. 3, 106; Stanton, *America's Tenth Legion*, 176–77.
22 Cleaver, *Frozen Chosen*, 144, 148; Wilson, *Retreat Hell!*, 71; Montross and Canzona, *U.S. Marine Operations in Korea*, vol. 3, 110.
23 Montross and Canzona, *U.S. Marine Operations in Korea*, vol. 3, 105.
24 Cleaver, *Frozen Chosen*, 141–42; Owen, *Colder Than Hell*, 117; Andrew Geer, *The New Breed. The Story of the U.S. Marines in Korea* (New York: Harper, 1952), 230–34.
25 Cleaver, *Frozen Chosen*, 147; Kenneth Jordan Sr, *Forgotten Heroes. 131 Men of the Korean War Awarded the Medal of Honor, 1950–1953* (Atglen, PA: Schiffer Military/Aviation History, 1995), 70–71.
26 O.P. Smith Personal Papers, Aide Memoirs, USMC Archives, Box 68, File 16.
27 Philip Chinnery, *Combat Over Korea* (Barnsley, UK: Pen & Sword Aviation, 2011), 39; Capt Keith Kopets, "The Close Air Support Controversy in Korea," in *Marine Corps Gazette* (May 2001), 42.
28 Chinnery, *Combat Over Korea*, 41–42; Henry Berry, *Hey, Mac, Where Ya Been? Living Memoirs of the U.S. Marines in the Korean War* (New York: St Martin's Press, 1988), 131–32; Simmons, *Frozen Chosin*, 120.
29 Tech Sgt James C. Jones Jr, "Mike's Puddle Jumper," *Leatherneck* magazine, March 1951.
30 July 1952, *Marine Corps Gazette.*
31 Shisler, *For Country and Corps*, 201.
32 John R. Bruning, Jr., *Crimson Sky. The Air Battle for Korea* (Dulles, VA: Brassey's, 1999), 39.
33 Simmons, *Frozen Chosin*, 74.
34 Kopets, "Close Air Support Controversy," 41–43.
35 Richard P. Hallion, *The Naval Air War in Korea* (Baltimore, MD: The Nautical & Aviation Publishing Company of America, 1986), 70–71; Cleaver, *Frozen Chosen*, 168–69.
36 Montross and Canzona, *U.S. Marine Operations in Korea*, vol. 3, 107–09.
37 Ibid., 110.
38 Montross and Canzona, *U.S. Marine Operations in Korea*, vol. 3, 110; Cleaver, *Frozen Chosen*, 147–48.
39 Spanier, *Truman-MacArthur Controversy*, 123–24; Manchester, *American Caesar*, 599.
40 Russell Spurr, *Enter the Dragon: China's Undeclared War against the U.S. in Korea, 1950–1951* (New York: Newmarket Press, 1988), 162; Roe, *Dragon Strikes*, 195, 199–201.
41 Montross and Canzona, *U.S. Marine Operations in Korea*, vol. 3, 112–14.
42 SAR RCT-7, Folder 7, 13-RR; Montross and Canzona, *U.S. Marine Operations in Korea*, vol. 3, 114–19; O.P. Smith Personal Papers, Aide Memoirs, USMC Archives, Box 68, File 16.
43 Appleman, *Escaping the Trap*, 7.
44 Roe, *Dragon Strikes*, 402.
45 Li, Millett, and Yu, *Mao's Generals*, 33
46 Ibid., 45.
47 Roe, *Dragon Strikes*, 230–31.
48 Simmons, *Frozen Chosin*, 22.
49 John Wukovits, *American Commando. Evan Carlson, His World War II Marine Raiders and America's First Special Forces Mission* (New York: NAL Caliber, 2009), 12; Korean War, USMC Archives, Box 9, Folder 3.

50 Wukovits, *American Commando*, 12.
51 Korean War, USMC Archives, Box 9, Folder 3.
52 Samuel B. Griffith II, *The Chinese People's Liberation Army* (New York, Toronto, London, Sydney: McGraw-Hill Book Co, 1967), 135; Stanton, *America's Tenth Legion*, 182.
53 Roe, *Dragon Strikes*, 252–53.
54 Clay Blair Jr, *The Forgotten War: America in Korea, 1950–1953* (New York: Times Books, 1987), 29; David Halberstam, *The Coldest Winter: America and the Korean War* (New York: Hyperion, 2007), 374; Sides, *On Desperate Ground*, 100–01.
55 Spurr, *Enter the Dragon*, 161.
56 Ricks, *The Generals*, 140–41; Blair, *Forgotten War*, 318–19.
57 Roe, *Dragon Strikes*, 98.
58 Stanley Weintraub, *A Christmas Far From Home* (Boston: Da Capo Press, 2014), 11–13.
59 Ibid., 20–21.
60 Cleaver, *Frozen Chosen*, 154.
61 Roe, *Dragon Strikes*, 224, 229.
62 Whiting, *China Crosses the Yalu*, 118–23.
63 Li, *Attack*, 56.
64 Roe, *Dragon Strikes*, 234.
65 Stanton, *America's Tenth Legion*, 179.
66 SAR RCT-7, 14-RR; Geer, *New Breed*, 258–59; Stanton, *America's Tenth Legion*, 179.
67 James Brady, *The Marines of Autumn* (New York: St Martin's Griffin, 2000), 48.
68 Spanier, *Truman-MacArthur Controversy*, 84–86.
69 Roe, *Dragon Strikes*, 98.
70 Spanier, *Truman-MacArthur Controversy*, 120–21.
71 Appleman, *Escaping the Trap*, 30.
72 O.P. Smith personal papers, Aide Memoirs, USMC Archives, Box 68, File 17.
73 Geer, *New Breed*, 255.
74 Cleaver, *Frozen Chosen*, 151; Griffith, *Chinese People's Liberation Army*, 147; Roe, *Dragon Strikes*, 233.
75 Simmons, *Frozen Chosin*, 34.
76 Roe, *Dragon Strikes*, 160.
77 Cdr Malcolm Cagle and Cdr Frank E. Manson, *The Sea War in Korea* (Annapolis, MD: United States Naval Institute Press, 1957), 167; Stanton, *America's Tenth Legion*, 189–90.
78 Spurr, *Enter the Dragon*, 164.
79 Simmons, *Frozen Chosin*, 40.

CHAPTER 3: THE MARCH NORTH

1 O.P. Smith personal papers, Aide Memoirs, USMC Archives, Box 67; La Bree, *Gentle Warrior*, 145–48; Roe, *Dragon Strikes*, 249.
2 Stanton, *America's Tenth Legion*, 184–85, 154–55.
3 Blair, *Forgotten War*, 387.
4 O.P. Smith Personal Papers, Aide Memoirs, USMC Archives, Box 68, File 16.
5 Shisler, *For Country and Corps*, 160; Lemuel Shepherd Jr, Oral History, USMC Archives, 166–69.
6 Simmons, *Frozen Chosin*, 34.
7 Russ, *Breakout*, 52.
8 O.P. Smith personal papers, Aide Memoirs, USMC Archives, Box 67; La Bree, *Gentle Warrior*, 145–48; Roe, *Dragon Strikes*, 249.

9 Appleman, *Escaping the Trap*, 33–34; Brian Catchpole, *The Korean War, 1950–1953* (New York: Carroll & Graf, 2000), 74.
10 Alexander, *First War We Lost*, 321; Brady, *Marines of Autumn*, 98.

CHAPTER 4: ARCTIC COLD ARRIVES

1 Donald Knox, *The Korean War, Pusan to Chosin. An Oral History* (San Diego, New York, London: Harcourt Brace Jovanovich, 1985), 471.
2 SAR RCT-7, 79-RR; Brady, *Marines of Autumn*, 75.
3 Wilson, *Retreat Hell!*, 77–78; Sides, *On Desperate Ground*, 114–15; Owen, *Colder Than Hell*, 161; Robert Leckie, *The March to Glory* (New York: Bantam Books, 1960), 7.
4 Stanton, *America's Tenth Legion*, 184; Geer, *New Breed*, 257–58; O.P. Smith personal papers, Aide Memoirs, USMC Archives, Box 68, File 16.
5 Roe, *Dragon Strikes*, 133.
6 Weintraub, *Christmas Far From Home*, 75.
7 Russ, *Breakout*, 63; Spurr, *Enter the Dragon*, 164.
8 Owen, *Colder Than Hell*, 162–64.
9 Ibid., 165–66; Leckie, *March to Glory*, 8–9; Cleaver, *Frozen Chosen*, 158; Eric Hammel, *Chosin: Heroic Ordeal of the Korean War* (New York: The Vanguard Press, 1981), 286.
10 Owen, *Colder Than Hell*, 166; Stanton, *America's Tenth Legion*, 200.
11 Appleman, *Escaping the Trap*, xi; Roe, *Dragon Strikes*, 238–39.
12 Cleaver, *Frozen Chosen*, 160; Geer, *New Breed*, 258–59.
13 Leckie, *March to Glory*, 8; Hammel, *Chosin*, 64; Roe, *Dragon Strikes*, 134.
14 Col Francis Fox Parry, *Three-War Marine. The Pacific, Korea, Vietnam* (Pacifica, CA: Pacifica Press, 1987), 165.
15 Ricks, *The Generals*, 135; Stanton, *America's Tenth Legion*, 200; Simmons, *Frozen Chosin*, 51.
16 Leckie, *March to Glory*, 10; Geer, *New Breed*, 258–59.
17 Berry, *Hey, Mac, Where Ya Been?*, 143.
18 Ricks, *The Generals*, 135.
19 Brady, *Marines of Autumn*, 98; Russ, *Breakout*, 50.
20 Owen, *Colder Than Hell*, 170–71.
21 Shisler, *For Country and Corps*, 184.
22 Appleman, *Escaping the Trap*, 15.
23 Montross and Canzona, *U.S. Marine Operations in Korea*, vol. 3, 135; O.P. Smith personal papers, Aide Memoirs, USMC Archives, Box 68, Files 16, 17.
24 Shisler, *For Country and Corps*, 184.
25 Simmons, *Frozen Chosin*, 37.
26 La Bree, *Gentle Warrior*, 150–51.
27 Geer, *New Breed*, 342–43; Alexander, *First War We Lost*, 321; Montross and Canzona, *U.S. Marine Operations in Korea*, vol. 3, 138.
28 Cleaver, *Frozen Chosen*, 218.
29 Sides, *On Desperate Ground*, 119; Shisler, *For Country and Corps*, 187.
30 Sides, *On Desperate Ground*, 122, 185.
31 Owen, *Colder Than Hell*, 174–77; Knox, *Korean War*, 484; Montross and Canzona, *U.S. Marine Operations in Korea*, vol. 3, 147.
32 Owen, *Colder Than Hell*, 180.
33 Periodic Intel Report 19, USMC Archives, Box 5.
34 Halberstam, *Coldest Winter*, 470.
35 Russ, *Breakout*, 64.

36 Geer, *New Breed*, 258–59; Shisler, *For Country and Corps*, 184.
37 Knox, *Korean War*, 469, 470; Montross and Canzona, *U.S. Marine Operations in Korea*, vol. 3, 148.
38 Knox, *Korean War*, 471.
39 Sides, *On Desperate Ground*, 127.
40 Simmons, *Frozen Chosin*, 40.
41 Ibid.
42 Griffith, *Chinese People's Liberation Army*, 139–40.
43 Montross and Canzona, *U.S. Marine Operations in Korea*, vol. 3, 144 (CinCUNC Communiqé 12, 24 November 1950).
44 Montross and Canzona, *U.S. Marine Operations in Korea*, vol. 3, 146.
45 La Bree, *Gentle Warrior*, 150; Hammel, *Chosin*, 6.
46 Blair, *Forgotten War*, 456.
47 Roe, *Dragon Strikes*, 299; O.P. Smith personal papers, Aide Memoirs, USMC Archives, Box 68, File 19.
48 Shisler, *For Country and Corps*, 188.
49 Roe, *Dragon Strikes*, 261–62.
50 Shisler, *For Country and Corps*, 187; Halberstam, *Coldest Winter*, 437–38.
51 Montross and Canzona, *U.S. Marine Operations in Korea*, vol. 3, 152.

CHAPTER 5: THE CHINESE PREPARE TO ATTACK

1 Russ, *Breakout*, 81.
2 Montross and Canzona, *U.S. Marine Operations in Korea*, vol. 3, 149; Roe, *Dragon Strikes*, 266–67.
3 1stMarDiv PIR 33 of 26 November, USMC Archives.
4 Montross and Canzona, *U.S. Marine Operations in Korea*, vol. 3, 149–50.
5 Li, *Attack*, 58–60.
6 Ibid., 59.
7 Ibid.
8 Russ, *Breakout*, 81.
9 Li, *Attack*, 60–61.
10 Whiting, *China Crosses the Yalu*, 27, 145.
11 Spurr, *Enter the Dragon*, 240–44.
12 Geer, *New Breed*, 262–64; Jordan, *Forgotten Heroes*, 80.
13 Montross and Canzona, *U.S. Marine Operations in Korea*, vol. 3, 151; Rose, *Dragon Strikes*, 258.
14 Geer, *New Breed*, 262; Montross and Canzona, *U.S. Marine Operations in Korea*, vol. 3, 154–56.
15 Montross and Canzona, *U.S. Marine Operations in Korea*, vol. 3, 154.
16 Ibid., 156.
17 Stanton, *America's Tenth Legion*, 208.
18 Montross and Canzona, *U.S. Marine Operations in Korea*, vol. 3, 156.
19 Hammel, *Chosin*, 46–48.
20 Halberstam, *Coldest Winter*, 438.
21 Hammel, *Chosin*, 40.
22 Owen, *Colder Than Hell*, 189.
23 Hammel, *Chosin*, 42–44.
24 Owen, *Colder Than Hell*, 190.
25 Ibid., 189–93.

26 Ibid., 193.
27 Hammel, *Chosin*, 44–45 ; Montross and Canzona, *U.S. Marine Operations in Korea*, vol. 3, 157; Geer, *New Breed*, 264.
28 Montross and Canzona, *U.S. Marine Operations in Korea*, vol. 3, 157.
29 Ibid., 160; Wilson, *Retreat Hell!*, 87–88.
30 Montross and Canzona, *U.S. Marine Operations in Korea*, vol. 3, 160.

CHAPTER 6: A NIGHT TO REMEMBER

1 Li, *Attack*, 67–68.
2 Fred Allison, *The Black Sheep Squadron: A Case Study in U.S. Marine Corps' Innovations in Close Air Support* (doctoral thesis, Texas Tech University, 2011), 576–77.
3 Ray Murray, Oral History, USMC Archives, 243.
4 Li, *Attack*, 66, 51.
5 Stanton, *America's Tenth Legion*, 200; Li, *Attack*, 52–53; Mahoney, *Formidable Enemies*, 34.
6 Li, *Attack*, 78–79.
7 Ibid.
8 Roe, *Dragon Strikes*, 285.
9 Li, *Attack*, 48–49.
10 Ibid., 67.
11 Roe, *Dragon Strikes*, 267; O.P. Smith personal papers, Aide Memoirs, USMC Archives, Box 68, File 16.
12 Li, *Attack*, 66.
13 Ibid.
14 Ibid.
15 Griffith, *Chinese People's Liberation Army*, 145.
16 Roe, *Dragon Strikes*, 234.
17 Li, *Attack*, 129; Roe, *Dragon Strikes*, 264–65.
18 Appleman, *Escaping the Trap*, 72; Roe, *Dragon Strikes*, 264–65.
19 Li, *Attack*, 70–71.
20 O.P. Smith personal papers, Aide Memoirs, USMC Archives, Box 68, File 18.
21 Li, *Attack*, 67–68.
22 Ibid., 71–73.
23 Ibid., 63–64.
24 Shisler, *For Country and Corps*, 192.
25 Warren Wiedhahn, Veterans' History Project (VHP) interview, 86209.
26 Gerald Boyd, VHP, 3356.
27 *Chosin*, Amazon Video.
28 John Smith, VHP, 101012; James Brown, VHP, 54946; Griffith, *Chinese People's Liberation Army*, 14.
29 Montross and Canzona, *U.S. Marine Operations in Korea*, vol. 3, 163–65.
30 Wilson, *Retreat Hell!*, 126–28.
31 Allison, *Black Sheep Squadron*, 576–77.
32 Arthur Gentry, VHP, 104908.
33 Hammel, *Chosin*, 55–58 ; Samuel Jaskilka, "Easy Alley," in *Marine Corps Gazette*, May 1951; Montross and Canzona, *U.S. Marine Operations in Korea*, vol. 3, 16.
34 Wilson, *Retreat Hell!*, 124.
35 Ibid., 136–37.
36 Simmons, *Frozen Chosin*, 54–55; Hammel, *Chosin*, 66–69 ; Wilson, *Retreat Hell!*, 109–10; SAR, 2/5, 18; Montross and Canzona, *U.S. Marine Operations in Korea*, vol. 3, 167.

37 Li, *Attack*, 68.
38 Davis, *Story of Ray Davis*, 117–18.

CHAPTER 7: THE LONGEST NIGHT

1 Li, *Attack*, 68.
2 Montross and Canzona, *U.S. Marine Operations in Korea*, vol. 3, 168.
3 Russ, *Breakout*, 214.
4 Montross and Canzona, *U.S. Marine Operations in Korea*, vol. 3, 158.
5 Appleman, *Escaping the Trap*, 59.
6 Cleaver, *Frozen Chosen*, 188–89.
7 SAR, 1/11, Appendices 1–5, 8; Parry, *Three-War Marine*, 168.
8 Parry, *Three-War Marine*, 174.
9 Li, *Attack*, 64, 56
10 Ibid., 68.
11 Roe, *Dragon Strikes*, 301; Montross and Canzona, *U.S. Marine Operations in Korea*, vol. 3, 167–68; Simmons, *Frozen Chosin*, 55–56.
12 Li, *Attack*, 78.
13 Hammel, *Chosin*, 84–87.
14 Appleman, *Escaping the Trap*, 54–55.
15 Simmons, *Frozen Chosin*, 55–56.
16 Li, *Attack*, 69; Montross and Canzona, *U.S. Marine Operations in Korea*, vol. 3, 168.
17 Joseph Wheelan, *Midnight in the Pacific. Guadalcanal: The World War II Battle that Turned the Tide of War* (Boston: Da Capo Press, 2017), 214–17.
18 Sides, *On Desperate Ground*, 142.
19 Hammel, *Chosin*, 88–89 ; Geer, *New Breed*, 277–80.
20 Russ, *Breakout*, 124.
21 Wilson, *Retreat Hell!*, 150.
22 Hammel, *Chosin*, 89 ; Wilson, *Retreat Hell!*, 150.
23 Wilson, *Retreat Hell!*, 153–54; Hammel, *Chosin*, 92 .
24 Russ, *Breakout*, 142 ; Geer, *New Breed*, 279.
25 Wilson, *Retreat Hell!*, 155.
26 *Chosen Few News Digest*, September 1989, 11–12.
27 Russ, *Breakout*, 142.
28 Hammel, *Chosin*, 92.
29 Schreier interview, 1995.
30 Wilson, *Retreat Hell!*, 167; Sides, *On Desperate Ground*, 169–70.
31 Hammel, *Chosin*, 93.
32 Geer, *New Breed*, 283–84; Hammel, *Chosin*, 120 .
33 1/5 SAR, Folder 6.
34 Knox, *Korean War*, 498–99; Montross and Canzona, *U.S. Marine Operations in Korea*, vol. 3, 182–84.
35 Win Scott interview, 1995.
36 Hammel, *Chosin*, 121.
37 Win Scott interview, 1995.
38 1/5 SAR, Folder 6; Alexander, *First War We Lost*, 346–47; Geer, *New Breed*, 285.
39 Geer, *New Breed*, 272.
40 Appleman, *Escaping the Trap*, 66–67; Thomas Cassis interview, 1995; Montross and Canzona, *U.S. Marine Operations in Korea*, vol. 3, 174–75.
41 Thomas Cassis interview, 1995.

42 Harold Dawe interview, 1995; Appleman, *Escaping the Trap*, 67; Hammel, *Chosin*, 122.
43 Montross and Canzona, *U.S. Marine Operations in Korea*, vol. 3, 170; Hammel, *Chosin*, 80–81, 84.
44 Montross and Canzona, *U.S. Marine Operations in Korea*, vol. 3, 171; Hammel, *Chosin*, 77–78, 81–83.
45 Adam Makos, *Devotion: An Epic Story of Heroism, Friendship, and Sacrifice* (New York: Ballantine Books, 2015), 278–83; Li, *Attack*, 70.
46 Li, *Attack*, 64–65, 70, 73, 137.
47 Montross and Canzona, *U.S. Marine Operations in Korea*, vol. 3, 382.
48 Makos, *Devotion*, 283; Montross and Canzona, *U.S. Marine Operations in Korea*, vol. 3, 166–67.
49 Roe, *Dragon Strikes*, 307; Simmons, *Frozen Chosin*, 47.
50 Murray, Oral History, USMC Archives.
51 Paul M. Edwards, *To Acknowledge a War: The Korean War in American Memory* (Westport, CN: Greenwood Press, 2000), 46.

CHAPTER 8: FOX HILL

1 Wilson, *Retreat Hell!*, 130.
2 Parry, *Three-War Marine*, 178.
3 Bob Drury and Tom Clavin, *The Last Stand of Fox Company* (New York: Grove Press, 2009), 28.
4 Cleaver, *Frozen Chosen*, 185.
5 Hammel, *Chosin*, 96; Montross and Canzona, *U.S. Marine Operations in Korea*, vol. 3, 180.
6 Montross and Canzona, *U.S. Marine Operations in Korea*, vol. 3, 180–81; Knox, *Korean War*, 492–93.
7 Russ, *Breakout*, 316 ; Wilson, *Retreat Hell!*, 99–100; Barber interview, 1995.
8 Berry, *Hey, Mac, Where Ya Been?*, 125.
9 Frank Kerr, "At the Reservoir: Through the Eyes of a Combat Photographer," in *Leatherneck* magazine, December 1990, 494.
10 Drury and Clavin, *Last Stand of Fox Company*, 152–54; Barber interview, 1995.
11 Wilson, *Retreat Hell!*, 100; Barber interview, 1995.
12 Wilson, *Retreat Hell!*, 130; Simmons, *Frozen Chosin*, 56.
13 Appleton, *Escaping the Trap*, 227–29; Simmons, *Frozen Chosin*, 57.
14 Barber interview, 1995.
15 Elmo Peterson interview, 1995.
16 Knox, *Korean War*, 502.
17 Ibid.
18 Barber interview, 1995; Sides, *On Desperate Ground*, 176.
19 Bob Kirschner interview, *Chosin*, Amazon Video.
20 Drury and Clavin, *Last Stand of Fox Company*, 53.
21 Sides, *On Desperate Ground*, 53–54.
22 Drury and Clavin, *Last Stand of Fox Company*, 52; Cleaver, *Frozen Chosen*, 192–93.
23 Montross and Canzona, *U.S. Marine Operations in Korea*, vol. 3, 181–82.
24 Cleaver, *Frozen Chosen*, 192–94; Sides, *On Desperate Ground*, 164–66.
25 Sides, *On Desperate Ground*, 181, Cleaver, *Frozen Chosen*, 194; Hammel, *Chosin*, 100–01.
26 Geer, *New Breed*, 297–98.
27 Elmo Peterson interview, 1995.
28 Ibid.

29 Parry, *Three-War Marine*, 177.
30 Geer, *New Breed*, 295–97; Capt Benjamin Reed, "Our Guns Never Got Cold," in *The Chosin Few News Digest*, January–February 1994, 12–13; Don Campbell interview, 1995; Wilson, *Retreat Hell!*, 137.
31 Parry, *Three-War Marine*, 178.
32 Reed, "Our Guns Never Got Cold," 12–13.
33 Elmo Peterson interview, 1995.
34 Barber interview, 1995.

CHAPTER 9: EAST OF CHOSIN RESERVOIR

1 Appleman, *East of Chosin*, 99–100.
2 Appleman, *Escaping the Trap*, 75–78.
3 Russell Gugeler, *Combat Actions in Korea* (Washington, DC: Center of Military History, United States Army, 1987), 60–61.
4 Cleaver, *Frozen Chosen*, 171; Li, *Attack*, 86.
5 Simmons, *Frozen Chosin*, 52–53; Blair, *Forgotten War*, 420, 458.
6 Appleman, *Escaping the Trap*, 82.
7 Gugeler, *Combat Actions in Korea*, 56–58.
8 Ricks, *The Generals*, 169–70; Cleaver, *Frozen Chosen*, 181–82.
9 Appleman, *East of Chosin*, 31; Matthew Seelinger, "Nightmare at Chosin Reservoir," at armyhistory.org.; Blair, *Forgotten War*, 389.
10 Appleman, *East of Chosin*, 31.
11 Ibid., 35, 60 (map); Appleman, *Escaping the Trap*, 85.
12 Stamford interview, USMC Historical Division.
13 Appleman, *Escaping the Trap*, 81; *Chosin Few News Digest*, May/June 1992, 36.
14 Li, *Attack*, 72.
15 Ibid., 87.
16 Ibid., 88.
17 Ibid., 88–89.
18 Li, *Attack*, 90.
19 Appleman, *Escaping the Trap*, 87–88.
20 Hallion, *Naval Air War*, 43.
21 Stamford interview, USMC Historical Division.
22 Simmons, *Frozen Chosin*, 8, 44–45.
23 Simmons, *Frozen Chosin*, 8, 44–45; Stamford interview, USMC Historical Division.
24 Appleman, *Escaping the Trap*, 89–90; Stamford interview, 72; Hammel, *Chosin*, 109–10.
25 Appleman, *Escaping the Trap*, 90; Stamford interview, USMC Historical Center, 72–73; Hammel, *Chosin*, 110.
26 Appleman, *Escaping the Trap*, 92–93.
27 Stamford interview, USMC Historical Center, 72–73.
28 Appleman, *Escaping the Trap*, 92–93.
29 Stanton, *America's Tenth Legion*, 265; Appleman, *Escaping the Trap*, 96. Later, the Chinese 27th Army awarded the 4th Company the "Combat Model Company of Sinhung-ni" for its performance; Li, *Attack*, 90.
30 Li, *Attack*, 91; Harbula personal papers, USMC Archives, Box 5.
31 John Gray interview, 1995.
32 Appleman, *East of Chosin*, 85.
33 Ibid., 80.
34 Ibid., 81–82.

35 Appleman, *Escaping the Trap*, 99–100.
36 Stanton, *America's Tenth Legion*, 265.
37 Appleman, *Escaping the Trap*.
38 Li, *Attack*, 91–93.
39 Ibid., 94.
40 Ibid., 61.
41 Appleman, *Escaping the Trap*, 101; Gugeler, *Combat Actions in Korea*, 66.
42 Appleman, *Escaping the Trap*, 106.
43 Cleaver, *Frozen Chosen* ,195; Li, *Attack*, 91–93; Appleman, *Escaping the Trap*, 104–05.

CHAPTER 10: OUT ON A LIMB

1 Roe, *Dragon Strikes*, 312–13.
2 Wilson, *Retreat Hell!*, 224.
3 Blair, *Forgotten War*, 464–65; Roe, *Dragon Strikes*, 320–21.
4 T. R. Fehrenbach, *This Kind of War. A Study in Unpreparedness* (New York: The MacMillan Company, 1963), 365.
5 Murray, Oral History.
6 Appleman, *Escaping the Trap*, 71; Stanton, *America's Tenth Legion*, 210–11; Hammel, *Chosin*, 133.
7 Hammel, *Chosin*, 131–32.
8 Wiedhahn, VHP, 86209.
9 Hammel, *Chosin*, 128–29.
10 Ibid., 124–25.
11 Hammel, *Chosin*, 128; Owen, *Colder Than Hell*, 195.
12 Davis, *Story of Ray Davis*, 109–10; Cleaver, *Frozen Chosen*, 196; Hammel, *Chosin*, 127–29; Simmons, *Frozen Chosin*, 56; Geer, *New Breed*, 288–91; SAR RCT-7, 21-RR.
13 Paul Robinson interview, VHP, 57807.
14 Shisler, *For Country and Corps*, 196; Sides, *On Desperate Ground*, 183.
15 O.P. Smith, Oral History Transcript, 222; Hammel, *Chosin*, 143–44; Simmons, *Frozen Chosin*, 47.
16 Shisler, *For Country and Corps*, 198; Smith, Oral History Transcript, 222.
17 Smith, Oral History Transcript, 222.
18 Ibid.
19 Hammel, *Chosin*, 211–12.
20 Blair, *Forgotten War*, 456.
21 Ibid., 464–65; Roe, *Dragon Strikes*, 320–21.
22 Manchester, *American Caesar*, 608.
23 Blair, *Forgotten War*, 469–70.
24 Li, *Attack*, 88–90.
25 Ibid., 91–92.
26 Gray interview, 1995.
27 Appleman, *East of Chosin*, 104.
28 Ibid., 105; *Chosin Few News Digest*, May/June 1997.
29 Appleman, *Escaping the Trap*, 102.
30 Roe, *Dragon Strikes*, 312–13.
31 Stanton, *America's Tenth Legion*, 217; Hammel, *Chosin*, 137; Sides, *On Deperate Ground*, 188.
32 Hammel, *Chosin*, 139; Brady, *Marines of Autumn*, 153; Blair, *Forgotten War*, 463.
33 Li, *Attack*, 68–69.

34 Brady, *Coldest War*, 265–66.
35 Li, *Attack*, 72.
36 Geer, *New Breed*, 293; Knox, *Korean War*, 509.
37 Russell Downs, VHP, 104067.
38 Montross and Canzona, *U.S. Marine Operations in Korea*, vol. 3, 192.
39 Li, *Attack*, 70.

CHAPTER 11: FOX HILL SURROUNDED

1 Sides, *On Desperate Ground*, 207.
2 Barber interview, 1995.
3 Wilson, *Retreat Hell!*, 187.
4 Appleman, *Escaping the Trap*, 227–29.
5 Barber interview, 1995.
6 Montross and Canzona, *U.S. Marine Operations in Korea*, vol. 3, 201; Hammel, *Chosin*, 151–52.
7 Drury and Clavin, *Last Stand of Fox Company*, 41, 49.
8 Sides, *On Desperate Ground*, 205; Drury and Clavin, *Last Stand of Fox Company*, 49.
9 Sides, *On Desperate Ground*, 207.
10 Leckie, *March to Glory*, 64.
11 Geer, *New Breed*, 301.
12 Wilson, *Retreat Hell!*, 186–87.
13 Ibid., 187.
14 Sides, *On Desperate Ground*, 208.
15 Drury and Clavin, *Last Stand of Fox Company*, 183.
16 Elmo Peterson interview, 1995; Hammel, *Chosin*, 182–84.
17 Berry, *Hey, Mac, Where Ya Been?*, 125–29; Appleman, *Escaping the Trap*, 230–31.
18 Appleman, *Escaping the Trap*, 231–32; Geer, *New Breed*, 302; Hammel, *Chosin*, 186–87.
19 Montross and Canzona, *U.S. Marine Operations in Korea*, vol. 3, 193; Hammel, *Chosin*, 184–86.

CHAPTER 12: HAGARU-RI

1 Wilson, *Retreat Hell!*, 224.
2 Weintraub, *Christmas Far From Home*, 133.
3 La Bree, *Gentle Warrior*, 169; Hammel, *Chosin*, 149–50.
4 Wilson, *Retreat Hell!*, 217–20.
5 Appleman, *Escaping the Trap*, 161–62; Montross and Canzona, *U.S. Marine Operations in Korea*, vol. 3, 203–04.
6 Hammel, *Chosin*, 148–51.
7 Appleman, *Escaping the Trap*, 208.
8 Li, *Attack*, 74–77.
9 Simmons, *Frozen Chosin*, 61; Wilson, *Retreat Hell!*, 223–24; Russ, *Breakout*, 205.
10 Wilson, *Retreat Hell!*, 224.
11 Russ, *Breakout*, 208.
12 Ibid., 209.
13 Hammel, *Chosin*, 156; Russ, *Breakout*, 206.
14 Wilson, *Retreat Hell!*, 224–25.
15 Montross and Canzona, *U.S. Marine Operations in Korea*, vol. 3, 210.
16 Hammel, *Chosin*, 158–59; Wilson, *Retreat Hell!*, 228.

17 Montross and Canzona, *U.S. Marine Operations in Korea*, vol. 3, 211.
18 Wilson, *Retreat Hell!*, 226; Geer, *New Breed*, 313; Li, *Attack*, 77–78; Russ, *Breakout*, 210.
19 Li, *Attack*, 78.
20 Ibid., 78–79; Russ, *Breakout*, 211–12; Appleman, *Escaping the Trap*, 165–66; Shisler, *For Country and Corps*, 199.
21 Li, *Attack*, 75.
22 Ibid., 77, 80.
23 Patrick K. O'Donnell, *Give Me Tomorrow. The Korean War's Greatest Untold Story – The Epic Stand of the Marines of George Company* (Cambridge, MA: Da Capo Press, 2010), 143–45; Simmons, *Frozen Chosin*, 60; Montross and Canzona, *U.S. Marine Operations in Korea*, vol. 3, 213–14; Weintraub, *Christmas Far From Home*, 132–33.
24 Montross and Canzona, *U.S. Marine Operations in Korea*, vol. 3, 213–15.
25 Simmons, *Frozen Chosin*, 62.
26 Cleaver, *Frozen Chosen*, 204; Simmons, *Frozen Chosin*, 62.
27 Appleman, *Escaping the Trap*, 172–73; Montross and Canzona, *U.S. Marine Operations in Korea*, vol. 3, 216–17; Hammel, *Chosin*, 165–71; Roe, *Dragon Strikes*, 318; Stanton, *America's Tenth Legion*, 225.
28 Weintraub, *Christmas Far From Home*, 133.
29 Stanton, *America's Tenth Legion*, 226.
30 Li, *Attack*, 76.
31 Simmons, *Frozen Chosin*, 62; Li, *Attack*, 75, 79.
32 Li, *Attack*, 75–76.
33 Wilson, *Retreat Hell!*, 189.

CHAPTER 13: SURROUNDED, LOSING HOPE

1 Knox, *Korean War*, 546–47.
2 Blair, *Forgotten War*, 506–07.
3 Shisler, *For Country and Corps*, 212.
4 Gray interview, 1995.
5 Appleman, *Escaping the Trap*, 107–09.
6 Li, *Attack*, 94–95.
7 Appleman, *Escaping the Trap*, 106–09.
8 Stanton, *America's Tenth Legion*, 218.
9 Gugeler, *Combat Actions in Korea*, 62–64; Toland, *In Mortal Combat*, 309.
10 Alexander, *First War We Lost*, 31.
11 Li, *Attack*, 96; Appleman, *Escaping the Trap*, 113.
12 Gugeler, *Combat Actions in Korea*, 64; Roe, *Dragon Strikes*, 315–16; Blair, *Forgotten War*, 506; Edward Magill, "Col. MacLean Captured," *Chosin Few News Digest*, Jan–Feb 1997, 16; Stanton, *America's Tenth Legion*, 218–19.
13 Gugeler, *Combat Actions in Korea*, 64.
14 Appleman, *Escaping the Trap*, 114–18.
15 Gugeler, *Combat Actions in Korea*, 64–66 ; Appleman, *East of Chosin*, 148.
16 Weintraub, *Christmas Far From Home*, 136; Blair, *Forgotten War*, 506–07.
17 Appleman, *Escaping the Trap*, 125–26.
18 Russ, *Breakout*, 228–29.
19 Hammel, *Chosin*, 199; Geer, *New Breed*, 333.
20 Hammel, *Chosin*, 227.
21 Shisler, *For Country and Corps*, 207.

22 Appleman, *Escaping the Trap*, 118–19.
23 Appleman, *Escaping the Trap*, 118, 126–29; Stanton, *America's Tenth Legion*, 217; Li, *Attack*, 96–97; Blair, *Forgotten War*, 461–63.
24 Knox, *Korean War*, 546–47.
25 Li, *Attack*, 95.
26 Maj Edward Stamford, "Recollections," at www.rcmcollection.com/Stamford.
27 *Marine Corps Gazette*, July 1952.
28 Li, *Attack*, 101.
29 Gugeler, *Combat Actions in Korea*, 68.
30 Appleman, *Escaping the Trap*, 132.
31 Brady, *Marines of Autumn*, 155.
32 Blair, *Forgotten War*, 510–12; Appleman, *Escaping the Trap*, 127.
33 Stamford, "Recollections"; Gugeler, *Combat Actions in Korea*, 68.
34 Li, *Attack*, 58–59.
35 Ibid., 97–98.
36 Ibid., 95–96.
37 Li, *Attack*, 85–86, 98; Richard Peters and Xiaobing Li, *Voices from the Korean War* (Lexington, KY: The University Press of Kentucky, 2004), 122–23.
38 Li, *Attack*, 83–87.

CHAPTER 14: HELLFIRE VALLEY

1 Sides, *On Desperate Ground*, 222.
2 Appleman, *Escaping the Trap*, 201.
3 Commando Veterans Archive, www.commandoveterans.org.
4 Berry, *Hey, Mac, Where Ya Been?*, 158; O.P. Smith personal papers, Aide Memoirs, USMC Archives, Box 68, File 18.
5 Montross and Canzona, *U.S. Marine Operations in Korea*, vol. 3, 225–28; Hammel, *Chosin*, 173–74; Sides, *On Desperate Ground*, 221.
6 Li, *Attack*, 81–82.
7 Silver Star citation; Zullo obituary, www.stringerfh.com/obituary/3323573; Toland, *In Mortal Combat*, 313, 319.
8 Li, *Attack*, 81–82.
9 Montross and Canzona, *U.S. Marine Operations in Korea*, vol. 3, 226–29; Shisler, *For Country and Corps*, 204; Appleman, *Escaping the Trap*, 188–91; Hammel, *Chosin*, 179; Sides, *On Desperate Ground*, 222.
10 Berry, *Hey, Mac, Where Ya Been?*, 158.
11 Montross and Canzona, *U.S. Marine Operations in Korea*, vol. 3, 230–31.
12 Ibid., 231.
13 Appleman, *Escaping the Trap*, 191–92; Toland, *In Mortal Combat*, 313–14.
14 Simmons, *Frozen Chosin*, 70.
15 Wilson, *Retreat Hell!*, 259–61.
16 Hammel, *Chosin*, 200–01.
17 Sides, *On Desperate Ground*, 223.
18 Montross and Canzona, *U.S. Marine Operations in Korea*, vol. 3, 231–33.
19 Wilson, *Retreat Hell!*, 264–65.
20 Li, *Attack*, 82.
21 Montross and Canzona, *U.S. Marine Operations in Korea*, vol. 3, 233–34.
22 Appleman, *Escaping the Trap*, 200–01; Hammel, *Chosin*, 210–11; Roe, *Dragon Strikes*, 319.

23 Wilson, *Retreat Hell!*, 269. Nash and several other prisoners escaped five months later, and were able to reach American lines.
24 Cleaver, *Frozen Chosen*, 215; Geer, *New Breed*, 323–25.
25 Shisler, *For Country and Corps*, 204.
26 Stanton, *America's Tenth Legion*, 254–55; Montross and Canzona, *U.S. Marine Operations in Korea*, vol. 3, 234.
27 Catchpole, *Korean War*, 88.
28 Shisler, *For Country and Corps*, 204–05.
29 Appleman, *Escaping the Trap*, 201.
30 Montross and Canzona, *U.S. Marine Operations in Korea*, vol. 3, 240; Li, *Attack*, 77.
31 Montross and Canzona, *U.S. Marine Operations in Korea*, vol. 3, 241.
32 Li, *Attack*, 79; O'Donnell, *Give Me Tomorrow*, 147–53.
33 Hammel, *Chosin*, 221–23; Sides, *On Desperate Ground*, 262.
34 Periodic Intel Report 36, USMC Archives, Box 5; Bob Harbula personal papers, USMC Archives, Box 5.
35 Montross and Canzona, *U.S. Marine Operations in Korea*, vol. 3, 242; Sides, *On Desperate Ground*, 262; Roe, *Dragon Strikes*, 340; Li, *Attack*, 77; Appleman, *Escaping the Trap*, 205–06.
36 Li, *Attack*, 76–77.
37 Ibid., 80; 1stMarDiv SAR, Korean War, USMC Archives, Box 9.
38 Simmons, *Frozen Chosin*, 74.

CHAPTER 15: THE AIRFIELD

1 Appleman, *Escaping the Trap*, 42.
2 Simmons, *Frozen Chosin*, 750.
3 Roe, *Dragon Strikes*, 380.
4 Shisler, *For Country and Corps*, 209.
5 Montross and Canzona, *U.S. Marine Operations in Korea*, vol. 3, 246.
6 Hammel, *Chosin*, 214; Appleman, *Escaping the Trap*, 118.
7 La Bree, *Gentle Warrior*, 169–70; Shisler, *For Country and Corps*, 209–10.
8 William Leary, *Anything, Anywhere, Any Time. Combat Cargo in the Korean War* (Washington, DC: Air Force Historical Studies Office, 2000), 18–19; La Bree, *Gentle Warrior*, 170.
9 lejeunenewriver.usmc-mccs.org/news/how-tootsie-rolls-accidentally-saved-marines-during-war#:~:text=Soon%2C%20pallets%20of%20Tootsie%20Roll,sealing%20them%20as%20they%20refroze; Sides, *On Desperate Ground*, 262–63; Stanton, *America's Tenth Legion*, 215.

CHAPTER 16: THE CHINESE DESTROY A REGIMENT

1 Appleman, *East of Chosin*, 243.
2 Sides, *On Desperate Ground*, 270–71.
3 Weintraub, *Christmas Far From Home*, 142–43.
4 Gugeler, *Combat Actions in Korea*, 68–69.
5 Li, *Attack*, 97–98, 101.
6 Ibid., 99.
7 Gugeler, *Combat Actions in Korea*, 68–69.
8 Appleman, *Escaping the Trap*, 134–36.
9 Knox, *Korean War*, 252.

10 *Task Force Faith: The Story of the 31st Regimental Combat Team* (Amazon, 2014).
11 Sides, *On Desperate Ground*, 267–68; Ricks, *The Generals*, 144–45.
12 Sides, *On Desperate Ground*, 268.
13 Blair, *Forgotten War*, 515–16; Gugeler, *Combat Actions in Korea*, 70.
14 Stamford, "Recollections."
15 Toland, *In Mortal Combat*, 328–29; *Task Force Faith* video.
16 Appleman, *East of Chosin*, 241–43.
17 *Task Force Faith* video.
18 Appleman, *East of Chosin*, 252–53.
19 *Task Force Faith* video.
20 Appleman, *East of Chosin*, 251.
21 Knox, *Korean War*, 553.
22 Sides, *On Desperate Ground*, 270–71.
23 Russ, *Breakout*, 280; Hammel, *Chosin*, 237.
24 Alexander, *First War We Lost*, 337; Ricks, *The Generals*, 147; Gugeler, *Combat Actions in Korea*, 73.
25 Gugeler, *Combat Actions in Korea*, 74; Stamford interview, USMC Historical Division, 85–87.
26 Stamford interview, 90.
27 Stamford, "Recollections."
28 Sides, *On Desperate Ground*, 271.
29 Stamford interview, 85–87; Knox, *Korean War*, 557–58.
30 Li, *Attack*, 100.
31 Hammel, *Chosin*, 239–41.
32 *Task Force Faith* video.
33 Weintraub, *Christmas Far From Home*, 142–43. Lieutenant Colonel Faith's remains were recovered and transported to the United States in 2004, positively identified through DNA in 2012, and interred in 2013.
34 Appleman, *East of Chosin*, 272–73; *Task Force Faith* video.
35 Appleman, *Escaping the Trap*, 150–51.
36 Toland, *In Mortal Combat*, 336–38.
37 Ibid., 336.
38 Li, *Attack*, 100.
39 Ed Reeves interview, VHP, 18290.
40 Ibid.; Toland, *In Mortal Combat*, 348–49.
41 Knox, *Korean War*, 559.
42 Russ, *Breakout*, 330–32; Geer, *New Breed*, 343–44.
43 Shisler, *For Country and Corps*, 212.
44 Russ, *Breakout*, 330–32; Geer, *New Breed*, 343–44.
45 Appleman, *Escaping the Trap*, 152–53; c 245.
46 Appleman, *Escaping the Trap*, 153.
47 Russ, *Breakout*, 333.
48 Blair, *Forgotten War*, 520–21.
49 Li, *Attack*, 102; Ricks, *The Generals*, 148.
50 Stanton, *America's Tenth Legion*, 243.
51 La Bree, *Gentle Warrior*, 167.
52 Li, *Attack*, 101.
53 Shisler, *For Country and Corps*, 212.
54 La Bree, *Gentle Warrior*, 166–67.
55 Cleaver, *Frozen Chosen*, 223–24.

CHAPTER 17: YUDAM-NI AND FOX HILL

1 Russ, *Breakout*, 324.
2 Roe, *Dragon Strikes*, 343.
3 Simmons, *Frozen Chosin*, 64.
4 Stanton, *America's Tenth Legion*, 211.
5 Weintraub, *Christmas Far From Home*, 101.
6 Sides, *On Desperate Ground*, 30.
7 Drury and Clavin, *Last Stand of Fox Company*, 206–07.
8 Ibid., 212; Sides, *On Desperate Ground*, 216–18.
9 Drury and Clavin, *Last Stand of Fox Company*, 213.
10 Ibid.
11 Ibid., 214–15.
12 Geer, *New Breed*, 304; Berry, *Hey, Mac, Where Ya Been?*, 128–29.
13 Drury and Clavin, *Last Stand of Fox Company*, 221.
14 Appleman, *Escaping the Trap*, 231–32; Geer, *New Breed*, 304.
15 Wilson, *Retreat Hell!*, 194; Appleman, *Escaping the Trap*, 332–33.
16 Hastings, *Korean War*, 157.
17 Knox, *Korean War*, 528.
18 Appleman, *Escaping the Trap*, 120–21.
19 Korean War Project, USMC -00107962.
20 Knox, *Korean War*, 527–58.
21 Montross and Canzona, *U.S. Marine Operations in Korea*, vol. 3, 195.
22 Roe, *Dragon Strikes*, 334.
23 Cagle, *Sea War in Korea*, 170–71.
24 Li, *Attack*, 83.
25 Hammel, *Chosin*, 216; Appleman, *Escaping the Trap*, 214.
26 Stanton, *America's Tenth Legion*, 212.
27 Hammel, *Chosin*, 253.
28 Geer, *New Breed*, 327.
29 Hammel, *Chosin*, 233.
30 Appleman, *Escaping*, 215.
31 Krulak, *First to Fight*, 182.
32 Warren Wiedhahn, VHP, 86209.
33 Russ, *Breakout*, 309; Appleman, *Escaping the Trap*, 215. In 1953, the bodies were exhumed and returned to the United States under the terms of the armistice ending the war.
34 Appleman, *Escaping the Trap*, 216.
35 Montross and Canzona, *U.S. Marine Operations in Korea*, vol. 3, 257.
36 Ibid., 251; Appleman, *Escaping the Trap*, 217–18.
37 Russ, *Breakout*, 323.
38 Korean War, USMC Archives, 1stMarDiv SAR, Box 9, Folder 1.
39 Russ, *Breakout*, 324.
40 Appleman, *Escaping the Trap*, 217–19; Hammel, *Chosin*, 245–46.
41 Hammel, *Chosin*, 189–90.
42 Russ, *Breakout*, 305.
43 Wilson, *Retreat Hell!*, 199.
44 Hammel, *Chosin*, 264; Appleman, *Escaping the Trap*, 224–25; Owen, *Colder Than Hell*, 206.
45 Roe, *Dragon Strikes*, 343.
46 O.P. Smith, Personal Papers, Aide Memoirs, Box 68, File 16.

47 Hammel, *Chosin*, 308–09.
48 Ibid., 250–51; Montross and Canzona, *U.S. Marine Operations in Korea*, vol. 3, 257, 266–67.
49 Hammel, *Chosin*, 256–58, 272; Geer, *New Breed*, 336; Appleman, *Escaping the Trap*, 222.
50 Appleman, *Escaping the Trap*, 219–20.
51 SAR, 3/5; Montross and Canzona, *U.S. Marine Operations in Korea*, vol. 3, 262–63.
52 Cleaver, *Frozen Chosen*, 229.
53 Hammel, *Chosin*, 281–82.
54 Lyle Bradley, VHP, 76421, and ibid., "A Close Air Support Blast," in *Naval History Magazine*, Vol. 14, No. 6, December 2000.
55 Wilson, *Retreat Hell!*, 212; Hammel, *Chosin*, 254–55.
56 Cagle, *Sea War in Korea*, 174.
57 Li, *Attack*, 114.
58 Murray, Oral History.
59 Keyes Beech, *Tokyo and Points East* (Garden City, NY: Doubleday, 1954), 197.
60 Hammel, *Chosin*, 278.

CHAPTER 18: THE RELIEF OF FOX COMPANY

1 Parry, *Three-War Marine*, 173.
2 Knox, *Korean War*, 541.
3 Owen, *Colder Than Hell*, 203–04.
4 Sides, *On Desperate Ground*, 22.
5 Hammel, *Chosin*, 265; Davis, *Story of Ray Davis*, 111.
6 Davis, *Story of Ray Davis*, 111; Parry, *Three-War Marine*, 174.
7 Parry, *Three-War Marine*, 173.
8 Davis, *Story of Ray Davis*, 111; Russ, *Breakout*, 287–88.
9 Owen, *Colder Than Hell*, 199.
10 Brady, *Marines of Autumn*, 204–05.
11 Russ, *Breakout*, 290–91; Owen, *Colder Than Hell*, 200.
12 Russ, *Breakout*, 293–94, 375; Lee interview, 1995.
13 Lee interview, 1995.
14 Owen, *Colder Than Hell*, 140–42.
15 Russ, *Breakout*, 290–94; Davis interview, 1995.
16 Lee interview, 1995.
17 Russ, *Breakout*, 295.
18 Owen, *Colder Than Hell*, 201.
19 Cleaver, *Frozen Chosen*, 227.
20 Li, *Attack*, 111–12.
21 Korean War, Box 9, Folder 3.
22 Harold St John, VHP, 105620.
23 Owen, *Colder Than Hell*, 200.
24 Lee interview, 1995.
25 Davis, *Story of Ray Davis*, 113; Davis interview, 1995.
26 Hammel, *Chosin*, 267–68.
27 Knox, *Korean War*, 540.
28 Davis interview, 1995; Knox, *Korean War*, 539.
29 Owen, *Colder Than Hell*, 201; Hammel, *Chosin*, 267–68.
30 Ricks, *The Generals*, 160; Owen, *Colder Than Hell*, 201.
31 Owen, *Colder Than Hell*, 201–02.

32 St John, VHP, 105620.
33 Appleman, *Escaping the Trap*, 235.
34 Hammel, *Chosin*, 269.
35 Knox, *Korean War*, 541.
36 Davis, *Story of Ray Davis*, 114.
37 Knox, *Korean War*, 540.
38 Davis, *Story of Ray Davis*, 113–14.
39 Ibid., 114; Hammel, *Chosin*, 269.
40 Lee interview, 1995; Owen, *Colder Than Hell*, 201–03.
41 Davis, *Story of Ray Davis*, 114–15.
42 Owen, *Colder Than Hell*, 203–04.
43 Leckie, *March to Glory*, 110.
44 Owen, *Colder Than Hell*, 203–04.
45 Ibid.; Sides, *On Desperate Ground*, 252; Peters and Li, *Voices from the Korean War*, 101.
46 Montross and Canzona, *U.S. Marine Operations in Korea*, vol. 3, 265; Appleman, *Escaping the Trap*, 235.
47 Sides, *On Desperate Ground*, 253; Knox, *Korean War*, 544.

CHAPTER 19: ENTERING HAGARU-RI

1 Geer, *New Breed*, 341.
2 Higgins, *War in Korea*, 190.
3 Shisler, *For Country and Corps*, 223.
4 Roe, *Dragon Strikes*, 342.
5 Cleaver, *Frozen Chosen*, 253; Simmons, *Frozen Chosin*, 119.
6 O.P. Smith, Historical Diary, Box 6, File 1.
7 Allison, *Black Sheep Squadron*, 580, 590.
8 Ibid., 589–90.
9 Hammel, *Chosin*, 282; Makos, *Devotion*, 320.
10 Davis, *Story of Ray Davis*, 115–16.
11 Montross and Canzona, *U.S. Marine Operations in Korea*, vol. 3, 270.
12 Ibid., 270–71.
13 Cleaver, *Frozen Chosen*, 230.
14 Appleman, *Escaping the Trap*, 236–37.
15 Hammel, *Chosin*, 280; Geer, *New Breed*, 340.
16 Geer, *New Breed*, 33–40; Montross and Canzona, *U.S. Marine Operations in Korea*, vol. 3, 270–71.
17 Elmo Peterson interview, 1995.
18 Russ, *Breakout*, 317; St John, VHP, 105620.
19 Geer, *New Breed*, 340–41; Montross and Canzona, *U.S. Marine Operations in Korea*, vol. 3, 272–73.
20 Simmons, *Frozen Chosin*, 88; SAR, 2/5.
21 Montross and Canzona, *U.S. Marine Operations in Korea*, vol. 3, 294–95.
22 Russ, *Breakout*, 319–20; Owen, *Colder Than Hell*, 210–11.
23 Cleaver, *Frozen Chosen*, 231.
24 O'Donnell, *Give Me Tomorrow*, 166.
25 O.P. Smith, Personal Papers, Box 47, USMC Archives.
26 Shisler, *For Country and Corps*, 223.
27 Ricks, *The Generals*, 163.
28 Geer, *New Breed*, 341.

29 Owen, *Colder Than Hell*, 211; Kerr, "At the Reservoir," 30–33.
30 Knox, *Korean War*, 534.
31 Elmo Peterson interview, 1995.
32 Appleman, *Escaping the Trap*, 243; Geer, *New Breed*, 346.
33 Geer, *New Breed*, 341; Roe, *Dragon Strikes*, 343; Knox, *Korean War*, 532.
34 Cagle, *Sea War in Korea*, 174.
35 Montross and Canzona, *U.S. Marine Operations in Korea*, vol. 3, 348–50.
36 Hallion, *Naval Air War in Korea*, 81–82; Simmons, *Frozen Chosin*, 113.
37 Major General John P. Condon (USMC Ret.), *Corsairs to Panthers: U.S. Marine Aviation in Korea* (Washington, DC: US Marine Corps History and Museums Division, 2002), 32; Montross and Canzona, *U.S. Marine Operations in Korea*, vol. 3, 296; Hallion, *Naval Air War in Korea*, 33–34.
38 Wilson, *Retreat Hell!*, 285.
39 Robert Edwin Kennedy, VHP, 93253.
40 Wilson, *Retreat Hell!*, 287–88.
41 Kennedy, VHP, 93253.
42 Montross and Canzona, *U.S. Marine Operations in Korea*, vol. 3, 281.
43 Beech, *Tokyo and Points East*, 197.
44 Toland, *In Mortal Combat*, 347; Beech, *Tokyo and Points East*, 188.
45 Toland, *In Mortal Combat*, 346; Russ, *Breakout*, 360; Beech, *Tokyo and Points East*, 186.
46 Montross and Canzona, *U.S. Marine Operations in Korea*, vol. 3, 322–23.
47 Spurr, *Enter the Dragon*, 33; Higgins, *War in Korea*, 190, 182.
48 Higgins, *War in Korea*, 186.
49 Shisler, *For Country and Corps*, 218.
50 Berry, *Hey, Mac, Where Ya Been?*, 107–08.
51 Li, *Attack*, 118.

CHAPTER 20: READYING THE BREAKOUT

1 Dawe interview, 1995.
2 Roe, *Dragon Strikes*, 386–88.
3 Hammel, *Chosin*, 304; Russ, *Breakout*, 355.
4 Li, *Attack*, 111.
5 Ibid., 118.
6 Ibid., 118–19.
7 Ibid., 111–12, 118–21; Appleman, *Escaping the Trap*, 251.
8 Li, *Attack*, 116–17.
9 SAR, 2/5, 5 December 1950.
10 O'Donnell, *Give Me Tomorrow*, 166–69.
11 Appleman, *Escaping the Trap*, 260.
12 Roe, *Dragon Strikes*, 382.
13 Li, *Attack*, 120–21.
14 Montross and Canzona, *U.S. Marine Operations in Korea*, vol. 3, 293.
15 J. Robert Moskin, *The U.S. Marine Corps Story* (New York, San Francisco: McGraw-Hill, 1982), 345.
16 Appleman, *Escaping the Trap*, 261; Russ, *Breakout*, 380.
17 Montross and Canzona, *U.S. Marine Operations in Korea*, vol. 3, 291.
18 Dawe interview, 1995.
19 Roe, *Dragon Strikes*, 386–88.
20 Appleman, *Escaping the Trap*, 260–61; Hammel, *Chosin*, 323–28.

21 Russ, *Breakout*, 377; Montross and Canzona, *U.S. Marine Operations in Korea*, vol. 3, 291–93; Geer, *New Breed*, 356–58; SAR, 2/5, 7 December 1950; Appleman, *Escaping the Trap*, 261.
22 Makos, *Devotion*, 334–61; Sides, *On Desperate Ground*, 290–94, 300–02; Appleman, *Escaping the Trap*, 243–45; Weintraub, *Christmas Far From Home*, 193.
23 Montross and Canzona, *U.S. Marine Operations in Korea*, vol. 3, 245–46.
24 Geer, *New Breed*, 343.
25 Montross and Canzona, *U.S. Marine Operations in Korea*, vol. 3, 279; Hammel, *Chosin*, 299–300; Sides, *On Desperate Ground*, 261–62; Appleman, *Escaping the Trap*, 50.
26 Appleman, *Escaping the Trap*, 246; Smith, Oral History, 238.
27 Montross and Canzona, *U.S. Marine Operations in Korea*, vol. 3, 246–47.
28 Weintraub, *Christmas Far From Home*, 178.
29 Shisler, *For Country and Corps*, 211.
30 Knox, *Korean War*, 563.
31 Russ, *Breakout*, 337.
32 Beech, *Tokyo and Points East*, 187–88.
33 Russ, *Breakout*, 338.
34 Smith, Oral History, 245.
35 Appleman, *Escaping the Trap*, 258.
36 Smith, Oral History, 231; Shisler, *For Country and Corps*, 217.
37 Appleman, *Escaping the Trap*, 247–49; Hammel, *Chosin*, 329.
38 Operation Order 25–50, USMC Archives, Box 6; La Bree, *Gentle Warrior*, 184–85.
39 Montross and Canzona, *U.S. Marine Operations in Korea*, vol. 3, 284.
40 Shisler, *For Country and Corps*, 219; Operation Orders, USMC Archives, Box 6, Folder 8.
41 Alexander, *First War We Lost*, 359; Hammel, *Chosin*, 303.
42 La Bree, *Gentle Warrior*, 175.
43 Hammel, *Chosin*, 304; Russ, *Breakout*, 355; Roe, *Drgaon Strikes*, 381.
44 Shisler, *For Country and Corps*, 217.
45 Russ, *Breakout*, 6.
46 Higgins, *War in Korea*, 181–82.
47 Montross and Canzona, *U.S. Marine Operations in Korea*, vol. 3, 287.
48 Shisler, *For Country and Corps*, 221.

CHAPTER 21: HAGARU-RI TO KOTO-RI

1 Smith, Oral History, 286.
2 Knox, *Korean War*, 569.
3 Hammel, *Chosin*, 307–10; Simmons, *Frozen Chosin*, 92.
4 Alexander, *First War We Lost*, 357–58; Montross and Canzona, *U.S. Marine Operations in Korea*, vol. 3, 286–87; Appleman, *Escaping the Trap*, 250; Geer, *New Breed*, 348.
5 Smith, Oral History, 286.
6 Ibid., 275.
7 Ibid., 287.
8 Heinl, *Victory at High Tide*, 567.
9 Cagle, *Sea War in Korea*, 175–76.
10 Condon, *Corsairs to Panthers*, 32; Cagle, *Sea War in Korea*, 178.
11 Appleman, *Escaping the Trap*, 252, 257; Simmons, *Frozen Chosin*, 96.
12 Ricks, *The Generals*, 163.
13 Simmons, *Frozen Chosin*, 94–95.
14 Montross and Canzona, *U.S. Marine Operations in Korea*, vol. 3, 283, 300–01.

15 Dawe interview, 1995; Murray, Oral History; Berry, *Hey, Mac, Where Ya Been?*, 52.
16 Appleman, *Escaping the Trap*, 262–63.
17 Russ, *Breakout*, 388–89.
18 Wilson, *Retreat Hell!*, 304.
19 Montross and Canzona, *U.S. Marine Operations in Korea*, vol. 3, 294–96; Appleman, *Escaping the Trap*, 253.
20 Stanton, *America's Tenth Legion*, 276–77.
21 Russ, *Breakout*, 365–66; Knox, *Korean War*, 570–71.
22 Russ, *Breakout*, 365–66.
23 Simmons, *Frozen Chosin*, 92; Wilson, *Retreat Hell!*, 295–96.
24 Wilson, *Retreat Hell!*, 295.
25 Hammel, *Chosin*, 335.
26 Appleman, *Escaping the Trap*, 255; Geer, *New Breed*, 351; Hammel, *Chosin*, 335–36.
27 Owen, *Colder Than Hell*, 206–07.
28 Russ, *Breakout*, 368–69.
29 Montross and Canzona, *U.S. Marine Operations in Korea*, vol. 3, 299.
30 Ibid.
31 Ibid., 296.
32 Wilson, *Retreat Hell!*, 306.
33 Hammel, *Chosin*, 313–14.
34 Russ, *Breakout*, 373.
35 Wilson, *Retreat Hell!*, 306.
36 Knox, *Korean War*, 569.
37 Wilson, *Retreat Hell!*, 306; Hammel, *Chosin*, 345.
38 Hammel, *Chosin*, 345 ; Appleman, *Escaping the Trap*, 256.
39 Russ, *Breakout*, 383; Parry, *Three-War-Marine*, 182–83; Reed, "Our Guns Never Got Cold," 36.
40 Murray, Oral History.
41 Russ, *Breakout*, 371; Hammel, *Chosin*, 121, 330.
42 Roe, *Dragon Strikes*, 382.
43 O.P. Smith, Historical Division, Box 6, Folder 1; Geer, *New Breed*, 353; Montross and Canzona, *U.S. Marine Operations in Korea*, vol. 3, 298; Appleman, *Escaping the Trap*, 256–57.
44 Russ, *Breakout*, 384.
45 Hammel, *Chosin*, 349; Appleman, *Escaping the Trap*, 264.
46 Genealogy Bank, Cleveland *Plain Dealer*, 11 December 1950, 1.
47 Geer, *New Breed*, 359.

CHAPTER 22: KOTO-RI

1 Roe, *Dragon Strikes*, 383; O.P. Smith Diary.
2 Periodic Intel Report No. 37, USMC Archives; Appleman, *Escaping the Trap*, 202.
3 Simmons, *Frozen Chosin*, 63.
4 Geer, *New Breed*, 266.
5 La Bree, *Gentle Warrior*, 62–63.
6 Russ, *Breakout*, 394; Simmons, *Frozen Chosin*, 97.
7 Roe, *Dragon Strikes*, 383; O.P. Smith Diary.
8 Knox, *Korean War*, 582–83.
9 Hammel, *Chosin*, 361; Condon, *Corsairs to Panthers*, 31–33; Simmons, *Frozen Chosin*, 96.

10 Montross and Canzona, *U.S. Marine Operations in Korea*, vol. 3, 307–08; Shisler, *For Country and Corps*, 223.
11 Montross and Canzona, *U.S. Marine Operations in Korea*, vol. 3, 308.
12 *Chosin Few News Digest*, January–February 1996, 26–27.
13 Ibid.
14 Russ, *Breakout*, 419; Hammel, *Chosin*, 365; Cleaver, *Frozen Chosen*, 247–48; O.P. Smith War Log, USMC Archives, Box 34.
15 Russ, *Breakout*, 419.
16 Shisler, *For Country and Corps*, 228.
17 Genealogy Bank: 11 December *Columbus Dispatch*, 11 December *Dallas Morning News*, 18 December *Washington Evening Star*, 17 December *Washington Sunday Star*, 12 December *Quincy Patriot-Ledger*.
18 Roe, *Dragon Strikes*, 361.
19 La Bree, *Gentle Warrior*, 179; Blair, *Forgotten War*, 525.
20 Halberstam, *Coldest Winter*, 468–69.
21 Heinl, *Soldiers of the Sea*, 568.
22 Appleman, *Escaping the Trap*, 288–89.

CHAPTER 23: THE BRIDGE

1 Knox, *Korean War*, 593.
2 Leckie, *March to Glory*, 145–46.
3 Hammel, *Chosin*, 415 ; Halberstam, *Coldest Winter*, 435.
4 Shisler, *For Country and Corps*, 224; Appleman, *Escaping the Trap*, 296.
5 Knox, *Korean War*, 593.
6 Leckie, *March to Glory*, 145–46.
7 Montross and Canzona, *U.S. Marine Operations in Korea*, vol. 3, 311; Appleman, *Escaping the Trap*, 297–98.
8 Appleman, *Escaping the Trap*, 296–98.
9 Russ, *Breakout*, 357–58.
10 Owen, *Colder Than Hell*, 221.
11 Montross and Canzona, *U.S. Marine Operations in Korea*, vol. 3, 307; Wilson, *Retreat Hell!*, 318.
12 Li, *Attack*, 121.
13 Ibid., 124–25.
14 Owen, *Colder Than Hell*, 223.
15 Lee interview, 1995.
16 Russ, *Breakout*, 401–02; Owen, *Colder Than Hell*, 225–26, 229 ; Lee interview, 1995.
17 Hammel, *Chosin*, 378 .
18 Russ, *Breakout*, 402–05 .
19 Li, *Attack*, 123.
20 Knox, *Korean War*, 593.
21 Simmons, *Frozen Chosin*, 103.
22 Montross and Canzona, *U.S. Marine Operations in Korea*, vol. 3, 321; Geer, *New Breed*, 368–70; Appleman, *Escaping the Trap*, 303; Knox, *Korean War*, 604.
23 Knox, *Korean War*, 604.
24 Russ, *Breakout*, 412–41.
25 Appleman, *Escaping the Trap*, 303; Hammel, *Chosin*, 379.
26 David Douglas Duncan, *This is War!* (New York: Harper & Brothers, 1951), 138.

27 Appleman, *Escaping the Trap*, 303–04; Weintraub, *Christmas Far From Home*, 204–05; O'Donnell, *Give Me Tomorrow*, 176; Hammel, *Chosin*, 390–91.
28 Appleman, *Escaping the Trap*, 303–04; Hammel, *Chosin*, 394; Montross and Canzona, *U.S. Marine Operations in Korea*, vol. 3, 322.
29 Knox, *Korean War*, 595; Montross and Canzona, *U.S. Marine Operations in Korea*, vol. 3, 323.
30 Sides, *On Desperate Ground*, 314; Hammel, *Chosin*, 392; O'Donnell, *Give Me Tomorrow*, 176.
31 Weintraub, *Christmas Far From Home*, 206–07.
32 Montross and Canzona, *U.S. Marine Operations in Korea*, vol. 3, 319.
33 Appleman, *Escaping the Trap*, 307.
34 Genealogy Bank, Evansville (Indiana) *Courier and Press*, 14 December 1950, 38.
35 Russ, *Breakout*, 422–25; Montross and Canzona, *U.S. Marine Operations in Korea*, vol. 3, 328–29.
36 Smith, Oral History, 253.
37 Montross and Canzona, *U.S. Marine Operations in Korea*, vol. 3, 330; Blair, *Forgotten War*, 542 (footnote).
38 Toland, *In Mortal Combat*, 365.
39 Montross and Canzona, *U.S. Marine Operations in Korea*, vol. 3, 332–33; Weintraub, *Christmas Far From Home*, 211–13.
40 Montross and Canzona, *U.S. Marine Operations in Korea*, vol. 3, 330.
41 S.L.A. Marshall, *Battle at Best* (New York: Pocket Cardinal, 1965), 145; Smith, Oral History.

CHAPTER 24: THE LAST FURLONG

1 Fred Braitsch Jr, "Dateline ... Korea," in *Leatherneck* magazine, Vol. 34, No. 3 (March 1959), 16–21; Simmons, *Frozen Chosin*, 99.
2 Genealogy Bank, 13 December 1950.
3 USMC Archives, Box 4, SAR MAG 12 and subordinate units folder; Cpl John Walden, "First Marine Division Magnificent Support," in *Leatherneck* magazine, April 1951.
4 Montross and Canzona, *U.S. Marine Operations in Korea*, vol. 3, 221–22.
5 Marshall, *Battle at Best*, 119.
6 Montross and Canzona, *U.S. Marine Operations in Korea*, vol. 3, 308–09.
7 Ibid., 314–15; Wilson, *Retreat Hell!*, 322; Appleman, *Escaping the Trap*, 290–91, 307.
8 Russ, *Breakout*, 408.
9 Montross and Canzona, *U.S. Marine Operations in Korea*, vol. 3, 315–16.
10 Ibid., 316.
11 Russ, *Breakout*, 409–10; Marshall, *Battle at Best*, 122–28.
12 Wilson, *Retreat Hell!*, 325–27; Braitsch, "Dateline ... Korea."
13 Li, *Attack*, 124; Simmons, *Frozen Chosin*, 105; Montross and Canzona, *U.S. Marine Operations in Korea*, vol. 3, 320–21; Wilson, *Retreat Hell!*, 327; Appleman, *Escaping the Trap*, 298–99.
14 Braitsch, "Dateline ... Korea"; Simmons, *Frozen Chosin*, 99. Barrow was awarded the Navy Cross and served as Marine Corps commandant from 1979 to 1983.
15 O'Donnell, *Give Me Tomorrow*, 178–82.
16 Li, *Attack*, 127.
17 Ibid., 124.
18 Montross and Canzona, *U.S. Marine Operations in Korea*, vol. 3, 324.
19 Appleman, *Escaping the Trap*, 308–10.

20 Li, *Attack*, 125.
21 Montross and Canzona, *U.S. Marine Operations in Korea*, vol. 3, 327; Appleman, *Escaping the Trap*, 309–10; Canzona, *Chosin Few News Digest*, January–February 1996, 26–27.
22 Li, *Attack*, 125–27.
23 Weintraub, *Christmas Far From Home*, 187; Toland, *In Mortal Combat*, 351.
24 Shisler, *For Country and Corps*, 195; Acheson, *Present at the Creation*, 514.
25 Roe, *Dragon Strikes*, 355.
26 Stanton, *America's Tenth Legion*, 290–91.
27 Roe, *Dragon Strikes*, 357–58, 363.
28 Spanier, *Truman-MacArthur Controversy*, 172–73.
29 Acheson, *The Korean War*, 514–17, 526.
30 MacArthur, *Reminiscences*, 374, 377; Sides, *On Desperate Ground*, 192–93.
31 Weintraub, *Christmas Far From Home*, 109.
32 2nd Battalion, Fifth Marines SAR, USMC Archives.
33 Appleman, *Escaping the Trap*, 316.
34 Xenophon, *Anabasis*, translated by Henry Graham Dekyns (independently published, 2021), lxx–lxxi.
35 Genealogy Bank, 13 December 1950.
36 Weintraub, *Christmas Far From Home*, 214.
37 Leckie, *March to Glory*, 179–77.
38 O.P. Smith Collection, USMC Archives; Shisler, *For Country and Corps*, 228.
39 Krulak, *First to Fight*, 201.
40 Knox, *Korean War*, 607.
41 Heinl, *Soldiers of the Sea*, 569; 1stMarDiv SAR, Korean War, Box 9, Folder 1; Simmons, *Frozen Chosin*, 119.
42 USMC Archives, Box 4, SAR MAG 12 and subordinate units folder; Walden, "First Marine Division."
43 Montross and Canzona, *U.S. Marine Operations in Korea*, vol. 3, 335–36; Cagle, *Sea War in Korea*, 186–90.
44 Cagle, *Sea War in Korea*, 180–86; Lowell Lein, VHP, 73525; Weintraub, *Christmas Far From Home*, 236–37; Blair, *Forgotten War*, 547.
45 Paul Robinson, VHP, 57807.
46 Weintraub, *Christmas Far From Home*, 238–39, 245; Cleaver, *Frozen Chosen*, 253, 255; Shisler, *For Country and Corps*, 239; Montross and Canzona, *U.S. Marine Operations in Korea*, vol. 3, 341; Stanton, *America's Tenth Legion*, 310–14.
47 Appleman, *Escaping the Trap*, 343.
48 Spurr, *Enter the Dragon*, 265; Higgins, *War in Korea*, 210–11; Appleman, *Escaping the Trap*, 340.
49 Appleman, *Escaping the Trap*, 340; Weintraub, *Christmas Far From Home*, 252–53.
50 Li, *Attack*, 328.
51 Ibid., 132.
52 Ibid., 136.
53 Higgins, *War in Korea*, 190–91.
54 Roe, *Dragon Strikes*, 265–66.
55 Spurr, *Enter the Dragon*, 268–69.

EPILOGUE

1 Shisler, *For Country and Corps*, 231.
2 La Bree, *Gentle Warrior*, 150, 224.

3 Allison, *Black Sheep Squadron*, 611.
4 3/11 SAR, USMC Archives, 12.
5 1stMarDiv SAR, USMC Archives, Box 9.
6 Korean War Project, USMC Archives, Box 9, Folder 3; Cleaver, *Frozen Chosen*, 256.
7 Montross and Canzona, *U.S. Marine Operations in Korea*, vol. 3, 351; O.P. Smith Historical Diaries, USMC Archives, Box 6, Folder 2; *Chosin Few News Digest*, May–June 1990.
8 Shisler, *For Country and Corps*, 231–32.
9 Sloan, *Darkest Summer*, 311.
10 Acheson, *The Korean War*, 76–77.
11 Manchester, *American Caesar*, 621–23.
12 Ibid., 627–28.
13 Ibid., 634–35.
14 Ibid., 638–48, 654–64.
15 MacArthur, *Reminiscences*, 411.
16 Manchester, *American Caesar*, 152.
17 O.P. Smith, Personal Correspondence, USMC Archives, letter from Colonel L.M. Fuller to Smith, 6 October 1950.
18 Krulak, *First to Flight*, 64–66, 68.
19 Peters and Li, *Voices from the Korean War*, 102.
20 Murray, Oral History.
21 Ibid.
22 Halberstam, *Coldest Winter*, 468; Alpha Bowser, Oral History, USMC Archives.
23 Li, *Attack*, 33, 36.
24 Simmons, *Frozen Chosin*, 124–27.
25 Li, *Attack*, 53; Spurr, *Enter the Dragon*, 265–67.
26 Li, *Attack*, 155, 162.
27 Shisler, *For Country and Corps*, 220.
28 La Bree, *Gentle Warrior*, 150, 224.
29 Ibid., 184; Marshall, *Battle at Best*, 111; Shisler, *For Country and Corps*, 132.
30 Allison, *Black Sheep Squadron*, 583, 553.
31 Ibid., 580.
32 Roy Sheil interview, Genealogy Bank, Canton (OH) *Repository*, 12 December 1995.
33 1st Division SAR, 8 Oct–15 Dec 1950.
34 Allison, *Black Sheep Squadron*, 611.
35 *Time*, Lvi, No. 25, 18–19, 18 Dec. 1950.
36 Montross and Canzona, *U.S. Marine Operations in Korea*, vol. 3, 358.
37 Hastings, *Korean War*, 329; Li, *Attack*, 154; Carter J. Eckert, Ki-baik Lee, Young Iek Lew, Michael Robinson, and Edward W. Wagner, *Korea Old and New: A History* (Seoul, Korea: Ilchokak Publishers, for Korea Institute, Harvard University, 1990), 345.

Bibliography

Acheson, Dean. *The Korean War*. New York: W.W. Norton, 1969.

Acheson, Dean. *Present at the Creation: My Years in the State Department*. New York: W.W. Norton, 1969.

Alexander, Bevin. *Korea: The First War We Lost*. New York: Hippocrene Books, 2004.

Allison, Fred. *The Black Sheep Squadron: A Case Study in U.S. Marine Corps' Innovations in Close Air Support*. Doctoral Thesis, Texas Tech University, 2011.

American Presidency Project. University of California-Santa Barbara, 1999. www.presidency.ucsb.edu.

Appleman, Roy E. *East of Chosin, Entrapment and Breakout in Korea, 1950*. College Station, TX: Texas A&M University Press, 1987.

Appleman, Roy E. *Escaping the Trap: The U.S. Army X Corps in NE Korea, 1950*. College Station, TX: Texas A&M University Press, 1990.

Beech, Keyes. *Not Without the Americans: A Personal History*. Garden City, NY: Doubleday, 1971.

Beech, Keyes. *Tokyo and Points East*. Garden City, NY: Doubleday, 1954.

Berry, Henry. *Hey, Mac, Where Ya Been? Living Memoirs of the U.S. Marines in the Korean War*. New York: St Martin's Press, 1988.

Blair, Clay Jr. *The Forgotten War: America in Korea, 1950–1953*. New York: Times Books, 1987.

Blair, Clay Jr. *MacArthur*. New York: Pocket Books, 1977.

Bowser, Alpha. Quantico, VA: US Marine Corps Oral History.

Bradbury, William C. *Mass Behavior in Battle and Captivity. The Communist Soldier in the Korean War.* Chicago: University of Chicago Press, 1968.

Bradley, Lt Col Lyle (USMCR). "A Close Air Support Blast," in *Naval History Magazine*, Vol. 14, No. 6, December 2000.

Brady, James. *The Coldest War. A Memoir of Korea*. New York: Pocket Books, 1991. Originally published in 1990.

Brady, James. *The Marines of Autumn*. New York: St Martin's Griffin, 2000.

Braitsch, Fred Jr. "Dateline ... Korea," in *Leatherneck* magazine, Vol. 34, No. 3, March 1959, pp 16–21.

Bruning, John R. Jr. *Crimson Sky. The Air Battle for Korea*. Dulles, VA: Brassey's, 1999.

Cagle, Commander Malcolm, and Commander Frank E. Manson. *The Sea War in Korea.* Annapolis, MD: United States Naval Institute Press, 1957.

Canzona, Capt N.A., and John G. Hubbell, "12 Incredible Days of Col. Page," in *Chosin Few News Digest*, January–February 1996.

Catchpole, Brian. *The Korean War, 1950–1953*. New York: Carroll & Graf, 2000.

Chinnery, Philip. *Combat Over Korea*. South Yorkshire, UK: Pen & Sword Aviation, 2011.
Chosin Few News Digest. Gainesville, FL:, Finster International. Published six times annually.
Chosin, Amazon Video. Veterans Inc. Expeditionary Media, 2010. thechosinproject.com
Cleaver, Thomas McKelvey. *The Frozen Chosen. The 1st Marine Division and the Battle of the Chosin Reservoir*. Oxford, UK, New York: Osprey Publishing, 2016.
Condon, Major General John P. (USMC Ret.). *Corsairs to Panthers: U.S. Marine Aviation in Korea*. Washington, DC: US Marine Corps History and Museums Division, 2002.
Davis, Gen Ray. *The Story of Ray Davis, General of Marines*. Fuquay-Varina, NC: Research Triangle Publishing, 1995.
Drury, Bob, and Tom Clavin. *The Last Stand of Fox Company*. New York: Grove Press, 2009.
Duncan, David Douglas. *This Is War!* New York: Harper & Brothers, 1951.
Eckert, Carter J., Ki-baik Lee, Young Iek Lew, Michael Robinson, and Edward W. Wagner. *Korea Old and New: A History*. Seoul, Korea: Ilchokak Publishers, for Korea Institute, Harvard University, 1990.
Edwards, Paul M. *To Acknowledge a War: The Korean War in American Memory*. Westport, CN: Greenwood Press, 2000.
Fehrenbach, T.R. *This Kind of War. A Study in Unpreparedness*. New York: The MacMillan Company, 1963.
Flower, Michael. *Xenophon's Anabasis or the Expedition of Cyrus*. New York: Oxford University Press, 2012.
Geer, Andrew. *The New Breed. The Story of the U.S. Marines in Korea*. New York: Harper, 1952.
Genealogy Bank. genealogybank.com.
George, Alexander L. *The Chinese Communist Army in Action*. New York: Columbia University Press, 1967.
Glenn, John. *John Glenn, A Memoir*, with Nick Taylor. New York: Bantam Books, 1999.
Gould, Joseph C. *Korea: The Untold Story of the War*. New York: Times Books, 1982.
Griffith, Samuel B. II. *The Chinese People's Liberation Army*. New York, Toronto, London, Sydney: McGraw-Hill Book Co., 1967.
Gugeler, Russell. *Combat Actions in Korea*. Washington, DC: Center of Military History, United States Army, 1987. First published in 1954.
Halberstam, David. *The Coldest Winter: America and the Korean War*. New York: Hyperion, 2007.
Hallion, Richard P. *The Naval Air War in Korea*. Baltimore, MD: The Nautical & Aviation Publishing Company of America, 1986.
Hammel, Eric. *Chosin: Heroic Ordeal of the Korean War*. New York: The Vanguard Press, 1981.
Hastings, Max. *The Korean War*. London, New York, Toronto, Sydney, Tokyo: Simon & Schuster, 1987.
Heinl, Robert. *Soldiers of the Sea. The United States Marine Corps, 1775–1962*. Annapolis, MD: United States Naval Institute, 1967.
Heinl, Robert. *Victory at High Tide: The Inchon-Seoul Campaign*. Baltimore, MD: The Nautical & Aviation Publishing Company of America, 1979.
Higgins, Marguerite. *War in Korea: The Report of a Woman Combat Correspondent*. Garden City, NY: Doubleday & Company, Inc., 1951.
Hoffman, Jon T. *Once a Legend: "Red Mike" Edson of the Marine Raiders*. Novato, CA: Presidio, 1994.
Hopkins, William B. *One Bugle, No Drums: The Marines at Chosin Reservoir*. Chapel Hill, NC: Algonquin Books of Chapel Hill, 1986.
Hoyt, Edwin P. *The Day the Chinese Attacked. Korea, 1950*. New York, St Louis, San Francisco: McGraw-Hill, 1990.

Jaskilka, Samuel. "Easy Alley," in *Marine Corps Gazette*, May 1951.
Jones, Tech Sgt James C. Jr. "Mike's Puddle Jumper," in *Leatherneck* magazine, March 1951,
Jordan, Kenneth Sr. *Forgotten Heroes. 131 Men of the Korean War Awarded the Medal of Honor, 1950–1953.* Atglen, PA: Schiffer Military/Aviation History, 1995.
Kerr, Frank. "At the Reservoir: Through the Eyes of a Combat Photographer," in *Leatherneck* magazine, Vol. 73, Issue 12, December 1990, pp 30–33.
Kim, Chum-Kon. *The Korean War*. Seoul, South Korea: Kwangmyong Publishing Co., 1973.
Knox, Donald. *The Korean War, Pusan to Chosin. An Oral History*. San Diego, New York, London: Harcourt Brace Jovanovich, 1985.
Kopets, Capt. Keith. "The Close Air Support Controversy in Korea," in *Marine Corps Gazette*, May 2001.
Krulak, Victor H. *First to Fight: An Inside View of the Marine Corps.* New York: Pocket Books, 1991. First published in 1984.
La Bree, Clifton. *The Gentle Warrior: General Oliver Prince Smith, USMC.* Kent, OH, and London: Kent State University Press, 2001.
Langer, William L., ed. *An Encyclopedia of World History*. Boston: Houghton Mifflin Company, 1940.
Leary, William. *Anything, Anywhere, Any Time. Combat Cargo in the Korean War*. Washington, DC: Air Force Historical Studies Office, 2000.
Leatherneck magazine. Quantico, VA: Marine Corps Association, 1917–
Leckie, Robert. *The March to Glory*. New York: Bantam Books, 1960.
Lee, Jongsoo. *The Partition of Korea after World War II*. New York: Palgave Macmillan, 2006.
Li, Xiaobing. *Attack at Chosin: The Chinese Second Offensive in Korea.* Norman, OK: University of Oklahoma Press, 2020.
Li, Xiaobing, Allan Millett, and Bin Yu. *Mao's Generals Remember Korea*. Lawrence, KS: University Press of Kansas, 2001.
Lone, Stewart, and Gavan McCormack. *Korea Since 1850*. Melbourne, Australia: Longman Cheshire, 1993.
Lowe, Peter. *The Origins of the Korean War*, 2nd edition. Oxfordshire, UK: Routledge, 1997.
MacArthur, Douglas. *Reminiscences*. New York, Toronto, London: McGraw-Hill Book Company, 1964.
Magill, Edward. "Col. MacLean Captured," in *The Chosin Few News Digest*, January–February 1997.
Mahoney, Kevin. *Formidable Enemies: The North Korean and Chinese Soldiers in the Korean War*. Novato, CA: Presidio, 2001.
Makos, Adam. *Devotion: An Epic Story of Heroism, Friendship, and Sacrifice.* New York: Ballantine Books, 2015.
Manchester, William. *American Caesar: Douglas MacArthur, 1880–1964.* Boston, Toronto: Little, Brown and Company, 1978.
Mao Tse-Tung. *On the Protracted War*. Peking: Foreign Language Press, 1960.
Marine Corps Gazette. Quantico, VA. Published monthly, 1916–
Marshall, S.L.A. *Battle at Best*. New York: Pocket Cardinal, 1965.
Marshall, S.L.A. *The Military History of the Korean War*. New York, Franklin Watts, 1963.
Marshall, S.L.A. *The River and the Gauntlet*. New York: Warner Books, 1952.
Millett, Allan R. *The War in Korea, 1945–1950: A House Burning*. Lawrence, KS: University Press of Kansas, 2005.
Montross, Lynn, and Nicholas A. Canzona. *U.S. Marine Operations in Korea, 1950–1953.* 3 vols. Washington, DC: Historical Branch, G-3, Headquarters, US Marine Corps, 1954–57.
Morris, Richard B., ed. *Encyclopedia of American History*, 6th edition. New York: Harper & Row, Publishers, 1982.

Moskin, J. Robert. *The U.S. Marine Corps Story*. New York, San Francisco: McGraw-Hill, 1982. First published in 1977.
Murray, Ray. Quantico, VA: US Marine Corps Oral History.
National Army Museum, United Kingdom. "Battle of Quebec," nam,ac.uk/explore/battle-quebec.
Naval History Magazine. Annapolis, MD: United States Naval History Institute. Bi-monthly, 1987–
O'Donnell, Patrick K. *Give Me Tomorrow. The Korean War's Greatest Untold Story – The Epic Stand of the Marines of George Company*. Cambridge, MA: Da Capo Press, 2010.
Oh, Bonnie B.C., ed. *Korea Under the American Military Government, 1945–1948*. Westport, CN, London: Praeger, 2002.
Owen, Joseph R. *Colder Than Hell: A Marine Rifle Company at Chosin Reservoir*. Annapolis, MD: Naval Institute Press, 1996.
Parry, Col Francis Fox. *Three-War Marine. The Pacific, Korea, Vietnam*. Pacifica, CA: Pacifica Press, 1987.
Peng Dehuai. *Memoirs of a Chinese Marshal*. Beijing: Foreign Language Press, 1984.
Peters, Richard, and Xiaobing Li. *Voices from the Korean War*. Lexington, KY: The University Press of Kentucky, 2004.
Reed, Capt. Benjamin. "Our Guns Never Got Cold," in *The Chosin Few News Digest*, January–February 1994. First appeared in the *Saturday Evening Post*, April 7, 1951.
Ricks, Thomas E. *The Generals: American Military Command from World War II to Today*. New York: Penguin Books, 2012.
Roe, Patrick. *The Dragon Strikes. China and the Korean War, June– December 1950*. Novato, CA: Presidio Press, 2000.
Russ, Martin. *Breakout. The Chosin Reservoir Campaign, Korea 1950*. New York: Fromm International, 1999.
Sang-Yong, Choi. "Trusteeship Debate and the Korean Cold War," in Bonnie B.C. Oh, ed., *Korea Under the American Military Government, 1945–1948*, Westport, CN, London: Praeger, 2002, pp. 13–39.
Scutts, Jerry. *Air War Over Korea*. London, Melbourne, Harrisburg, PA: Arms and Armour Press, 1982.
Sears, David. *Such Men as These. The Story of the Navy Pilots Who Flew the Deadly Skies Over Korea*. Cambridge, MA: Da Capo Press, 2010.
Seelinger, Matthew J. "Nightmare at Chosin Reservoir," at armyhistory.org.
Shaara, Jeff. *The Frozen Hours: A Novel of the Korean War*. New York: Ballantine Books, 2018.
Sheil, Lt Roy. "Air Support Saved Marines, Lt. Sheil Writes," from Genealogy Bank, *Canton (OH) Repository*, December 12, 1950.
Shisler, Gail B. *For Country and Corps. The Life of General Oliver P. Smith*. Annapolis, MD: Naval Institute Press, 2009.
Sides, Hampton. *On Desperate Ground. The Epic Story of the Chosin Reservoir – The Greatest Battle of the Korean War*. New York: Anchor Books, 2018.
Simmons, BrigGen Edwin USMC(Ret). *Frozen Chosin: U.S. Marines at the Changjin Reservoir*. Washington, DC: History and Museums Divisions, US Marine Corps, 2002.
Sloan, Bill. *The Darkest Summer. Pusan and Inchon 1950: The Battles That Saved South Korea – and the Marines – from Extinction*. New York, London, Toronto, Sydney: Simon & Schuster, 2009.
Smith, General Oliver Prince. Oral History Transcript. Washington, DC: Historical Division, US Marine Corps, 1973.
Smith, General Oliver Prince. Historical Diary. Quantico, VA: US Marine Corps Archives.
Smith, General Oliver Prince. Personal Papers. Quantico, VA: US Marine Corps Archives, Boxes 23–68.

Smith, General Oliver Prince. War Log. Quantico, VA: US Marine Corps Archives.
Spanier, John W. *The Truman-MacArthur Controversy and the Korean War*. New York: W.W. Norton & Company, 1959.
Spurr, Russell. *Enter the Dragon: China's Undeclared War against the U.S. in Korea, 1950–1951*. New York: Newmarket Press, 1988.
Stamford, Maj Edward. "Recollections," at www.rcmcollection.com/Stamford.
Stanton, Shelby L. *America's Tenth Legion: X Corps in Korea, 1950*. Novato, CA: Presidio Press, 1989.
Steward, Richard W. *Staff Operations: The X Corps in Korea, December 1950*. Fort Leavenworth, KS: Combat Studies Institute, 1991. armyupress.army.mil
Stuck, William. "The Coming of the Cold War to Korea," in Bonnie B.C. Oh, ed., *Korea Under the American Military Government, 1945–1948*, Westport, CN, London: Praeger, 2002, pp. 41–60.
Sun Tzu. *The Art of War*. London, Oxford, New York: Oxford University Press, 1963.
Task Force Faith: The Story of the 31st Regimental Combat Team. Amazon Video, 1:44. 2014.
Time magazine. New York: Time Inc. Weekly, 1923–
Toland, John. *In Mortal Combat: Korea, 1950–1953*. New York: William Morrow and Company, 1991.
Truman, Harry. *Memoirs of Harry S. Truman: Volume Two, Years of Trial and Hope*. Garden City, NY: Doubleday & Company, 1956.
US Marine Corps Historical Branch. "Marine Air Covers the Breakout," in *Marine Corps Gazette*, August 1952.
Walden, Cpl John T. "First Marine Division Magnificent Support," in *Leatherneck* magazine, April 1951.
Weintraub, Stanley. *A Christmas Far From Home*. Boston: Da Capo Press, 2014.
Wheelan, Joseph. *Midnight in the Pacific. Guadalcanal: The World War II Battle that Turned the Tide of War*. Boston: Da Capo Press, 2017.
Whiting, Allen S. *China Crosses the Yalu. The Decision to Enter the Korean War*. Stanford, CA: Stanford University Press, 1960.
Wilson, Jim. *Retreat Hell! We're Just Attacking in Another Direction*. New York: William Morrow, 1988.
Wukovits, John. *American Commando. Evan Carlson, His World War II Marine Raiders and America's First Special Forces Mission*. New York: NAL Caliber, 2009.
Xenophon. *Anabasis*. Translated by Henry Graham Dekyns. Independently published, 2021.

1995 INTERVIEWS

William Barber
Don Campbell
Thomas Cassis
Ray Davis
William Davis
Harold Dawe
John Gray
Chew-Een (Kurt) Lee
Ernie Pappenheimer
Elmo Peterson
William Schreier
Win Scott

VETERANS HISTORY PROJECT INTERVIEWS

Harry Adams, #107300
Gerald Boyd, #3356
Lyle Bradley, #76421
James Brown, #54946
Ray Davis, #89653
Billy Devasher, #66119
Russell Downs, #104067
Arthur Gentry, #104908
Donald Griffith, #4925
Thomas Hudner, #2938
Robert Johnson, #60169
Robert Edwin Kennedy, #93253
Chew-Een (Kurt) Lee, #80441
Lowell Lein, 73525
Joseph Peters, #116
Ed Reeves, #18290
Paul Robinson, #57807
Harold St. John, #105620
John Smith, #101012
Charles Stockhausen, #85352
Warren Wiedhahn, #86209

MARINE CORPS HISTORICAL DIVISION INTERVIEWS

Robert Barrow
Ray Davis
Chew-Een (Kurt) Lee
Ray Murray
Lemuel Shepherd Jr.
Ed Stamford

Index